Dedicated to all the supporters
who ensured that there would be
a physical copy of the 4th edition of
Self-Management for Actors for you to hold.

Listen to the mustn'ts, child. Listen to the don'ts. Listen to the shouldn'ts, the impossibles, the won'ts. Listen to the never haves, then listen close to me: Anything can happen, child. Anything can be.
—Shel Silverstein, writer

SELF-MANAGEMENT FOR ACTORS

GETTING DOWN TO (SHOW) BUSINESS
4th edition

by

Bonnie Gillespie

Cricket Feet Publishing
Los Angeles

Self-Management for Actors: Getting Down to (Show) Business
© 2014 by Bonnie Gillespie
Fourth Edition, Fourth Printing

Cricket Feet Publishing
PO Box 1417
Hollywood, CA 90028
323.397.7576
publisher@cricketfeet.com
cricketfeet.com

SCB Distributors
scbdistributors.com

Unattributed quotations are by Bonnie Gillespie.
Contributed essays are used with permission of the copyright holders.

Cover design by Shelley Delayne.
Bonnie's headshot by Holloway Pictures.
Printed in Canada.
LCCN 2012946170
ISBN 978-0972301961

Self-Management for Actors and Brandprov are registered trademarks.

WHAT OTHERS ARE SAYING ABOUT
SELF-MANAGEMENT FOR ACTORS

"Beyond mastering your craft, Bonnie Gillespie believes actors should learn how to manage the business side of the industry to establish a successful career. This straightforward guide offers advice about marketing yourself as well as managing your acting career."
—*Team Tom Cruise, tomcruise.com*

"I'm blown away by Bonnie Gillespie's wealth of industry knowledge. She makes us believe that it is possible; it's just a matter of having the tools and the knowledge to be proactive."
—*Stef Dawson, actor*

"What a great resource for actors! The advantages this book gives you are endless. Bonnie's advice and insight will enable you to have the leading edge over many actors. This book is a must-read if you are ready to turn acting into a career, yourself into a professional, and auditions into roles!"
—*Michelle Metzner, casting director*

"Bonnie Gillespie is one of the most prolific and readable writers out there. A must-have book, I give *Self-Management for Actors* my highest recommendation. Few books are as well-written as this one, and even fewer cover this critical information in the caring and concerned manner. *SMFA* is filled with specific action advice and thoughtful strategies. Every actor who has a tenacious desire to succeed in our little biz needs this excellent book."
—*Bob Fraser, author-producer-showrunner*

"*Self-Management for Actors* is a practical, usable, insightful book that every aspiring actor and every working actor should absorb in detail. This will be the best money you'll spend this year."
—*Bob Souer, voiceover artist*

"It is so crucial that actors realize they have to take control of their careers. Each chapter covers the actions to take and examples of how to take them. I love Bonnie's writing! *Self-Management for Actors* is really wonderful!"
—*Judy Kerr, actor-author-coach*

"At last! Someone who tells it like it *really* is. Bonnie has a handle on this mysterious process of *being* an actor. Bonnie's book is the best demystifying of this wacky industry and a must for every actor, beginning as well as advanced. Brilliant!"

—Joel Colman, director

"Bonnie Gillespie's wonderful book should be required reading for all actors! Every word, every sentence, and every idea is so clearly presented to help actors take charge of and manage their own careers. It's pure gold! Bonnie's eminently qualified, pure-gold advice should be treasured and followed."

—Lawrence Parke, Acting World Books

"The author's common sense and good humor make reading this book like having a long chat with an experienced friend in the business. Whether you're just starting out or a seasoned veteran, you will surely find both useful advice and amusingly identifiable anecdotes to keep you motivated and prepared for that next audition. Gillespie's smart and savvy expertise smiles through on every page."

—Nelson Aspen, Sunrise *Australia*

"I really had an epiphany thanks to *SMFA*. I was able to start thinking about my career and this industry in a totally different way."

—Lindsay Hollister, actor

"Between the specific advice and the anecdotes that prove their effectiveness, *SMFA* comes across more as a conversation than a mere how-to list. There's really something for actors at every level. There are the very practical and extremely helpful tips for those just starting out, through the insights best described as: 'I never heard it stated just that way before. Now I understand!' to the countless realizations: 'I never thought of that. That's something I should do immediately.' *Self-Management for Actors* is an indispensable handbook that should be in every actor's possession."

—Richard Riehle, actor

"This book has changed everything about the way I think about the industry, the way I do business, and the way I market myself. When I moved to LA from Orlando, I hit the ground running. I started booking right away thanks to *SMFA*."

—Mike Kalinowski, actor

"Bonnie Gillespie's book is insightful, informative, and nurturing. This book should be read by producers as well as actors to make that process as productive and creative as possible."

—*Nancy Meyer, producer-television development exec*

"Finally, someone—and it's no secret it's Bonnie Gillespie—has laid out in a clear, concise manner a way for writers, producers, casting directors, and even your own mother to see your work and hire you. Because remember, if we don't see you, you don't get hired. Not even if your mother owns the studio."

—*Mark Troy, writer*

"*Self-Management for Actors* is the ultimate step-by-step guide to success in the industry! There is no reason to find yourself adrift in the industry when you have expert guidance at your fingertips. Bonnie is well researched, intuitive, and wise beyond her years."

—*Lynn Stallings, Atlanta Workshop Players*

"Miss Bonnie will blow your mind. Her genuine passion, focus, and kindness is contagious. I credit her as my secret weapon."

—*Cassie Silva, actor*

"Bonnie Gillespie has the best hair in Hollywood!"

—*José Eber, celebrity stylist*

Don't ask what the world needs. Ask what makes you come alive, and go do it. Because what the world needs is people who have come alive.
—Howard Thurman, author

TABLE OF CONTENTS

FOREWORD

Shortly after receiving my MFA in acting, I came to the realization I was not particularly interested in the gypsy life of a regional theatre actor—I needed roots. The four people in the world that have ever heard me sing will tell you that Broadway wasn't the answer. I had been told, however, that my "unique look" (a nice euphemism for being weird-looking) might be well-suited for film and television. Everything was settled. I moved to Los Angeles in 1992 with the intention of pursuing a career in film and television and perhaps doing some supplemental theatre to prevent any "artistic stagnation."

I had received excellent training at a well-regarded institution. I had played clowns and villains, lunatics and straight men. I also vaguely remember wearing rope sandals and some kind of tunic but that memory is foggy. I was a good actor with a professional attitude and an interesting character face. How could Hollywood resist? Well, they were about to show me.

I'm embarrassed to admit it now, but I thought it would be relatively easy. I was sure that reputable talent agents all over town would be clamoring for a well-trained theatre actor, particularly one with no film credits and some tunic-sandal thingy on his resumé. I was convinced that the doors to casting offices would swing open and scripts would be handed to me from all angles. What I recognize now as absurd cockiness (or at least naïveté) is in some ways attributable to the Ivory Tower mentality of so many BFA and MFA programs.

We are taught in school that it is all about *craft*. If you have the talent and work on your voice and movement and rehearse your monologue enough times, then you will win the role. There are 28-year-olds all over the country playing King Lear. And some are doing it very well. What we don't realize at the time is that we are competing in a talent pool of 15 to 50 people, most of them within a 10-year age range. Audition slots are guaranteed; all you need to do is pick a time and sign up.

What I discovered after moving to Los Angeles is that I was competing with 10,000 people just to *meet* the person who *might* sign me and subsequently *try* to get me an audition. It was a whole new ballgame.

I don't mean to disparage these programs at all. They are invaluable and I applaud every actor that devotes his time and energy to the honing of his craft. I do believe, however, that many programs are remiss in teaching the realities of the business, particularly with regard to the world of film and television.

When an actor leaves school he is a *manufacturer* of a product (good acting). When he arrives in Los Angeles, he needs to learn to *sell* the product. As with any industry, manufacturing and sales require very different skill sets. I know many actors here who have a marvelous product but little ability to sell it. Conversely, I know lots and lots (and lots) of actors who are terrific salesmen but their product sorta stinks.

When an actor arrives in Los Angeles, he is hopefully the manufacturer of a good product, but many actors soon discover that there is a steep learning curve on the sales end. It can be extremely frustrating to know that you have a good product and find that nobody will even consider "buying" it. This frustration can lead to great bitterness and many good actors will "jump ship" before their time. I personally spent four years in a muffin factory. Although I look superb in a hairnet, I would have been quite content to cut those four years to one or two!

This is where Bonnie's book comes in. I believe it is geared toward actors that have some real training and a strong sense of craft but need to know how to transition into the "sales" arena. This book will teach every actor how to efficiently and effectively market himself as an actor, which can mean shaving years off the learning curve and saying goodbye to that crummy temp job just a little bit sooner.

—Bob Clendenin
SAG-AFTRA, AEA
ex-muffin employee

Introduction

For the fourth edition, I considered retitling this book *Self-Management for Creatives* or *Self-Management for Artists*. Truly, we're all creative freelancers, small business CEOs, brilliantly talented artists who may not have entrepreneurial brains.

But we must. Gone are the days of "I signed with *X* agent fresh out of conservatory so now I'm testing on a pilot." Sure, that *can* happen, but it's not the norm. And while you wait to see if you're one of the lucky ones for whom that type of success comes, you're missing loads of opportunities to tier-jump on your own.

So, you want to be an actor. Great! Welcome to one of the coolest, scariest, most exciting, adventure-filled, emotionally-fulfilling, and delightful careers out there. History is filled with people who have chosen to be the storytellers of their generation, charged with making sense of (or commenting on) the politics, social issues, and psychology of the world around them. By choosing to inhabit other people for moments, hours, or weeks at a time, actors shine a light on all sorts of things we can't—or won't—put together on our own about the mysteries of the human condition.

Whether you're pursuing acting as a hobby in community theatre somewhere or packing up and moving to Hollywood to become a full-fledged movie star, there are some elements that are universal. There are a few rules in this business. Many will tell you there are *no* rules and that's true too, which is *also* one of the rules. This is a confounding, confusing, crazymaking business and no two people will have the same journey, ever. That's a guarantee.

The pursuit of a creative career is a lot like the quest for fitness, and many folks want the magic pill, the secret diet, the easiest exercise that will suddenly give them the body of their dreams. There's a reason people spend bazillions of dollars searching for shortcuts rather than just doing the work. And just like within the fitness industry, success as an actor comes with hard work and discipline over time. It's not glamorous. Sometimes it's not even fun. But doing the work has great value, and that's where *Self-Management for Actors* comes in.

Many will say that you must have representation in order to succeed. Sure, a team is a great asset to your career—at the right time. Sign too soon or with the wrong rep and you could make mistakes from which recovery will be difficult. There is plenty of work to do before signing with a manager or agent. The *SMFA* goal is to turn you into your future rep's dream client!

Casting directors and producers generally do not care *at all* where submissions come from if you are the right actor for the role at the exact moment they need you. But—and here's where the whole "there are rules but there are no rules" thing gets ramped up—this *is* a relationship business, and especially in offices where it's difficult to get seen without representation (studio feature films and episodic series), casting directors rely heavily on relationships with agents and managers. We don't simply seek submissions of actors' headshots and resumés from agents and managers; we seek well-thought-out recommendations based on relationships cultivated over years of experience.

Let's be clear: This is *not* a book about how you *don't* need representation. It's a guide for all those career moves you can make to get you to the point at which you find the *right* agent or manager. I encourage actors to enter the game higher. Let's shave years off "the struggle" by controlling those elements we can, and by teaching the buyers what we do best.

While I freakin' love that *SMFA* has become a textbook in acting programs worldwide, I take issue with much formal acting training because it concentrates almost entirely on the craft and not much *at all* on the business of acting. Sure, maybe there was *one* day when resumé formatting was covered, or there was discussion of writing a decent cover letter, but did you discuss brand management? How about handling junkets? Or getting in the room when "the usual stuff" isn't working? If you're reading *SMFA* because your school requires it, thank your professor! There's a generation of actors out there who received no business guidance in their formal training. You—equipped with ninja tools—can change this industry and the world!

The ninja actor isn't afraid of doing research. You know it's not just about the craft—it's about being able to share your craft with the broadest audience possible, and that comes from building relationships and getting access to opportunities at the higher tiers. Use the vast resource that is the online acting community to start building up your knowledge base and your relationships. Attend every free panel discussion, seminar, or class audit that you can find. Information shared at these events—while more limited than what may exist in ongoing classes—is both valuable and motivational. Don't ever let the excuse for inaction be: "If only I had more information." Knowledge is free. Go get yours!

Take classes wherever you feel the most comfortable *and* the most challenged. Work out parts of your craft you haven't explored yet and make sure that you always audit classes before you plunk down registration fees. Auditing ensures that you connect with the instructor and allows you to talk with current students to make sure the classes are a good fit to your needs. Don't get in a rut with any one instructor or technique. Explore your options and have fun!

Now for that big, ridiculous question everyone asks, when consulting actors: *Can you be happy doing anything other than acting?*

I actually despise this question. It's so weird to me, when I read so-called experts saying, "If you can be happy doing anything other than acting, do it." I get why they say it. They're trying to keep you from experiencing all of the rejection and heartbreak that comes with a career in acting. But honey, there's rejection and heartbreak in *every* life. To believe that choosing to pursue a career in something *other than* your life's dream is to steer *away* from heartache is ridiculous. It's flat-out ignorant about what life itself contains. You're not going to *spare yourself* feelings of hurt by leaving your dreams behind. You'll always wonder "what if" and that's a recipe for a life filled with bitterness.

Oh, and in case it matters, I don't really believe rejection exists in this business. It's just the matter of a paradigm shift, actually. Every time you are invited to submit a headshot, asked to audition, or requested for a callback, you are being *included*, not rejected. Being *rejected* would mean hearing, "You're not an actor! Go away!" and that's not what's happening when we cast someone else after you made it all the way to final callbacks. That's not rejection *at all*.

Want to try acting? Great. Everything you need to do to succeed in this business starts with getting out of your own way. There is nothing linear or fair about the way success is found in this industry, so to try and make statistics or even logic apply—or worse, to believe you've earned or you deserve success— is to drive yourself nuts (and to give your family ammunition with which to pester you about choosing some "safer" career).

My first professional acting credit was in the summer of 1977, right after my seventh birthday, and I've been infused in this business ever since. If there's anything I know 100% for *sure*, it's that there is no one way to crack this nut. There is no one way to become a success in this business. There is no one *thing* that if everyone did it, they'd be instantly famous. (Believe me, if there were such a thing, I'd have written *that* book and I would retire to my private island.) The reason it's **SELF**-*Management for Actors* is because the journey is an individual one. Sure, there are patterns. Sure, there are some "rules" this industry has about how it operates. But it's changing every day, and the ninja move is to be plugged in and aware of how our business is changing, be well-versed in the history of how "it's always been," and be smart enough to track when you're encountering someone with whom you have to go "old school" vs. someone with whom you can go "next generation."

Case-by-case is your best friend, here. Believing there's just one way to "make it" is to ignore every great success story you've ever heard. *SMFA* is not about overturning a system. It's about mastering one: your *own*. Your path— like you—is unique. How freakin' awesome!

When I first moved to LA there were no casting directors sharing their toys like they do now. Today, in the era of CDs (and agents and managers and showrunners and producers and directors and writers and publicists) blogging, vlogging, tweeting, writing guest columns for publications, being interviewed in DVD behind-the-scenes extras about their process, showing up on reality shows, authoring books, hosting livestream panels, etc., we are *overloaded* with actor advantages, since actors now have *no excuse* for not studying up before a first encounter. The information is out there, and free, and that is truly badass.

The biggest shift of it all, I believe, is that we're seeing a generational handing off of the baton from a group of people who had the mindset of, "I walked uphill in the snow both ways to and from school every day," or—for our industry—"It was *hard* for me to get where I am so I'm certainly not sharing my *how* because you'll steal jobs from me," and, "I had to scrap and scheme and hustle to get my SAG card and you kids today have no idea how easy you've got it just walking up and creating a new media project and becoming union eligible," yada yada yada (Tell that story again, grandpa!) and that baton is being passed to a generation of "open source."

A generation of, "Hey, here's a lifehack I've tried that has helped me in my productivity. Hey, here's something I found useful and maybe you will too. Hey, if I like this information, I'm gonna hit the *share* button because it's not nearly as much fun for me to hoard the good info for myself." It's a generation of, "My jobs are my jobs and there's no one who will *steal* my job just by knowing how to join the union or how to format a resumé or how to organize a show bible. If I don't get it, then I *hope* it's you, because I love my community and the resources I've shared to help build it."

Just like the on-camera union merger finally went through, just like the Internet has become a legitimate source of original programming at the professional—and Emmy-winning—level, just like *Self-Management for Actors* has become a textbook in schools all over the world, the resistance that creates the "I know nothing about actor branding" statement is going to die off soon, in favor of pulling back the curtain and saying, "Yeah. The reason that actor gets in front of me is because he's so well-branded both for what he delivers creatively and the consistency and professionalism with which he delivers it."

We're building a better Hollywood every day that we make choices that include one another, that embrace the collaborative process, that celebrate the "yes, and..." of it all. Clutching "trade secrets" is as effective as trying to hold on to a fistful of sand. I say, let's all get in there and build castles together!

Start now. Even if you're at the very beginning of your creative journey, share your toys. Your ability to pull back the curtain on your process *today* will make a difference in someone's life down the line. Believe that. Don't wait 'til you're at the top tier to decide it's time to give back. Be "open source" today. Not only will it *not* cost you work, it'll help you transform this industry into one you're ridiculously more proud to be a part of, every day.

Be excited that you are living your life as a working actor. The work is more than what you do on a set. Stay inspired every day! As you learn to market yourself, if you're not excited about that process, how can anyone else be? It *is* overwhelming. I know! I've seen many really talented actors burn out from trying to keep up with the business end of things. It's not an easily-developed skill, but it is essential. In the pages that follow, I—with the help of some of the most brilliant people I know, who so generously contributed words of wisdom—will try to break it all down into a process that is easier to follow and less intimidating than it appears when you're on your own, looking at the many business-related tasks all at once.

That's my goal: to present information in such a way that you think, "Man! Why didn't I think of that?" Then I want to see you move forward with the advice in little steps and, hopefully, remember to give me a shoutout when you hold up something gold and shiny, right after you thank the Academy. Not too much to ask, is it?

Another request I have is that you keep me posted on how things go for you (join us at smfa4.com to get plugged in now). I'd love to keep up with your progress. It will help me give better advice when I know what is working for you and what snags may come up along the way.

Remember that there is nothing magic or even a little mystical about the business side of the business. There is, however, a cloak of protection around some industry information. As one casting director told me, "This is *not* classified information! Most of it is common sense and the rest of it is all available through research." Sure. But research can be tedious, and as an artist, you are trying very hard to balance the muse that helps you create, the inspiration that keeps you going, *and* the organizational skills that allow you to navigate it all.

Oh yes, and you're trying not to take it personally, when you don't get cast! Forget about keeping all those balls in the air at once. Reward yourself for *each* success you have in the complex life that is the actor's.

One of the best things Keith Johnson—my partner—taught me was that you have to launch at 85%. If you wait for everything to be perfect, you'll never start. Because nothing will *ever* be perfect. And, babe, what if you *could* get it to be perfect? Let's think about that!

If you *could* reach perfection on something (your marketing tools, your target list, your script for your self-produced short, your personal pitch) and then it failed (because sometimes, no matter how great it is, it will fail), what would *that* mean to your ego? Ouch. A lot of crushola, if you ask me.

We are all gonna fail. We are all gonna scrap and struggle. We're all gonna have amazing, blissed out days in which everything is all kinds o' perfect. And none of those bad or good or just vanilla days came about because of anything having been *perfect* before we got going.

Get going. Whatever it is you're hoping will line up exactly right before you hit "launch," stop waiting for it. Start. Just go. Take a step in the right direction and learn from it all. You'll be better equipped next time. And the next. And the next. But you'll never launch at 100%. There's just no such thing.

Please note that, throughout this book, any specific mention of a company is simply that: a mention. I have not been paid to represent any company or service in good favor and you should make no assumption as to the reputation of such companies and services. Always verify information from *any* source before taking big leaps of faith or finances. Additionally, the information provided herein does not represent a recipe for success, a guarantee of a job, or even a promise of increased confidence in audition situations. Application is up to you!

Finally, you'll notice that I have chosen to refer to casting directors using the female pronoun. This is not due to some feminist agenda, but due to the fact that casting is one of the only female-dominated segments of the entertainment industry. In an attempt to balance the scales a bit, I have chosen to refer to actors, agents, and managers using the male pronoun.

Throughout the book, you'll see calls to action for visits to smfa4.com to get *SMFA* Hot List downloads that round out your *Self-Management for Actors* experience. If you do not have access to our website, just drop a self-addressed, stamped 9x12 envelope in the mail to us at Cricket Feet Publishing, PO Box 1417, Hollywood, CA 90028, and we'll get you all the freebies via snail mail.

Enjoy this fourth edition of *Self-Management for Actors*. If you have borrowed this book from a friend and would like one of your own, please visit smfa4.com. Heck, maybe even add the audiobook version to your collection! Break a leg, have fun, don't suck, and remember: Live your dreams! If you don't, someone else will..

ACKNOWLEDGMENTS

It is impossible to list off every person whose fingerprints are on the success of *Self-Management for Actors*, both as a book and as a lifestyle. Still, I will attempt to single out some of the folks whose participation in the evolution of *SMFA* has had enduring impact. Wish me luck!

Let's start with the illustrious members of Team Cricket Feet, past and present: Ellie Abrams, Ryan Angel, Ryan Basham, Camille Bennett, Christina Blevins, Verona Blue, Anna Borchert, Kathi Carey, Ana-Julia Cavana, Candice Marie Flournoy, Emily Gibson, Carolina Groppa, Kevin Hartley, Julie Inmon, Jermaine Johnson, Lindsay Katai, Erich Lane, Jill Maglione, Dave Manship, Jeff Michael, Mandi Moss, Daniele Passantino, Chari Pere, Amber Plaster, Jennie Roberson, Jay Ruggieri, Mae Ruling, Nick Sayaan, Tamika Simpkins, Jacqueline Steiger, Beau Wilson, and Brian Wold. Gold stars for the ninja angels I so treasure: Jen Losi, Mércedes Manning, and Erin Zapcic.

The companion "Bonnie in your pocket" guide to this fourth edition— SMFA: The Ninja Within—came together thanks to the research team and proofer patrol of Rose Auerbach, Ben Blair, Joni Harbin, Claudia Hoag, Dan Knight, Eric Olson, Brian Smith, Karl Stober, Mary Torio, Naomi Vondell, Dina Wilson, and Denise Winsor.

For this delicious fourth edition itself, I had a ton of help from several of the rockstars listed above, as well as from my team of advisors, promoters, and proofers: Jennie Ahlgren, Leah Cevoli, Dave Conrey, Deb Cresswell, Christina Gray, Amy Harber, Konstantina Mallios, Deb Mellman, Lenka Šilhánová, Claartje van Swaaij, Sean Walton, and Ross Watkins. Of course, the cover design for both books was lovingly crafted by Shelley Delayne, and without the leadership of super proofers Hannah Knudsen and Marie Watkins, neither book would exist. At least not yet! Team, I thank you from the bottom of my heart. It has been a joy to jam with all of you.

Without the mentorship, friendship, and inspiration provided by Bob Brody, Twinkie Byrd, Paula Dorn, Mignon Fogarty, Leslie Gornstein, Marg Haynes, Anne Henry, Blair Hickey, Deborah Jacobson, Lesly Kahn, Gary Marsh, Lawrence Parke, Dan Poynter, Faith Salie, Aaron Silverman, Lisa Soltau, Anna Vocino, and Rob Weinert-Kendt, Self-Management for Actors would be a completely different book. I am so very grateful to you all for the significant influence you've had in my life.

My physical and spiritual fitness exist due in no small part to the loving encouragement of Sabrina Bolin, Lisa and Laura Bunbury, Louise Flory, Mark Gantt, Steph Gaudreau, Melissa Hartwig, Esther Hicks, Judy Kerr, Bree Melanson, Mary Grace Montemayor, Chrystal Rahmani, Drea and David Roers, Colleen Wainwright, Bex Weller, and Amanda Wing. Whether you've helped me dream bigger, coached me to push harder, or simply reminded me that my work is to weave dreams, I am a better person thanks to your gifts.

I am especially grateful to the brilliant folks whose essays and quotes are shared throughout this book. Your "yes, and..." action inspires me! Of course, this book would not have thrived since 2003 without the many professors who have added *Self-Management for Actors* to course curricula around the world. To every actor (and every hyphenate) with whom I've worked online and in person: You have become a part of *SMFA* just by sharing your journey with me. And to all the generous contributors to our campaign to keep this book in print—most notably Mara Grace, Austin Sloan, and Elizabeth and Brandt Stevens—well, this book is yours. Literally. Thank you for the support. I am humbled by your belief in an edition that didn't exist at the time you raised your hand to say, "I'm in."

Finally, I'll sign off my sappy thank-yous with a sweet kiss to the people who live closest to my heart, every day: Kim Estes, Jean Hull, Quinn Johnson, Laurie Records, Katie Swain, Charlsie and Art Weaver, and of course, my beloved husband Keith Johnson. You are the only one who knows exactly what goes into 424 pages of my life's work. Thank you for honoring the process with as much grace as is spousily possible. I love you.

PART ONE: MINDSET

We don't see things as they are; we see them as we are.
—Anaïs Nin, author

1 : WHAT'S IMPORTANT

A healthy mindset is perhaps the most important element in a working actor's ability to self-manage. There will be times you will have to work "outside yourself" in order to be your own best advisor. A manager or an agent will have a vision of how to market you that you may not see. While self-management is a term that implies you do it all for yourself, there certainly will be ample opportunity for you to consult with mentors, experts, and peers. So, make sure you have a mindset that allows for constructive criticism without allowing feedback to land with an ego-shattering blow.

How best to do that? Remember that your acting career is, in fact, a business. Some people recommend that actors see themselves as products, with the casting director as the shopper, the producer as the buyer, the agent or manager as the marketing director, and the audience as the product's end consumer. If that analogy works for you, by all means, go with it. I'll just remind you that you're operating a business every day and that requires not only the lovely creative mind that allows you to embody other characters, but also the organizational skills of a successful business owner. If the idea of becoming organized or developing managerial skills repulses you, then self-management is not for you. You will need to rely on luck, talent, and timing to have your creative dreams realized. Those who self-manage, though, have the added benefit of a certain level of control over their own career paths.

Marketing is a major part of an actor's success. Yes, of course, there's craft, there's raw talent, there's a look, there's luck... but there is much more staying power among those with business sense and marketing savvy. It really can give you an edge over someone else who may be evenly-matched with you in every other element.

Breaking It Down

What factor has the most impact on whether an actor is called in for an audition over another actor? Is it training? Look? Special skills? Union status? Credits? Agency representation? I like to answer that question with a quip shared by CSA soap opera casting director Mark Teschner. When asked what the *one* most important factor for getting called in was, Teschner responded, "Shirt color!" And what is that shirt color? "Blue." Of course, that's a joke, but it really summarizes the way casting directors feel about the minutiae actors tend to place emphasis on, when dissecting the "call-in" factors.

There is no *one* thing. There are so many things—and there are no things—that make the difference in whether a certain actor is called in for an audition. So, rather than focusing on breaking down those indefinable elements, which differ based on who you ask, I'd like to focus on breaking down the few things actors *do* control—shirt color being one of them, of course!

I am a recovering academic and would *love* to apply science (or at least empirical statistical analysis) to the casting process. Sadly, the process is more of a "gut instinct" than anything else. Casting directors take a look at your headshot and say, "Yep. That's the *type* we need. Ooh, there's something going on in the eyes. There's a life there." Then we start skimming the credits. "Hmm. He's worked with so-and-so. That's a great director! Oh, trained with what's-her-name. Ooh! Improv! That's great. He's repped by this-and-that-agency. Super! We have a relationship with them. Call him in!"

Before there's a relationship on which to bank, getting called in is more about an overall *feeling* the casting director gets when she first sees your headshot. That's why everything in your marketing arsenal should come across as clearly representative of your brand.

As for what single element carries the most weight, relationships are everything. If you have studied with, have worked with, or are repped by someone with whom the casting director has a connection, you're a lot closer to "in" than you might imagine.

Don't focus on what might be the most "important" item on your resumé or the value any one casting director may place on your training or the agency logo you're sporting. Focus instead on putting together an overall marketing plan that you can be proud of and that you feel *really* represents your brand accurately. Your "vibe" should come through all of your materials. After that, it's just a matter of what you're putting out there connecting to something in the casting director.

Is a good headshot important? Yes. Is it even more important that the headshot looks like you? Yes. Can a headshot get you in the room? Yes. Do credits matter? Yes. But remember, your headshot will be looked at first. I don't know a single casting director who *first* looks at a resumé and *then* checks to see if the actor's look is of any interest to her.

Does representation matter? Sure. If you are signed with a great agent who has a fantastic relationship with a casting director who just *happens* to be looking for your type *right now* and who happens to reach out to your agent asking for your type, then yes: Your representation just got you in the room. But, since I'm assuming you're working on the whole self-management concept *because* you don't have that perfect agent with that perfect relationship at that perfect moment (not yet anyway), I'll continue with the rest of what matters.

Naturally, you want to be sure you're getting into the right casting directors' offices. The *best* way to be sure that happens? Make connections in the industry. Network. Meet people who know people who know people and invest in your relationships. It's not about who you know. It's about who *they* know. You may have connections you don't even realize yet.

Once you begin connecting with people who work in the industry, you'll learn that a casting colleague has mentioned a new project for which you'd be perfect to a contact you share. Your friend will call you and say, "Get your headshot over to so-and-so's office and tell her I sent you." Need an agent to make that happen? No way.

> *Your submission nominates you (agency submissions are like belonging to the right political party, a much stronger nomination). Your headshot seconds the nomination. Your cover letter is your campaign speech. Your resumé and reel vote you into office. Your audition is your term. Callbacks are how you're doing in the polls. Booking the job is your re-election. Once you're an incumbent, it's easier to stay in office. A string of jobs is your political career.*
>
> —Robin Gwynne, actor

Remember, there will always be the next job and the next job and the next job. Don't ever focus on how much you could be doing "if only" you had an agent, "if only" you had league school training, "if only" you were taller, "if only" you were younger. You are who you are, where you are, and opportunities are out there. You're in this for the long haul and you can start whenever, wherever you are. Always move forward to the next tier. Just get started!

> *It never gets easier. At first, you're trying to land an agent. Then, you're trying to book that first speaking role on TV, then all you need is that first guest-star credit to launch you. Then it's a recurring role. And of course, the series regular, the promised land. People get frustrated there too. Sure, by the time you're a series regular you're making great money, but you're also prevented from booking all kinds of features and other television roles due to your contract. Many series regular actors have abandoned their steady gigs because of the "grass is greener" complex. Is the grass truly greener? Sometimes. Sometimes not. It depends on you.*
>
> —Assaf Cohen, actor

Bitter Actor Syndrome

Your energy walks into the room before you do. Most people who study social interactions can tell you about "vibes" that enter spaces before an encounter between two parties. Call it an aura, a mood, energy, whatever. It's fascinating to observe the shifts in tone the room takes in an average day of casting sessions, as actor after actor comes and goes. If your energy is toxic, we're going to feel that and possibly get defensive toward you before you even begin your audition. We may not know why, but we'll say later, "He just rubbed me the wrong way."

Because this energy thing can be an obstacle that stands between you and the role—and it's an obstacle you control—let's look at how bitter actor syndrome begins and how to prevent it.

People in general become bitter when they believe the world owes them something they're not getting. Someone who has "done everything right" and still "gets nowhere" risks becoming bitter, simply due to the fact that he has that perception. A little myth-busting: There is no "doing everything right"— not in this business (and not in life, really). Everyone has his own path and every actor would share a different story about the road and its obstacles, even if the destination each actor reached were the same. There is also no "getting nowhere." Even if you stand still, you have made some progress just by attempting a career in this industry—something many people wish they had the courage to do.

Bitter actors seem to do things like compare themselves to others of their age, of their type, of their look, from their hometown, who they see in audition waiting rooms, who they see accepting Oscars. Of course, non-bitter actors will do a little comparing too, but they don't obsess on comparisons. They *observe* them. When you find yourself overly-concerned with how someone else is doing, ask yourself if you are obsessing or observing. If you can't tell, here's a tip: Observation is fleeting and judgment-free. Obsession sticks around a long while and packs loads of judgments.

Most of the time that people grouse about nepotism or favoritism, they neglect to notice that there is a requirement that *talent*—at a sustainable level—exist on the part of those who are granted chances "unfairly," or else they will never maintain the success to which they were given access. The first shot at it may come easy, but these folks won't endure if they can't deliver the goods.

Even as we study the successful, we can't just "do what they did" because we are not who they are, were not born into the era into which they were born, don't have the same charisma or smarts or *whatever* it is that existed for them when they did those things. This is one of my favorite principles in Malcolm Gladwell's *Outliers*, and it's what I always say: It's not the one thing you do; it's all the things you do.

Sometimes it's that random thing that just happened to happen, irrespective of the work you put into your career or how much you tried to make happen. So much of what you do can put you up against that thinnest line (the line between "struggling actor" and "ultimate success"), but what pushes you past that line has much less science to it. It's magic.

The unpredictability of what makes for a *huge* success is actually one of my favorite things in this business. It's the "there's a chip on the floor as you walk through the casino. You *have to* play it. To which table do you take it and what skill do you bring to *that* game you chose, to make it so you *at least* get two chips from that amazing opportunity? And then how do you use those chips?" thing.

I really effin' love that. It's why everyone has a shot at being a success story for others to study.

What are you doing to get as close to that thinnest line as possible? What are you preparing to bring to the table, so that when you stumble upon that chip in the casino, you make the most of your time? And what will you give back to the world, as it asks if it may study your success, once you've gotten to the top tier? Map it out now. It's good for you, and for the world.

The process of getting cast is crazymaking and always will be. Absolutely, you need to stay mindful of the business and its many rules, non-rules, idiosyncrasies, and nonsensical jolts, but what you control is your performance. When you find yourself mired in what I call "monkey mind," fixated on the unfairness of this industry with a chatter that will not stop, shift your energy. Work on a character, dust off a monologue, get better at a special skill, write up a scene to do in class, or transcribe a bit of dialogue from a favorite movie. Go get in a play that no one will ever see at a hole-in-the-wall theatre. Do open mic night at a stand-up comedy club. Sing karaoke and scare yourself silly over how well you can belt out some classic rock. Get inspired and get out of your head about the process using anything in the chapter called **Your Business Plan**. There are infinite potential factors involved in your getting an invitation into any audition room, almost none of which you control. Bitter actors spend a lot of time focused on those issues. Non-bitter actors work on their craft and keep a healthy perspective on the rest of the process.

The reason we don't want to work with bitter actors is the same reason we don't want to deal with bitter DMV representatives or bitter bank tellers. Bitter people are *not fun* to spend time with. And when we have so very many options regarding who we choose to spend time with (as is the case when casting a role for which thousands of actors have submitted), we will almost always choose to populate the set with the equally-talented actor with the better energy. It's human nature for us to want to get along with those we *choose* to spend time with. No one cares why you're bitter, we just know it doesn't feel good to be around you, and we *will* choose to work with someone else.

If you're really stewing in bitterness, consider taking a break for a while. It's not a bad idea to get recharged *personally* before giving the biz another go. I did that when I went to grad school and I think that's part of the reason I'm successful "this time out" in Hollywood. Because this industry is very open to people stopping or starting at any age, at any time, it's not the end of the world if you decide you need a year or two "off" to get your head together. Oh, and a "break" can be as short as a long weekend.

Conspiracy of Yes

I get hundreds of pictures for every role. The number of people who I can't hire is mind-boggling to me. So, when someone comes in and it feels like they don't want to be there, I think, "You must *pick another career." Your job as an actor is to audition. And if you audition well, your reward is getting the part.*

—Lisa Miller Katz, CSA

When you think about all of the factors that go into casting a single role, it becomes clear that it's a conspiracy of events that lead to a *yes*.

There's the breakdown going out in a place you have access to it, for starters. Assuming you have no representation out there pitching you on projects that come through "the real Breakdowns," that means the project needs to show up on Actors Access (or any of the places covered in the chapter called **Become a Booking Machine**) or your personal networking needs to have landed the project on your radar despite its absence from Actors Access or other legitimate direct-to-actors project listing services.

If you do have representation (yay, you), that means you need those folks who rep you to see the breakdown, think of you, and submit (or even pitch—again, yay, you) you on the appropriate role. Then that submission needs to be seen by the casting director who put out the breakdown. Easier said than done.

Looking at submissions on a union feature film project I cast in Los Angeles, but shooting outside of Hollywood, we received 13,389 electronic submissions via Breakdown Services and Actors Access in just two months. (Most of 'em arrived in the first week, as instructed, of course.)

Okay, so let's assume your headshot has made it to the computer screen on a project someone is casting. What are the odds your submission is given any sort of quality time, as page after page of thumbnails cross in front of us? The odds are better if your submission comes from an agent or manager with whom we have a great relationship, or if we already have had a positive experience with you via previous audition, networking encounter, marketing efforts on your part, or even our online awareness of you and your work. Obviously, if your look is a slam-dunk for the role, you'll stay in the mix through that first headshot thumbnail pass.

At this point, you've already crossed a few hurdles: awareness of the project, submission on the appropriate role, and acknowledgement by us that you're in the mix. Even now, it could turn out that you're not right for the part, or we've already cast the role by the time you've gotten on our radar, or they've written scenes out, or the project's funding has fallen out, or the union status of the film now prevents you from participating, or the role now calls for nudity and that's not your thing, or any number of other issues.

So, let's say none of that stuff has happened (but still, respect that it could, as we're calculating the conspiracy of yes, here) and somehow you've made it farther than another several hundred (or several thousand) actors to stay in the mix with a few dozen who will be more seriously reviewed. If you're at this point not due to an existing relationship (yours or that of your agent or manager—which would put you ahead without as much of the "little stuff" I'm about to mention), that means your look is right on. Your credits inspire confidence in us that you'd be low-risk for this role. The work on your reel lines up with what we need on this project. You're a good "family match" for someone we've already cast. Everything is lining up enough that the thought of an audition for you isn't too far-fetched.

Yeah, I've called all of that "little stuff," but it's not. Not at all. It's all a part of the conspiracy of yes, and we're not even at the yes, yet! We're just at the "you're still in the mix and we're just now scheduling auditions" stage of things. Yikes! Much more to go.

Okay, so you get the call that you have an audition. Awesome! More with the "yay, you" of it all. Assuming you're the type to do all the right things, in terms of actor prep (which means you research the team on this project via the trades, IMDb-Pro, CastingAbout, and good ol' Google; get your sides—or, better yet, get a copy of the entire script—and get to reading; and begin making creative choices about your audition way in advance of walking into the room), you help yourself toward your yes with each of those bits. Of course, you also make sure your schedule can accommodate the audition; get off work if you have to; switch a shift. Find out where the audition is and, if you've never been there before, find out how to get there, how long the commute will take, where to park, and whether you need coins for the meter or if you'll need your ID for on-lot access that was granted ahead of time.

Phew! Exhausted yet? You haven't even entered the room! So, you do that. Yay, you! You've found your way there, made it on time, shown up prepared and ready to rock. You've signed in, made it through any waiting room games your colleagues are playing, and didn't let anything shake you when you walked in the room. That means stuff like a change in sides, a change in character description, a change in whether you're being taped or not, a change in who's in the room during your read, a change in the location of the audition itself—any of that!

Then you do a good job. You have fun; you don't suck. Best possible audition you can have, since you've shown us your work and your work was good.

More conspiracy going on: *Alllll* of that goes right and you're also the perfect type. There was no awkward small talk (or if there were, it went unnoticed by the folks you worry you offended). You don't look like the producer's ex. Your talent, your choices, your chemistry, your work, your vibe all lines up. And even though there are several people on the creative team who have a favorite, you're the one who comes out on top. You get the offer. The role is yours.

Ah, not so fast. Then there's the schedule, the negotiating of the deal itself. The terms and the timing can be some of the biggest elements to the conspiracy of yes! This stuff is where casting falls through many times, and you may never even know it.

Let's say everything works out. You're free during the shoot. It pays what your team agrees you need to be paid for this level of work. You sign off and begin packing for your trip to location, or your trip to the lot for a one-day guest. Whatever. Point is, you booked it. Time to celebrate!

Now, I'm not even getting into conspiracy of staying in the project. Not getting cut before you shoot, or after. Or of staying in the project but having the role rewritten and suddenly it's much smaller than what you had agreed to accept. To even begin going into the myriad things that *keep* an actor in a part would be another few pages in this chapter. You get the point, right?

It takes a huge conspiracy of many, many things for anyone to get a *yes* in this business. For an actor to be cast, for a show to be picked up, for a film to be greenlit, for an agent to land a top client, for an exec to be named a studio head. It's a conspiracy of too many things to even calculate sometimes. Think it through—and I mean *all the way* through—just once and then find a way to stay grateful for *however* far you get in the process, every single time. It's a miracle anyone ever gets their "big break." Yet every day, someone does. Let's help make that someone be you!

On Fairness

Now, I'm all for standing up for violation of rights (you signed a contract that said you'd get a copy of your footage, you are due that footage and need to make noise to get it if they don't make it easy for some reason; you were told there would be no nudity and then you're on set being told to strip, that's your cue to exit stage left; you are held way too long at a commercial audition and the union has fought for you to get paid for that, and you should), but I'm also a fan of being *happy*. I think a lot of things that actors choose to get upset about are things that *aren't* going to change—no matter how much energy we throw at them—and there's just far better use of that energy, in my opinion. Especially when the focus on the unfairness of it all pulls you out of happiness.

Sometimes what smarts is a room full of gruff attitudes, in an audition. I'm reminded of a brilliant take on that from showrunner Jonathan Shapiro. When we talked about "the room" and warm rooms vs. cold rooms and last-minute changes and how actors are treated, Shapiro stressed that we're looking for actors to come in, do a job, do it well. Sure. We all know that. But when he shared an analogy about how *everyone* in a position to kill the series, fire the showrunner, or end a career is behaving about the importance of *every* decision and *every* moment, it became crystal clear to me.

He said, essentially: "When my house is on fire, if I'm less than polite to the firefighters, it doesn't mean I don't appreciate them. They have one job to do, and I'm in a panic about 100 things." No, we're not saving lives as we produce content to entertain people, but because the higher-ups treat it as such, those who are hoping to get hired, make a good impression, or be asked back need to at least understand the mindset, as unfair as it may feel. Come in, do your job well, and don't *need* love. Enjoy it if you get it, but find love in other places. Don't go looking for it in the casting room. Or in Hollywood, for that matter.

Complaining is a choice. Social networking makes that choice easier, it seems. This industry is a machine that's been in place for a long time, and even though in many ways we're in the Wild West of the entertainment industry, it's still easier to change this beast from within. And that means understanding it—unfairness and all—and then *getting inside*, where we can make changes and turn this into the business we *want* it to be.

High Self-Esteem, Low Ego

A "no" isn't personal. A "yes" is personal.

—Allen Hooper, CSA

You pretty much have to have high self-esteem to pursue a career in this business. It's an exhausting pursuit that will make you question your sanity sometimes and you *have* to feel somewhat special to believe you can outlast and outshine the competition, most of whom leave this career with their dreams broken and hearts sick over all that time, investment, and belief that *it could really happen* spent with little return. If you feel as though you can make it, you probably have high self-esteem. You feel special. You know you're tougher than those who pack it in and go home. You're here for the long haul and you know there will be dips in the road along the way.

Low ego is the balance that those who *truly* succeed seem to have attained. Because an ego—which inherently feeds on validation and outwardly-confirmable benchmarks for success—also has the power to derail you, if it's out of control. It presents as entitled. It charges into the room as a challenge to all: "How can you *not* cast this? I am perfect and you're too stupid to have realized that by now. What's wrong with you, peasant?" Perfectly talented actors find themselves constantly wondering "what's wrong with this town" for not recognizing their brilliance, when what we're actually doing is absolutely recognizing their brilliance, but knowing there are dozens—if not hundreds—of other actors of the exact same type and talent level who *don't* bring the beast of the ego to set with them. Guess which actor we'd rather spend time with?

> *Your ego is like your stage mom. Leave her in the lobby for auditions, rehearsals, classes, on set, etc., or she will eff you up!*
> —Lesly Kahn, acting coach

Dichotomy Required

You must be vulnerable so that you can freely access your emotions, yet hard-shelled enough to deal with the criticism, rejection, and exhaustion of pursuing this career.

You must care enough about a role to prepare with gusto and have confidence in the product you're offering up, but care so little that it's easy to forget you were on avail, had a pin in you, or booked the gig before the money fell out or they cut the role.

You must be both creative and business-minded and know when to switch from one to the other, as creatives scare the bejeezus out of suits, but people who don't know how to negotiate because they're so busy dreaming get eaten alive in this business.

You must know how to spin the projects you have coming up without stealing focus from those you're promoting right now, since your enthusiasm for the latter was at its peak months or years before you're being asked to give good mic on the red carpet.

You must be encouraged by love and adoration from the fanbase you worked so hard to create, but not so tied up in whether anyone gives a crap about what you're doing that *you* give a crap about the hate some will spew, the more high-profile you become.

You must be able to hear endless advice about "how this works" and both take the advice that will help you and throw away the advice that doesn't apply, wouldn't help, or simply isn't right for you *right now*.

Yes, there is craft, but there is business. Yes, there is art, but there are numbers. Yes, there is vision, but there is product. And if you can ping-pong back and forth between each world, you're well on your way to enduring all of the "stuff" that confounds the rest of the world (those who watch entertainers and scratch their heads—both because they're in awe of the talent required in what we do and because they're confused as to how we can be so irresponsible as to hang a career on a dream).

Throughout this book, I'm going to ask you to do meticulous research, to study your potential buyers, to become an expert on those with whom you hope to jam, creatively, over the course of your career. And then I'm going to tell you to let all that work hum quietly in the background, while you have fun with your pursuit. You're not going to try to *become* what the buyers want; you're going to be your authentic self, telling the stories you most want to tell, confident that you've identified the buyers who most need to know you (since they help populate the stories you were born to tell).

That's the ultimate dichotomy required of those who endure this beautiful business: Care a lot. And let it all go.

In a world where you hear no *much more than* yes, *you've gotta find some way to make friends with* no.

—Julie Bowen, actor

2: THE COSTS OF ACTING

Wait. The chapter called "The Costs of Acting" is in the Mindset section? Yeah. And it's not about monetary costs. For that, hop to the chapter on **Money Management**. This chapter is all about helping you and your family cope with your career choice, getting you set with commitment, and avoiding the shady stuff that you may encounter along your journey.

What are the costs you can expect, in choosing a career as a performing artist? They'll be emotional, mental, and spiritual in nature, and for some actors, these costs will add up to far more than any dollar amount spent on pursuing acting in any given year. There are costs to your relationships and to your sanity. Yet most actors could never choose another career. Despite the fact that the pursuit of acting at a professional level in a major market is one in which the odds will never be in your favor, many people will give up everything in order to give it a shot.

I would never discourage anyone from living his dreams. I am living mine, and I know that I would've chosen to do so no matter how many people tried to tell me not to risk so much on a "maybe." But the thing is, to me that word "maybe" means just that: It *may be*. Not: It *may not be*. Right there, there's a chance! And I'm a glass-half-full kind of gal. So, while this chapter may depress you (and perhaps be used against you by your family, when they're lobbying for you to think it over and choose a safer life), I know that it will also inspire you to make it happen, no matter what the costs. And there are costs. Don't ever think this career choice will be an easy one. That doesn't mean it won't be worth it all, but it sure as heck will challenge your spirit sometimes.

Your Relationships

You start off by moving thousands of miles away from your family and closest friends. Jealous partners can't handle seeing you in love scenes with other actors (or you fall in love with every new co-star and dump your significant other with each new film). Friends you had back home won't *get* you anymore, since you've "gone all Hollywood" or can't talk about anything "normal" anymore, don't eat when you go out to restaurants with them, or never visit without a script in your hand and a cell phone attached to your ear. Actor friends you used to sit around and rant with about the worst parts of the industry will find themselves envious of your success (and it doesn't even have to be a significant amount of success for this to start happening). Family members will actually take pleasure in your failure, because that's when you fly home to get your spirit recharged, eat lots of home-cooked meals, and cry in the arms of those who otherwise never get to see you anymore. Man, that stinks!

There are basically two types of people: those who live their dreams and those who watch others living their dreams and feel resentment and jealousy over the fact that they can't do the same. (Of course, it's not that they *can't*, it's that they choose not to, but that doesn't matter when they're flinging negativity all around you.) Lyn Mason Green—actor and founder of Canadian Actor Online—once said, "There is no virtue in pessimism. There is no superiority in espousing the negative in every situation so that you can say, 'I told you so.' We want to encourage 'dreamers' to understand that there *is* work involved in achieving their dreams and that, if they are willing to do that work, they certainly *can* do what they dream of doing."

Regarding the "actor friends you used to rant with" issue, I'd like to suggest that you—early on—develop an understanding of the difference between friends and colleagues. Friends are people who loved you before you decided to try your hand at acting and who would love you if you gave it all up tomorrow. Friends are happy when you succeed and are there for you when you fail. They are also generally very supportive of your *attempts*. Friends are not so into results. They are in your life because it's fun for them to be there. Everything else is just *stuff*. Even if these friends are actors, they are okay with seeing your career take off when theirs stall out. How many actor friends do you have about whom could you say the same? Be honest! How many of your actor friends could fly off to shoot a feature film with Samuel L. Jackson tomorrow and have you be happy for them without any twinge of jealousy or bitterness about how it "should've been" you instead?

Most of your actor friends—once you are pursuing acting professionally in a major market—are not actually friends. They're colleagues. These are people for whom you're generally excited when they're having career success, but who may very well move on to another tier of professional relationships and leave you behind. Similarly, you may begin to travel in different circles than you used to, simply because your career is advancing faster than the careers of some of your colleagues and slower than the careers of others. Getting okay with this sort of thing *now* will be a huge help to you, when you wonder where your "friend" went. If you're really just colleagues, it's no big deal that you begin to socialize less at certain points in your careers. About 90% of your actor friends are actually going to be colleagues. That's just gotta be okay. You're not being "used" by a friend. You're being bypassed by a colleague who has moved a tier beyond. It's not personal. And it won't be when your career spirals up past that guy's career someday.

Does it turn you into a cold, uncaring shark with no deep friendships to think this way? No! Not at all! What it allows you to do is focus your energy on deep, true friendships that will withstand all manner of career checkerboard jumps, rather than mistaking colleagues for friends (an issue that can hurt you, them, or both of you). The quality of your friendships (and the professionalism of your colleagueships) will improve, once you know which people fall into which category.

The Results

It will be hard to explain your first milestones to friends and family back home. They are waiting to see you on TV or the big screen. It is hard to explain how a second callback for a job you didn't land was the highlight of your month and a very valid reason to celebrate.

—Jenna Fischer, actor

When you're looking over the alumni newsletter or the family holiday bulletin, having been on avail for a national commercial suddenly pales in comparison to the valedictorian's third corporate takeover or your cousin's new baby taking his first steps. Sitting across from your overachieving sibling at Thanksgiving isn't so much fun either, when he's getting praised for having been named partner at the law firm and your biggest news is having finally gotten all of the footage together for your reel.

I'd urge you to only compare yourself to *you* (a year ago, where you hope to be this time next year, etc.) and never compare yourself to others, inside or outside the industry. If people around you have a hard time understanding what to celebrate in the life of an actor, it's possible that it's because *you* haven't learned exactly what little things are worth celebrating!

As for perspective on what "counts" (and perhaps, what may help, the next time you're feeling grilled by those who need more traditional-looking benchmarks to know you're succeeding), consider this: No one is "given" a callback as a favor. Certainly, there are actors who get "favor" prereads or first meetings, but you won't get a callback unless the decision-makers legitimately believe you have a shot at winning the role. Being put on avail or going on hold is a very big deal. Each of these accomplishments is "worth" being very proud of. No, people outside of the industry may not *get* that, but that's okay.

You won't always have the kind of success that people are going to really respond to! When you're pursuing acting in a major market, it is assumed by everyone in your life that you have the opportunity to "make it" and make it big (like they've seen on TV). If you've been compared to any famous actor your whole life, your family and friends back home probably watch that actor's career with great interest, assuming you will have the same measure of success and on the same timeline. Either teach your civilian friends and family from the very beginning that every *audition* is confirmation that you are a professional actor or—if it's too late for that—do what many actors do: Stop telling your family and friends that you've had significant auditions altogether. It's hard enough for actors to let go of how badly they want to book certain gigs without those questions along the lines of, "Have you heard yet? Do you think you'll get it? When will you know?"

Imagine if we were to call our family members who were regularly interviewing for promotions at work or trying to score big clients. "How did that meeting go? Do you think they liked your presentation? How big will your raise be if you get this promotion?" *Never* would such specific questions be considered appropriate! But because people are fascinated with the public, creative life actors choose to live, they have many questions, and the media assures people that there are *no* lines to worry about crossing. All access, all the time! Since keeping a healthy mindset is difficult for even the most balanced artist out there, choosing to play your cards a little close to the vest about projects you're going for is a pretty good idea, as it'll contribute to your sanity level.

The Fear

Fear can block your creativity. But you can't seem to banish fear from your life even though it can cost you work. Vicious cycle, eh? All creatives must find ways to cope with the financial insecurity that comes with any artistic endeavor at the professional level. Sure, there is amazing financial success to be had for those who reach the highest levels in this industry, but there are many years—even for those who reach *A*-List status—when paying rent looks iffy. That sort of thing really takes its toll.

Even for actors who have booked work, there is some of the, "I'll never work again" mantra swimming around. The very fact that you continue to audition (even after you've proven yourself, won awards, reached the top) puts you in a position to fear for your status. You begin to question: "What if I have an *off* day? Does that drop my name from the list? What if my agent gets bad feedback about me? Do I get shelved?" All of that confidence-eating actor mind taffy—more on that later—can really work a number on you! Some actors deal well (exercise, therapy, meditation, personal retreats, self-produced projects) others don't (drugs, alcohol, reckless behavior, suicide). Get good at dealing with fear right away. There's potentially too high a price otherwise.

That Fairness Thing

This business is *not* fair. You *will* be strung along while casting directors attempt to hammer out a deal with the first-choice actor, keeping you around in case things fall through. You *won't* hear back about an audition you really nailed, even though you're sure you earned a callback. You'll make it all the way to the network test for a series regular on a sitcom and learn that you *aren't* the one who got cast by reading about the actor who *did* get the role in the trades the next day. I know it sucks, but it's just the way it is (until you run Hollywood and make all of the changes you want to see) and it's not personal. I can't stress that enough. It's *not* personal!

As Jenna Fischer wrote in her blog: "It's not like other businesses where, if you show up and work above and beyond everyone's expectations, you are pretty much guaranteed to move up the ladder." Right. You can be *the best* at what you do *every single time* you audition and still *never* get cast. Know that going in and you'll save yourself a lot of grief. It's not about who deserves the part, who did the best work, who has the most credits, or whose life is basically identical to that of the character. Casting is a business decision almost *every* time. Don't take business personally. It'll make you crazy.

No matter who you are, you're not going to be treated like you have great value until you're famous (at which time, your butt will be kissed like never before). After that, if you're suddenly not hot anymore, you'll be a pariah. And it's not because you've done a dang thing wrong. It's just the way this fickle, image-obsessed, who-can-help-me-today business can be. (And I'd love to say that it's all Hollywood's fault, but there are people all over the world buying the tabloids and watching the scandal-filled celebrity news items to credit with teaching the culture of celebrity where to place its collective priorities.)

How are we to survive this? Find value in yourself, don't look for your own self-worth in what others have to say about you, and always take a moment to remember that *life* is a whole lot more than just this industry and the people in it.

Why We Do It Anyway

At this point, you're either really pissed off or really charged up. Me too. Yes, both. And part of the way those of us who choose to continue the pursuit of performing arts at the professional level in a major market deal with that conundrum is by letting all of these costs become "reasons to kick ass" at this career.

Artists know that choosing to create is not *really* a choice. What *is* a choice is *where* we pursue it. When actors say, "I didn't choose this career. It chose me!" but then complain about how hard it is, pursuing acting at the professional level in a major market, I am tempted to say, "Okay, you didn't choose the path, but you did choose *where* to walk it." See, you can be an actor *anywhere*. Pursuing acting at the professional level in the largest market for entertainment on the planet is a choice. If you find the costs of acting to be too extreme but you have no intention of giving up the craft, that's cool. Just relocate. (See: **Mastering Your Market**.) There is nothing wrong with being a big fish in a small pond. And, if you think about it, to the fish, it's all just water anyway.

Some people will try to discourage you from pursuing this career. And with good reason. It's hard. It's ego-crushing. The odds are terrible that you will ever find financial success whatsoever. The reason people will discourage you from putting yourself through such things is because they care about you and do not want to see you struggle. It's not because they don't want to see you succeed. They'd actually love to see you succeed, and if the odds were better, they may be more likely to tell you to stick with it. I still have relatives who ask, "Now Bonnie, when are you going to stop this Hollywood foolishness and come home?" I have friends who work as series regulars whose family members are happy for them, but still wish they would get "real jobs" with benefits and a *predictable* sense of security.

When it comes right down to it, you have to reach a point at which you decide it's *your* life you're living and not anyone else's. I did this. For me, it was The Age 28 Epiphany, but it can happen at any age for any individual. That's when I sold everything I owned on eBay and moved to Hollywood to give it "one more shot" before I woke up 40, wondering whose life I was living, always asking "What if...?" about my choices.

It's impractical to think that people don't make life decisions based on their dreams. And I think that's one of the coolest parts about this whole business. It's based on a whole lot of dreams—some of which happen to come true. But here's the question you have to ask yourself, in choosing to go for it at the professional level in a major market: Can you find joy in the *pursuit* of acting? Would you consider that pursuit to be "living your dream"? If the answer is yes, and—whether you succeed or fail when you go for it—you're okay, then rock on! Get to it! Take the harsh but realistic information about the truth of pursuing this career and—knowing what to expect—go and *go big*! Why is having the realistic information such an important part to the equation? Because it's a *dream*, not a *delusion*. Even the most fantastic dreams are based in a foundation of reality. Be realistic, be ambitious, be happy!

Commitment

Working actors have to juggle a freelance schedule. You may say yes to a role that keeps you from accepting another. Or, you may choose to break your first commitment in order to take the later-offered role. What's my take on that? It's better business to state your availability up front and honor your commitments. It's okay to *not* be available, but to say that you are and then renege on an agreement is just not cool.

I'm certainly aware that it's just easier to make the plan and then, when something "bigger, better, wow" comes along, to accept *that* offer and risk killing the relationship with the people on whom you cancel. However, it is important to remember that you are moving toward the goal of being a working actor. Attaining that goal requires years of building healthy relationships. (See: **The Web of Trust**.) Keeping your word is key to accomplishing that goal.

Yes, actors do have to juggle a lot of various money-making endeavors in order to make ends meet between regular acting jobs. I think that's a large part of why an actor's life is a courageous existence. It requires faith in the dream, but that must be balanced with practical issues about paying rent and making choices that further the dream—bringing it more into reality with each choice. No doubt, it's tough. But earning a reputation as a professional who keeps his word is gold.

There was this TV actor in her twenties who began hating her series regular high school student role. To demonstrate her displeasure, she started showing up late to set, costing the production time and money while they waited for her. She bragged about this behavior in an interview! Rather than being a professional and working through the term of her contract (a contract no one *forced* her to sign), she earned a healthy reputation as an unreliable brat. Funny... despite her talent, I haven't noticed her booking beyond the guest-star level since then. Think word got out?

Actor Flake Factor

> *My agent goes, "Oh, this is too stressful—if I were you I'd just take it easy on your first day and don't feel we'll hold it against you if you don't go in—there'll be plenty of others...." (Subtext of which reads, "Are you the kind of actor who is ready to bring it on five minutes' notice?") There was no way I was not going to this audition.*

> —Frances Uku, actor

A friend who founded a nonprofit organization did some research on the average percentage of no-shows for fundraising events. When I was lamenting the fact that many actors no-show their audition appointments, she said that the numbers are not encouraging—in any industry—for people who like to count on folks being where they say they will be when they say they will be there. Turns out that the national flake factor (percentage of people who will, on average, *not* show up after having RSVP'd "yes" to the event) is around 30%. The Los Angeles flake factor is closer to 40%. I suspect that the entertainment industry flake factor may be even higher than that. Of course, actors who've held seats in the theatre for their friends who say they'll be there to support them in their local plays would agree it's an embarrassingly high percentage.

This might explain why casting directors tend to over-schedule prereads. The practice of over-scheduling certainly frustrates actors who arrive at a time when everyone is showing up as planned (causing a backlog, a delay, a less-than-smoothly-running session). But if you've ever been around during that window where five people have no-showed, you also know that you can end up being seen far ahead of your scheduled appointment time.

I run sessions on time. I pride myself on being able to accurately gauge the pockets of time during which the most no-shows will occur (no-shows will *always* occur, no matter what efforts we've made to keep them from happening) and try to build in opportunities to discuss the work we've seen so far, powwow with the director and producer, and give actors who are present during that period of time a chance to do a little more work for us. Due to careful pre-screening of actors I'll bring to prereads, I average a flake factor of about 20%. So, if a director wants to see 100 actors on a particular day, you can be sure I'll schedule 125 actors. That tends to be 100 actors whose work I know (from previous auditions, showcases, reels, plays, etc.) and another 20 or 25 who will be totally new to me. Most casting directors tend to "go with what we know," otherwise, we risk no-shows.

Why do actors no-show auditions? Who knows! I've heard stories of actors waiting to audition and saying, aloud, "Man! It's such a pretty day. I need to hit the beach," and then signing out and leaving without reading for the role. What I like to tell actors who worry about the vast numbers, in terms of competition, is that you *must* keep in mind that among your so-called competition is a chunk of flakes. *Show up* and you'll have beaten those folks right out of the gate! Don't be a *flactor*.

Casting director friends have told me about actors no-showing final producer callbacks when it's down to only three actors. There are tales of actors who no-show after *begging* to get in to be seen for a particular role. Generally, the actors we make the most effort to accommodate (scheduling and rescheduling the appointment time in order to make sure the actor can be there) turn out to be the ones who blow us off. That makes it all the more valuable to be the actor who is easy to work with, professional, and accountable. We already assume that you're talented. That's why you're here. The ability to rise above the flakes is sometimes the *talent* that sets you apart.

The Shady Stuff

The pursuit of acting costs money. We all know that. But there are some shady players out there, hoping to separate you from more of your money than is necessary. It's important that you know what to look out for and what's a worthwhile investment in your dream.

Never pay an agency or management firm in which an "administrative fee" is required to get your headshot into their book, onto their website, or the like. Getting onto an agency's "house reel" should not come at any charge to you. They want you in their book, on their sample demo, or on their site because your work could get them a commission. All of the costs involved in representation by legitimate companies are covered by the commission the agent or manager receives upon the booking of your first job. Never pay up-front fees!

Watch out for any group that wants you to pay up front or without any prior audit or orientation so that you know what it is you're getting into. Avoid package deals (photo sessions, reel editing, acting classes, and representation all from the same source), as most of those are sketchy. Go online and check out the companies with which you plan to do business before handing over your hard-earned money. Just Google the name of the company or its principals and add "+scam" to the search!

Sadly, when people are scammed, they become ashamed and are not likely to share their experiences for fear of how stupid they may look, having fallen for the scam to begin with. Please, if you are scammed, file a report with the Better Business Bureau and the state attorney's office, then be sure to write a letter to the editor of your local paper and the trade publications. There is no reason to think that your "one little voice" won't make a difference in closing down scam artists.

If you have been suckered into a shady program and now have a resumé filled with training from a group with a murky reputation in the industry, consider listing only the instructors' names on your resumé, rather than the program. Casting directors will see some "schools" in actors' training sections and toss the headshots right out, since the credits are equated with "new, duped, doesn't know better, non-pro" so much of the time.

Once your headshot is out there, you'll start getting requests for headshots from people supposedly working on projects—as well as requests for autographed photos (usually from "some child who has suffered some debilitating tragedy"). Here's what you need to know: I am not being overly-cynical. *Every* request for an autographed headshot I ever received from someone with a sad story turned out to be from either a prison inmate or a collector of photos and autographs intending to do nothing but sell my autographed headshot on eBay down the line.

You have a phone number? Someone's gonna get it. And sell it. And pass it around. Same with email addresses. Especially when the seller of your number and your email address can verify that you are a member of a particular demographic or customer base, your contact information becomes valuable to advertisers looking for marketing lists.

Companies that are marketing actor services aren't always buying actors' contact information from those who collect and resell information. Sometimes they're putting out casting notices in order to have you mail or email your headshot to them, then getting your contact info and using that info to pitch you actor services of all kinds! *Backstage* did an exposé in which they created a headshot and resumé for a non-actor staff member and submitted it per a casting notice on which the mailing address was a suite away from a casting director workshop facility. Well, wouldn't you know it! Within weeks, the non-acting *Backstage* staffer began getting pitch calls for workshops, with the line "a friend referred you."

Sometimes, skeevy agents will have side deals with workshop facilities. They'll allow the workshop folks to come by and pick up unsolicited headshots that have been mailed over by actors seeking representation. Then the workshop facility personnel start calling. How can you prevent that from happening? I mean, you aren't going to *stop* submitting your headshot to agencies when you're looking for representation, right? How can you know which groups are in cahoots with which agencies? It's not like anyone advertises this stuff!

They can also gather trash. Yup. Dumpster diving has been known to happen outside major casting facilities. That's bad news for your contact info, of course. But you also need to be careful about what you write on sign-in sheets and size cards. Your Social Security Number doesn't need to be given out until you are hired! Don't risk identity theft just by signing in for your audition. It's one thing for shady players to have your phone number. Quite another for them to steal your identity and screw up your credit!

Of course, there's also the old-fashioned method of collecting contact information. People who work for these workshop facilities, acting studios, demo reel editing companies—pretty much any actor-related service provider might do this—will attend shows and ask for industry kits, saying they're "producers," and then they'll grab the actors' phone numbers right off their resumés and add them to their own lists. More work involved that way, but it happens. Regardless of how they got your number, most of these folks will say a "friend" referred you. Yeah, right.

Outside of never sharing your contact information, ever, there's really no way to prevent this sort of thing from happening. So, rather than worrying too much about *how* this happens, just be ready with your response when it does. My philosophy is this: If someone is providing a really great service, actors are going to hear about it and buy it, use it, attend it (whatever) just through word-of-mouth and traditional means of advertising. So, anyone who is picking up the phone or sending unwanted emails to someone who never opted in for such a thing is probably not getting enough business on the merits of his service.

That means—to me anyway—that I already know everything I need to know about a company that cold calls or blasts emails. "No thank you," is the best answer they're going to get out of me, if they're not a company whose reputation has already secured them a great spot on my radar. I thought going into casting would keep cold calls about entertainment industry services from coming my way, but sure enough every time I put out a breakdown, I get a few calls and emails from companies that offer competing or support services for casting directors. They want me to list my breakdown at their website. They want me to force actors to use their service in order for me to be able to view and share the session videos. They want my business (even if it costs me nothing to use their service) because then they can use my name when selling the cost-based part of their service to actors. Nope. No thanks. I'm covered.

As an actor, if you're covered (meaning, you're happy with your current acting class, reel editor, headshot photographer, marketing coach, or CD workshop facility of choice), it's as simple as a, "No thanks," for you too.

As for the time-sensitive angle they're usually hustling, that's just so you'll commit to checking them out before you've had a chance to do any sort of homework. They figure they're more likely to sell you their services if you walk through the door and see all of the photos of famous people on the walls and read the glowing testimonials they plaster in their brochures. Don't fall for it. Take your time. Check 'em out. Do your research. Talk with fellow actors who can share firsthand experiences. And then decide whether you want to take the meeting.

Watch out for industry "experts" whose own success in the industry is unverifiable (a trip to IMDb-Pro should suffice). Experts whose only cred exists on their own websites specialize in the high-pressure time-sensitive offer. The realization that you fell for slick marketing usually only comes after the expert has separated you from your money. Only after buying what is being sold, following the rules the seller has claimed are fail-safe, and then failing miserably because of following those rules (potentially damaging fragile industry relationships) will most people realize that these "experts" are making it all up when they say there are *any* 100%, all-the-time, no-matter-what rules about this industry.

As the great producer-author-studio exec Peter Guber loves to say: "There are no rules, but you break them at your peril." Anyone who tells you there is only their once-in-a-lifetime-deal way of doing anything is putting their need to sell you something over the truth of what this industry is: complex.

Why Scams Work

Scammers say all the right things. They tell you everything you've ever wanted to hear about your talent, your chances, your marketability. Then they tell you that the only thing standing between you and the career you've always dreamed of is the one thing they can provide—for a fee. Look, legitimate agents and managers want your money too, but they earn it by collecting commissions on your bookings. Legitimate schools and coaches want your money, and they earn it by providing a certain number of classes over a finite amount of time.

Because there will always be a new crop of hopefuls entering the industry, there will always be scammers hoping to catch those newbies before they know better. All the more reason to spread the word if you've been scammed!

Red Flags

➢You submitted your headshot on a *project* and are being contacted for representation, classes, headshots.

➢You live in a market other than the one from which you've been "scouted."

➢Auditions are located at a private residence rather than in a public casting office.

➢The company claims to have pull in a major market, but is headquartered nowhere near a major market.

➢The email you received confirming your appointment is filled with typos, misspellings, and grammatical errors. Also, you are encouraged to bring a friend. This is so your cynical friend can get caught up in the hype and sign up as well. Your cynical friend is far more likely to convince you this is a scam if you go alone and then tell him about it later, so they want him there with you, getting the well-oiled sales pitch.

➢Your appointment turns out to be an open call with many other hopefuls excited about this "opportunity."

➢The company's website lists no principals' names, only extreme and unverifiable claims of success and power in the industry.

➢The company's principals (if disclosed) are nowhere to be found on IMDb-Pro.

➢You are guaranteed paid work before you even sign up for

whatever it is they are offering (management contract, package deal, workshops).

➤You've been told to come to LA to get seen by agents during pilot season. (Agents are busy pitching their *existing* roster during pilot season; they are generally *not* looking to sign anyone new.)

➤You can "win" an event and then travel to LA for pilot season at a discount, since you were the winner.

➤You Google the name of the program along with the word "scam" in the search and find *pages* of hits.

➤You're sent a check for more than the amount of the booking and are asked to pay back the overage (that check is bad, you'll later learn).

➤You've been told you'll score big if you spend $10,000 to come to this company's month-long "intensive."

➤You've been told you'll be "scouted" by top industry players (unnamed, of course), if you spend $2000 to attend this company's weekend conference.

➤Your "manager" wants you to pay for participating in an industry showcase, guaranteeing that you will be seen by top agents and casting directors. (Of course you will! They have all been *paid* to be there. Paid with *your* money. And then what kind of agent have you nabbed? One who, instead of pitching his current clients or negotiating their best deal on projects is out doing paid scouting trips to sign more new, out-of-market talent? What a winner!)

➤You've been provided *Mad Libs*-style templates and one-size-fits all career solutions.

➤You're feeling manipulated as a marketer "sells to the pain" or tries to activate FOMO (fear of missing out) in you with limited-time-only offers.

➤You've agreed to meet with a producer to discuss a project and now it's cocktails instead of coffee, and you're wondering if he thinks this is a date. (Tip: Bring a friend, meet during the day, and keep your headshots out on the table.)

So What? It's My Money!

One of the most popular arguments among those who have been scammed is, "So what? It's my money and I'll spend it where I want to." You're absolutely right. You are entitled to spend *thousands* of dollars on unnecessary classes, unprofessional photos, and totally bogus showcases in front of people who are just collecting a check for doing something that is *part of their job*. The problem is, in doing so you help perpetuate the scam! These folks can continue to operate because so many people are willing to throw good money after bad, and then folks who maybe *don't* have thousands to spare will think they *have to* spend the money in order to compete, when the truth is they could just do their own legwork and have *better* results (and the added satisfaction of having gotten savvy about the business, rather than having paid someone to tell them everything they wanted to hear about how special and uniquely talented they are).

When to Say No

Actors become so accustomed to saying *yes* to every offer (especially when just starting out), that you often forget the importance of knowing when to say *no*. Say no to scams. Say no to anything in the red flag territory 'til you can do more homework. Say no to roles that are too good to be true. Some gigs just *aren't* worth taking. What makes an offer one to pass up? That can only be answered by one person, of course. That's you.

Establish your personal policy *before* the offer is in front of you. Will you do nudity? Will you work for "copy, credit, meals" when other actors on set are getting paid? Will you cut or dye your hair for a role? Is there a particular product or cause for which you will not pitch? Will you work "off the card" (do nonunion work) despite your hard-earned union membership?

The answer to these questions—and to any of the others of this type that may come up—should be clear in your mind *before* the issue is staring you down. The pressure of coming up with a quick answer (especially when money is being offered) could cause you to make a decision that you otherwise wouldn't make. That's why it's amazingly helpful to have your personal policies on such subjects clearly stated (whether in your journal, on a Post-It Note on your mirror, or in your blog). You can then consult those policies when the offers start coming.

It is one of the many responsibilities of actors—or anyone out there who is both building a brand and hoping their reputation will lead to future work that aligns with that brand—to be absolutely certain you know exactly how your work, your image, your very brand itself is being exploited.

I'm no conspiracy theorist, but I was educated very well in journalism school that there are many ways in which the media—not to mention producers of "agenda" films—can manipulate its messages (and, sadly, make unwitting participants the face or voice of its manipulated messages). Limiting the use of your brand—especially when it is being rented for very little (like copy, credit, meals, for instance)—to a specific, contracted term is not only your right, it's your responsibility.

It's no different than my days as a journalist for *Backstage*, which started me out in 1999 at 10 cents per word. For that rate, I was only renting my words to the publication. I granted rights to my work, which would revert back to me after six months. Similarly, when actors are getting paid minimal amounts—or worse, not getting paid a thing, but are granting rights to the unlimited commercial use of their image via Terms of Service (TOS) for the privilege of using a free site like Facebook—there needs to be a limit to the use.

How are you to build a brand in which the top-tier producers cannot wait to invest if you are unwittingly the face of something so very off-brand for you? As actor, voiceover artist, and former political consultant Anna Vocino shared with me, "We as talent have to be in charge of covering our own asses. Folks on the outside watch ads and have emotional responses so great, it can cost you some dings to your career if you don't protect your brand by aligning with ads that you can believe in and stand by."

Sometimes there is no script, sometimes there are only sides, and sometimes there are valid reasons given on set as to why that's the case. It's one thing if that's something you're experiencing on the set of the latest hush-hush JJ Abrams project. It's quite another if you're experiencing that at the audition or on the set of a project brought together by producers with no IMDb presence who post casting notices on Craigslist.

I have a friend who makes no bones about being a bit of a pain in the butt when it comes to protecting herself. "I say, 'Sorry, guys. I'm an attorney's daughter, so I'm overly cautious,' and then I require a script, a contract, explicit detail about our work together," she told me. I love that!

When we respect ourselves, we protect ourselves. Absolutely, we can all get duped. We can take all the precautions in the world and still have the wool pulled over our eyes in this business. But it comes back around to respecting what you're building—long term—before saying yes to a project. Look up everyone on IMDb. Google them. Demand a contract and a script. Research the agenda, the angle, the political campaign for which you are about to become the face or the voice. Read the TOS before hitting *like* all over the place. Be sure you're being paid ridiculously well if you're granting commercial rights to your image in perpetuity on some stock photography gig. Don't be so hungry for work—for a paycheck or footage—that you ignore the red flags that what you're signing up for does not align with your brand.

Only say *yes* to being a part of the stories you *want* to tell in this business. That is the ultimate protection.

The Stench of Desperation

Every new breakdown I put out, I'm reminded that—in addition to the thousands upon thousands of wonderful, professional actors that fill my days—there are some actors who are really desperate. "I *have* to be cast in this movie. This is *my* story. I'll do anything. I'll work for free. I'll *pay you*. Please, Bonnie, please. *I have to be cast in this film!*"

Do you *really* want to come off like someone who so desperately wants a gig that you'll *do anything*? Or worse, if you're the parent of a child actor, do you really want to come off as someone who will pimp out *your child's services* for free? Do you realize that this sort of offer, if put in front of an unscrupulous casting director or shady scam artist, is the scariest and most seductive bait? This is how the casting couch was created. Not so much because there are scummy people in positions of power looking to manipulate those who want something so badly, but because there are many people out there so *desperate* to get the gig that they will offer up *anything* (and I do mean *anything*—you would be shocked and disgusted) in order to get a shot at it. The most power-hungry producer wannabes in the mix will absolutely take advantage of that much desperation being flung in their direction.

You don't need to buy things for people. You don't need to sleep with them. You don't need to offer up working for free. While it *may* be true that you'd pay to get to be a part of a certain project, that you'd *do anything* to have this opportunity, that you—deep inside—do *desperately* need and want the next job, you cannot say that. Save those details for *after* you've booked the gig. Gush about how much booking this one means to you *after* the check has cleared.

Everyone in this business is secretly terrified he will never work again, to some extent. Even if it's never really dwelled upon, *everyone* knows this is a fickle, freelance career choice. There's a way to submit that exudes confidence, and in the end, that's far more attractive than desperation.

Unprofessional Behavior

Let me make it really clear, here: No agent, no manager, no casting director, no writer, no director, no producer, no headshot photographer, no coach, *no one* in this business makes a buck without *you*. Yet for some reason, actors walk into auditions, CD workshops, classes, networking events, negotiations from a position of weakness: sheepish, timid, and worried about what others are thinking. You stress over how to impress people in the room, before showing up. You obsess over what you might have done wrong when you aren't the one cast. You spend way too many hours of your life focused on ways in which these other folks "control your destiny." You give away your power. Daily.

An actor spoke with me about an atrocious meeting she had with an agent. She'd been called in for a meet and greet and read after he "found her headshot in a stack of trash from months ago" (which isn't likely, since she only moved to LA and started mailing submissions to LA agents weeks before). She'd been given less than 24 hours' notice for the meeting. She'd been emailed four pages of dialogue-heavy sides for the read. And she showed up anyway, because she is a committed pro, was not going to flake, and was so excited to sign with her first LA agent that she was thrilled with the invitation to start that potential process.

Rather than thinking, "Why are there red flags here? Why is this a time-sensitive offer? Why is he lying about how he got my headshot?" or saying, "Hey, you and I both want me to do my best work when we meet up. Let's do this next week," she said, "Okay!" and busted her ass to make it work. And that's when things got really ugly.

He was the total cliché "bad audition" recipient. He spent the entire time she was reading the sides either on the phone or eating a sandwich, a finger in the air toward the actor, prompting her to either keep going or stop—like he was some traffic cop at Sunset and The 405 at rush hour. Obviously, it was not her best audition ever (How could it be?), but she was going to show him she was unflappable. She was going to keep her chin up and continue the meeting, during which he let her know there was just no chance he was going to sign her anyway, so this really was a favor opportunity and probably a waste of time.

But the meeting continued. This guy continued to make her feel bad about her photos, her credits, her union status, her weight, her lack of footage, her look, her everything! And why? Just so she could hopefully have the honor of printing the logo of this bozo's agency on her resumé? This agency that—if I were asked to list my "Top 200 Favorite Agencies" in order—would come in somewhere around the 180-mark? Are actors so totally hungry for a logo—any logo—on that resumé you'll ignore the absence of simple human decency in order to earn it?

There will never be an end to the number of folks in this business who try to separate you from your money and who try to lessen your level of power. As soon as you realize that you—being the one in the position of power to begin with—have the right to say no, deserve the best representation possible, can create your own heat, and are the reason any of us puts food on our tables each meal anyway, you'll audition better, you'll take meetings better, and you'll feel better.

Never make business decisions from a place of fear. Stop giving your power away. Your power is worth more than anything "Hollywood" has to offer. Believe it.

Courage doesn't always roar. Sometimes courage is the quiet voice at the end of the day saying, "I will try again tomorrow."
—Mary Anne Radmacher, author

3: PREMATURE MOVES

There are a few key moves actors will have the opportunity to make early in their careers. Unfortunately, these are moves actors often rush to make. And premature moves like these can stunt the natural process of development in an actor's *lifelong* career. They can also *prevent* future progress and breed bitterness.

As you know, bitterness is one of the most unattractive things to bring into an audition or encounter with anyone. If you have yet to make some of these moves, consider taking a little extra time in the decision-making process. Some of these things may look like the Holy Grail for actors. Based on the number of actors out there who feel they're "stuck" for having made these moves, that's just not the case.

Joining a Union

So many otherwise intelligent people advise actors to hurry up and join the union. I really wish they'd stop doing that. Sure, there are many more upper-tier opportunities available for actors once you are a union member, but until you're ready to compete at that level, your premature union membership could be cutting you off from a steady stream of paid nonunion work that builds credits, footage, and relationships that will help you—organically—get to the next tier.

Once you join SAG-AFTRA, you're cut off from doing student films at institutions not working under a blanket union agreement, you're prevented from doing nonunion blackbox theatre work, and any spec content your friends put together without attaining signatory status. What?!? "How can SAG-AFTRA tell me that I'm not allowed to work a nonunion play (which would be AEA's jurisdiction, not theirs)? That's not fair!" Well, it may not seem fair to you, but when you *choose* to join a union that is a sister union to AEA, you may not work nonunion—even in a right-to-work state!

Be *really* sure it's the right time to "go pro." When is it time? When you are regularly having more union auditions than nonunion auditions, it's time to *begin considering* joining a union. When you have been union-eligible and have enjoyed the benefits of being able to go out for union roles without having to turn down nonunion work, *begin considering* joining SAG-AFTRA. But until you have "hit a ceiling" in the nonunion world, don't even *consider* joining a union. Why? Well, by doing so, you'll be a few grand poorer (initiation fees) and, if you join too soon, you may find yourself considering "working off the card" or going FiCore, neither of which are reasons you joined the union in the first place. (See: **Union Membership**.) It's like getting married so you can have an affair. Don't do that.

You join a union to be considered a professional in your industry. Until you have the career momentum to leave your paid-amateur status behind *forever*, stay where you are, because once you join the union, that's it. You're *in* the higher tier. While there are some low-budget union contracts on which both union and nonunion members can work, for the most part, as a union member, you'll be competing with people who *may* have more relationships, more footage, more training, more experience than you do, and that'll start feeling like crap. Say *yes* to the next tier when it's knocking at your door.

Pursuing an Agent

Of course, I feel strongly about actors remaining self-marketing, self-submitting professionals even after signing with an agent or manager. That said, there will certainly be a time in every actor's career in which he will benefit most from having someone handling the contracts and advising the major career moves. The problem is, many actors think it's time for that relationship *long before* it truly is.

"An agent will help me get work." No. An agent will pitch you for roles of your type in projects at your level (or just above, hopefully) if you are ready for that sort of thing and if you have signed with an agent who does more than "sign and shelve" you until he drops you. An agent can certainly get you into offices you might not have been able to get into on your own, but your resumé *must* measure up in order for that to happen.

An agent can get you bumped from co-star to guest-star billing and an agent can help increase your rate quote for each new job, but those are issues actors have somewhere *after* the beginning of their journey. Still, I hear complaints from countless actors about how no theatrical agent will take a look at them. I then check out their resumés and I understand why. There is a time for building a resumé and there is a time for using the resumé you have built to assemble a team to advance your career. These are not simultaneous activities, when you're starting out.

Too many actors believe an agent will *get* them somewhere. No. An agent will help you get a better deal once you're pretty close to that "somewhere" already. Signing with an agent too early can make you bitter about all of the things your agent isn't doing for you. It is entirely possible to get yourself out there so much that you are *approached* by an agent who wants to have you on his roster. Wouldn't that be a better scenario than doing mass submissions to hundreds of agents and hoping that someone, somewhere agrees to meet you, only to shelve you once the ink on the agency agreement is dry?

Enter the game at a higher tier. This book is designed to help you do that. Don't settle for the agent who'll sign you without meeting you. Wait for the agent who hustles for you like his rent depends on it.

Moving to Los Angeles for Pilot Season

Many actors from other markets believe that Los Angeles is "calling" them for pilot season before that is true. *Most* actors who move to LA for pilot season end up leaving after three months, angry that they spent all sorts of money for temporary housing and a long-term rental car, never having gotten out for more than a handful of auditions—and rarely on any pilots.

Move to Los Angeles *for good* when you are ready to pursue a film-and-television life in the Super Bowl of Acting fulltime. Now, before I go into all of the qualifiers for that statement, let me say that I *do* support the idea that some actors are perfect for pilot season *visits* if they are busy, working actors coming in from one of the larger markets (New York, Chicago, London, Sydney, and the Pacific Northwest—including Vancouver) with bi-market representation. There absolutely *are* actors who can—and do—come to town and take LA by storm, head back to their hometowns, and live as even bigger fish for having had great experiences here. Those aren't the folks I'm talking about.

I'm talking about the actors who believe they can pick up from wherever they live with no agent or manager, no union membership, very few credits, no reel, and a clearly out-of-market headshot and come to LA for pilot season expecting something to happen. *Can* something happen? Of course. Legends are built upon the fact that lightning does, occasionally, strike. But until you have significant credits in your local market, coming to Los Angeles to pursue a film and television performance career during pilot season is simply a dream killer.

It's much better for you not to attempt a pilot season short-term move but instead to build credits (and your bank account) to a point where a permanent move to pursue a lifetime career as an LA-based actor is feasible. (See: **Moving to Los Angeles**.) Then, it's not about pilot season (which is crazymaking for even the locals, in terms of volume of auditions and hectic scheduling constraints); it's about the long haul. And you want to be an actor who "made it," right? Not an actor who "made it to LA for three months and came home bitter about it."

Be sure to give LA (or any new market, for that matter) at least 18 months, never "just a year." That's a setup for failure, as it takes a year just to learn the freeways, here, and longer than that to get the feel of the place and really know what you're doing, no matter where you live! Consider your lifetime goals carefully before making big moves. Pro athletes train for many years before they suit up professionally. Make sure you're ready for the big game before you get yourself here as nothing but a benchwarmer.

4: Actor Mind Taffy

According to Breakdown Services, there are approximately 125,000 actors in the Los Angeles branch of their system and 64,000 in New York, with around 340,000 actors in the system worldwide. Subscribing agencies in Los Angeles number just under 250, while over 700 management firms are getting breakdowns in LA. (The New York numbers are just over 100 and approximately 420, respectively.)

Why am I sharing this with you? Well, because the numbers are overwhelming. The odds are staggering. And we go for it anyway because we can't *not* try. What's important is that we do whatever it takes to avoid getting stuck in actor mind taffy territory. *Self-Management for Actors* is all about controlling those few things we do control and letting go of the rest. But we can't ignore the realities of this delicious industry we've chosen.

I was once asked by an actor friend, after he interned in my casting office and saw typical submissions: "Why do we spend all our time trimming resumés to fit the headshots, stapling precisely in four corners, or any of those other little things?"

"Oh, well, you do that because it's one of the few things you control about this whole process," I replied.

The next day, as if on cue, another actor asked in an online discussion forum whether casting directors prefer stapled-on to glued-on resumés. *Are you kidding?* Do you really think casting directors have a preference? Heck, maybe some do. But *never* in my life have I heard of a casting director falling in love with an actor's headshot and resumé, feeling eager to bring that actor in to read for a role, and then stopping cold, saying, "Oh, wait. I can't bring this actor in. He used a glue stick." C'mon! Nobody cares! If you're the right actor for the role, you could have a handwritten resumé done in crayon on the back of your photo. We'd still bring you in.

I find that actors like to concern themselves with these tiny details because they've gotten in the habit of asking casting directors in workshop settings what their pet peeves are. Heck, when I interviewed casting directors for what was then called *Back Stage West*, one of my weekly questions was about pet peeves. It's an easy question to ask. It's also pretty irrelevant. Most casting directors would rather talk about what brings them joy in their day-to-day life, what makes an actor really stand out, and why they choose to cast the projects they cast. But actors ask what bugs casting directors, and that's why casting directors say things like, "Horizontal headshots bug me." Truth is, they don't bug anyone so much that the right actor won't get seen because of having chosen a horizontal headshot. Ever.

That said, let me state for the record that I do believe actors should give great attention to detail when submitting to an agent or manager for representation. What you're showing an agent in a submission is, "This is how I promote and market myself. Wouldn't you like to be a part of my team?" So, in that case, a sloppy submission or lackluster cover letter could cost you a meeting. More on that in a few chapters. But with casting submissions, we're generally looking to solve an immediate problem. If you're the right fit, we're generally not going to refuse to bring you in just because you submit "wrong." This is *not* permission to do stupid stuff like call producers and pitch yourself, ignoring the fact that the producers *hired* a casting director to deal with actors! Be smart. The filtering process exists for a reason.

So what does this have to do with the title of this chapter? Well, I first used the words "actor mind taffy" when talking with a lifelong actor friend about her career in 1999. She was the worst when it came to spending days wondering how an audition went, rather than just doing the work and then moving on. I finally told her, "Look, you're just pulling actor mind taffy by trying to figure out how you did or what they're looking for. It's not going to get you anywhere and you're just going to end up with sticky fingers. Stop playing with it and move on."

I really love the visual image of an actor sitting around, pulling taffy all day, thinking it's going to give him some great insight into the process. So, the next time you try to get into the head of a casting director to figure out whether your submission method is effective or if the choice to tweet the casting director before your audition was somehow the deal-breaker on a particular gig, just know that you're engaging in actor mind taffy. It may feel like fun, but it's not particularly productive in the long run.

Think Like a Producer

In speaking with actors worldwide, I often find a common answer to questions is: "Think like a producer. Then that decision makes sense." Actors want to know why one actor gets cast over another. You want to understand the value placed on a *name* actor over an equally talented, brilliantly prepared, up-and-coming actor. We all want to know why runaway production exists. The bottom line tends to be, well, the bottom line! If you think like a producer, you'll understand a lot more about the way things work in this industry.

Producers make a seemingly infinite number of decisions during the course of production. They're thinking about issues that most people won't ever even know exist. What may be an investment of a few days or months on a project to someone in any other job has actually been years for a producer. By the time casting is going on, a ton of money has already been committed and every bit of savings counts. The reason it's important for actors to at least understand the producer's POV is because doing so will help remove some of the actor mind taffy. And anything that can remove an obstacle between you and the role you hope to book is worth exploring.

Why didn't the breakdown go out to actors via Actors Access? Why is it only being put out to subscribing agents and managers through Breakdown Services? Or, even more exclusively, why is the casting director only releasing the breakdown to a short list of a dozen key agents? The producer isn't interested in non-*name* actors. The producer needs to attach *name* actors to particular roles in order for this project to get distribution and recoup any of its production costs. Is it fair to the non-*name* status actor who might be perfect for the role and whose performance could be exactly what this project needs to really take off? Nope. But nowhere in the Hollywood rules is the word "fair."

Why didn't the casting director allow you to come in a day later than your scheduled audition appointment? (You know, the one you couldn't make due to a booking on another set.) Because the producer wasn't going to pay to staff sessions for a second day, and there were dozens of other actors the casting director could choose from, once you said you weren't available for that original slot. Sure, you're at the top of the casting director's list, but the producer wants tape at close of business on that one day you're not available. Tough. Rock beats scissors and producer beats casting director. Every time.

Why is this particular film casting in Los Angeles but shooting out of the country, where the non-stars will all be hired locally? It's cheaper. There are financial incentives for films and series to shoot all over the world (and in cities all over the US outside of Hollywood), and even if the talent pool in Hungary is not as densely filled with professional actors, there are coaches to take along for the shoot who will do whatever it takes to get those actors looking and sounding just as good as the more expensive Hollywood-based non-star actors. Yes, even the expense of importing dialect experts, acting coaches, and creative consultants comes out to less money than a producer would lay out to take a bunch of union dayplayers out of the country to shoot a film. Absolutely, there are producers who will stand firm about shooting locally and hiring locally, but for every diehard union-label type there are another dozen producers who just want to save a buck and make money on a movie, geography be damned. Don't hate 'em for that.

Why was the most beautiful scene cut from the finished film? It would require too much "clean up," in the producer's assessment. Cut it, let it go, and move on. What did they mean when they said that an actor was "more commercial" and therefore a better choice? More commercial means more money. Think like a producer. Are producers more likely to know what will be commercially successful than non-producers? Well, successful producers are! That's how they become successful producers: They predict correctly more often than incorrectly what will sell.

As for what you can do (once you're thinking like a producer) to help maximize your chances of getting cast, that'd include things like making yourself look bankable, being all about the professional mindset (and never about bitterness or personal drama), and maintaining industry relationships in which we can all help one another. Appear like someone who isn't a big risk. Read scripts, look at your audition clothing, and choose your headshots through a producer's lens. What's going to sell? What's going to make a producer more inclined to take a chance on you? What qualities make you a good investment (and how can those qualities become obvious to those with the money to invest)?

Yes, you're an artist. Yes, you're creative and passionate. But to navigate a business in which those juices inside that allow you to create fictional worlds so beautifully are safe from the cutthroat decisions made here every day, you need to at least be able to think like a producer (even if you only do it from time to time, just for the sake of perspective).

If you had "ponies for everyone" money, would *you* cast yourself? Or would you offer the lead role to a *name* actor—guaranteeing distribution—and give yourself some juicy co-star scenes? Think like a producer. Think about the bottom line.

5: THE WEB OF TRUST

Every booking comes from a relationship. Period. Discouraging information? It shouldn't be. It's true. And what's *also* true is that you probably have more relationships in the industry than you realize.

A fellow casting director once told me that he brings people in for their first auditions with him feeling as though he already knows them. By the time he brings an actor in, he may have received that actor's headshot and resumé dozens of times. He may have seen a stack of postcards, show flyers, and headshots from that actor. He may have heard the actor's name from agent pitches, buzz about a show, conversations with other casting directors about who is up-and-coming. The actor may have done a show and the casting director may have attended the first act only, having never picked up a kit or dropped off a business card, and may have scribbled a note about the actor in the playbill. The casting director may be a fan of the actor's latest webseries. Since one would never know about any of that, there is no reason to assume that you have *no* relationships in the industry, just because you haven't been in a particular office *yet*.

You're building relationships every day. With every mailing, every panel discussion, every show invitation, every networking event, every online encounter, every festival screening, you are creating and developing relationships that could result in bookings.

Of course, you don't go into any relationship expressly with the intention to develop it *for the purpose of gaining work*. That is the surest way to be considered a climber, a phony Hollywood type, a person with no longevity in the industry. And isn't it a *lifetime of work* you're looking to build? If you have the intention of building a reputation as a consistently-working actor, you must acknowledge that you are building a foundation to that end every day.

The book *How to Make It in Hollywood* by Linda Buzzell is one I read decades ago, before heading west to pursue my entertainment industry dreams. One of the tactics the author recommends is that you keep an action log of your conversations, meetings, and networking activities. This is to remind you that you are investing in yourself and your career with what may seem like "uneventful" coffees, lunches, and mailings. When you begin to feel as though you've done nothing to move your career forward (perhaps because you've had no auditions or callbacks that week), take a look at how many people with whom you've connected. I don't mean people who can cast you, I mean people who are in the industry, working. Add all of this action to your show bible.

We've all heard the stories about actors who are offered acting jobs without even having to audition, simply because someone involved with the project has worked with a particular actor before (or knows someone who has worked with that actor). That's no accident. Frequently, there is no time to hold full-scale casting sessions, and a few phone calls will get a project cast almost immediately. We'll call agents and managers from within our web of trust—these are all people we love to do business with and whose clients have served us well in the past. We'll call actors we've cast before and who always receive great feedback from the directors of the projects in which we've cast them. We'll call our favorite acting coaches to say we need someone very specific and end up bringing in an actor from their classes who matches the criteria.

Return on Investment

If you knew, from the beginning, that it was going to take thousands of hours of effort on your part before you would begin to see a return on your investment into yourself as an actor, would you still choose to be an actor? Most would. We've all read advice from veteran actors about the hard road they've taken: "If you can be happy doing anything else, do it." Of course, most actors know better. You're an actor. There *is* nothing else.

But there is a process of career investment for actors that is dissimilar to that which is required by those in every other occupation. The number of hours, the amount of money, the emotional expense—the true cost of a career as an actor is impossible to accurately calculate. And so what if you could calculate it? Would it make you feel *better* to quantify the hours, the dollars, and the emotions you invest in something that, most years, leaves you needing a survival job in order to afford rent?

Of course not. So, this isn't about quantifying the investment. It's about developing perspective. Consider that, at the beginning of your career, you are putting in one thousand units of effort for every one unit of reward. That's when you feel as though you are sending headshots out into an abyss and occasionally getting one line in a student film. There will be a time when you are putting in one unit of effort for every one unit of reward. That's when you get called in from your well-earned reputation and book pretty regularly. Perhaps most exciting, there will be a time when you are putting in one unit of effort for every one thousand units of reward. That's when you no longer audition. That's when your rep fields offers on your behalf. Yay, you!

Unless lightning strikes, it takes going through the 1000:1 ratio before you make it to the 1:1 ratio or come anywhere close to the 1:1000 ratio. Therefore, you have to find a way to feel rewarded by something other than that one measly unit of reward you get, after expending one thousand units of effort. Keeping score is a waste of energy. Keeping score is for wannabes.

An industry friend told me about a group of masterminds from Wharton who came to Hollywood to study the business model, figuring they could analyze and demystify it. They applied every "rule" of business to what they witnessed in agents' offices, pitch meetings, casting sessions, producer lunches, and studio powwows only to leave Hollywood scratching their heads. There is no science to the entertainment industry. That is why it's so important to remember that your path is unique. Reading about others' experiences is of value, commiserating with other actors is also fun, but none of it provides a recipe for *your* success. You will learn how many units of effort yield how many units of reward in your life as an actor as you go. Enjoy "those crazy days" in which you have to do one thousand things to make one thing happen. If you don't enjoy those days, how will you feel that you can rightfully enjoy the 1:1000 days that come to you in the future? Let the investment be the reward.

You are gonna get burned. You'll get screwed. It's like cooking bacon.
It'll pop and grease will land on your hand and you'll cuss and yell... but
you'll make bacon again. You will *get burned. Just don't stop makin' bacon.*
—Keith Johnson, actor-writer

Breaking It Down

My husband and I have a relationship that is built on two fundamental principles. One: Always trust that we each have the other's best interests at heart (that way, even when we're fighting, we *know* it's because we both want a result that improves our relationship or current situation). Two: Always go for the funny. I say that the second one is the more important of the two, but it's really because of the first one that the second one works so well.

This chapter is about the first principle: *trust*—trusting your fellow castmates, trusting your director and producer, trusting your agent and manager, trusting your acting coach, trusting yourself, all while pursuing a career in an industry where self-doubt and cut-throat tendencies seem to crop up. No, it's not gonna be easy, but it sure will be wonderful, once you embrace trust in your career's path.

It takes smarts to *really* trust those around you. You *must* keep your eyes peeled for scammers who will take advantage of too much misplaced trust. Also watch out for folks who'll lead you into a ditch because they simply don't know any better (but they talk a good game). If you start off by building your relationships on a foundation of research and common sense, you're on the right track for having a professional community you can easily trust at every turn. But if you're so eager to get a team in place that you aren't choosy when assembling it, you're much more likely to have your trust misplaced down the line.

Take the time to know who you're dealing with. Only sign with agents you've researched incredibly well. Try to put yourself in the hands of directors whose visions you share. Study under coaches who *get* you and your career goals. And constantly reassess to be sure you're in the best possible partnerships as your needs change and your career path leads you up a tier or two. Once you surround yourself with people you trust, you must then *trust them*. Don't micromanage their process. If you did your research and prepwork correctly, you've got to know that you've put yourself and your career into capable hands. Let these folks do their best for you, unfettered by your anxious chatter.

There are some directors who are gonna ask you to do weird stuff. The specifics might not make sense to you, but if you've done your homework before getting involved in a project with any particular director or producer, you're going to trust that this person has the best overall finished product in mind, when asking you to perform in any particular way. (Now, of course, if you are being asked to do anything that jeopardizes your safety or crushes your spirit, you need to check with your union or your support network to really examine whether you *did enough homework* before signing up to work with this loon.)

In most instances, the directors and producers you work with are going to have a broader view of what the overall finished product is supposed to look like, and while you may be certain that "it'd be better if I got to say this word on this beat instead of that one," you're only privy to a portion of the overall project, and you'll need to trust that a director is going to pull out your best performance *in context* that you might not have access to just yet. This is not to say that you should throw out your values *at all*. This is just a point about how important that early research can be, as it is the cornerstone for the trust required when you're on set and being asked to provide what may just turn out to be a brilliant performance.

Stay involved in what your representatives do on your behalf but don't ever micromanage your team. If you avoided a premature move and only signed with someone after you did research and targeted, then landed that *hell yes* rep, you're okay. Yes, even when times are slow or you're wondering if your agent is out there hustling for you, if you signed on with a team you trust, you can focus your energy on things you control, rather than worrying about whether your rep is doing his job.

Before you started spending loads of money on acting classes, you spoke to other actors whose work you enjoy about who their coaches are, right? You audited classes so that you could see, by sitting in and observing, how the coaches work and whether they'd meet your needs, right? Okay, so assuming you've not signed up for classes with some soul-crushing, "watch me break you down and then build you up in my image so that you'll walk around like a drone telling the world how much of a guru I am"-type coach with all that research you did, you're in a good class. Now, because you're with a coach you trust, *trust* him. Let him bring out the best in you. Test your range. Have fun.

Sure, there are times when you need to check with someone outside yourself to know you're on the right path or making the right choices, but if you've surrounded yourself with people you trust in all of the above scenarios, the number of times you actually doubt their guidance will reduce significantly. So, that means you need to trust yourself. Trust that you've made good choices. And trust yourself to check in with your progress in case your team begins to no longer mesh with your needs as an artist. That's growth. It's a good thing.

Finally, *trust that you're enough.* You don't need to lie on your resumé or beef up your first credits. Enjoy being a beginner while you're a beginner! It's the only time when you can freely be open to learning so much from so many others who have been down the same path. There is room for everyone in this business. Your patience with your process, your willingness to treat this career as a long-haul experience rather than something you can quickly master, and your enthusiasm for the opportunities you get every *day* in this business will be *more than enough* to get you started. Rather than ever looking at an audition in terms of, "What are they looking for and how can I be that?" focus your energy on, "This is who I am and now let me show them that."

Trust me: You, yourself, are enough. I know it sounds "Stuart Smalley" in nature, but it's the truth. You don't have to be anything other than who you are in order to make it in this business. In fact, the harder you try to figure out what we want and the more you stray from your bullseye in order to *be that*, the less trust we're going to put in you to deliver the goods as an actor who gives voice to our projects' characters in the first place. Trust that.

Energy Vampires

There are people in this industry—in this life—who are best described as Eeyores. Yes, from the world of Winnie the Pooh. Negative Nellies, Poison Playmates, Debbie Downers, Complainey Janies, Energy Vampires. Don't invite them in on your journey. Have no stress about letting them go if they've been a part of your journey and now need to be shown the door. Every hour you spend working on someone else's drama is an hour you're not investing in succeeding in the life of your dreams.

Spend no time trying to help folks who *don't* get you understand you. Invest your time in folks who get you—they'll invest in you. Spend no time in conversation with those who've committed to being bitter. Bitterness is the most uncastable quality and you must avoid having the stench of others' bitterness on you.

The only appropriate response when a toxic person asks, "Would you be interested in some constructive criticism?" is, "Oh, absolutely not." Certainly welcome all sorts of solution-based feedback from people whose souls light up the world. Poison people? No interest. The second you leave your high-achieving, focused, goal-filled road to walk along a path of sadness with someone else, you're losing footing in your creative journey. Don't sacrifice. Wallow with someone who's having a tough road a moment. After that, have empathy, but get out of their drama and get back to building your empire.

Web of Trust 101

All this "relationship" stuff works the opposite of the way you're thinking about it. You need to look at it from the position of the people handing out the favors, the people giving the hands up.

Let's say you're a semi-established entertainment industry professional... an actor, director, crew-type, or something like that. You make your living in the industry, no survival job at all for the last two years or so. You know enough people that you get regular work. You're a pro, and the people you work with are also pros.

Now, let's say you're also in a personal relationship with a partner who is giving you the best sex you've ever had in your entire life. Best! Sex! Ever! Let's call this person "BSE." BSE is an actor, a decent one, mostly talented but not working at your level. That's not a criticism; it's an observation. It's just a fact. BSE needs a few more years of experience before being ready to play in your league.

One day, BSE sees that there's a project starting up, notices that a couple of people with whom you've got existing, professional relationships are heading it up. BSE points out that there's a perfectly-suited character in the project, and suggests that you make introductions to the team. You know the caliber of people that these guys are looking for and you know that BSE isn't even close.

The conundrum: Are you—a competent industry professional with years invested in your career and the relationships that make your career work—going to put your professional reputation on the line by making this introduction?

Because that's what you're considering doing. Think about it. Every time you make an introduction between people in this industry, you're putting your reputation on the line. Your judgment is being tested. You know that if you set up a dog of a meeting, your producer friend is never going to trust your recommendation again.

The answer to the conundrum, when the stakes are the best sex you've ever had—and probably will ever have—in your entire life vs. your professional reputation is, of course, *no.* You would not take the hit to your rep for BSE. It's not that you don't care about BSE—you do—but you also understand what's important.

When the stakes are lower than the best sex you've ever had, it's even more obvious that you don't make connections between people if it's going to damage your professional relationships and thus your career. One of the things you *do* do is make every effort to connect people who will rock each other's respective worlds.

One of your main goals as an industry pro (other than being a consummate professional in your area of expertise) needs to be to make synergistic connections between other industry pros. You need to be out there hoping that by putting good people together, you are making that magic happen.

Here's where a lot of self-absorbed actors lose track of what's really important. Most of the time, making these connections helps the people you connect directly. But you? Not so much. Someone is looking for the perfect actor to play a specific role, you know someone who'd be perfect, you make the introduction, they hit it off and go make a movie together while you sit at home with nothing more than the knowledge that you're the one that made it happen. You need to keep in mind that so much more than that is *actually* going on.

When you make a good call, your reputation improves. When you make a mistake, your rep takes a hit. And that hit is proportional to the stakes involved in the judgment call.

See any and all of your industry relationships as strands of spider silk, strung between you and the industry person with whom you have the relationship. The strength and thickness of the strands is analogous to how good your relationship is, how strong the relationship is, how much trust exists between you. All of your relationships—along with all of their relationships—form your web of trust.

When you try to make a connection between two people who don't know each other (and thus have no trust between them), you borrow from your existing strands of silk to make the initial strand between them. They'll trust each other based largely on how much each of them trusts you. If their relationship takes off—if you've created a synergistic match—the bonds of trust between them grow and strengthen on their own and their trust in you gets stronger. The synergies you create make more strands of spider silk flow between all of you.

If, however, you've made a bad judgment in making the introduction (for any number of a million reasons that you may never learn about or have been able to predict), the connection doesn't fit, the strands get severed between them, and you don't get those strands back; they fall away, broken. Each party has been bitten by your (in this case) poor judgment call, and as a result, they trust you less next time.

Sounds pretty simple, right? Truth is, it's exactly that simple. Disgustingly simple. And with the strands of spider-silk imagery, it's easy to see too. When you understand the web of trust, you understand why it takes patience in this industry. It takes time to establish working trust with people. It takes time to evaluate the people with whom you've established trusting relationships to determine if they're worth hanging on to and then prune away those that aren't worth it. Sometimes, you cut people out of your web—or they cut themselves out—and you have to rebuild with different folks. Sometimes you'll make a call that's so bad it takes a long time for your colleagues to trust you again.

Opportunities to develop synergistic trust with other industry pros happen by chance. But taking advantage of those opportunities doesn't. Your ultimate goal needs to be to expand your web of trust until it can feed you enough work to have a self-sustaining career.

You must be the kind of person (have the skills, talent, and attitude) that others will gain a good rep from through their recommendations of you. I don't know how to make you one of those people. No one but you can control whether you're that kind of person or not.

—Keith Johnson

The web of trust is only as strong as the people we connect are *good* together. Sure, sometimes we misfire. But if, over the years, we consistently put great people together, our web of trust is healthy and we regularly hear, "You know so-and-so? Oh! I love her! She's the best!" because the connections made are *good* ones.

The web of trust is in use when you're asking for a referral to an agency for possible representation. The web of trust is in use when casting directors bring an actor in front of producers for a larger role than the actor may seem ready to book. The web of trust is in use when a manager picks up the phone and says, "You've gotta see this new client," to a casting director. And how well the web of trust works hinges upon the strength of those strands of spider silk. A manager who sends a casting office an actor who is late, unprepared, and bitter? That manager will have a harder time getting the next actor through the door. The manager who continues to *only* send in the very best actors a certain CD has ever seen? Red carpet, baby. That's a casting office that is wide open to actors within that manager's web of trust.

Using your show bible, map out your web of trust today. Yes, even if all you've done are a few indies, some student films, self-produced projects, and loads of training. You have a web of trust and you would be crazy to think that some of the folks currently in your circle will have no impact on your future in this business. Sure, a lot of the folks you connect with at the beginning of your career will move along and leave the biz, but others will rise right along with you (or faster than you, or slower than you) for decades. To this day, I do business with people I worked with in the 1980s in Atlanta, right here in Hollywood. You betcha.

Who, in your web of trust, is someone for whom you cannot wait to help make something happen? Start looking at your friends and colleagues that way and focus on how *you* can make connections *for others*, first. Being a connector between creative collaborators is a beautiful thing! You'll find people looking for ways to repay the favor in no time. Fact.

The champion wins first, then walks into the arena. Everybody else walks into the arena and then tries to figure out what to do.
—Jim Fannin, business coach

PART TWO: PREP

The way you make it is you just tell them: "This is who I am."
—Alec Baldwin, actor

6: Your Bullseye

I was at lunch with an actor friend when one of those alerts came over his phone for a casting that matched his online profile. He opened the message and followed the link to the breakdown, and started reading aloud: "This guy's a loser. A schlub. A sad sack whose mere presence makes everyone else uncomfortable. He's losing his hair and gaining a gut. He can't win."

We looked at each other and burst into laughter. "Yeah. I go out for this guy all the time," he said. I asked, "How do you take that, emotionally, when you're not in such a good place, and those words land in your inbox?" We looked at each other, then after a beat, both said, "take it all the way to the bank."

I say that phrase a lot. I also add the phrase, "wipe your tears with hundred-dollar bills," sometimes, because the visual is so delicious. Yeah, it may hurt your heart a bit when you get that call from your agent saying, "I've got you going in for the role of the vapid model. She's really stupid and gets used a lot, but she's too dumb to notice. Break a leg!" but if you focus on the "I've got you going in" part, it's all good news.

Actors who are cast as the creep, the bad guy, the wannabe, the never-was, the fatty, the uggo, or the loser, need to stay focused on the fact that they're *cast* that way, and not get down about the rest of it. There's an episode of *Family Guy* in which Peter Griffin talks about Steve Buscemi's looks, noting "every one of his teeth is in business for itself." When you think about how many times Buscemi probably heard comments from others about his looks over the course of his career, think about how it felt when *you* heard comments about your weight, your hairline, your acne scars, your *whatever*. Multiply that by the number of times Buscemi must hear it all, and think about how tough-skinned one must get, to survive.

Wiping tears with hundred-dollar bills; dedicating each of your gold, shiny statuettes to those who've said negative things about you; playing roles with unflattering adjectives in their descriptions—all the way to the bank—makes it all so much easier. Start conditioning yourself for success by depersonalizing any part of this pursuit that feels personal (because, remember, it's never personal). Getting down with this sooner will only help you, later. Start by adding "all the way to the bank" to anything that makes you uncomfortable to hear, about the roles you inhabit. Cash those checks, baby!

The key to being an actor in Hollywood: Never think about the sheer volume of people who have basically said, "Nah, I don't particularly like you."

—Phil LaMarr, actor

Specializing

Actors get into this business feeling as though they'll be able to play all sorts of roles, try on many characters, inhabit various worlds. True, but it's those who specialize who really "make it." Using your primary brand, your specificity, your bullseye actually gets you farther faster—and to a place where you absolutely can, *eventually*, show your range. But it's knowing, selling, and living your bullseye—that thing you do better than anything else and that thing no one else does as well as you—that gets you the shot at showing the world what *else* is on your dartboard.

Being paid to do the same boneheaded character between "action" and "cut" for years on a top series is a lovely thing to do—all the way to the bank. But for those who want to be everything, play everything, and never specialize, I simply ask that you reflect on the careers of the successful actors you love most. They probably specialized 'til they reached a certain point in their careers, at which point they were invited to show the world what else they could do.

Eventually, you'll be a specialist who gets to show the world other specialties you have. You'll have so many *different* specialties that your fans will follow along and check out your range. Some may love it. Some will want you to stick to your specialty. Think about how you feel, as a consumer of music, when your favorite band has an album in which they "try out something new." Sometimes you hate it! You want them to deliver that thing they're known for. You want them to provide you with more brilliant music in the style that is their specialty.

I get the reluctance. I remember seeing an ad for the next in the latest "blow everything up" film franchise. Before I even knew what the ad was for, I said, to myself, "Pff. Michael freakin' Bay." How did I know it was Michael Bay (or at least, Michael Bay-like) from the first seconds? He's well-branded for his specialty. It may not be for everyone, but it's a brand that served him while he was starting out and got him to where he is today. It's his bullseye, and my "pff" means nothing to him. He wipes his tears with hundred-dollar bills.

Whatever it is you're providing—if you're an actor, that's your interpretation of the sides at your audition; if you're a writer, that's your well-crafted sentences that take readers on a ride; if you're a producer, that's your detail-oriented logistic ninjaosity that saves everyone money and time—when you make it look like it's just "no big thing" that you created the intended result, you've made it look *effortless*. And the buyers want that. That's you hitting your bullseye, over and over.

I saw an infomercial for something called a Magic Bullet and actually decided I *could* be a fine cook (even though I am not to be trusted in the kitchen, ever) because this thing made prep, cooking, and clean-up look *effortless*. Now, I know better, because I have an entire closet filled with gadgets, each bought with the enthusiasm of "look how easy it is" that didn't measure up to the truth of actually *using* the dang thing. But the point is, when it's made to look *effortless*, it is *desired*.

When athletes are in the zone, they can pull off a half-court shot at the buzzer and make it look like they sink that shot *every* time. Same with the hole-in-one, the amazing endzone catch for a touchdown as the clock ticks over to 00:00, the outfielder's gravity-defying leap to catch a ball destined for the seats far above his head. Effortless work looks phenomenal. It makes us cheer. What is effortless is your bullseye.

Your Youness

You'll build toward your bullseye by way of celebrating your "youness"— you know, that stuff that makes you uniquely you. The ninja actor celebrates authenticity. Others show up for auditions and immediately start angling, based on what they think we're looking for.

One of these choices makes you an actor. The other puts you in the psychic business, and *that's* not anywhere close to what we're looking for! I get that it's tempting. You *are* a chameleon, based on years of actor training. You *can* change up your choices, based on years of practice doing so. You *are* an intuitive critter and you *do* want to please others—especially if pleasing someone gets you this gig right now!

But I'll recommend that you get out of the habit of trying to get into our heads—or worse, hustling for info in the waiting room, or taking seriously whatever other auditioning actors are saying about what *they* believe we're looking for in the room—with the goal of changing up your read to please anyone. Get information, sure. But don't let *anything* throw off the hard work you've done in prep for your time in the room.

Beyond the auditioning room, this advice goes for selecting headshots, designing your website, or putting together your reel! By trying to be everything to everyone, you successfully accomplish only one thing: Not being yourself to anyone.

Visualizing a dartboard, the bullseye is your ultimate youness. It's where you are, at your core, when you work on a role. Sure, you may play the creepy bad guy and not truly *be* a bad guy, but that bad guy is your bullseye and a trusted clergyman is somewhere in the outer rings of the dartboard. Doesn't mean you can't hit that role—of course you can, you're an actor—but it means it's a bit off the mark of what you do, effortlessly. More importantly, it's someone else's bullseye.

Sure, you can walk in, read the room, figure we're looking for someone younger to try and come off younger in your read. But someone else is going to walk in younger, be younger, *bullseye* younger. Why compete with that? Instead, chalk it up to one of those auditions where you got to show us your take on the role (even if we're going to cast someone younger, creepier, quirkier, whatever) and, most importantly, you got to show us your youness, so that we can call you in "better" next time.

Okay, but what if you don't yet know your bullseye? You have an idea. You know who you are, pretty much. But you hear so much about *type* and you see so many words in the breakdowns and—because of your training as an actor—you know you can *do* just about anything, so you do the same thing that most actors do: Submit on anything that marginally fits, show up, do your best, and then wonder why you've not been successful in building a *brand*. Ah. Well, type is a tool to lead us to your bullseye (which is where your brand lives, by the way). So, let's start with an easy, fun, fairly common typing exercise to build toward the good stuff at a tier above that simple foundation.

Type Yourself

How do you type yourself? You get outside help. You provide a list of words—visit smfa4.com for a downloadable and printable list you can take with you as you conduct this research—approach others (especially folks who know you not at all), and get them to tell you how you present in the room. Take copies of the list, a clipboard, and a pen, and go take a survey! A note of caution, before you begin: Do not seek out so-called "experts" and rank their opinion of you higher than anyone else's. The self-typing exercise is meant to operate on patterns that are established the more people you survey. The results will be a bell curve, with certain words repeating often enough to make it clear what you bullseye (and what's just on your dartboard).

Once you've downloaded your master type list from smfa4.com, you may be feeling overwhelmed. Great! Let's get the list to a manageable state. What are you supposed to do with all of these words? Get rid of words that will *never* describe you as you now are—but don't limit the list *too* much—make copies of the list and whenever you have time to kill (you're early for a CD workshop, you're on a break during acting class, you're at rehearsal for a play, you're in the lunchroom at your day job, you're on campus between classes, you're in line for EPAs, you're commuting on the train, you're waiting at the

DMV), start asking folks to circle the half-dozen words that best describe you. Over time, you'll see patterns emerge. You'll learn which themes align for the storyteller you are. Clusters of words will keep coming up and you'll soon realize that you're way more small-town than big city. Or you're coming off as an intellectual when you've always felt you were a doofus.

Why does this matter? Well, when casting directors put out a breakdown, sometimes we ask actors to submit on the one role for which they're best matched only. When an actor instead submits on all seven roles, it conveys three things: 1. He can't read; 2. He's desperate to play any role, no matter what; and 3. He doesn't know his primary type, because clearly he believes he could be both a 20-year-old nerd and a 45-year-old punk rocker, which simply isn't likely.

Whatever market you're in, knowing your specialty is going to help you communicate your brand to the buyers. Most folks don't want to know *all* the things you can do. We want to know about the one thing you do *best* and we want you to do that every time we call you in—all the way to the bank. We like to know that *you* know your strengths. It's not impressive to see that you think you could play *every* role equally well. It's impressive to see that you know where *you* rock the most and we love it when you rock exactly like that, every time we call you in. Once you've been at it for a while and have built fans out of the buyers, you can spread out and show us the other amazing things on your dartboard. But actors who *lead* with that "No, really, I can do anything" agenda are seen as scattered, unfocused, and *desperate.* Don't be one of those actors!

Now, about Your Headshot

You don't have to wait until you've nailed your bullseye to find out what *type* your headshot is selling. Yes, your headshot is a placeholder for those of us who already know your work, but because you may be trying to get in front of casting directors who don't yet know you, it's also important to be sure your headshot sells exactly what you're going to be able to deliver when you walk through the door in person.

Create a survey and post a link to your most-used headshots on your blog or your Facebook page or your Twitter stream or whatever space you use to interact with folks the most online. These people don't have to be in the business. These "friends" don't have to know you (in fact, the less they know you in person, the more effective this exercise will be, because they're going to be able to tell you what type your headshot *says you are*, irrespective of what they know about you as a person). As with the in-person typing exercise, there's no one authority whose opinion "wins." You're looking for patterns in the results, here.

Is your headshot selling what you're selling? If the resulting words don't align with the words you get from the in-person typing exercise, you're running the risk of committing the number-one top sin mentioned by casting directors worldwide: You don't look like your headshot. You're misrepresenting yourself with a headshot that doesn't sell what you're selling. It's like having a business card with a misprint in your phone number. What's the point?

A great tip on typing (especially if you're shy and don't want to do typing exercises as we've outlined, here) comes from actor and type-based headshot photographer Mark Atteberry, who suggests you pull out your old yearbooks from high school and make a list of all the things folks wrote about you back then. It's eerily accurate! Did your besties call you "my rock; my go-to when things are tough" or "silly, funny, quirky" in your yearbook? That stuff is *great* typing information, because your essence never goes away.

Interview Your Bookings

Let's map out exactly what's *already* going on in your career. Let your previous bookings help you define your bullseye! For each project you've gone out for in the past two years, explore the *typing words* you were given in the breakdown, then look at how far you got through the casting process. You'll score each audition for how deep into the casting process you got. So an avail weighs more than a callback, which weighs more than a preread. To download a worksheet to help you easily complete this exercise, hop on over to smfa4. com and grab your handy PDF. Now, do not use this exercise as a way to beat yourself up for what you didn't book, but instead as a tool to see how the buyers value what you do, so you can walk toward that and get to the money faster. Yay!

For specific classifications (paid vs. non-paying gigs, union vs. nonunion projects, on-camera vs. on stage roles, major market vs. minor market bookings), I recommend the following: If you have a *ton* of bookings, start segregating. If you only have a few, clump 'em all together for now. What we're looking for here is patterns, and you can't track patterns with too little data. You have to have enough information to start to see where the keywords keep coming.

You're going to have broader range on stage, both in type and age. Does that help you learn how the buyers for on-camera work see you? Nope. Not at all. So splitting those up is a great idea. If you've moved from a minor market to a major market, you'll want to separate out your old home's bookings because they only tell you how you *were* cast, not how you'll be valued in your new home.

If you've recently joined the union or transitioned out of copy-credit-meals gigs into the paid ones in your market, same thing. The information about your previous tier is only helpful historically. Once you've made a tier-jump, your need to study the data from the lower tier becomes lower priority. Notice I didn't say it's not important at all! Just that it's a measurement of something less in step with where you're headed. And, of course, where you're headed is what you really want to focus on.

Make sure every booking you interview is something you could still book (or would want to book) today. Being in love with your old credits after you've aged out of them doesn't help you. It's a sentimental thing that won't lead to your next booking, and I'm all about helping you get farther faster.

How specific, how narrowly focused do you want to be? That's up to you. In some markets, you can have a larger bullseye, because there's less competition and therefore less specificity required to build a brand among fewer buyers. In larger markets, however, the more narrowly focused you are, the easier brand-building becomes. You're threading a needle either way, as you submit on roles and attempt to get cast. Whether you choose to use a single string or a strand of yarn to thread that needle is up to you. Narrow focus makes it easier, though, and clears the clutter of all the other roles out there, to which you'll eventually stop paying attention.

If the words are stumping you (like, you keep getting "bitch" and that word rubs you the wrong way), use a site that provides a visual thesaurus to get better words that still tell the same story. Once you have a nice list of typing words that describe *you*, track your data visually by using websites that generate a "type cloud." We have great resource sites for this part of the task at smfa4.com, of course. Import the results of your typing exercises, retain the number of times that each word or phrase was provided, and watch the most-repeated words and phrases appear largest in the "type cloud" you create! This is just like a tag cloud on a blog and it's a great visual depiction of your bullseye to post at your actor workspace. The words that come up the most, in typing yourself, your headshot, and your bookings (whether in different exercises or clustered together)—that's your bullseye. With the type cloud, you'll always remember how to submit on-brand, at a glance.

This visual, with your bullseye clearly largest, begging for your attention, will keep you focused on how to submit, project to project. It'll help you refine your target list (more on that later). It'll help you with your logline (more on that later, too). It'll keep you focused in such a ninja way that you start seeing the rest of the characters, the rest of the breakdowns, the rest of the projects out there as *noise*.

What a beautiful place to live, as an artist: Focused. Completely aware of what you bullseye, daily. Ready to deliver the goods—effortlessly—when invited in to do so. Never hustling to try and prove anything to anyone. Confident that your brand is, indeed, castable. It's all about lining up with those who most need to know your bullseye exists, then showing 'em how it looks when you hit it. All the way to the bank.

Typing Tips

Resist typing yourself. You know yourself too well. Others may see the scar above your eyebrow and classify you as someone who gets in fights. You see that scar and remember the horrific car accident that nearly took your life. Your association with everything about you is too intimate for you to be an accurate judge of "type," when we're hoping to mimic the casting process. The less people know you, the better their typing words will be, for you. That's not to say there's no value to self-awareness or that folks who know you best can't help! But because casting directors won't generally get to know you, deeply, before making their first casting decisions about you, start on the surface.

Keep in mind that people love to classify types by creating hybrids. It's just easier for people to take a known commodity and tweak it to their current needs. Think of two actors (past or present) whose blended qualities would be *you*. What would your hybrid cross be?

Pay attention to the roles you're given in acting class. Don't get weirded out by reading parts in class that are "against type." One of the goals in class is to push your boundaries in an attempt to stretch your range. So, even if something is very much *not* your type, go ahead and give it your all. You may surprise yourself. Of course, that's an in-class thing. When you're out in the real world, your brand-building work is more important than showcasing your range. This is not to limit you as an actor; it's to get you to the next tier, faster!

Write your own character breakdown. What words would a writer use to describe the character that *is* you? Once you know *your* character breakdown, you are well on your way to matching yourself up for the right roles, something we do in casting every day. Remember: Play your look and be yourself.

Type Me Please

Because discovering your type can sometimes provide a jolt, I'll now share a heartbreaking story about how I discovered my type, back when I was pursuing acting. My first ongoing on-camera class as an adult was a very telling experience. I'd been marketing myself as the kid I'd been rather than the adult actor I'd grown into. It's hard to know you're doing something like that, but it's *so* much better when you do know it—even if you have to hear it from someone else.

I was in the first session of a four-week class with a casting director instructor and I went into the class pretty sure of how I came across on camera and in my work. My marketing plan reflected that, and I was working plenty as a college kid type, but not as much as I did after "the incident."

The casting director left our headshots on a chair in the room before the break. She'd been sitting near me while each actor read audition sides. At the break, I looked over to my headshot, which was resumé-side-up. There was a notation on the resumé (as is common practice. Casting directors will make notes of our first impression of actors, so our memories will be "jogged" after it's been a while since meeting the actors). It read, "Good ol' gal."

I was devastated! "Good ol' gal?" Hell no! Not me! I am elegant and statuesque and voluptuous and funny and brilliant! I am a diva! I am *not* some "good ol' gal!"

Then I took a good hard look at myself and realized, "Wait! I am an Atlantan, through and through. I am not a *Cosmo* Girl. I am not a Valley Girl. I am a Southern Belle but I am also one of the guys. I know more about SEC football than any other chick with such a gorgeous pedicure. I shoot pool, I throw darts, I bowl, I swear, I drink, and I am quick-witted, cynical, and sarcastic. The most formal piece of clothing I own is the pair of jeans *without* a hole in the knee. Y'know what? Maybe I *am* a good ol' gal!"

Holy cow! That changed everything. I went out and shot new headshots while wearing jeans instead of "dressing up" for the shoot (more on that in the chapter on **Your Headshots**). Instead of sitting up straight, perfectly poised in my pose, I just relaxed and said, "Hey! How's it goin'?" which gave me a great, friendly, accessible, *good ol' gal* look on my face. Suddenly, by not fighting what casting directors were already seeing in me, I started booking like mad! Once I stopped resisting what was *most* marketable about my look, I was able to go out for the roles I was more likely to book.

So, brace yourself and really listen to what others are saying when you get comments about how you might be different in the room than you appear in your headshot.

It is a gift to know who you are, truly. Your self-awareness will permeate everything you do, and that's a big plus for your acting—no matter what your type may be.

Remember how the other kids made fun of you in middle school and high school? Of course you do. Try to figure out what specifically that was about because that's your money ticket! Are you seven feet tall? Do you have a big gap in your teeth? Got a strangely-pitched voice? These are things that get you noticed. Don't run from your uniqueness. Build on it.

—Assaf Cohen

But I Have Range!

Casting directors do *not* want to see four different headshots from you, showing us all the different types you *can* be. Agents and managers may want to see such range, as that helps them market you in several different ways. Casting directors, however, want to see the one headshot that shows you as the exact right type for the role we're casting at that exact moment. Don't talk us out of it with headshots of conflicting type! While you think you're proving range by having lots of different looks in your online profile, what you may be doing is talking us out of believing that any of those looks is truly representative of you today. We begin to wonder if perhaps the one look we're crazy about for a project is one from a years-ago photo shoot. We're staking our reputations with the producers who hire us every time an actor walks into the room, so we're not likely to take a risk if we're not sure which headshot accurately represents you *right now*.

So, what do you do? You *are* versatile. You *do* look both 15 and 23. You *have* that great a range and your photos are all from the same shoot. Do you *only* market yourself one way? Sometimes, yes. If you're constantly going out for 23 even though you *can* play 15, perhaps you're better off marketing yourself as 23 and letting go of the "but I also look 15" headshot in the bunch. Sure, have that headshot in case you ever need it, but don't include it when you are submitting to casting directors.

A confused mind says NO. Too much information can cloud a casting director's view of you and get you put in the "no" category, in favor of an actor who has provided exactly *one* headshot: the one that sells that actor in *this role at this moment*. Think about logos for your favorite brands, as a consumer. Apple doesn't use 10 different "looks" to convey its brand. Be careful when you're tempted to showcase loads of looks. You could be eroding the brand loyalty you're hoping to build.

> *The biggest mistake actors make when it comes to their look is not having one. Create one!*
> —Marki Costello, manager-casting director-host coach

Type vs. Brand

Visualize your brand as the umbrella under which all the various type of roles you can play live. You may play a misunderstood genius who works at a major university. Then you take on the role of a societal outcast who lives on the streets. The next project has you playing a serial killer who lurks in the shadows, preparing his next conquest. You may say to me, "See, Bon?

I have no one specific type! These roles are all over the map!" To which I reply, "Consider the thruline. All of these characters are loners. They're on the outside, trying to look in. These are different types that all live under the umbrella brand of *outsider*.

Does that mean you can only ever play the outsider? Of course not. It means—if you do your work to build a brand that includes a career of having played loads of roles with this thruline—you're working on building loyalty and lowering the perceived risk in casting you, cementing relationships in the industry, becoming the go-to actor for roles of this ilk, and elevating to the next tier faster. When you interview your bookings, note what they all have in common. That's the foundation of the brand you've already begun building.

Consider someone like Betty White. Every role in her decades-long career could easily be put under the brand umbrella of what it *is* that everyone thinks of, when considering "Brand Betty White." That doesn't mean there's been absence of range and experimentation within those roles! But there is no mistaking her bullseye.

Your Brand Filter

One of the surest ways to head in the right direction for the brand you hope to put out into the world is to make brand-based decisions from the very beginning. You know where you want to end up. You can see the goal that's many tiers above. You have an idea of how you'd like the world to see you, once you've found some success. But it's looking at the steps to the very first tier jump, then the next one, then the one after that, that will help the most right now.

At each level, there's an opportunity to do work that's on-brand and to do work that adds to brand confusion. The latter makes the buyers less sure of what they're going to get when you walk into the room, because it's so far off the mark from what you showed them you could do last time. And the time before that. Or if you're just starting out—like, *really* just starting out—there is no "time before that," and that's why it's so dang important to have your bullseye to rely on, when making those foundational choices.

The bigger issue when you're starting out is that there are so many opportunities to work for free, many of which you'll *need* to accept, simply because you're building your credits, you're getting footage for your reel, and you're investing in relationships by saying yes to freebie gigs. However, if you never want to be associated with violence because you see yourself as the new face of Disney down the line, your brand filter had better help you know when to say no.

Having an overarching mission statement for yourself as a creative in this industry is very important. Because, while it may cost you an immediate opportunity in your established brand to do a risky role, it could—bigger picture—give you the decades-long career growth you're hoping for to be choosy. You're planting seeds with choices at every stage in your career. Each immediate decision must be in service of your overall career brand, to be most effective as a tool for your career trajectory.

Does filtering your choices take all the fun out of the pursuit? Remove the mystery from the journey? Pull the artist away from the art and diminish the love of it all? No. Not even a little bit. Just like having a religion or a moral code makes some folks' decisions easier, because they have a set of rules or guiding principles with which to check in, running career decisions—especially ones that seem challenging, that look really sparkly and shiny and exciting and profitable at a time when you're hungry for work or money or both—through your brand filter can be the easiest way to stay on target for your overall career goals, rather than constantly correcting an oversteer in one direction, then the other.

Rebranding

Stalling out between jobs is not an uncommon experience in Hollywood. What's an actor to do? One option is rebranding. I'm a big fan of the style and class Michael Chiklis showed in rebranding himself as an actor.

He made a choice to change the course of his career. Chiklis had done *The Commish* and then the oh-so-bad sitcom *Daddio*. He was overweight, balding beyond help, and always playing the lovable goofball roles far older than his actual age. After *Daddio* was cancelled, he found little work because he really wanted to start playing roles his own age.

He got depressed with the options available to him, having convinced the industry he could only play "that schlubby type." Still, he kept trying, kept looking for other options, and then had a heart-to-heart with his wife about considering no longer accepting the loser roles.

His wife assured him that she would be by his side, no matter how tight money got, while he rebranded himself. They put a plan of action into place: weight-loss regimen, lifting weights and training every day, working with scripts he had never been considered for previously, and shaving his head. Then, in a serendipitous trip to Gymboree to pick up their child, Chiklis and his wife reconnected with friends from Miami: Cathy Ryan and her husband Shawn, the creator of "this new, edgy FX series," *The Shield*.

When Chiklis' agent followed up with a call to the casting office for the show, Ryan expected he'd be asked to make an offer—something he was not ready to do, based on what he knew of Chiklis' prior work. But Chiklis was willing to *read* for the role—something actors of that level tend not to do.

He knew he'd need to show the buyers he could do something different than what they might be expecting, based on his body of work. He needed to show the buyers this *new* bullseye. Yes, it had always been on his dartboard, but he was well-branded by his old bullseye. Even though he had cred as a booking machine, he read for the role of Vic Mackey.

While Chiklis refers to the dark, dry spell of his career between series as a crossroads, he also knows that it took getting to a certain level of depression to enable him to make such a major change in himself and book the lead role in a groundbreaking cop drama. A year later, Chiklis was thanking Emmy voters.

This is an awesome story about the importance of taking control of your career when it has stalled out. Important to note, of course, is that Chiklis was already low-risk as a leading actor on multiple series before rebooting the brand. Build your fanbase *before* you start shaking things up. That goes for drastic changes in hair color, weight, personal style, and even your name. Don't "shuck and jive" to try and figure out what will work. Build your brand, create a fanbase, and know when it's time to shift gears after you're perceived as low-risk.

Consider someone like Tom Cruise. Early on in his career, he was regularly cast as the young, dimwitted cutie (in *The Outsiders, All the Right Moves, Risky Business*). Had he said at the very beginning, that he only intended to play roles such as the Vampire Lestat, he would've been laughed out of casting offices all over Hollywood! Get "in" the way your type is selling the *best*, then show the world what *else* you can do.

The point of understanding your brand (which comes from getting clear on your type, your targets, the vibe of the stories you like to tell, and where all these things intersect in current opportunities) is that it clears the clutter of all the overwhelming *noise* out there. That noise comes from hundreds of casting directors and hundreds of agents and managers, not to mention the thousands upon thousands of actors, all sure they know exactly how it works, but of course they'll change up their headshots again in three months, and then their hair, and then their team, and then their stage name because, well, "nothing's working." The people who do it best—and who have been doing it for decades—are so well-branded that the *work* of it all disappears into the background. That's ninja.

Casting directors prefer working with specific upper-tier agents *because* of the brand that the agents have built: They're easy to deal with, they always supply wonderful actors who are both talented and the exact right type for the role as described. The top agencies on the planet wouldn't have "branded entertainment" as a main menu item on their websites if branding weren't a part of this business. Brand has long been a "guy behind the curtain" bit of work done to help Hollywood "sell" the giant head of "The Great and Powerful Oz" story.

People who say they know nothing about "actor branding" are either hoarding information about what happens with that "guy behind the curtain" or they're so completely wooed by brand that they don't even realize it. Why will I pay more to fly Virgin, when I grew up a "Delta brat" due to my dad's 40 years with that company? Because I'm down with the Virgin brand. It speaks to me. Why are some actors *everywhere* for a year (like, in every single commercial, it seems, plus on these two shows, and in this feature film, all at once)? Because everything lined up for the buyers to jump on board—and fast—and the actor was smart enough to take advantage of as much of it as he could, right then.

Your brand is something you can manage, your brand message is something you can put out into the world, your fanbase is something you can build—or your buyers can tell you who *they've* decided you are. Either way, the labels are on you. I say, choose yours (and work it) rather than letting the industry—or the world—define you.

7: YOUR SHOW BIBLE

I spend a lot of time talking about the importance of understanding that this is a business built on *relationships*. I also spend a lot of time talking about the importance of doing *research* so that your marketing is targeted, your plans are specific, and your type and your vibe are aligned with your promotional efforts. When I speak to actors about this research, I see some eyes glaze over as I get to the part about setting up Google Alerts on the casting directors you're targeting based on your research about the projects that align with your bullseye. It's not that setting up the Google Alerts or keeping tabs on the folks who populate the projects most likely to consistently need your vibe and type is too confusing. It's that the whole point of getting into acting—for many folks—is to avoid a lot of math and number crunching and stats and logic puzzles.

Ah, but in Hollywood, there is *always* math involved. So, why am I using the concept of a "show bible," here? Looking at what Wikipedia says about show bibles—*Show bibles are an optional part of the television series development process... they are meticulously-maintained archives of everything known about a show's characters*—it may not seem to track. Stick with me. When you walk into the writers' room for any television series, you'll see multi-colored index cards up on cork boards, outlining plot points and story arcs, character development and inciting incidents. At the root of the information on those cards for any particular episode or season or series is the information in the show bible. The characters' *lives* are there. Their every relationship and intersection is mapped out. (Y'know, Ross and Rachel were going to end up together when *Friends* ended whether the series ended after season 1 or season 10—or anywhere in between. It's because that was mapped out in the show bible, and that intersection was *going to* happen. Same as your intersections throughout your career.)

Who are the characters in your show bible? I'd guess they're the casting directors who populate the shows you're targeting, the agents and managers on whose rosters you'd love to appear, and all the folks vital to success in show business that you'll encounter many times over the course of your decades-long career.

Back in 1992, when I came across the book *An Actor Succeeds* (the first casting director interview book I'd ever seen), I started keeping a notebook with a list of casting directors' likes and dislikes, based on information right from their own mouths, as transcribed by the authors, Terrance Hines and

Suzy Vaughan. Each in-person encounter, each book, each article, each behind-the-scenes interview segment on an entertainment magazine show I saw after that was a source for information that would end up in my little notebook. I was an actor, and that meant these were my potential buyers. I needed to research them and keep up with what I learned about them: This one has a dog in her office. That one works from her house unless in sessions. This one hates perfume. That one loves postcards. This one started out in the theatre. That one was once an actor too.

Stands to reason that I would score a kickass survival job interviewing casting directors in 1999, huh? Before IMDb made it easy, I had my own three-inch thick three-ring binder of pages of data about all the casting directors out there. I knew who had worked on what, with whom, and for how long, so I could track which sort of audition experiences were a result of the boss' choices and which were organic to the casting associate's innovative approach. I learned which casting directors were actor-friendly and which were downright unpleasant to all people. I knew before I ever walked into a room to audition *exactly* what I was about to experience.

I had a show bible. I just didn't know it was called that, back then. But that would become *Casting Qs* which went from a weekly column in *Backstage* to a book and on to a web-based series. Who knew!?!

So, how does your show bible look? Whether you use online organizational tools or a good 'ol fashioned notebook filled with handwritten notes, your show bible is a powerful tool. (Since technology moves faster than published books, visit smfa4.com for your *SMFA* Hot List of productivity and tracking tools.) Acting classes have private, web-based discussion forums with threads dedicated to the buyers out there, so actors can share information that may help when it comes time to get in front of any particular casting director, when nerves might be running high and anything that comforts you could make the difference in nailing the read. We have convos like this at smfa4.com all the time.

Are you already keeping tabs on the folks you're targeting? Do you note when you get a business card from someone where you met and which mutual friend did the introductions? Better than that, do you transfer that information into your show bible so it's always there when you need to look someone up before a meeting?

When a casting director is interviewed in behind-the-scenes DVD extras, take notes. When a director talks about the casting process in one of the various cable interstitials, look up whose office they were talking about, thereby connecting the dots. Head over to Google Images and do a search to see what people look like if you're only finding print interviews with no photos. Hit Facebook. Go to LinkedIn. Check YouTube for any behind-the-scenes interviews your targets have conducted. Scour podcasts. Any place where you can hear, see, or read interviews with the people with whom you hope to do business is gonna be a fabulous resource for you! Set up Google Alerts on your targets, and then when Google does its job and notifies you about a panel discussion on which your favorite potential agent is appearing, get there, take notes, and add them to your database.

Yeah, yeah, yeah, I'm taking the fun out of the whole acting thing, by asking you to do homework (and regularly) about your potential buyers and teammates in this industry. But think of how much fun you'll have—and sooner—when you get on set because you nailed the audition that your rockstar agent got you, because both the casting director and the agent were folks you researched—and targeted—years before! Of course, you know your job includes ninja work like this, or you wouldn't have picked up *SMFA* to start with, right? Next up, let's get to targeting buyers so we can really level up!

Talent hits a target no one else can hit; genius hits a target no one else can see.

—Arthur Schopenhauer, philosopher

8: Targeting Buyers

I'm about to walk you through the process of targeting co-star roles on ongoing television series. What if you've set your sights on film, stage, webseries, or commercial castings? No problem! This method works for all types of casting, but requires different—more advanced—tools. Visit smfa4.com for some ninja tips on taking this targeting process to the next level *after* you've mastered everything I'm outlining here.

The reason it's important to know how to target buyers for television is simple: TV is predictable, it's trackable, you get your footage faster, and there's no better way to prove you can handle being on the set of a major studio feature film than displaying that you were considered an asset on the set of a television series. If you're in a major market, the television casting directors—as well as their associates and assistants—are generally more accessible than casting people who work in film. I wanna get you to the money faster, and that means the more you do this targeting work—especially early on in your career—the sooner you get the gig that gets you the rep who gets you to the next tier.

Targeting specific shows—based on the ninja goodness you identified about yourself in plotting out your bullseye—will keep this task manageable and your efforts focused. Slinging spaghetti at the wall and hoping something will stick is what most actors tend to do. They send materials to casting directors just because we are casting directors! Most actors do no research on what projects we cast and whether there's synergy between those stories and their type, their brand, or their vibe as storytellers.

Not you, though. You're getting very clearly focused on which casting directors work on the projects you most line up with, as an actor. It's not about making a list of the shows you fantasize about being on, although that may come to pass. It's about finding true clarity in who is out there working on projects that line up with your bullseye, and then making sure those folks know you exist, because you solve a casting problem they have every week.

Of course, there may not be a bullseye role for you in every episode of your target shows (in fact, that'd be really weird to see happen, statistically, and probably pretty boring to watch, if you think about it), but you can certainly learn which shows are more likely to populate their stories with actors like you. Get started by watching a little bit of everything that's out there. Watching the co-stars, then the guest-stars, then the recurring players, and those lovely series regulars, you'll begin plotting out a map to the next set on which you need to play. Let's assume we're beginning with co-stars (those one-liners, maybe one-sceners that go to actors whose names you probably don't know yet) and get going.

Why not start with the series regulars? Well, unless you've tested on pilots as a series regular before, had your share of top-of-show guest-stars, or are so regularly booking guest-stars that you will certainly be on shortlists at networks next pilot season, you need to be watching shows with an eye toward the co-stars. Not the leads. And not even the meaty recurring or major guests. Yeah, yeah, they're fun to watch. You see where you could totally do that guy's job and be that character, if they had just gone less "namey," and it's not a bad idea to look into all of that too (it's all research), but assuming you're looking at turning a run of co-stars into that eventual series lead booking, we *start* our work in co-star land.

How specific do you need to get, in targeting? If you're in a major market, you need to get *really* specific. If you're in a market where only one or two shows shoot, well, there you go! Those are your target shows. But still do this homework for shows in Los Angeles, because it's a great way to get very clear on targeting projects of all types on which you may eventually work. For an updated list of all shows actively casting in major markets, visit smfa4.com for your *SMFA* Hot List.

Once you've downloaded the current show list, print it out, but don't be overwhelmed by it, even though it *is* somewhat overwhelming. Instead, be empowered at the thought of *so much opportunity*, because it's out there. Our next step is to get specific with this massive chunk of information. You will be engaging in this process multiple times in your career, so get used to building your own list using data from the Devwatch section of thefutoncritic.com, the In Production section of imdbpro.com, and the most fabulous resource for actors who love to do this sort of research, castingabout.com/smfa (ninja special, there). The status of your target shows should be easy to track, using those resources. There are even more resources listed in the **Become a Booking Machine** chapter, when you're ready to kick targeting into high gear. Again, if you don't want to build your own list, but want our smfa4.com master list as a starting point, come to ninja headquarters for your download.

While I don't want you to get into the habit of targeting only shows that are actively casting (because that's so dang results-oriented and not at all big picture, in nature), a show that is far too early on in its development process may be something you target peripherally, since filling your show bible with details will pay off later, but getting really clear on your first target, first, is best. Especially on these "untitled projects," you are looking at our TV schedule a couple of years from now. Even if *these shows* don't get picked up, people who get development deals *are low risk* in this business, and there will be more where these came from. Getting clear on who these people are will only serve your ninja badassery!

For any show you're not familiar with, spend some quality time with your DVR, your TiVo, on Hulu+, at Netflix, on iTunes, on network-on-demand apps, or on YouTube, to catch at least enough of an episode to get a sense of the show's tone and vibe. Because of the upfronts, most shows will have some sort of preview (or trailer version) available online, and that's a great way to get clear on a show's tone and vibe. Watch as much as you can, while looking for your brand in the stories.

Taking the master show list, cross off any show that's just *not* gonna work for you. That could be due to its geographical location—like, it shoots in Canada and you don't have papers that would allow you to work there (but keep on shows that are a slamdunk for you, type-wise, even if they shoot out of market, because you never know what your options might open up to include, should the right opportunity arise for you to work as a local hire). Lose shows with no characters that are in the territory of your bullseye anywhere in the world of that show. Consider losing shows not yet in production (or shows that have been shelved on some extended hiatus). Survey your friends, your classmates, those folks in your social networking connections, and your community at smfa4.com, because they may identify shows that you would never even think of targeting, because maybe they have small children and are intimately aware of the *schmacty* family shows that perhaps you would never watch. Hey, you may not aspire to be the next big Disney star, but if there's a great co-star slot for you on one of its new shows? Grab it. Show the buyers that you can book!

At this point in the process, you may want to arrange the "votes" each of the shows gets into some sort of visual representation. As with most statistical analysis, throw out the "outliers" that only get a vote or two. Get excited about trends you're seeing and add the words "all the way to the bank" to any show you feel tempted to judge because it's not your style. Book it. Cash the check. Don't bitch.

After you've narrowed down your target list beyond the pages and pages and pages of shows that are actually *out there*, pick two to target. Yes, two. Believe me—especially as we get into targeting agents and managers—you will be very glad you took my advice to start with only *two* shows here. You're learning a research skill that you'll be able to use at many different tiers of your career, so don't rush to study all the shows that exist, at once. You'll make yourself nuts!

Using CastingAbout, show sheets from your local union office, guides like *Call Sheet* (formerly *Ross Reports*), or an app like Actor Genie (IMDb-Pro can be a little slower with this information, and truly, CastingAbout is my highest recommendation of these, by a longshot, but I don't want to micromanage your process), you're going to look up the casting team for these two shows. Also note the showrunner and any other core personnel while you're at this, and enter all the data into your show bible. The more targeting you're doing, the more ninja your web of trust and the relationships you will start to build.

For each of your target shows, identify the following, at minimum: show title, tone, casting director, casting associate, casting assistant, showrunner, producers, writers, other key personnel, other information about the show, and note any history you have with any of these folks.

Once you've started loading juicy details into your show bible, hit Showfax and download sides for your target shows. Yes, even if there's not a role for you. You are about to start *majoring* in these two target shows. You're going to be so dang aware of what their sides look like, how the assistants mark them up, whether they cobble together multiple scenes or do long monologues or hold auditions for one-liners with loads of instructions written in the margins that when you finally get into the office for your audition, you'll be a master at those sides. Trying to figure out what their handwriting means on the day of your session won't even be a consideration.

Because you'll be watching the show every week, you'll see the difference between how the sides look at the time of the audition and how the lines end up flowing in the finished episode. You'll also get to see *how* they cast certain roles after you've seen them described a certain way in the character description area of the sides. Practice creating choices with one or two lines from your target shows without suffering from "one line fever," wherein you attempt to make, "Can I get you anything else, sir?" into Shakespeare. Fire up your webcam and start shooting yourself doing these sides, not because you expect to send the footage to the casting office to "crash" an audition, but because you need practice doing the thing you're eventually going to be invited into the office to do!

You don't want anything to feel like a steep ramp when you're headed into that office for the first time. You want to be so confident that you've got the system *down* that all you have to do is prepare the material and make some choices that line up with what you've seen *work*, due to all your research.

Meanwhile, set up Google Alerts on all the people whose names you've added to your show bible. Data will start coming into your inbox about these folks who need to know you exist. You'll hit film festivals in which there are panel discussions featuring your targets. If you're in LA or New York, you'll go to WGA Foundation events that are open to the public to hear writers on your target shows talk about their process. You'll visit the Paley Center to soak up as much as you can about the creators of your target series. Wherever you live, you'll load the livestream of events the unions put on, featuring stars and creators of these shows. Every chance to get information that gives you an edge, *take it*.

If the show is a new one but it's being put up by a showrunner whose work you always love—and in whose worlds you could easily fit (since a particular showrunner always tends to have a certain *tone* to his work, even on what appear like vastly different shows)—check out that person's history at IMDb-Pro because people in this business are loyal. April Webster casts everything that JJ Abrams does. Period. When you see in *The Hollywood Reporter, Daily Variety, Studio System News, Deadline Hollywood Daily*, or any other industry news source (yes, it's your job to keep tabs on these publications, too) that a new JJ Abrams show has been ordered, sending a note of congratulations to the casting office is a ninja move.

Every actor will be reaching out when it's been announced that casting is starting up. *You* get on the radar before that moment, and not in the creepy, "I'm an actor, please cast me" kind of way. You are just a colleague who wants to be in business with this person for decades to come, acknowledging a victory and celebrating it! No need to point out, "Hey, I have this bullseye that really lines up nicely with the types of stories your boss likes to tell. You should bring me in," because your bullseye already looks effortless to the buyer, and your targeting research lets you put yourself in front of someone who needs to know you exist. No reason to "lead with need," here. Just put it out there: "We're in this together and, yay, *you*, on another career victory." Let the buyers figure out how dang on-target you are for what they're about to start casting!

Yeah, yeah, yeah, this whole targeting thing is a lot of work, but pretty early on in the process, your competition will feel that it's a lot of work too, and *stop*. As long as you feel that impulse but then *keep going*, you've got the edge. It's truly ninja!

Taking Research to a Whole New Level

Finally, it was happening. I was in. I was signing with a "big time" agency, one with prestige, clout, and multiple headset-wearing assistants. I had arrived; my ship had come in. I signed the contract, left them with a stack of headshots, went home, and waited for them to do their thing. Twelve months and eight auditions later, I was out. They called to let me go. "Sorry. Good luck." Just like that.

I was stunned. I was hurt, shocked, angry—all the usual post-dump emotions. I blamed them; I blamed myself; I swore revenge; I called my mother. Eventually, I calmed down enough to take a hard, cold look at the situation. I realized, with some embarrassment, that I had just spent a full year sitting on the sidelines, entrusting my entire career to other people—people who honestly didn't know me very well and who, ultimately, didn't believe in me. I'd done very little to support my work and nothing to help the agency promote me. The truth was, while I was waiting for them to do their job, I hadn't done my job. And, for most of the casting directors in town, I simply no longer existed. Gone. I had fallen off the radar, lost to the sea of submissions, mailings, and new relationships that fill their offices every day. It was a wake-up call for me. And it was time to get busy.

Over the next several months, I dedicated all my time to creating and nurturing relationships with casting directors. (Agent or no agent, I wasn't going to let the same thing happen twice.) I didn't do it through mass mailings—which is like driving down The 405 throwing postcards out the window and hoping they land on somebody's windshield—but instead through specific, targeted messages to casting people who needed me.

To keep things manageable, I focused on television, where the need for new actors is greatest. I read everything on TV production I could find. I found out who was casting which show and who their associates and assistants were. I learned the show's schedules, whether a new show had been picked up, and when a casting office had been attached. I attended casting workshops for people who cast projects needing my type, then closely tracked their careers. When a casting director was hired for a new gig, I'd send the office a congratulations note. When an associate got a promotion, I'd send her a note as well.

In short, I took control of my career by actively getting in the game; by knowing who the players were and making sure they knew me. It wasn't easy. There was a lot of research and it quickly turned into a fulltime job. But that's the point: Managing my career *is* my job. And over time, it worked. Casting offices began to think of me when they needed my type, calling me at home and asking me to come in. The fact that I didn't have an agent didn't matter; casting directors knew my name, they knew my work, and if I was the best guy for the part, they were happy to call off their search and sign me as a "direct hire." I started booking again, my resumé grew, and eventually I attracted the attention of both theatrical and commercial agencies. I've since signed in both areas—but continue to do my work, with a *much* healthier understanding of an agent's role in my career.

The fun and completely unexpected postscript to the whole story is that my research paid off in a lot more than just acting work. As I really got into it and my database grew, friends started calling me asking for current casting info—knowing, as I did, that the pre-printed info available to actors was often incomplete and out-of-date. Soon, I was encouraged to "do more" with my information, to find a way to expand it, and make it available to others. I sat down with an Internet-genius friend to brainstorm some ideas. Before long, with a small group of investors, partners, and programmers, Brian Wold and I launched castingabout.com, a bigger, web-based version of my database which is now kept current by teams of researchers in LA and New York.

I feel very lucky. I now get to spend my days running two businesses—my acting career and CastingAbout—both of which are still growing. More importantly, I now see myself in a whole new light—not as a passive "wannabe" at the mercy of the All-Powerful Hollywood Gatekeepers, but as a professional working actor with a true sense of empowerment and excitement. And for that, I will always be grateful to the agency that cut me loose.

—Blair Hickey, actor-CastingAbout co-founder

What about Pilots?

I don't advise you *start* the targeting process with pilots, but to start tracking them when your career is at a tier in which pilots are in your sights. That's more likely after you've had more than a few co-stars and guest-stars on existing series. Over 100 pilots are ordered to network each year and only a few will make it more than a few episodes. If you're targeting pilots, I have a formula to map out series success. Now, I don't *really* like to call it a "formula," simply because that connotes a good deal of statistical certainty which we all know is not native to the Hollywood landscape. Still, here's the nitty-gritty of the tracking system I've devised, whatever we want to label it.

We're going to create a "point system" that will represent a predictor of which shows will do well. In the version I do, the points are weighted based on years of my research and data stored in *my* show bible. For the purposes of this explanation, just count points evenly and let the shows with the most points at the end of this exercise "win." Believe me, it'll still get you "close enough" and it'll be much less geeky than the sort of statistical analysis I do for fun. (Yes, really.)

First, take a look at who owns what for a simple "likelihood of airtime" factor that you can add to what we learn during upfronts. Note: If you go ahead and do this homework before the upfronts, you'll have a quick list of top shows to target based on points. Then, when you add the sales data from the upfronts to your list, you should have very clear "winners" to target, in terms of locating (and getting in front of) the shows' casting directors during episodic season (which you now know is far more likely than getting in on the pilot, at first).

The first, easiest thing to determine is whether the studio producing each show and network on which each show will air are owned by the same parent company. I've got a great infographic at smfa4.com for a visual depiction of these relationships. If ownership is the same, you're looking at a show that will be given a little extra time to find an audience simply because the parent company is making money either way. While there are many complexities to the ownership structure of each entity, a basic understanding of the players will do, for our purposes here. That means, for example, you need to know that the network ABC is a Disney property and the studio-production company Touchstone is also a Disney property. So, for any ABC pilot produced by Touchstone, that's a point.

Okay, so now for the part of the "system" that gives shows a second "point." That's going to be whether the principals in the team of these pilots are owners of one of the studios-production companies producing the show. This is where you're looking for things like Brian Grazer on the team and Imagine TV as the studio. Since the principals of the company are directly involved in these particular productions, they're going to throw more money at a floundering show than folks who exec produce but don't sign the checks at the production company (they have to ask nicely first).

Criteria for a third point: Does the production team include the star? This becomes important because someone like Patricia Heaton, for example, could elect to take a hit on her "star salary" for a show on which she's making money as the exec producer in order to help it stay in production a bit longer, should it come down to such a moment of truth.

Fourth point comes from the reputation built by exec producers and showrunners. This is where your membership at IMDb-Pro pays off. Doing a little research on the folks on the teams of these pilot order lists will yield information on the staying power of the last series Shonda Rhimes exec produced or Bernie Su's industry cred. Not sure whether Carol Mendelsohn's new series is going to be given a little breathing room? I'm sure. It will be.

Next, has the star of the series been a series regular or series lead on a hit primetime series previously? That's a point. This is important because network brass will allow for a bit more time when it's just a matter of a star's audience finding him on his new series. That star's publicist (in conjunction with the network's publicity department and studio's team) may kick things into high gear to try and help that along.

Take a look at whether the show is being developed for a cable channel— or if the parent company of this project has a history of shipping its less-successful offerings to a cable channel within its family of networks. If a show can't sell well at upfronts for NBC, maybe it'll be given a home on Bravo. Another point. The number of projects that get "adopted" by TV Land or TBS should show you that even a "no" from a network doesn't really mean a *hard* no for TV altogether. And of course, there's always the web, gadget-based VOD, and airline offerings. If a target pilot sells well at upfronts, you don't need to do the point system I'm outlining here, because that upfront money will usually keep a new show on the air long enough for your targeting to pay off—if you are at the pilot level at this point in your career.

The upfronts are the annual presentation of series roll-outs for media buyers in New York each May. Programming execs present the networks' lineups to advertisers who then begin spending billions of dollars on that next season's shows. Business-minded actors who keep up with which shows "sell best" to advertisers have an early idea of which shows will stay on the air longest. This is a pretty logical train of thought: If advertisers are spending big bucks *up front* on a show, the networks will keep it on the air a little longer than other shows with similar ratings for which ad dollars have not yet been received. It's not costing the networks money to give a borderline show a little time to ripen on the vine if its up-front ad sales have been good. For the updated *SMFA* Hot List of my favorite sources of information on ad sales during upfronts, visit smfa4.com.

Finally, any pilot that already has a series commitment or series order gets a point. This is not to say these will be the *hits* (or even that they'll sell well at upfronts). This just means they do well on the point system I've detailed here, indicating they'll be given more time than shows that don't score well to hit their groove, once they are on the air.

> *There may be patterns for the things that succeed, but that doesn't mean there's a formula for success.*
>
> —Simon Sinek, author

Bringing It Back to Casting

So, now that you've gotten your homework done about which shows have the best shot at staying on the air for more than a week or two once they debut, how do you go about finding out who's casting them? First, check CastingAbout. Also visit IMDb-Pro to see whether a series casting director is listed. Note: A pilot will likely be cast by one CD while the regular episodes of that same show will be cast by another. If you strike out there, visit showfax.com to see whether sides have been posted for the project in question and, if so, by whose office. Since you already have a short(er) list of shows to target based on the point system, you could even return to Google and set up Google Alerts for the titles of the shows and the casting offices you're most specifically targeting.

If you strike out on all fronts because it's still too early for any of that juicy info to be out there, get back to IMDb-Pro and look at the track record of each series' exec producer and showrunner. Remember, these people have history with casting directors from previous projects, and this is a very loyal segment of the business. It's a part of your work as an actor to track these folks' web of trust in action. You will thank me for this bit of homework, and it's fairly easy to do (though time consuming).

In addition to consistency in their teams, you'll find there's consistency in the style of storytelling, among those whose projects get a shot at the small screen. When *Glee* was announced, I remember suggesting that everyone check *Nip/Tuck* for the tone, the absurdist style, the homoeroticism, the insider-outsider themes. Sure enough, these shows had way more in common than you'd imagine a high school singing show could have with a sexy plastic surgery show. Why? Brand Ryan Murphy.

Showrunners, creators, exec producers, they all have brands—bankable brands—and it will behoove you to study those, as you prep for collaborating on stories you'd like to tell together someday. Since there will be a point of intersection in your future, your ability to map out where it's likely for that to happen will benefit you. Filling up your show bible with details about your targets—whatever job they have in the industry—will be hugely helpful!

9: YOUR BUSINESS PLAN

Let's start by talking about inertia, shall we? The truth of it is, every good thing that becomes a habit in our lives does so because we mindfully choose it, regularly. We brush our teeth when we get up in the morning and before we go to bed because we were taught to choose to do that and we continued to do it so regularly that it became a habit. We exercise regularly because we choose to show up for the workout. I don't know about you, but I can feel the force of inertia when I *don't* exercise for a few days in a row. I get out of the habit. I think about how hard it'll be to get back at it. I stress about how difficult everything will feel. Inertia wins.

Or, I get back at it. I go to that first "Oh, man, this is gonna kill me" workout and I get the endorphin rush. I feel great after. My muscles are "the good sore" the following day. I can't wait to go back for more, so I go back, and after a few days in that direction, inertia wins. Either way, inertia wins. It's just a matter of inertia for *not* building a habit (or, let's say, for building a habit of *not* doing that positive thing) or inertia for building that good habit.

Developing and then consistently following a business plan will likely cause you to stress out a bit. You may find yourself feeling a ton of resistance. That's okay. One of the things I want you to plan for as you build your business plan is failure. You *will* try to build some structure into your artistic life and just flat-out *not* be able to make it work. That's gonna happen. Leave room for that, and don't turn it into a snowball of a whole month of not brushing your teeth. You just stumbled a bit. We all do. Get back at it.

Just like a professional athlete simply *cannot* go weeks without a workout and still be at the peak of his game, an actor hoping to advance—quickly—from tier to tier needs to get down with some daily practices, some career management strategies, and some regular work on the scary things that most creatives *don't* want to do. Imagine what you'll accomplish after just a few months of staying disciplined with your actor business plan. Try it out and stick with it long enough to have some actor habits your colleagues covet!

Better yet, involve your colleagues in the experience. Find projects on which you can collaborate, "yes, and..." one another's thoughts, and be stronger together than you are on your own. If you live in a place where there are few co-conspirators for success in the entertainment industry, join in the convo at smfa4.com to jam with your fellow ninjas for masterminding and supporting and "yes, and..."-ing all sorts of things. Don't be shy! Dive in! Your business plan is all about a series of daily practices that allow your inner ninja to thrive.

The following list is broken down into five major categories. Choose one item from each category for a single day each week. That covers five days. The sixth day should always be one of "The Biggies," irrespective of others that are similar to them, on a categorized list (see below). And that seventh day—you guessed it—is one in which you can relax, take time off from managing your acting career so intensely, catch up if you failed on one or two of the days earlier in the week (and, again, that's totally okay). Many times, people say "do something for your acting career *every* day," as if you have to be reminded to treat your career like a business. I say: You *know* your career is a business, and you know how seriously you need to treat it. Being reminded that taking a day off, giving yourself a day to catch up, knowing you're building a muscle— that's what that seventh day is for.

Please download my sample *SMFA* calendar as well as a blank one for mapping out your business plan at smfa4.com. Of course, you can use your own calendar, but I have a blank one and a sample one for you, if you need them! I also have downloadable versions of these lists—The Biggies and the categorized lists that follow—for you at smfa4.com if you want to print 'em out! If any of these concepts are fuzzy, take heart: They'll be covered later in this very book, and rounded out at the site. Until we see you online, here the big lists are! Let's go.

The Biggies

➢Audit, enroll in, or move up in a class, so your craft is never stagnating.

➢Write, shoot, or edit a scene with fellow ninjas, even if it's popping up on a categorized list (below) frequently.

➢Update your show bible using more detail than you do when it pops up on a categorized list (below).

➢Wrangle a thing that currently feels unconquerable by doing a little more of it than when it pops up on a categorized list (below).

Craft and Your Instrument

➢Download sides from Showfax, learn how that casting office marks up their material, and practice cold reading for a target show.

➢Self-tape your cold reads from a set of sides on a target show, watch the footage back for tics or unconscious choices that don't serve your work, organically.

➢Work on memorization by committing a block of text to true off-book status.

➤Create physicalization for a character by doing mini workouts you normally wouldn't choose for yourself.

➤Stay fit by doing yoga, Pilates, meditative stretching and deep breathing—or just go for a walk.

➤Read an article from a magazine (popular, political, how-to, fashion, technical—whatever kind of magazine you'd like to use) aloud and take on different characterizations as you work through the text.

➤Do vocal warm-ups and tongue twisters, speak in hums and hisses, really work your voice.

➤Dialect day: practice your favorite monologue or scene using a new dialect or accent, then move on to new material so that you can improvise and perfect that new skill and add it to your resumé.

➤Audit a class that's way outside your comfort zone: tap dancing, stand-up comedy, stunt training, Krav Maga, improv, pole dancing, screenwriting—and if it really scares you, enroll in ongoing classes.

➤Sit and "people watch" for a half hour, making notes about personalities, conversation styles, accents and dialects, emotional intensity, physicalization.

➤Change up your rhythm, whether in your acting life or in your non-acting life, by playing with your words and your thoughts as if you're conducting a symphony, expressing nuances via crescendo or a change in pacing.

➤Break down a character: objectives, intention, backstory, status.

➤Break down a scene: structure, subtext, dialogue, story arc.

➤Audit a craft class.

➤Go see a play.

➤Attend an open mic night.

➤Go to—or even participate in—an improv jam.

➤Sing karaoke.

➤Attend the table read of a work-in-progress (participate if you can).

Research and Prep

➤Read a play you've never read before.

➤Read a chapter in a biography or autobiography of an actor whose career and craft you admire.

➢Read a script written by someone whose work you hope to voice someday.

➢Read three pages in a trade publication—every word—and mark names of players about whom you want to know more someday.

➢Hit the local library and read a chapter in a book you're not sure you want to buy; people-watch while you're there.

➢Watch a great movie or episode of a TV series on DVD with the director commentary turned *on*.

➢Explore a new podcast about the entertainment industry and listen to a few archived episodes.

➢Update your show bible using Google Alerts that have been flowing into your inbox.

➢Update your show bible using notes from your recent networking activities.

➢Update your show bible using recent news in the Twitter feeds of both trade publications and those folks you're targeting.

➢Spend an hour tracking the career moves of the "tier above" *you*; that person who is just one or two seasons ahead of where you currently sit—look at what roles they were taking on a few years ago and where they were planting seeds to get where they are now.

➢Do a lap at Actors Access and Casting Networks (See: **Become a Booking Machine**) to be sure you've self-submitted on projects that line up with your bullseye.

➢Check your Actors Access and Casting Networks messages for any requests for self-taped auditions or visits to the session room.

➢Study your targets: spend time watching the resources that your targets are putting out there via blogs, vlogs, printed interviews, and their own social networking profiles.

➢Watch an archived livestream from the SAG-AFTRA Foundation library (even if you're not yet a SAG-AFTRA member).

➢Watch an episode of a TV show from which you previously downloaded sides to track how the finished product looks (which lines are thrown away, what type of actor booked the role, any relationships you can track on IMDb-Pro) and consider choices you can make in future reads that may make you feel like a booker.

➢Watch an episode of each new series that makes it to TV to track trends and keep tabs on what your targets in show-running are up to; also check in on hot webseries and "alternative platform" series that go straight to Netflix, Hulu, Amazon, etc., and update your show bible accordingly.

Mindset

➤Build your brain in ways that Facebook cannot by doing a half-hour of Lumosity, Words With Friends, Sudoku, or a pen-and-paper logic puzzle.

➤Face your fears by writing down three things that terrify you about pursuing a creative career (save conquering those fears for another day; for now, just dissect 'em a bit).

➤Do something "little" differently, y'know, like brushing your teeth with your non-dominant hand or driving a different route than you always do between two points.

➤Do some non-acting enrichment using a site like CreativeLive, Skillshare, Udemy, Coursera, Media Bistro, or iTunes U; then watch a TED Talk on something you imagine might be boring.

➤Mentor a newbie—and if you have no access to young, up-and-coming actors who could benefit from your expertise, contribute to the collective knowledge base that exists at free message boards online, where simple words of encouragement or reminders that actors are *never* to pay up-front for representation can be hugely helpful.

➤Set goals for the week, the month, the quarter, the year, 5 years, 10 years—leave yourself lots of dreaming room here, and don't get so rigidly locked into anything that this task becomes torture.

➤Write a list of those to whom you will always be grateful, as you continue to succeed in your creative career; especially note those who will be thanked in those "holding up something gold and shiny" moments to come.

➤Journal, write freely, do the "morning pages" à la *The Artist's Way* by Julia Cameron.

Tools of the Trade

➤Test various pieces of your auditioning wardrobe on camera using your self-taping set-up; discover what each color and neckline and pattern does to your skintone and overall vibe.

➤Test your self-taping set-up at different times of day to see what the existence of natural light at various hours does to your artificial lighting.

➤Style your hair and makeup different ways as you self-tape to track the impact of a little shine-reducing powder.

➤Make sure your receipts are organized and categorized so it's not a bear of a task come tax time.

➤Revisit your recent paystubs to be sure your agency commissions are being properly calculated and reported.

➤Accounting analysis: tally up your union dues, photos, acting classes, membership on submission sites, and marketing materials.

➤Contact a producer from whose project you've not yet received your footage; be polite and professional, yet firm in asking for an expected date by which you will receive your scenes for your reel, even if the team is not yet finished with final edits on the project.

➤Perform some resumé feng shui. (See: **Your Resumé.**)

➤Update your bio. (See: **Your Bio and Cover Letter.**)

➤Revamp your cover letter. (See: **Your Bio and Cover Letter.**)

➤Tighten up your reel. (See: **Your Reel.**)

➤Update your social networking presence—spruce up that "about me" logline, refresh your photos, check your Googleability.

➤Reach out to your fans—shoot an email, write a new blog post, put together some postcards for an upcoming targeted mailing.

➤Do a targeted mailing of postcards, general submissions, or career updates—again, a *targeted* mailing.

➤Update your website. (See: **Your Online Presence.**)

Mastering the Game

➤Watch a half-hour of junket footage from a recent movie's press tour using the "related videos" feature at YouTube; learn which interviewers employ what style, observe which actors handle curveballs best, note when answers are crafted by publicists or improvised by the actors—think about what your style will be. (See: **Working It.**)

➤Visit WireImage or Getty Images' editorial-entertainment galleries and search out the fashion choices of actors in your type and vibe, to see what they wear to red carpet events, charity appearances, upfronts, luncheons, or any other time they're photographed (and not just by *TMZ*). (See: **Working It.**)

➤Search out discount versions of key items you'd like to add to your networking wardrobe—get smart with the best colors for you and add *one* great piece to your closet (while purging the items that simply don't work for on-brand *you*) periodically.

➤Drill yourself on your monologues—yes, even if you are never asked to perform them; don't let 'em get rusty.

➤Drill yourself on your 16 bars—yes, even if you don't really audition for musical theatre any more; you may need 'em someday.

➤Drill yourself on your pitch, your logline, your answer to, "So, tell me about yourself," and all other Brandprov prompts at smfa4. com, so you're ready for every possible networking scenario. (See: **Working It**.)

➤Write a scene for yourself and two friends. (See: **Content Creation**.)

➤Shoot a scene—do it for your reel, do it for the practice, do it for relationship-building, just do it. (See: **Content Creation**.)

➤Transcribe and practice like a ninja; that means, if you're targeting a show written by Aaron Sorkin, you transcribe a lesser-known Sorkin scene and practice its pacing, its rhythm, its style (also avoid iconic characters).

➤Watch actors on everything from *Inside the Actors Studio* to *Watch What Happens Live* to study the art of Brandprov. (See: **Working It**.)

➤Watch a "dumb reality show" that you otherwise would never care about, and pay particular attention to the music, and how producers are branding good guys and bad guys with their choices in sound editing—master producer-end branding by deconstructing it and considering what your theme music might be.

➤Hit up a local film festival, panel discussion, theatre company fundraiser, or student film showcase for some low-stakes networking experiences. (See: **Working It**.)

➤Engage in a DIY power group—find other creatives (start at smfa4.com) who might like to jam about what's happening in the industry, your community, your personal and professional lives and then do so, regularly; split up targets and share the research load, thereby creating a beautiful mastermind experience.

➤Do something from your "things I love to do for my acting career" list that's not otherwise represented on this list.

➤Do something from your "things I hate to do for my acting career" list that's not otherwise represented on this list.

Phew! Feeling good? Yay! Feeling overwhelmed? Also yay! You have a starting point. You have a recipe for where to restart when you falter. It's okay. You're building a muscle and that takes time, consistency, and patience. An actor who fails at even 75% of the things mapped out on a year's calendar of the above items is *still* advancing more, controlling more, tier-jumping more than most actors out there! Promise me you'll give yourself room for success to happen. I want you to have many ideal actor days, in your life.

So, what *is* an "ideal actor day" after all? It's one in which you're moving forward, it's one in which you're giving yourself room to grow as an artist, and it's one in which you feel connected with your process, aware that there are definitely places where you have power and control, and you take it on! Don't get bogged down in feeling that any particular day *has to* look a certain way. Just continue advancing your creative business, continue building good habits, and continue enjoying the ride! That's how you succeed in the long haul, after all.

10: THE RIGHT TRAINING

The only thing that you have control over in this business is becoming the best actor you can be. The rest of it is the lottery.
— Eugene Blythe, casting director

Do not let the length of this chapter fool you. Training is *important*. So important, it's a no-brainer. Professional athletes train every day—even in the off-season. Professional performers must also train whenever they are not regularly working. The craft is built on muscle tone, so to speak. To keep your abilities sharp, you must continue to train, to explore new methods, and to improve your stamina through various classes. It's important to find a coach who challenges you, but with whom you feel comfortable enough to take risks. It's about balance, and you'll probably work with many coaches over the course of your creative career.

There are more types of training available to actors than I could begin to cover fully, here, and training is an incredibly personal decision. Instead of attempting to get into every possible type of craft coaching you might encounter along your journey, I'll suggest that you check out the most recent *Backstage* guide to schools and coaches, call around to do some comparison shopping, and always do a class audit (sit in on a current class without enrolling) before investing in ongoing training. Don't be swayed by political campaigns that yield "best coach of the year" status, so-called "gurus" whose philosophies are the *only* path to success, or a list of famous alumni on a coach's website or marketing materials. The coaching experience has to be a good fit for *you*, and you'll only figure out whether it is by getting started.

Examine ongoing scene study classes, on-camera intensives, improvisational training, commercial classes, cold reading courses, Meisner technique, sitcom workshops, voiceover workout groups, Method acting, and everything in between. There is no one type of training that will unlock your most creative self. It's going to take a combination of classes over time to reveal your talents, fully. And especially in a market like Los Angeles, you'll have a lot of options from which to choose!

The best way to know whether any class is right for you is to audit first. Auditing is important because you can get a sense of the teacher's style and personality, plus know if the students he attracts are on your level. If a coach has a policy of not offering free audits, he had better have enough *out there*— via free vids at YouTube or books and articles—that you have no question what you're going to experience, should you work with him. Do your homework, keep learning from every possible source, and remember that opinions are just that, opinions—not fact. Firsthand experience and research will pay off!

> *Taking care of yourself as an actor—training and coaching on a consistent basis—is the best way to assure that when you are called upon to perform in an audition or performance you will be in peak form.*
> —Arnold Mungioli, CSA

How Important Is a BFA or MFA?

Basically, a BFA or MFA in acting is important to the people to whom it's important. Here's what I mean by that. Some people will *really value* seeing the letters "BFA" or "MFA" on your resumé. Others won't even notice them. Nope. Not even if you graduated at the top of your class at one of the most prestigious programs on the planet. It's just one of those things that matters to some folks and doesn't register a blip on the radar for others. Anti-conservatory casting directors will figure that you spent a few years in a bubble doing things that have absolutely no relevance to the way you have to hustle in order to pursue an acting career in the real world.

Where your time in school can really pay off, once you're pursuing acting in a major market, is in the networking realm. This is where you can get an edge just because you happen to be in front of an agent, casting director, or filmmaker who also called your campus home, long ago.

It's not just the school, though! I joke about the Atlanta Posse that's in Los Angeles, but it's not a joke. We all love to make a very large, very scary world feel smaller and one of the best ways to do that is to find something we have in common with others. Your choice to get an advanced degree is what you make of it. There's no one who is going to call you up and cast you outright, just because you *have* a BFA or MFA. It's all about the common threads you weave with others, in this business.

> *Do directors these days have the time or patience to deal with a Method actor? Some directors I've worked with won't hire Method actors on the basis that it's just "too much work." So, what are you left with? Most actors love their coaches, but that doesn't mean they're learning anything. If actors would just trust themselves, their work would be more significant. A good coach who is smart will guide the actor through the scene but leave room for adjustment.*
> —Matthew Barry, casting director-manager-actor-coach

Workshops

Let's be clear, there are a bunch of cold reading workshops, casting director workshops, representation showcases, and one-offs in many markets. Casting directors and their assistants attend or even run workshops, and so do agents and managers. These are NOT (all caps, *whoa*) a substitute for training. They don't get listed on your resume as a class you took, even if you did a multi-week intensive with a particular CD. Sure, you may learn *something* doing workshops, but you should see short-term casting director workshops as part of your marketing plan, not your craft workout.

Will Work for Class

One of the most amazing—but most expensive—classes I ever took, I took for free. How? I managed the class. I went in (with recommendation—you generally must have a referral from someone who has history with the instructor) and, in exchange for arranging chairs in a circle, collecting class payments, cleaning up, locking up, and setting the studio alarm at the end of the night, I got the best cold reading intensive I've ever experienced. Free! Check into it. Not all studios offer this option, but it's worth asking about. Class management is a wonderful way to take classes on the cheap. If you excel at graphic design or web design, your skills may be worth a trade for acting classes. Just ask!

***

Because new coaches hit the scene and have an impact faster than books are published, I've moved my list of recommended coaches to smfa4.com. Check in for the *SMFA* Hot List of coaches in several major markets. Woo!

It's easier to pull work out of your files when an opportunity presents itself than it is to pull it out of your ass. Do the work.

—Keith Johnson

PART THREE: MATERIALS

It's not what you are that holds you back; it's what you think you're not.

—Denis Waitley, author

11 : YOUR HEADSHOTS

The number-one most important tool in an actor's kit is the headshot. It's the logo for your small business. It's your most consistent brand manager. It's your key to unlocking doors to opportunities.

Then why do so many actors get it wrong? Vanity? Perfectionism? Fear of disagreeing with the photographer, with an agent, with a coach?

Whatever the reason, the fact is there: The majority of actors do not use headshots that accurately represent them. I should know. I interviewed hundreds of casting directors before becoming one. I've seen for myself what all these folks told me for years: The reason 80% to 90% of audition appointments go to actors whose work casting directors already know is because those "new" actors (new to us, not necessarily beginners) *may* look nothing like their headshots. The risk is too high. When time is tight and a problem needs to be solved quickly, those precious slots go to very few actors based solely on their headshots.

This means we have to work to recondition casting directors, agents, managers—all buyers—to believe that actors *do* look like their headshots, that actors have *not* over-airbrushed their proofs, that the vibe that is being presented in the still image is precisely how it will *feel* when the actor enters the room.

Let's start now, shall we? I'll begin with a story from my actor days. Like for most actors, "headshot shoot day" was a *huge* deal for me. It only came around once every couple of years or so, and the dieting would begin a month before, as would shopping for all sorts of different outfits. I'd be sure to get my hair done and even make a trip to the Merle Norman counter at Perimeter Mall so I could get a refresher on the best way to contour and shadow and blend. Plus, samples!

I'd get very little sleep the night before my headshot shoot, because, well, y'know, new headshots! The pressure was *on*. But I would be sure to be very well-hydrated, because I had heard that would make my skin look its best. (All it meant was I had to take pee breaks all through my shoot, but whatever.)

First, we'd shoot me in my most flattering silk blouse. My hair would be curly and my makeup would be subtle. Next up, the curls would start falling out of my hair and I'd apply a bit more eyeshadow, as I changed into my black tanktop and ex-boyfriend's leather jacket (it always did look better on me). Finally, I'd pile my hair up into a tight bun, shellac it all back with Aqua Net (purple can), and throw on my pretty pink powersuit with the shoulder pads. Exec all the way!

Wow! What a great shoot! Three looks, all sorts of different castabilities, and all for a couple hundy. The proofs would come back and I'd dutifully print up 4x6s of my favorites, and cart them around to my agent, my coach, anyone who'd look at 'em. All opinions are good ones, right? And the opinions were great: "You look beautiful here." "Great cheekbones." "Your eyes are sparkling." "Love this one." "Ooh, this one is nice." So, off to the repros the masterprints would go. And hundreds more bucks later, I'd have a stack of headshots that made me look great. Some in a silk blouse with curly hair. Some in a leather jacket with heavy eye makeup. And some in a pretty pink powersuit.

Such a shame. Not one of those perfectly lovely headshots sold *Brand Bonnie Gillespie.*

When I had my "good ol' gal" type epiphany (See: **Your Bullseye**), I immediately reshot. I showed up in jeans and a fitted but casual shirt, wearing very little makeup, and with my hair the way my hair falls on its own. I brought a CD of my favorite music and I talked with the photographer ahead of time to let him know, "I'm a good ol' gal. I drink, I swear, I throw darts, I shoot pool, I stay out too late, and I have more guy friends than gals. Let's shoot!"

When I sat on the steps of his back porch, bathed in natural light, the line running through my head was, "How y'all doin'? How's it goin'? What's up? Let's hang out. Next round's on me." *Bam!* Best headshots of my life. I wasn't trying to play "Dress-Up Barbie Bonnie." I wasn't trying to show range. I was being myself, 100%, and that shined through my shots.

The *best* thing you can do for your headshots is to be comfortable in your skin; to be fully who you are; and to stay present despite all the hair and makeup retouches, the distraction of the lights, the art direction of the photographer, and all the things that are running through your head about all you need to prove with these shots.

Just like a small business owner must meet with a graphic designer to create and refine a corporate logo, you must connect with your photographer about what *feeling* you're going for in your headshots. Logos of successful companies are not merely graphic depictions of *things*; they are specifically-crafted, stylized, well-thought-out, and hopefully fully-authentic representations of the brand in question. You—the actor—are creating a logo for *brand you* with your headshots. Huddle with your photographer about the feelings you want to convey, about the roles you most often book, about your bullseye. A great headshot photographer will not only understand the importance of this conversation, he will be thrilled that you've put more thought into it than most of his clients.

Your Headshot Is Not a Photograph

Huh? *Of course* your headshot is a photograph. Uh-huh. But if you think that's all it is, you're missing the point. *Your headshot is not a photograph. It is a marketing tool.* Therefore, if your headshot is not helping you get work, it is *costing* you work.

Look, I know you want to choose the headshot in which you're beautiful. But when you come into the room and lead with *quirky*, we're just pissed that we called you in on the *beauty* role. We'd rather call you in on the *quirky* role and then note, "Ooh, she's also a beauty," as there's often a benefit to casting a pretty actor in a quirky role. There is *rarely* a role in which we seek out the beauty and decide to "go quirky." You need to lead with what you lead with.

If you come into the room quirky, we want your headshot to sell that. If you're the leading man's wingman, we want your headshot to sell that. Getting called in *incorrectly* because your headshot doesn't match your *primary casting type* is just going to frustrate you—because you won't earn a callback, no matter how much you rocked the audition, since the role was never intended for someone of your type—and us—because we saw you read for something you have no shot at getting, rather than the role for which you would've been perfect on the last project but for which we never called you in because your headshot didn't show us how perfect you were for *that* role.

Most actors suck at choosing their own headshots. It's because they're letting their egos help with the decision-making process, rather than thinking about their "actor self" as a product and a headshot as advertising that brand. In your headshot, don't try to sell us what you look like under perfect conditions, with perfect lighting, at the perfect angle, on your most perfectly-airbrushed day. Sell us exactly what we're getting when you walk in the room on a moment's notice. Believe me, it will make a difference!

What to Do Way Before the Shoot

Get down with your bullseye. It doesn't get much simpler than that, really. Until you know your type, your vibe, the world you inhabit as a storyteller, *your brand*, having (even great) photographs won't serve you as well as killer, on-bullseye headshots will.

So, revisit the chapter on **Your Bullseye** as you start this process. Get very clear on what it is you do better than anything else—and better than anyone else—so that you can begin idling at that speed with intention (rather than doing so just because it's easy). Remember, when you make it look effortless, that's ninja. It only feels easy to you because that's where you live.

If you want to do things like meet with an image consultant, have your colors done, get a makeover so you can learn some on-camera tricks that may serve you, all of that is fine. It's just not required. If, however, it boosts your confidence to have any of that going for you, go for it. I would advise against crash dieting to "look your best" during your shoot. It's not about looking your *best*; it's about looking your most castable!

As you research photographers, think about *brand you* and look at the various photographers' galleries at their websites. Don't get wowed by their celebrity clients or glamour shots. Instead, find the gallery of actors who come closest to selling what you sell, in terms of type. How well does this photographer shoot actors like you? Does this photographer *get* that you don't need to be shot like an ingénue just because you're young? Does this photographer treat *every* quirky male the same way? Is this photographer shooting people in costumes, with props, or in over-the-top charactery poses? Or can you see the care this photographer is taking in his ability to listen to the client and create "logos" that get the job done?

Does this photographer over-crop so that you have no options about how *you* should crop your own image? Does this photographer care about his brand more than the actor's brand? (This is rampant in Los Angeles, by the way—headshot photographers forget that they are *headshot photographers* and it's not about their brand; it's about the actor's brand. Watch out for this!)

Once you've narrowed down your photographer choices to a handful, set up meetings—in person—with these folks so that you can sit down with one another, see if you click, and know *before* you've plunked down money whether this is the right fit for your "logo design" needs. This is an investment in the most vital of your marketing tools. You must be sure the following questions are answered.

Does the photographer share your goals for the session? Does he agree with how you see yourself and how you hope to market yourself? Are you comfortable in his studio? How long will your photo session last? Do you know whether you'll be shooting in-studio or outdoors using natural light? How long will it take to get your proofsheets back? Will you be provided with a CD right away? How long after you have selected photos will it take to get 4x6 prints? 8x10 prints? Do you have to get those printed off your CD elsewhere? Do you own the copyright of the photos, once you've paid for them? If shooting on film, do you retain the negatives? What is the cost for the photo session and does the price include hair and makeup? What is the cost for the master prints? Is retouching included? Will the photographer help you choose the best shots? What is the policy on reshoots if you are dissatisfied?

Get all of these questions answered up front and weigh all of these factors from each of the photographers you meet before booking a session. Knowing what to expect will make the photo session a much more relaxed experience.

What to Do Immediately Before the Shoot

Brainstorm not only typing words that consistently show up in your life, but also that really *feel* right for you. Using the master type list at smfa4.com, try to narrow the list down to a few keywords that do the job best, when it comes to describing you. Let's do me: Folksy, wise, relatable, happy, no bullshit. Yup. Done. Those are qualities I can't "take off" or "put on." They're woven into my soul's fabric. Get *that* clear on what you can't lose. This is *not* to limit you as a performer! I repeat: *This is not to limit you* as a performer! This is to get you into the headspace that will get you some rockin' headshots.

If you are motivated by music, create a playlist for your shoot. Pull out your clothes—not your pretty pink powersuit (unless that's on-brand), but instead those clothes that make you feel amazing, while representing your brand fully. Have a few options, but not so many that you're doing that whole costumey thing. No one needs to see you in a cop uniform to *get* that you can play a cop. A dark blue dress shirt, pressed, is plenty to suggest the vibe. A *Law & Order*-style shot needn't be taken in front of a bookcase to convey that you can play a lawyer.

Get good rest. Be hydrated. Bring your own makeup and hairstyling supplies not just to protect your health but so that the makeup artist and hair stylist don't turn you into something you could never replicate, since you don't have their fancy tools.

What to Do During the Shoot

Relax. Have fun. You arrived early (Right?) so you're not stressed about time management. You have all your supplies and clothing, as well as your music and your mental keywords. Have another quick convo with the photographer about your brand and your goals for the shoot. Start running your keywords through your mind, and have a few great phrases that get you in the headspace that makes your face light up in the way that only being totally authentic and on-brand can create for you.

When the photographer tries to put you in front of a brick wall, ask about depth-of-field so that the lines of the wall aren't the focal point, but instead muted texture behind you, out of focus. When the photographer tries to get you to put your chin down (a common photo "trick" that casting directors are hip to—you look younger and thinner in this flattering pose, and it's a useless headshot you get, with this pose, because CDs don't trust it), ask for a few more shots with a more direct angle. When the photographer gets you contorting into uncomfortable poses, ask for another few shots in which you're relaxed, after which you've taken a deep breath, in which your body just feels *better*.

It's not about "running the shoot," because—of course—if you've done your pre-shoot homework well, you've chosen a photographer who is going to work with you in a lovely partnership. But when those habits of "chin down" or "brick wall" or whatever start to pop up during your shoot, respectfully asking for a few more shots done "your way" is totally fine. Blame your manager: "My manager also wants a few shots chin-up. Can we do a few before moving to the next outfit?" Same with an open-mouthed smile, a belly laugh, an intense stare. Get 'em all! This is *your* session and this photographer is being paid to deliver the results *you* outlined in your first convos.

What to Do After the Shoot

Before you click on the link to view the proofs from your glorious, on-brand shoot, revisit that list of adjectives and essences and type words! Remember the line of dialogue you were repeating during the best moments of your shoot to help you stay on-brand and in the moment. Take a deep breath, then dive in. Find the shots that *feel* like those words. Sure, you'll naturally gravitate toward some gorgeous photos that are very flattering and not at all on-brand—you can't help it—and on this first pass of the proofs, that's totally fine. Just be sure to keep a running list of which shots are flattering and which ones are castable.

Go back through the proofs again and get more selective. Toss out the ones that come close to getting the job done but don't do as well as others. Once you get your list of favorites down to a few dozen, it's time to connect with your trusted advisors—an acting coach, your manager, the smfa4.com community, your mastermind group of fellow ninjas—and get some feedback.

Once you have a few winners, print them up to see what they look like at 8x10, in hard copy. Sure, most of the time, you're going to be using electronic versions—thumbnail sized ones—of your photos, but the 8x10 really pulls out flaws that you may miss, when you're looking at the teeny version of the same shot, or just blowing it up on your computer screen.

Whatever you do, do *not* retouch the life out of your shots. We *want* to see your wrinkles, your laugh lines, your freckles, your moles, the gap in your teeth, your strands of silver hair. Remember, to teach the buyers we can trust that actors look like their headshots, you start with *not* retouching your headshot in order to minimize something that *will* enter the room with you when you get called in. Blemishes, stray hairs, a dollop of mascara that should've been cleaned up before the shoot? Yes, airbrush those away. But don't turn yourself into an unattainably perfect version of yourself in a photo. Not only will you never be able to replicate that in the room, we actually will assume your shot is *sooo* retouched that the likelihood you get invited into the room becomes lower, because we have to assume there's a higher-than-average risk that you look nothing at all like your headshot.

Always keep in mind that your headshot—the logo for your small business—is meant to convey your brand. It's meant to teach the buyer not only what you look like but how you *feel*. That extends even to the font you choose for printing your name on the hard copy headshot, and whether you choose borders or not. There's no one "right" choice, only what's on-brand for *you*.

Changed Your Look?

What if you've changed your look—whether for personal reasons or for a role—since getting your headshots done? If you're submitting your old headshot make sure to note: "I've dyed my hair for a role. I will be going back to the color in my headshot when we wrap, but I just wanted to be sure that you were aware I'll be coming in with a new look."

What if you've simply cut your hair? If your headshot is close-in enough that your hair length isn't obvious anyway, you could be okay using an older headshot that still looks like you. If, on the other hand, you have gained or lost weight, changed your hair significantly, or simply matured in your looks, be prepared to get new headshots. In general, you should get new headshots at least every two to three years, regardless.

It's All Online

Yeah, even though the majority of your headshot submissions will be happening online, you'll still need to have hard copy headshots printed up to take with you to every audition, every time. You should always have several copies in case the casting director has another project for which you'd be right and would like to show that extra headshot to the producer on that one. Best bet: Always keep a stash of 20 or so headshots in your actor bag. You never know when you may need a few. Restock after every audition, just to be sure you never run completely out.

Rules

You'll hear a lot about "don't wear stripes or bold patterns," "no logos or slogans on your clothes," "no hats, no props, no wacky expressions, no glasses if you don't wear glasses," and a bunch of other headshot *rules*. Here's what's ninja: You get to blow off every rule you've ever been taught about headshots *if* it's on-brand to do so.

Run every marketing tool through the brand filter. You can break the rules if being a rule-breaker is on-brand for you. Don't do it to be different, to be gimmicky, or to stand out. Do it if one of those delicious brand words for you happens to be *rebel*. Remember that you're teaching the buyer how it feels to be in your presence—not just what you look like—with your headshots.

12: Your Resumé

The format of your resumé is important. In general, the standard is as follows (from top to bottom): Name, contact info, stats, union status; **Film Section** (with three columns: Title of the film, your role's billing, and then the director or production company or studio), **TV Section** (with three columns: Title of the show, your role's billing, and then the director or production company or network), **Commercial Section** (this one's easiest. Just list "Conflicts Upon Request"), **Theatre Section** (again, back to the three-column style, but now it's: Title of the show, your character's name [*not* billing], and then the venue that put the play up [unless there's a really prestigious director's name to mention] including a parenthetical notation of the city if it's not where you're currently pursuing acting), **Training Section** (up top should be your current class, then most impressive), **Special Skills**, and a footer that lists your website's URL (where we can find more photos, your reel, additional credits if we're holding onto an old resumé, your updated representation status, etc.).

We're gonna hit everything you need to know to have a great resumé here, but—especially because our industry is changing and its platforms are constantly evolving—please visit smfa4.com for downloads of updated tier-based resumé templates. Being nimble about this industry is the muscle you want to build, here. Also, please always remember, the ninja move is to have various versions of your marketing tools to use in different scenarios. Dropping breadcrumbs down the path to your next booking is essential, and that means a different resumé for different buyers. Don't be afraid you're going to get this *wrong*. Learn basic structure so you have freedom to improvise.

Resumé Feng Shui

Ready to have the most rockstar resumé of your career? It's time to do a little resumé feng shui. First, a few core principles you'll need to get down with, to really clear the clutter and rock this like a ninja.

Just like your headshot is not a photograph, but a marketing tool, your resumé is not a list of everything you've ever done. It's a recipe for how to cast you next. It too, is a marketing tool. If you treat your resumé like a list of everything you've ever done, you neglect to use your credits in the way they were meant to be used: To get you your next opportunity. The more junk you cram onto that page, the more you tell us you're simply desperate to work, to show us that you belong. Go *simple* with your resumé and you tell us you're confident in your credits and your abilities, even if there are few of each. Teach us how to cast you. Show us where you're headed, not everywhere you've ever been.

Just like clearing clutter from your home can shift the flow of energy in all areas of your life, cutting credits and training and skills from your resumé can create a shift of energy in your career. You won't believe me 'til you try it. But if you try it, you'll see. I get buttloads of email from actors who've taken my advice, trimmed the fat from their resumés, and increased their flow because of it. This works! Do not fear the white space.

Next, your credits don't need to be presented in chronological order. Someone somewhere decided that "corporate rules" aligned with "Hollywood rules" and told actors to list their credits in chronological order. Nope. Don't do it. There is very little similarity between Corporate America and Hollywood. That's not news. These are different worlds.

The inverted pyramid is something they taught us in journalism school, and it's all about leading with the meatiest part of your story, then tapering off to the stuff that's less important. Yup. It's unlike any writing you were taught in your composition classes, where that conclusion paragraph had better be a real winner. You let the less-awesome stuff go last because the story may be cut for space in the newspaper or magazine in which it appears. (Ah, print journalism. The good ol' days, grandpa.)

Just like you don't want to "bury the lede" in your hot story, you don't want to put your hottest credits under the ones that are less badass. Lead with your strongest credits. Lead with your largest roles. Lead with your biggest studios. Lead with your most prestigious directors. Lead with the *power* items on your resumé (and end with the crap credits that you're simply unwilling to lose yet, no matter how much I beg you to slice 'em). Listing your credits in order of strength makes it very easy to trim credits in the future; you're always cutting the bottom credit when you're adding a new, stronger one up top.

Booked a top-of-show guest-star on a top network series? Great! Off goes the one-liner in the spec pilot no one ever saw. Booked a studio feature film? Great! Off goes the student film which never yielded footage for your reel anyway. Show us how to cast you next. Lead us to your next booking. Don't get sentimental over the old credits as you delete them. We sure don't!

And finally, no one has the same emotional attachment to your credits that you do. This is a guideline (hopefully) for the detachment with which you should approach this process. Just like sitting through someone else's home movies is exciting only for them (because they remember how it *felt* to live those moments) and is mildly interesting (at best) to those who are spectators, your sentimental credits mean nothing to 99% of the people reading your resumé. Yes, you remember getting your union eligibility on that indie film. We see a microbudget direct-to-video project no one will ever see and that doesn't show us that we can take a risk on you as the lead of a studio blockbuster.

You remember falling in love with your co-star. We see a one-liner on a cable series that got cancelled in its first season, and that doesn't show us that you could be qualified for a series regular position on a new project at network. You loved that role. It was your breakout moment on stage. Good for you. You're never gonna be cast as that type, that age, that character again. It's been 20 years. Let it go! Show us how to cast you *today*. Now, let's get to some resumé feng shui *musts*.

Include Contact Information

Please, even if you have an agent or manager who requests that you do not, include your cell phone number, a Google Voice number, or your email address. At bare minimum, include your website's URL. Why? Well, we want to book you. We want to schedule you for an audition. We want to contact you for work or the possibility of work. And as much as your agent rocks, his *life* is not consumed with your career goals. He goes on vacation. He takes a day off. He has other clients. He's not interested in low-budget (low-commission) projects that tug at your creative heartstrings. Sometimes he's just unreachable, no matter how much he has assured you he will *always* be reachable. Rather than having us go to the next actor on the list, make it easy for us to get to you when we can't get to your rep.

An agent or manager who *requires* that you remove your own contact info from your resumé is usually operating from a place of fear. He is concerned that you will cut him out of commissions on projects you book directly. There is so much wrong with that mindset. This is your teammate. You're gonna pay him commission on *everything* you book because that's the deal. And some stuff you want to go after might not even yield a commission (or much of one, anyway). Fine. If your rep will not budge on this, then give him the stack of headshots and resumés without your contact info, but bring to auditions the ones *with* your contact info.

Besides, how sure are you that this will be your agent or manager forever or for as long as we might hold onto your resumé after an audition, a showcase, a great play? Are you certain? Casting directors are packrats when it comes to the headshots of actors whose work we love. Say I pull your headshot and resumé out a year after your agency folded (or after your agent left the agency and you went with him somewhere else, or after you upgraded to a bigger agency, or after you were dropped during lean times at this agency). If

I contact your *former* agent trying to find you for a new project I'm casting, it's not your former agent's job to help me find you. It's his job not to let me off the phone 'til I agree to see the *new* version of you he now has on his roster. And if I already have a "you" by the time I hang up with him, why do I need to keep trying to track you down when you couldn't be bothered to share your cell number on your resumé to begin with?

Sure, we could go to IMDb-Pro and look you up, but if we have two actors' resumés and one of you provided us with exactly what we needed and the other expected us to go look you up (and hopefully know which of the four credited people who share your name is you, and then further trust that the contact info at IMDb-Pro has been updated recently), who is making our job easier? As voiceover casting director, coach, and producer Nancy Wolfson says, "Never give an opportunity provider homework." When we're looking for anything to help us cut down the number of actors we're considering, you making it more difficult for us to find you is just a little actor Darwinism in action. We welcome the assistance in thinning the herd!

Speaking of herd-thinning, if your business number is your cell phone, keep that sucker charged and always pay the bill on time! We can't reach you if we get a "temporarily out of service" message when we call. Be sure your outgoing message is brief and professional. We'll hang up on long, silly, music-filled outgoing messages if we're in a rush to cast a role.

Including your URL on your resumé (even if your URL is just redirecting to your profile page at Actors Access, IMDb, or another online service) is a great idea also because you can list, right there in the footer of your resumé, "additional photos, credits, reel, and updates available at www.whatever.com." That communicates with us that you have additional photos (duh), will probably update your credits (yay), have credits that aren't the "selected" ones on your hard copy resumé that you'd like to share if we're interested in seeing more (smart), have a reel (awesome), and have a website in case we need to see updates! C'mon, that's a no-brainer and an efficient use of space at the very bottom of your resumé.

If you have no current representation and are submitting your materials to agents and managers, there is no need to put "seeking representation" on your resumé. The absence of representation on the resumé lets them know you're on the prowl, just like the absence of a wedding band is enough, if you're at a singles' club. No need to wear a T-shirt that says "single and ready to mingle" too.

That Third Column

Okay, so you use the three-column structure (again, visit smfa4.com to download templates of actor resumés for various tiers of your career) in the film, TV, and theatre sections of your resumé. (In the training and special skills sections, you can just go all the way across the page; no need for three columns there.) But within the third column is another of those Corporate America structure things about which I'd like to shake your perspective.

At some point, someone decided that if you listed a director's name in that third column on one project (perhaps the one on which that director's name was really impressive), you now had to list directors' names on *every* project. Nope. Total myth. You go with what's strongest. Remember, lead with the powerful information!

So, that means if you did a supporting role in a no-name-director's film for a major studio, you list that *studio* in column three. If you did a pilot for a "gun for hire" at ABC and his name is now mud in this town, you list "ABC" in column three. If the production company is the most prestigious item, go with that. *Mix and match*, baby! There is no reason to be *forced* to advertise the name of a director on a project if the director's name isn't nearly as impressive as the fact that this film was a USC grad film. List "USC grad." That's your production company, and it can mean a lot more than a director's name if that director decided to stop pursuing filmmaking after producing that thesis film. Hey, it happens!

Billing

I see this mistake probably more often than any other on a resumé. Well, actually, that's not true. The biggest mistake I see, is use of the word PRINCIPLE on a resumé instead of the only freakin' version of the homonym that could possibly be an adjective—which is what you want, since you're *describing* the size of the role: PRINCIPAL. You can remember it's an adjective because of that handy *A* right there in the word. *A* for Adjective, get it? Same for "the start of principal photography" in shooting a film. And while I'm ranting, it's spelled PREMIERE, not PREMIER. You're welcome.

Anyway, the second most frequently made mistake on an actor's resumé is the use of character names in the second column instead of billing, for on-camera credits.

Film Billing—*Lead*: principal role in the film, in most scenes, name is often in the on-screen credits that start the film (as well as in the complete end credits). *Supporting*: principal role in the film, in one or more scenes but not a lead character although important to the storyline. *Featured*: principal role in the film with one or more lines but easily cut from the final version of the film. Unfortunately, many extras use the term "featured" to describe their extra work and that means casting directors are less and less convinced that a job listed as "featured" actually was a featured principal role. *Extra*: non-speaking role in the film with no on-screen credit. This billing does not belong on an acting resumé.

Television Billing—*Series Regular*: contract role with exclusivity to the series, network, and production company for a term of one season or more; paid for a predetermined number of episodes produced, on contract for all episodes, even those in which the character doesn't appear. *Recurring*: character returns over multiple episodes, either on standing contract or contracted periodically, based on negotiations and number of appearances. *Guest-star*: one-episode guest whose character's storyline is central to that episode, works at a weekly rate (and is under contract for the week, even if only shooting a day or two). Remember, billing helps with quote bumps later. At some point, you may receive average-range co-star pay on a gig but be billed as a guest-star, which allows you to negotiate for guest-star pay on your next gig. Ninja actors will accept lower pay for higher billing, since that helps ramp them up for better pay on the next project. *Co-star*: one-episode guest whose character's storyline may or may not be central to that episode (since co-star billing actually depends more on negotiation than size of the role), anywhere from one line to multiple scenes. *Extra*: non-speaking role with no on-screen credit. This billing does not belong on an acting resumé.

Internet Billing—Ah! This is fun. If the Internet, branded content production, or direct-to-gadget project is a one-off (like a short film), use film billing protocol. If the Internet project is an episode within a webseries, use television billing protocol. Cool, huh? I predict, eventually, that resumé sections will simply be "on camera" and "on stage." So, if you're ready to lead the field, you can cluster like that to keep it clean. Of course, if the piece is overtly commercial, treat it like a commercial (see below).

Soap Opera Billing—*Contract Role*: daytime series regular or recurring character. *Principal Recurring*: an actor who recurs over time but is not under contract and can therefore work on other soap operas. *Dayplayer*: a character with five lines or more. *Under-5*: a character with between one and five lines. *Extra*: non-speaking role with no on-screen credit. This billing does not belong on an acting resumé.

Canadian Billing—Canadian billing includes the terms *Principal* and *Actor* (and I've seen abbreviations of *PP* and *PA* for *Principal Performer* and *Principal Actor*). As I understand it, the ACTRA billing of Actor corresponds to our Under-5. An ACTRA Principal would have five lines or more.

Theatre Billing—While billing can be used in on-stage credits (*Lead, Featured, Ensemble, Multiple, Swing, Understudy*), most theatre credits include the character name, as role size is generally known by those buyers who love theatre. Definitely, if the production is of an original work or relatively new play, include a parenthetical notation of "lead" or "supporting" after the character name. Also note that you originated the role, if that's the case. Depending on how well-known the play becomes down the line, this could be especially impressive information.

With all issues of billing, when in doubt, check your contract. If you are working a union television contract, your billing will be spelled out specifically in your contract, so there is no room for error. If you do not have a contract or deal memo for your work, check the original breakdown for the project, as the billing for the role will likely be listed after the character description. If you're still not able to nail it down, check with your agent or someone in casting or production for the project. You do not want to mistakenly upgrade yourself on your resumé and then meet up with the casting director in the future.

Always remember that you're trying to help us with risk assessment and that means you need to show us that you're right for a guest-star because you've already done a guest-star. You're ready for your second co-star because you already scored that elusive first one. It's time to consider you for a lead in a studio feature film because you've had leads in a half-dozen indie films. *Billing* is all we care about in the on-camera sections of your resumé.

So, about Those Theatre Credits

Look, I know you love theatre if you love theatre. Heck, I love theatre. I started out as a stage actor as a kid and I have great fondness and respect for stage actors. Their discipline, stamina, and devotion to the craft and unpredictability of daily performances in front of a live audience are all awesome qualities. But almost everyone—especially in Hollywood—who is looking at you for an on-camera role doesn't give a poop about your theatre credits, and your insistence upon keeping that section packed full on your resumé simply tells the industry you're *not* working on screen.

Since our business is risk assessment, we need to see evidence of your work in exactly the area we're looking to hire you. Show us how to cast you. List your "biggies" in theatre (and that means Broadway, Chicago, and London stage, maybe a few major LA or Off-Broadway theatres, very few regional houses and only then when award-nominated productions) and change the header to say: "Theatre (selected)," so we know we can ask you about what else you've done, if we happen to be theatre types. (Be prepared to rarely be asked about this section. I know. It hurts your heart. Mine too.)

Remember that your goal is to show us how to cast you next, and that means you don't want to distract us from the meaty credits you have that relate to how we *want* to cast you, in order to show us children's theatre or summer stock or even off-Off-Broadway credits. You do that stuff to build relationships, feed your soul, and keep your craft sharp. To reduce the level of importance of your one and only network co-star by surrounding it with a half-page of stage work is to tell the industry you're happy working on stage and don't really care whether you ever get your name left at the gate of CBS Radford again. Think it through. What's your goal? Show us a map to *that* goal via your resumé rather than providing a list of *all* the things you've done.

Now, I'm not advising that you cut so much stuff that your resumé is left looking like a tree stump. Just prune the branches back. You know the difference between getting a trim so that your hair is healthy and shaving your head. Be smart. Do as much trimming as is required to show us how spectacular you can look.

You can note that these are *selected* credits, if you want to spark conversation about the other credits you do have. The best part of listing *any* section of your resumé's credits as "selected" is that you open the door for a rich conversation during an audition or meeting. "Oh, your theatre credits are fabulous! But it says here these are selected credits. Obviously, you have chops. What else have you done?" Hey, cool! You've just encountered a member of the industry who loves theatre and wants to talk shop with you. That means those credits you lopped off the resumé are actually *helping* you in that room.

Commercial Conflicts Upon Request

Don't list your commercials. Even if you no longer have a conflict airing, don't list 'em. Commercial clients and ad agency reps worry when they see the word "Verizon" on an actor's resumé that the actor might have been as recognizable and as product-associated as "The Verizon Guy" even if you were only a hero mom in a regional spot and never even actually touched the product, much less said, "Can you hear me now?" to camera. Doesn't matter. You scare folks off when you list the commercials you've done, and you don't need to add obstacles to a career that already has a ton of 'em. If you have done *zero* commercials, that "conflicts upon request" line is fine. When requested, your reply is, "Oh, I have no current conflicts." Yay, you.

Minimize All the Other Stuff

Here, I'm talking about voiceover, stunt, background, corporate, industrial, non-broadcast, stand-in, modeling, singing, stand-up comedy, hosting, directing, writing work of any kind showing up on your acting resumé. Consider getting rid of it. And if you cannot bring yourself to get rid of it, then relegate it to your resumé's special skills section.

What?!? I know. Calm down. You worked hard to become an amazing hyphenate. But this is an *acting* resumé and the buyers looking at it are trying to decide whether you should be invited in for a shot at an *acting* role. Sure, having TelePrompTer skills is awesome if you're a host. Create a host resumé. And if you're sure you should keep your host info on your acting resumé, then include in special skills that you have "extensive host experience—reel and credits available upon request," and leave it at that.

Anything that distracts us from your juiciest *acting* credits and takes us down the mental road of, "Oh. So desperate to be in the industry that he'll do *anything* to get on our radar," is potentially costing you acting work. So what if it's true that you've done a thousand different things? An acting resumé needs to be focused on your acting credits and skills, teaching us where you're headed. Period. Everything else is a potential distraction.

Yes. I know you're certain that your years of background work proves to a principal casting director that you have valuable on-set experience. No. It doesn't. You might as well have spent those same years as a PA. It's a totally different skill set. That doesn't mean that the experience doesn't have value (since it absolutely does); it means it doesn't belong on an acting resumé. Of course, there's a whole chapter in this book celebrating **Life as a Hyphenate,** but until you've built a bankable brand, you need very specific tools and an acting-specific resumé is what we're working on right now.

The Training Section

In your training section, if you're currently studying somewhere, note that! Just a simple parenthetical notation after the name of the coach with whom you're studying is plenty. For example: "Lesly Kahn: Comedic scene study (ongoing)."

Done. That lets me know two things. One: You're actively working on your craft, keeping your instrument tuned up, and pushing yourself as an actor, even when you're not on set. Two: There's someone with whom I can check in if I want to know whether you've got the chops to handle something I'm casting.

"Les, hi. I'm thinking of casting Chris in this really hilarious comedy and I only see dramatic roles on the resumé. What's the work like in class lately?" The answer helps me know whether the risk (there's that word again) is worth a slot on our audition session calendar. Now, that sort of thing might not happen often, but it happens enough, so it's worth the notation on your resumé. You never know what makes up any one buyer's web of trust, as we're reviewing your resumé.

Should you note your college degree—even if it has no relevance to your acting career? I say that you should note your degree somewhere below all of your relevant theatre training. Here's why: Some casting directors like to see that actors have a full life outside of acting. We like to know that you have lived a well-rounded existence and have spent time on the development of other areas of your world. So, don't list it because it shows anything relevant to the actor you are, but because it gives a little insight into who you are as a person.

The Special Skills Section

Balance your special skills listings between personality-driven and actual, marketable skills. Include dialects, language proficiencies, sports, vocal range, recreational activities you enjoy, and any licenses or certifications you have that could be applied to your acting (weapons training, horseback riding, black belt). Make sure you list things you'd be able to do *today* if asked. Many casting directors will ask you to demonstrate a special skill while in the audition room. If you wouldn't be able to do it today, remove that item from your resumé until you've brushed up. Most folks in casting would appreciate two very important things regarding special skills: Be specific. Don't lie.

Being specific is important because we don't just want to know that you can throw darts. We want to know whether you played on a dart league in college. Sure, you can do a southern dialect. Is that South Carolina or New Orleans? Didn't know there was a difference? Then you have no business putting "southern accent" on your special skills list. The same goes with any regional dialect. Your level of proficiency in sports is especially appreciated. You practice karate? Awesome! What level belt? You speak Russian? Fantastic. Are you fluent? Are you a native speaker? And if you are a native speaker of another language, when you speak English, can you do so without an accent? Firearms? Yippee! Which ones? And when was the last time you fired a gun? If you sing, we want to know what your vocal range is (actual notes you can hit aren't necessary for most casting directors, but if you frequently audition for musical theatre, of course you should be that specific). Wheelchair basketball? Cool! Do you play for a team every week or just think you could probably do it, if asked? Improv? Great. Did you tour with a major comedy troupe or are you just quick on the "yes, and..." draw? You can juggle? Super! Are we talking small balls or flaming chainsaws?

The more specific you are, the better, as long as you're describing a special skill that may be of use to us, in casting you. The fact that you can list all state capitals in reverse alphabetical order is more of a "fun fact" than a true special skill, at least in the casting sense. A personality item, a "stupid human trick" you can do, something you can either do in the room or be asked about in the room could go here, but be prepared to be asked to do this thing on command, happily. When you leave, we will discuss you as "that guy who played the William Tell Overture on his cheeks" when we're down to our top four and trying to decide who we liked best hours before.

Eventually, upper-tier actors leave off special skills altogether, assuming that your body of work speaks for itself, in its diversity and skill requirements. Also, when actors are working at a tier filled with studio projects, you can expect to be given training time as necessary in order to get ready for the big-budget action picture. If you're still going in for indie films, though, keeping "can drop and gain weight quickly" on a special skills list is cool. We may just need you to do that (and not have a nutritionist to supervise your progress).

Young actors should include "can cry on cue" and "can play dead" only if you seriously can shed a tear (not "mock cry") in a believable, non-overwrought way and if you truly can slow your breathing and lie still for an extended period of time. More important on a child's resumé are items that give us insight into the actor's "real life." What are your interests? What is your best subject in school? What do you like to do when you're not acting? These are the best items for the special skills area on a young actor's resumé. Of course, we also need to know if you're 18 TPY and whether you have a current work permit. (See: *SMFA* **for Young Actors**.)

I regularly see "bartending" or "typing 85 WPM" listed among actors' special skills. All that tells me is that you have a survival job as a bartender or as a temp. You don't want to remind me that you even *need* a survival job, when I'm wondering whether you're the best actor for the role. (Sure, we know you do need a reliable way to make rent. Just don't remind us about it while we're looking at your acting marketing tools.)

Share Those Good Reviews!

The last play I did before retiring from acting yielded an *LA Weekly* review that included the words: "Bonnie Gillespie is excellent." Can't ask for a better four-word review than that, I'd say. (Especially when they didn't really dig the play.)

You bet those four words, followed by, "*LA Weekly*, August 2000," went on my resumé right under my name, union affiliation, and contact number. Had I kept acting, I'd have lopped off the date after a year, because you don't want to draw attention to the fact that your last amazing review was more than a few months old.

Same with film festival wins. If a film in which you starred went to a major festival, find a place to say that on your resumé. Some actors will note it parenthetically after the film's title. Others will use an asterisk and resolve it at the bottom of the page or section. **Best Narrative Short, Sundance, 2017* is a great blurb. Until 2018. Then you just delete the year and leave it as a conversation starter. "Oh, wow! When were you at Sundance?" "In 2017. We won Best Narrative Short that year." "I see that. Awesome!" "It really was. Thank you." "Did you catch the Best Doc while you were in Park City?" and so on.

You earned the goodies. Share 'em with the folks who care enough to look at your resumé (or website, for that matter). Don't go overboard and get all "glowy" about yourself. Pick the best of the best. Don't let the review from a rag no one has ever heard of distract us from the fact that *Variety* called you talented. Shine spotlights on the biggies.

Proofing!

For the love of all that is holy, please do this even if you ignore everything else I've suggested (but please don't ignore it, it's all really good advice): Have someone else proofread your resumé. You're too close to the work of art to see its flaws. You don't realize you've used the wrong word, misspelled a director's name, didn't align your tab stops in Word, or left off your contact information altogether.

Just as those really cool home-buying shows do, have someone who knows whether you're "staging" your space in an optimum way to attract buyers take a look at your product before you put it in front of the buyers. Have 'em tell you whether the font *feels* like you.

Making Sure the Whole Dang Thing Is On-Brand

Let's "interview" your resumé. Next to every credit currently on your resumé, answer the following question: "What do *you* tell the buyers about me?"

Hold off on passing judgment on yourself, your credits, the space you were in when you agreed to work on that crappy student film or that no-budget indie for which you got horrible footage and a parking ticket while on set. This first step is just about asking the question and writing the answer down. If I were interviewing my old casting resumé, I would put next to *Death By Beaver* the answer: You tell producers that I signed on to cast a $150,000 SAG Limited Exhibition film in 2005, cast eight actors, and then got word that the producers had parted ways and the project would not be going forward. There is no footage. There is no IMDb entry. Yes, I did the work, but the "story" of this credit is one that ends badly.

If I were to interview my current casting resumé, I would put next to Machinima's *Bite Me* the answer: You tell producers that I can sign on for a groundbreaking nonunion indie webseries for a site that had never before done scripted content and get such a rockstar cast that—along with all the other stars that aligned for this gamer zombie apocalypse project—for season two, we were transported to "the big leagues" when Lionsgate acquired the series, the series went union, the series aired weekly on television, and the project got profiled in dozens of international publications as an example of the new wave of production tier jumps, from web to TV to feature film to merchandising, and landed me an invitation to join the Television Academy.

Now, when I compare these two "interview" answers, there's no question where I'm headed when it comes time to do a little resumé feng shui. How about you? Remember: All of the items on your resumé are telling a story about your past. Only *some* of the items on your resumé tell a story about your future.

I want you to experience a feeling that you can begin to associate with every credit, going forward. As you amass work, I want you to start asking yourself, "Will this show buyers how to cast me next, when it's a credit on my resumé? Or am I doing this project for some other reason?" It's totally fine to do projects because you're not otherwise busy that day, you like the crew and want to do a favor, you'll get to stretch as you play against type, or you just need some money and this schlocky horror film gig pays. You'll start realizing that there are some projects that never get added to your resumé. That doesn't mean they didn't have value in your life! It just means their purpose was not to show people how to cast you next.

Once you've had a paradigm shift—that your resumé is not a list of everything you've ever done; it's a recipe for how to cast you next—this process gets really easy, and you start to enjoy yourself more on sets, or when you audition, or even when you submit! Because you'll not feel the stakes are so high and that you desperately need to add to your "list of credits," but instead that you're free, you're an artist having fun, and when the project *also* helps buyers understand how to cast you next, it can come hang out on your awesome resumé, with all the other badass credits you're so proud to share with the world!

Don't worry that you're "not enough" when others have crowded resumés and that old way of thinking tries to creep back in. Those folks are hoarding credits just like your grandpa kept too many old newspapers. Clear the clutter. Remove sentimentality from the items on your resumé and think like a buyer, assessing risk. Trust the power of the most powerful credits on your resumé. Simplify. Live on-brand. Lurk then lead. You'll know *for sure* that it's a better, stronger resumé when casting directors who didn't "get" you before start calling you in. Resumé feng shui at work!

File Type

Be sure to save a copy of your resumé as yourname.pdf (yes, as a PDF—use the "print to PDF" function in your word-processing software; yes, with your name as the file name, not something generic like resume.pdf), so it is descriptive even as it lives on someone else's computer. Should you ever need to email a link to your resumé, or the file as an attachment, to multiple recipients at once, use BCC to protect the email addresses of the folks to whom you are blasting the email. Oh, and really, think it over before doing anything resembling a mass email blast. It's so *not* the ninja way, to sling spaghetti at the wall and hope something sticks. Target, target, target!

For hard copy versions of your resumé, printing your resumé directly onto the back of the headshot is a great idea. In general, it's most cost effective to do this from your own laser printer. If you don't have a laser printer or don't care to put it through the rigorous task of putting card-stock lithographs through its rollers, you should be able to get about 100 copies printed up at your local copy shop for around $20. Note: You generally cannot print directly on the back of a photographic print (vs. litho) of your headshot using a laser printer. The printer's heat will melt the photographic paper and ruin both the headshot and the printer itself. Some actors find ink jet printing to be an economical option for photographic paper headshots. Just be sure to let the ink dry before stacking the photos up.

One thing to watch out for, in the printed-on version: If you're doing a lot of work and would need to update your resumé more quickly than you'd run out of the number you have printed up, you will find you're having to write in your new credits. If it's more than just one new thing, it could start to look sloppy. An option then is to print a new resumé on paper and staple it to the headshot, covering up the printed-on version of the resumé, if updates are coming so fast. Yay, you!

Many casting directors prefer printed-on resumés because credits and contact information cannot get separated from the headshot. Glue dries up and resumés fall off, or staples get snagged and rip resumés off. Then, when we want to bring you in or contact your agent with an offer, your contact information is nowhere in sight. If you decide to go with the non-printed-on version, trim your resumé to the size of the headshot. The easiest way to handle this is to set the margins in your word processing program to leave the most room on *two* sides, so that you're not trimming all four edges (major time-waster). Staple the resumé at the two top corners and once at the center bottom of the headshot, under your name. Voila!

13: YOUR FOOTAGE

Your demo reel is the trailer for the feature that is *you*. Look at every bit of your potential footage through the lens of the buyer, so that only the most castable footage is what remains. As you make decisions about content, length, and distribution, make sure you "advertise" yourself accurately and in such a way that leaves the viewer wanting more (just like the best trailers make you *really* want to see the movie). It's all about making sure the viewer knows how to cast you. Make that clear, from start to finish.

Especially for the audience of buyers that are casting directors, demo reels have gone from a linear presentation of an actor's history of work to an à la carte selection of clips, which better show the folks casting your *next gig* that you can do what we need you to do, because you did it on a *previous gig*. That we can experience this without being distracted by the *other things* you have done is ninja!

Credit the Internet. Once upon a time, there were physical *things* delivered to the buyers: VHS cassettes, then DVDs. Now it's a link that shows buyers what actors can do. That means we've gone from putting a tape in a machine and pushing play—watching start to finish—to clicking a link and choosing only what we *need* to see. This is what informs our very next action. And that's huge. That you—as an actor—can provide a potential buyer with an exact formula for how to cast you, how to understand your essence, how to *get you*, is fantastic. It's pretty dang empowering, but it means you must get over the old-school way of thinking about your reel. For the actor who understands how best to use nonlinear presentation of footage, this is incredibly empowering and gets you closer to your next role faster. And isn't that the goal?

I asked Gary Marsh—owner of Breakdown Services, Showfax, and Actors Access—to weigh in on the way reel footage is being used these days. Here's what he shared with me: "Just think of the casting process. You get over 1000 submissions per role. You are on a deadline and are selecting actors. How long can you watch an actor's reel (especially for episodic television) and why are you watching it? A: You don't know the actor; B: You know the actor but you know him doing drama and you need to see him do comedy, etc. You are really looking at these clips to quickly determine whether to bring in the actor or not. Once you've made the decision, you either select the actor or not. Nothing fancy, just efficient."

I also talked with Dave Manship—owner of Edit Plus—on this topic. Here are his thoughts: "Effective demo reels today are not 'one-size-fits-all.' They are specific video tools chosen to get a specific result. Think of your demo as a set of the finest kitchen knives. Each has a use. There is probably one knife that is used 80% of the time, but when you need a boning knife, a paring knife, or a cleaver, it makes the job easier if you have those available. Today's demo reel should be thought of as a set of video tools."

What do actors need to know about best practices, in putting their clips online? Marsh says: "Casting needs to see your face first when they are watching your clip, not the monologue of the lead actor, then you. Remember actors are marketing themselves, not the person they are doing the scene with. It is an absolute must for actors to label and describe the scene. As a casting director, you are casting the role of an attorney grilling a witness in court and you see a description such as '*Law & Order* (played role of attorney badgering a witness).' Okay, as the casting director, I want to bring in actors who know how to play that; I watch the scene and, *bang*, the actor has an audition. If the reel was labeled 'Demo Reel,' well there's just no attempt on the part of the actor to market what they do well and the actor loses the audition and the casting director loses the opportunity to bring in the right actor."

Manship also has opinions on this issue: "An actor should have a general demo for marketing to new reps and CDs that need to know the range of their work. This is something that could be posted at IMDb-Pro, at one's website, and at Actors Access. It allows the actor to have professional, searchable online video presence. An actor should post individual clips to Breakdown Services and Actors Access. The clips should be no more than one minute long with specific descriptive naming that helps the CD know what they are about to watch. '*Grey's Anatomy* clip' as a description doesn't work. 'Entitled Bitch' is a winner—especially if that is the character description they are looking for."

I'll take it one step further and say "*Grey's Anatomy*: Entitled Bitch Scene" is even better! With that description, we know the vibe of the show, the tone of the scene we're likely to see, the type of role you're playing, and that's all fantastic information, just due to smart labeling!

Work your brand words into your descriptive titles of individual clips. Let us know exactly what we're going to get, and know that your use of those phrases that describe your bullseye actually help cement your brand in the minds of the buyers, even if we don't click to watch the footage! You've effectively reminded us that you have this particular thing in your arsenal, should we ever need it. Label well. It's a part of your overall marketing strategy, believe it or not!

Do You Still Need a Linear Reel?

Yes. Just like agents and managers still accept hard copy snail-mailed submissions for consideration, they are the last holdouts on wanting to see old-school, linear demo reels, as they offer a broad overview of what you can do. Still, I'm going to recommend strongly that you get specific about what you're offering to your primary buyers, always. With à la carte clips, you actually *can* have more range "out there" and just show what needs to be seen to the right people at the right time. You won't talk us out of how to "get you" by overcrowding a single demo reel. So, consider your branding—and not your concern about trying to be everything to everyone—to create the best reel presence possible.

Have your reel available on your website, your online actor profiles, and your IMDb page, as this allows potential buyers to bump into it, and it provides you with an easy link to email around, when your reel is requested. Of course, if you are submitting yourself electronically on a specific project through a breakdown (or your agent or manager is submitting you), a specific clip can be attached to the submission from right there within the system. Super easy!

Are the days of sending a DVD of your reel to a casting office over? Yep. As CSA casting director Debra Zane says, "There's just no time to look at an unsolicited demo. It's not a top priority." Still, having your reel (as well as headshot and resumé PDFs) on inexpensive thumb drives is great, in the rare instance that someone requests something physical. Come to smfa4.com to see my favorite ways to share this stuff (my current nontraditional favorite is a business card thumb drive—yes, really). But for the most part, you'll be asked to direct someone to an online version of your reel, so make sure you've got it up somewhere you can easily access it, and not require folks to put in passwords or download copies to their local drives in order to see your goods!

Submissions to agents and managers for representation should arrive without physical reels because your cover letter can include the URL to a website at which the agent or manager can access your footage. Before going to the expense of including a thumb drive of your reel with your submission for representation, call the office and ask whether they would like to have something like that included. They'll let you know, so you don't waste supplies or resources.

Should you ever need to email a link to your reel to multiple recipients at once, use BCC to protect the email addresses of the folks to whom you are blasting the email. Oh, and really, think it over before doing anything resembling a mass email blast. It's so *not* the ninja way, to sling spaghetti at the wall and hope something sticks. Target, target, target! (Sound familiar? Good. Learn it. Know it. Live it.)

That Inverted Pyramid, Again

So, you know I love to apply the inverted pyramid to the actor's resumé, thanks to your resumé feng shui work at this point. Can the inverted pyramid help you get your reel in order too? You betcha. If you insist upon keeping a linear demo reel available, there's a hierarchy of material, ranked badassiest to suckiest. You want as much of the former and as little of the latter as possible. And if all you have is the latter, you have to decide if it helps you at all, or if it just hurts you.

Sometimes it's better to be perceived as "so new there's no footage" than to have something that gets you excluded from those first little auditions you could get based on your credits, if not for that horrible little monologue or in-class scene that just makes the buyers say, "Not ready yet."

What's considered "best," as footage goes? Studio-produced material that got distribution. Network TV scenes that aired nationally. Maybe a really fantastic little project that happens to be indie, but is done with a professional cast and crew, stars recognizable folks, looks wonderful, and does well at festivals. Web-based projects can sit at this tier if they meet the same criteria as the fantastic little indie I just described.

Next tier down? Indie stuff that's less awesome. Spec pilots, the majority of web-based projects out there, most student films, shorts—basically anything on which people are learning and you can *see* the learning in the finished product. A boom shadow, jump cuts, continuity errors, lighting issues, sound-sync problems, poor writing, less-than-stellar acting by your co-stars (or even by you; be honest with yourself about how much you grow as an artist every day) are the typical sins of these projects. It doesn't mean their footage is useless! It just has to be very judiciously edited and sometimes some of the "learning" still shows.

Keep in mind that self-produced footage should be some of the tightest stuff on your reel! It's where you have ultimate control of the way you are seen. Make it count. As former casting director (now author-director) Ellie Kanner says: "You *must* have a demo reel; however, bad footage is worse than no footage. So, unless your footage is of broadcast quality, with good writing and talented actors playing with you, don't use it. Remember that the reel could be the last thing a producer sees on you."

What's lower on the inverted pyramid? The student film in which you're on-camera in a principal role, but not heard (or only heard in voiceover), your very first self-produced project (the short you did to learn, but which has a lot of flaws), industrials, reenactments, commercials, and anything you paid money to have shot at one of those production facilities that does reel packages (we can *always* tell, with those). Again, none of this is—by classification—useless on a reel! It's just lower-ranked than the juicier stuff I led off with. Used sparingly, these items can be helpful in rounding out a reel. But if they're all you've got, well, think about what you're teaching the buyers about what to expect from you, should they cast you.

The lowest? Stage work. Scenes done in class. Self-taped auditions. Monologues. Live improv or sketch shows. Stand-up comedy. Anything that's not acting but that you may keep on a reel in a minor market: singing, dancing, modeling, appearances at tradeshows, hosting, interviews you've done about your acting, appearances on the local news, your extra work in which you walk by a famous person in a huge film, etc. These items are almost never on a "real" reel, and I find that new-to-town actors will include them on their first LA reel, hoping it helps prove, "Hey! I've worked! See?" without realizing that's not the function of a reel (more on that in a sec).

It's not that you cannot have any of the so-called lowest stuff on your reel, it's just footage you should use sparingly and get off your reel as soon as you have higher-tier material. Why? Because your reel is not a retrospective of everything you've ever done on camera; it's the story of how to cast you next.

Sure, if you want a career as the next top industrial actor with the occasional non-sync sound undergrad student film, keep those clips prominently featured on your reel. But as soon as you have footage—even in a quick one-liner—on a major network show or a studio feature film, you are confusing your buyers by cluttering up your reel with work you no longer hope to book.

It's not about proving you've been on set or that you didn't get left on the proverbial cutting-room floor. It's more about educating buyers on what you can do and where you're headed. If you're on the newer side, good. You absolutely do not need to represent yourself as someone who has loads of footage that is at the lower end of the inverted pyramid. Hustle to get footage that's higher up. Enter the game at a better tier.

Remember how I asked you to interview your bookings, earlier? Great. You're going to go through your footage the same way right now. Rank it, inverted pyramid style. Yes, it all needs to still look like you (reasonably; we do understand that hair changes and all that jazz), it all needs to be on-brand so that we fully understand what you bullseye as an actor, and it all needs to be as badass as possible. Rank it all. Then start cutting from the bottom.

No, this does not automatically indicate the *order* in which the clips should be presented on your reel, but it lets you know where to start "losing" footage. Yay! That's exciting! Even if it only leaves you with one really amazing clip, so what? It may be enough to do the job on its own. How awesome is that?

Who Are We Watching?

Don't highlight someone else's performance in your reel. There are many tales of actors who have been cast from *other* actors' demo reels. Make sure when you're doing the inverted pyramid ranking of the material you plan to use on your reel that you're choosing scenes in which your performance is the focus. If your partner's work is stellar and cannot be edited down without compromising the flow of the scene, make sure your partner is not someone of your *type* or category. Why should your reel put you out of a job?

If your first scene includes multiple people, unless you started with a freeze-frame on your headshot, you run the risk that we don't know who to look for, in that first scene. Make it easy for us to get connected with you!

What Are We Watching?

Commercials are so narrative in tone that there's less reason to exclude them from a reel than once was the custom. Of course, if you're a pitch person doing a direct-to-camera testimonial for a product or service, that may feel out of place on a theatrical reel. But if you're the hero mom in a narrative commercial that just happens to be cementing the brand of whatever product helps your character save the day, consider including that footage! Especially if it's a great, on-brand representation of *you*, that's worth keeping. With the non-linear presentation of clips, you just need to label with as much specificity as possible. "Hero mom for major cable provider," "Doofus dad in home repair commercial," "Eager co-ed with a cool new smart phone," and so on.

There's no hard and fast rule on how long you can keep using a particular clip. The important thing is to be sure the footage still represents how you could be cast today. Even if it's a few years old, as long as you still—realistically, now; not just in your dreams—look the same and your brand is well-depicted in the footage, and you're not drawing attention to how long it has been since you've actually *worked*, the footage may be of service to you. Always revisit your clips to see where they rank, in terms of showing the industry how to cast you next. Eventually, older material will work its way out of the rotation.

Be consistent. If you're going to put the show title (or film title) in the lower-third of the screen at the start of the clip, to let us know what we're watching, please use that device on all of the footage. If it's only on one clip, it'll feel out of place when we don't see it on the other clips.

How Long Are We Watching?

For a long-form, linear demo reel, industry standard is 90 seconds to three minutes. Sure, there are some great 60-second reels. There are some great four-minute reels. But in general, you should be able to get the job done in under two minutes. And, of course, for your individual clips, you're able to show the buyers that you bullseye exactly what they're looking for in under a minute. That's ninja!

Montages

How about montages (those clips with music playing, just showing a bunch of things you've done)? Here's what Marsh had to say: "Whatever you do, please please please, no montages! Montages are loved by editors but hated by casting when they need to see and hear you ASAP."

Robert Campbell—owner of Quick Nickel Editing—had similar thoughts to share about montages:

> ➤ *They suck.*
>
> ➤ *They do not equal range. Watching a bunch of quick clips of an actor doing a lot of random jumping, kissing, laughing, running, etc., does nothing to show you can believably convey a character's emotional life.*
>
> ➤ *They are an obvious attempt to steal the energy of the band, or song, and transfer it onto you. I call it trying to sell the sizzle, and not the steak. The problem is, you're trying to sell sizzle to people whose job it is to sell sizzle.*
>
> ➤ *They implicitly state: I have nothing worth watching so I'm going to try to delay you from seeing my work as long as possible.*
>
> ➤ *If you absolutely have to have a montage, I strongly suggest putting it at the end. That way if the viewer doesn't want to watch it, they can hit stop, and they won't miss seeing any of your actual work.*

Yes! Please! If you're going to use a montage—I agree—throw it at the end of the reel. That's just fine. Your reel answers all sorts of questions that your headshot and resumé alone cannot. CSA member Peter Golden agrees that a demo reel is more representative of what to expect from an actor. "I don't judge an actor on just their experience in the room [during a casting session]. That's such an uncomfortable setting for so many actors. That's why you *must* have footage. If you don't audition well, your most valuable tool becomes one great scene, even from a student film." With footage, we get a quick sense of you, your vibe, the way you sound, how you connect with others, what to expect when you walk in for your audition. That's all stuff we can *get* very quickly, so be sure to start off strong.

Killing Off Babies

I know it feels like killing off babies to lose footage you love. I do. I understand that it totally breaks your heart to remove the clip of your work on *M*A*S*H*, but y'know what? That was a generation or two ago and no one is going to cast you like that now. I loved playing Cha-Cha in *Grease* when I was a teenager. And I clung to that credit on my resumé for over a decade. "I won a local theatre award for it, for cryin' out loud! That was awesome! I'm not losing that credit and you can't make me!" Yeah. But no one in Los Angeles was looking to cast a nearly-30 plus-sized character actor as "the best dancer at St. Bernadette's," so it *had* to go.

It's the scrapbook syndrome. You don't want to choose a favorite among your babies. You don't want to omit footage from projects that were important to your career trajectory. Okay, I get that. But it's very simple: If it's not helping you get cast today, it's actually *costing* you work. So, if you have a dozen co-stars and three guest-stars, get rid of half of the co-stars to show the industry you are now a working guest-star. If you have studio films, start losing those indies that didn't do the festival circuit. And those student films should be long gone at this point.

Avoidable Sins

I want you to review your footage specifically checking for these sins. Note: Having these sins does *not* make the clip unusable! It just makes it lower-ranked than something that doesn't have as many sins. This footage review will help you know which "baby" will be killed off first, once there are higher-tier options available to you. Yay!

> ➢**Are you highlighting someone else's performance instead of your own**? The fix: Re-edit to make it all about you. Yes, even if you're sharing the screen with the star of the show, make them your co-star. We don't need to see what *they* can do.

> ➢**Is the clip not on-brand**? The fix: If it can't be edited to somehow stick with your brand and show the buyers how to cast you next, it may have to go. Yes, you want to show range, but it needs to be range that exists within your brand, for it to do you the most good long term.

> ➢**Does it suffer from scrapbook syndrome**? The fix: Let go of the sentimental clips. If there are benefits to keeping something that's way sentimental, try an edit that minimizes the schmaltz factor and ups the "here's how to cast me next" quotient.

➢**Is the scene too short?** The fix: If it really is just a blip of a scene and you'd have to show it in slow-mo to really get a lot out of it, you may wanna let it go. But if there's some lead-in, lead-out footage you could use to buffer it, there may be hope.

➢**Was the scene obviously produced at a reel-for-pay facility?** The fix: Require that they shoot you with another actor, and not just for "over the shoulder" rough singles. Real scenes move from establishing shots to masters to two-shots to close-ups. If all you have are a series of close-ups or rough singles with long, lingering shots of *only you* (uninterrupted screentime even Oscar winners don't get), we know you paid for your material. It's not horrible to have *one* of these scenes among other "starter material" on your reel, but if it's all you've got, get going on getting *more*, ASAP, so you can move this stuff off the reel.

➢**Are you showcasing extra work posing as principal work?** The fix: Lose it. Extra work doesn't belong on a reel, no matter how "featured" you were. If you were a non-speaking principal, that's one thing—think Paul Dano in *Little Miss Sunshine*, for context—but all seeing you make eye contact with Brad Pitt does for us is show us you can be trusted on a studio set, but not to speak.

➢**Is the clip of poor quality?** The fix: If it's sound, see if you can bump it up, remove hiss, or contain whatever the issue is—but it'll be tough, most likely. If it's light, see if you can change the saturation—again, tough, but doable. If the footage looks like a third-generation off-air copy from local TV, all you're showing us is that you can be trusted to do crappy local TV work, because we're going to go with how it *feels*, and those tech elements can factor in, greatly. Be really sure the quality of the work—acting, technical quality, production quality, all of it—lines up with where you're headed.

Selecting an Editor

A demo reel should reflect the strengths of the actor, not the creativity of the editor. The right editor can absolutely elevate your demo reel so be sure to put some time and effort into picking the right one for you. Check out the editors' websites for samples of their work. If they don't have a website, pass on that editor. Call four or five of them to get a feel for who you might be working with, and have a list of questions ready. If an editor doesn't have the patience and professionalism to answer all of your questions, keep looking.

Do you have to hire a professional editor? No. If you're a do-it-yourselfer with some computer savvy, you can put together a perfectly fine demo reel.

But there are advantages to hiring a professional, as well as factors to consider.

<u>The high cost of free</u>. Yes, you can get your friend or your cousin or your cousin's friend to edit your reel, but, you can't push them to hurry up because they're doing it for free; you can't complain about the quality because they're doing it for free; and you can't ask them to do it again because they're doing it for free.

<u>Time savings</u>. If you're not already familiar with not just the editing program, but how to bring your footage into the computer, and how to troubleshoot problems (which crop up all too frequently), then you could be looking at a learning curve that easily stretches 30 or more hours. On the upside, after the first go-round, the next time you edit your reel it may only take you two or three hours.

<u>Industry awareness</u>. A good demo reel editor has spent lots of time examining what works and doesn't work, and why.

<u>Dispassionate opinion</u>. Probably the biggest advantage an editor brings is that we're not emotionally connected to your work. We look at it with the "fresh" eyes of both a prospective audience member and an industry professional. This is a much greater asset than simply knowing how to work the software.

<u>Editorial branding</u>. There shouldn't be any. Don't let whomever edits your reel put their name, logo, website, or email address on any of your marketing materials. It's not their reel or career, it's yours.

—Robert Campbell

Editing the Dang Thing

If you're a DIY editor, well, that's awesome. If you're meeting with a professional editor, make sure you have a conversation about your brand and where you're headed, as an actor. It's important that your editor understand your goals, and not just slap together a reel that's filled with all your footage. A good demo reel editor can help craft your footage so that it showcases you as "next-tier-ready," making you appear lower-risk to the buyers at that tier. Show up to your reel editing appointment with all of your tapes cued up and ready to go, or the timecode logged if you're bringing in digital files. Plan the flow of the reel, from segment to segment, and decide on stylistic elements such as title cards and credits, music, and whether or not you will use a montage.

Edit your headshot and contact information into your reel! Make it at the start or the end. Matters not. But the way to be sure your info cannot be separated from the footage is to edit it in there. Use caution in editing in info about your representation, because you may leave that agency or the management firm may drop you or who knows how long 'til you'll next edit your footage, right? Putting your URL in the reel is a great way to be sure we can always find your current representation, since you'll be able to keep it updated there.

If you're going to store your vid at YouTube, note that you need to have clearance on the clips you use and the music you choose for any montage, intro, or outro segments (or the music needs to be in the public domain). Actors will post a demo reel and then have it flagged as infringing a network's copyright because it contains too much of a scene that the network hasn't cleared for use outside of its network's online properties. Same with music. So, rather than facing the frustration of having your goodies taken down after you've proudly posted 'em and started sending the link around, just keep it all squeaky clean or post it on a site where you control the rights (like your own site) or where it is clear to all involved that it's a reel for demonstrative purposes within the industry only (like on IMDb or Actors Access).

Getting Footage

Commit to getting copies of your on-camera work. It's your right as a performer. Show up to set with a contract like the one available from Holdon Log at copyprovided.com (a PDF) so that a producer on the set goes on record with you as pledging to get you your footage. Build relationships with the people most likely to be able to provide copies *while* you're on the set. If you're working on a commercial, speak with a representative from the ad agency. Exchange business cards and make sure to stay in touch, asking for a copy of the spot even if it never airs. If you're working on a student film, get the name of the student filmmaker's professor. Many times, a request of the professor will aid your quest to get a copy of the student film, when your requests of the student filmmaker go ignored. With film, work with the production company. With episodic television, have a video service (such as Edit Plus, which does Aircheck Services in conjunction with Breakdown Services) record the episode as it airs, if you haven't been able to get an advance copy of your footage. At the very least, set up your DVR and acquire your footage on your own. Yeah, you may end up having to scrape a copy off YouTube months after you were promised footage sometimes, but at least you'll have it.

What If I Have NO Footage?

Good news! You're going to be able to get footage specifically for your reel while knowing exactly what purpose your reel serves, what value to place on what type of material, and where to rank each new piece of material that comes into your life by using the inverted pyramid, so you'll know its position on your reel and how to label the individual clips as you receive them, so they can do their best service of your career goals! Fab!

Technology is more affordable than ever and it's not like you have to wait for some big break to get footage. You can have your own footage ready in a matter of weeks, if you produce it yourself (more on that in the **Content Creation** chapter). Get to it!

As you amass work, I want you to start asking yourself, "Will this show buyers how to cast me next, when it's a clip on my demo reel or à la carte at my online profile? Or am I doing this project for some other reason?" Just like with your resumé, it's cool to do work that doesn't end up on your reel!

A final thought: Start strong! Consider the number of seconds you give yourself before changing the radio station in your car, even if the song is a perfectly good one, if it's not the one you want to hear right then. That's how buyers are going through demo reel footage: Fast. Make sure you lead off with great footage of fantastic, on-brand work so we *get you* even if this isn't your role right now. That's how your reel can help build your brand even when you're not booking because of it. Teach us how to cast you so that you become our go-to when we next need exactly what your reel shows us you bullseye.

14: Your Bio and Cover Letter

haiku precision,
the perfect cover letter
says much... with little
　　　　　—Tegan Ashton Cohan, actor

It's not often that you'll be asked for a bio. You aren't doing submissions that require cover letters every day. But it feels so delicious when you *are* asked for a bio, or you do need to do a mailing, if you know—with confidence—that your materials are their on-brand best.

First, let's cover some principles that exist no matter which element we're dealing with—mini-bio for a playbill, "about me" statement in social media, bio for your professional website, professional summary for a media kit, cover letter for an agent submission, note for a role-specific casting submission, or a general letter of introduction to anyone in the industry.

Your Tools Are in Service of Your Brand

Just like your headshot, your resumé, your reel, your website, and everything else about your marketing package, your bio and cover letter are a part of teaching us how to *get* you, how to *cast* you. Why go formal when you're clearly casual otherwise? Why use "rules" that you were taught about letter-writing when they don't jibe with what the rules of your *brand* might be? Be your authentic self! That's who we want to get to know. If your cover letter starts us off down the wrong path about how to understand you, you're making the already-existing hill steeper than it needs to be.

Before you tackle your bio and cover letter, revisit the chapter on **Your Bullseye** and refocus your typing words. Because your materials are an extension of your brand, a read of your bio or your cover letter should *feel* like you. If you're not the type of person who would say, "I knew I was born to be an actor from the tender age of five when I first picked up a bottle of shampoo and accepted an Academy Award in the bathroom mirror," to someone in person, keep it off the bio. If you're not the type of person who would say, "It is with great pleasure that I reach out to you today for the potential of collaborating on your upcoming theatrical project," to someone in person, keep it out of your cover letter. Truly, so very many "sucky" bios and cover letters could suck less with one quick read-through, aloud.

Don't Be Afraid to Have Several Versions of Your Tools

There is no such thing as a one-size-fits-all version of your goods. I have at least four versions of my bio. They vary in length because sometimes someone wants something shorter than my most frequently-used version. They vary in tone, because sometimes I'm going to be speaking at a university, other times I'm going to be a guest on a cheeky latenight BBC talkshow. Now, don't let that last bit make you think one is overly formal and the other is crazy casual! Among my bios, there are slight variances within the same, on-brand message.

If you do a lot of theatre but also want to break into on-camera acting, your website should feature prominently the bio that teaches people where you're *going*, but always make available that very specifically tailored one. If you have a huge voiceover career but recently released a single at iTunes, you'll want to create bios that complement one another, not ones that conflict with one another. Remember, you don't want to talk us out of being excited about your acting career just because the short you wrote made it to the Sundance Film Festival. You want to focus our attention on the fact that you are a hyphenate who is *building* on success in one area to make a tier-jump into another.

There is even more room for variation when it comes to cover letters, because you're never going to send the same one to a casting director that you would send to an agent. I say that like it's a "no duh" type thing, but I've received countless cover letters that say, "Dear Sirs, I am hopeful to be represented by your company." No targeting research there, huh?

A major reason for having several versions of your tools is because— where cover letters are concerned—mass mailings *feel* like mass mailings. We *know* we're being sold to without any consideration for who we are or what we're working on, what level of actors we represent, etc. For casting, it feels general and sometimes desperate, as if the goal is *getting work* not *letting us know how you solve a problem your research shows you we have*. For representation, it feels, well, general and sometimes desperate, as if the goal is *getting representation* not *laying down roots for a mutually-beneficial relationship that will last decades*.

Think about how special you feel when you receive mass mail of any kind. Whether it's a sale circular in snail mail, a restaurant's take-out menu on your door, or email spam, you certainly don't feel like a relationship is being created when you're on the receiving end of these goods. Ours, of course, is a relationship business!

Research Your Recipients

This is another one that seems like a no-brainer, but you'd be amazed how many creatives send out their materials with unfocused cover letters. Hey, I was one of those actors, back in my early LA acting days! I bought the mailing labels and did a mass mailing to every agency in the pack, and that meant my oh-so-clever cover letter detailing my minor market career accomplishments in theatre, industrials, and voiceover would go to agents who only repped writers. Or camera operators. Or athletes. What was I thinking?!?

Researching your recipients takes time, patience, focus, and discipline. And while that's not at all glamorous, the extra touches you're able to add to your materials based on the research you've done will make a huge difference.

Knowing *why* your bullseye might be of value to the recipient of your cover letter is of utmost importance. Explaining to the recipient of your materials exactly how you see a collaboration being a good fit is a ninja move. Because the majority of the packages crossing desks all over this industry will not have such specific focus, yours will stand out—even if your credits are less impressive than you'd like them to be right now. Does this mean you'll start getting meetings like never before? No. A beautiful cover letter alone will not make all the difference. But it will make *a* difference.

Ask Yourself This Question:

"Why does this person need to know I exist right now?" Note: That last bit—"right now"—is specifically important because you may decide, after researching your targets, that the time is *not* right for making contact. The ninja way is all about "lurk then lead." You'll study your targets, you'll observe where the work they're doing aligns with what you hope to do, and you'll check out how they prefer to receive actor contact by watching their interactions in social media or asking smart questions at networking encounters. You'll use your show bible and sometimes map out that the intersection between you and this industry professional makes more sense at the next tier. When that happens, hold on to that chip. Don't cash it in yet. Keep collecting data on your target and choose your moment wisely. That moment will be something beautiful about which to write in your cover letter, *at* that time.

So, back to the question: "Why does this person need to know I exist right now?" If the answer is, "Because he's an agent and agents need actors and I'm an actor," *do not send that submission.* If the answer is, "Because she's a casting director and I need to be cast," *do not send that submission.* If the answer is, "Because this is my dream and everyone needs to know I exist so I can start living it," *do not send that submission.*

Wanting it is not enough. You will not convince someone you're the solution to their storytelling problems because you are determined to make it, this is your life's big dream, you want it more than anyone else. Think like a producer and reframe that drive, that sheer will to succeed, and come up with a position that puts you powerfully, confidently in the business of solving problems, not begging for access.

If you're coming back to me with, "Aw, it's just an email. It doesn't cost me anything. What could it hurt?" please let me remind you that your goal is not to blanket the world with submissions. You are building a brand and hoping to work for a lifetime. That requires way more care and focus and discipline than flinging out ads for random pharmaceuticals.

If you're able to answer the big question with something specific like, "This agent is one I've researched enough to know represents actors one tier above where I currently sit. My research also shows that he has clients who regularly book in my target casting offices. He has no one on his roster of my age, type, and credits level but has a history of having been open to actors with my level of credits. He respects improv training, and I have a ton. I have booked paid work. I can list relationships I've built with personnel in casting offices. When it's not terribly busy, this agent does try to attend industry showcases, and I happen to be in one next month. This person needs to know I exist right now because he can attend the showcase, see my work, decide if I'm a good fit for his roster based on the on-brand, target-specific performance I'll be doing there, and then—if he would like to meet with me—I am ready to discuss my target casting offices in an eloquent way, and—due to my consistent training—my craft is at a level where I could book the room if he were to start sending me out to my target casting offices the next day. Further, if I'm not currently a good fit for his roster, he will at least know what it is that I bullseye, and we can begin to lay the foundation for a relationship that will last for decades, potentially."

Um, hi. That's some ninja specificity!

Brevity Is the...

Shorter is better. No one has ever read a bio or cover letter and thought, "Wow. I sure wish this were *longer.*"

Proof It!

The number-one most essential favor you can do for yourself is proofreading. Better yet, it's having someone else proofread. A bio, a cover letter, anything you're sending out in front of people with whom you hope to collaborate and make tons of money should not be treated as casually as a tweet, a blog post, or a Facebook status update.

It's appalling the number of *intelligent* people out there using the wrong "it's" or "its," using "then" when they mean "than," even creating words like "I's" (*trying* to be proper, saying "Steve and I's new play..." I suppose). *shudder* I remember being shocked to see a bio in which a top exec at one of the most important companies in this industry used the phrase "segue way" (because I guess he didn't know that the word segue is pronounced "seg-way") and it seems strange to me that *no one* mentioned it, despite that bio having been in front of many recipients and certainly a team of assistants over the years.

Even if you're absolutely certain you remember everything from grammar school, there's probably something you've forgotten. I'm sure there's at least one typo in this book, despite the efforts of a team of ninja proofers (tweet me when you find one). Because you could potentially turn off otherwise interested agents, managers, casting directors, producers, directors, writers, showrunners, etc., by writing "use to" instead of "used to" or "should of" instead of "should have" or misspelling the word whoa (it is absolutely NOT spelled woah), I strongly recommend you have others proof your goods before calling your materials "ready" for the world! No, we're not casting you because your grammar is perfect, but the professionalism you convey by catching typos can make a difference in how your brand is perceived.

Preflight Checklist

Visit smfa4.com for a downloadable version of this checklist of *musts* before you start your next marketing blitz. I'll ask that you run your actor marketing goodies through this checklist before letting them out into the world. Remember, these tools you're spending so much time and energy and care and love creating are going to be representatives of *brand you*. Arm them to do a good job by making them strong enough to really do that.

> ➤Feels like me. Sounds like me. Represents *brand me*.
> ➤Highlights where the recipient and I intersect—or should— and how that benefits the recipient.
> ➤Is specific, without getting too dang long. Seriously. Pretend you're Coco Chanel: Lose a sentence.
> ➤Shows where I'm headed more than where I've been, but uses my history as a foundation for the next tier.
> ➤Does not contain any of the following clichés: "from the tender age of," "literally since birth," "born to act," "the stage

was calling," "received glowing reviews," "passion for theatre," "Hollywood beckoned," "to name a few (credits)," "projects *like* (and then a list of credits)," "take my career to new heights," or even, "I'm seeking representation," since—of course—that would be why you're approaching an agent.

➢Isn't cutesy, precious, formal, overly quirky, or anything else that isn't on-brand for *you*.

➢Doesn't use the overused word "quirky" or near-meaningless phrase "girl next door" to describe you.

➢Includes contact information—at the very least, your website's URL, where the reader can go for more information, but hopefully also a phone number.

➢Includes information about where your work can be consumed (an upcoming show, an episode airing on TV next week, regularly at showcases by the improv company with which you train, weekly at an open staged reading jam, online at your YouTube channel).

➢If being emailed, the bio, cover letter—anything that starts out in Word or another word-processing application—was generated using "print to PDF" to retain formatting. Further, the file name is "YourNameBio.pdf" so that its description has value when saved on the recipient's computer.

➢Contains minimal links—ideally *one*—which sends folks to a space you control (your website, a URL you redirect to your IMDb page or Actors Access profile, a page highlighting your latest award win, big news, etc.). Since few folks will actually go all over the web to learn more about you, keeping it simple will help with brand management.

➢Minimizes "the name drop" while still including anything remarkable (an award-winning performance opposite a legend, a hot industry referral).

➢Is written in either first-person or third-person, but not both. All issues of grammar, voice, consistency, capitalization, spelling, and punctuation are consistent and double-checked by another person.

➢Comes from your *why* (passion for storytelling, desire to tier-jump, lifelong goal to succeed, etc.), but doesn't *detail* your why. Instead, it details why aligning with you is a brilliant idea for the reader.

➢Has been read aloud—multiple times—and still feels both on-brand and like something you would absolutely say, verbatim, in a face-to-face encounter.

Gimmicks, Gifts, and Silly Stunts

Do gimmicks work? Work at accomplishing what, exactly? Some people will respond to the unique letterhead choice or an odd-shaped or brightly-colored envelope. Others—whose assistants or interns may open everything and discard such items that make a mailing unique—may never even see the trouble that you've gone to and then the point is moot. Basically, everyone on the receiving end of your mailings is going to have *seen it all* by now. You'll hear the story about the casting director who received a roll of toilet paper with an actor's credits written all through it. You'll hear the tale of the actor who sent a life-sized cardboard cutout of himself to a casting director. You'll hear about the actor who had a tin of custom-made magnets created (those poetry magnet-style sets) using only words that described her. You'll learn about the actor who sent a pigeon to the casting office with instructions to set it free to let it return to the actor for acknowledgement that there was interest.

Actors get drawn in by these wild ideas and decide to try them and they forget the punchline: Stunts don't work! I've heard so many stories about crazy things actors have tried to be "different." It's shocking! Special paper, custom letterhead, or some slightly unusual presentation can be fun, but remember that professionalism is key. Be a pro and we notice that you rock. Clutter up your submission with glittery junk and we wonder what you're trying to hide. Let what rocks about you shine through!

I believe people are basically good. Unless you enable comments.
—Dave Wiskus, designer

15: Your Online Presence

Hey, no surprise here: Everything that exists about you online should be in service of your brand. Everything on sites you control especially should be 100% on-brand, since you choose the fonts, colors, photos, and content of all kind. If you choose to use a template-based website to get started, at least customize the template to get some of your brand's blood flowing through it. There is no *wrong* way to have an online presence. There are only more on-brand and less on-brand ways to present yourself in the web-based arena.

Snatch your domain name even if you have no website at this time. This should cost $8 to $13/yr. for domain registration and around $100/yr. for hosting. Grab (ideally) YourName.com if you can. If you can't score your ideal URL, try YourNameTheActor.com or CastYourName.com or something like CreepyBadGuy.com or TheWackyNeighbor.com before you go to a .tv or .net or .org or .info choice. Register using a PO Box as your primary address or choose domain privacy to protect yourself.

Some services offer free website hosting if you register your URL with them, including one-click WordPress installation, which is great if you choose to use a WordPress-based website. WordPress is easy to keep updated and there are thousands of templates from which to choose when coming up with the starting point for your website. Customizing your template will ensure that your site doesn't look like everyone else's. Again, since you're communicating *brand you* with your site, it *shouldn't* look like anyone else's, right?

Even if you aren't ready to launch a website of your own, you can redirect your registered URL to your IMDb page, your Actors Access profile, or some other page at which your basic info exists, 'til you can get your well-branded site up and running. Owning your own domain name helps reduce off-brand stuff about you that may be out there. When you're at the next tier, a publicist can help push down old credits and clean up any pre-*SMFA* missteps from your web presence. A steady stream of content hosted at your own site is one of the best, cheapest remedies for reputation issues as well as brand management, of course.

As we get into design elements, remember to treat every page on your website as if it's the only page anyone will see. Does it do the job, where brand management is concerned? Does it *feel* like you? Does it provide links to the most important facets of who you are? Does it compel visitors to stick around, rather than to click away?

Have you chosen colors that *feel* like you? Using a site that creates palettes, check your colors (no more than a five-color palette is standard, but even a single color with an accent or two is delightful) and be sure the colors you've chosen sell *brand you* and that they also work well together. Avoid colors that challenge colorblind visitors. If you want to start with your headshot as the basis for the first color you select for your website, there are sites that allow you to upload your photo and discover which colors create the best palette for it. If you want to include photos on your website with text overlays (like, your name or the title of the project from which a still was captured, for example), we have suggestions for sites that do that too at smfa4.com of course.

When it comes to font choice for your website, don't get too funky! There's a *reason* the most frequently-used fonts are straightforward. There are some browsers out there that will turn your very cool, bizarre font into good ol' Times New Roman if the font isn't something those browsers can interpret. One of the best sources for finding fonts that work on almost all browsers, all platforms, with consistency is Google Web Fonts.

Absolute Musts, on Your Website

➢Your contact information (your phone number, a Google Voice number, a way to reach *you*).

➢An HTML and PDF version of your resumé.

➢An embedded demo reel or selection of clips, meticulously labeled.

➢Thumbnails of headshots (but not too many).

➢Your bio.

Only If It's On-Brand, on Your Website

➢A blog or news section (consistently updated).

➢A photo gallery with stills from the set, or photos of you in non-acting situations.

➢A feed of your tweets, Facebook posts, YouTube vids, or Instagram photos.

➢Fantastic reviews of your work.

Be Cautious with These, on Your Website

➢Racy photos that aren't on-brand.

➢Too-personal *anything* (blog entries, photos, overly-political tweets feeding directly into the sidebar, anything that makes you appear higher-risk to the buyers than you may wish to be perceived).

➤Links that take buyers away from your site to see something that you could embed instead (video content, voiceover audio files, photo galleries, your resumé), especially if you send visitors to a place like YouTube or Facebook, where the potential for distraction and for bumping into other potential candidates for the role that made them check out your site in the first place is high.

➤Having too many of *anything* (photos, tabs labeled similarly, vid clips). Keep it simple! A confused mind says *no*. Focus visitors' attention exactly where you want them to look: at whatever it is that makes you most castable.

➤Handing off the controls of your website to another party. Plenty of well-intentioned webmasters may get too busy to keep your site updated (or worse, may hijack your site for additional payments). Your online presence—like your career itself—should remain in your control.

Never Ever, on Your Website

➤A landing page with a "click to enter" button. Visitors meant to come to your site. Don't make anyone confirm that fact *again.*

➤Flash. Even Adobe no longer supports the platform they developed, and many gadgets won't run Flash at all.

➤Auto-playing media files. This is one place where we *do* want to click to start the experience!

➤Ads, survival job-related moneymakers in the sidebar, things that erode our perception of you as a professional actor.

➤Pages that say "under construction." It's okay to have things in development, but go with "coming soon" or "check back by [date]" since *all* of the web is constantly "under construction" by definition.

Best Practices

Test your site on all browsers from both Mac and Windows-based platforms, on mobile devices and gadgets of all types, using Wi-Fi and cellular connections, and with various browser window size settings—which you can do from your own computer, using a "Resize My Browser" tool.

Check for extended load time on long, text-heavy pages or on any page with images. Check from someone else's computer, since the images may be cached at yours, making load time much faster than what a first-time visitor will experience. Resize those images and store old stories on archive pages, to have a lean, fast-loading site.

Your site is all about brand first, and buyers second. Check everything from that perspective and be sure you're good to go, then drive traffic to your site and *enjoy* having that brand manager out there working for you, 24/7.

Give your URL out every chance you get. Put it in your signature file for your outgoing emails. Put it in your cover letters. Put it in your "about me" area of all other websites at which you have memberships. Print it on your business card. Add it to your IMDb page. Print it on your hard copy resumé. List it prominently in social media. When submitting on projects with "notes" open, if you can do so, include your URL along with your comments about how you're right for the project. Drive traffic to your well-branded site!

Web Presence Outside of Your Own Website

Google yourself! Are you findable? If you're not showing up on the first page of results (even when you use quotation marks around your first and last name and then add the word *actor*), get to blogging or vlogging so that your brand starts entering the first page of results, due to your active and consistent presence in places Google loves to index, no matter what algorithm they're using lately.

Similarly, if the first you-related results are not *acting* related (like, your Facebook page or Twitter feed or crafting hobby blog comes up first), your actor-focused efforts need to start taking center stage. They should be the *right* actor-focused efforts, on-brand creations that help the buyers get excited to cast you, clear on exactly what it is you bring to any project.

Do you have too many actor profiles out there? If you were in a minor market in which you needed a profile at legitimate, regional casting submission services but you've moved to Los Angeles and are shifting your brand toward professional actor at the next tier, it may be time to close off those old profiles. Remember, you're trying to focus the buyers' attention on the *one* place you want them to go, not "be everywhere" hoping they'll bump into you. High-powered agents and publicists will kill off their clients' presence outside of IMDb to drive up brand control and mystique. There's a reason for that!

On your Actors Access profile (and any other casting submission profile you determine is beneficial for you to maintain, at any point in your creative career), don't have too many photos or too many clips. Again, you're focusing our attention with your choices. How do you *want* us to cast you? Don't try to be everything; be your most castable self. Label everything meticulously— especially if you're offering up multiple clips featuring the various types of roles you can nail.

Are you using the IMDb *bio* section masterfully? It's more powerful to steer visitors to your website, where you control the brand experience, than it is to use the resumé function of your IMDb page to add credits. Of course, it's fine to do both, but you control context, formatting, font, flavor, and overall experience when you get buyers over to your own website.

Social Media

Do you *have to* have a presence in the world of social networking? Of course not. One of my private coaching clients booked a very big film with an Oscar-winning director and she was lamenting how much she *hates* updating her Facebook page (which had something like 1100 fans). "Kill it off. Kill it off immediately," I told her. First of all, *anything* that makes your face tighten up, that quickens your heart-rate, that makes your stomach turn because of how much you *don't* enjoy doing it—you must immediately stop doing! It cannot be good for your career to "do social networking" because some of your actor friends swear by it. So what if it works for them? That's their brand, those are their buyers, and if you've done the work to get clear on who you are, what you bullseye as an actor, who the target buyers are of that bullseye, and social networking doesn't feel right for you, *having* that presence isn't helping you.

Run everything through the brand filter, be sure your entire online presence helps focus the buyers' attention on you as you wish to be perceived as an artist. Be consistent. Be unapologetic about your decision to *not* be on any particular social networking site. And on those sites you choose to use, be consistent and on-brand, always. That's gonna be defined differently for every actor, of course. Just because you see someone else posting photos from set doesn't mean it's on-brand for you to do so. *Always* run your social sharing choices through the brand filter—and any NDA (non-disclosure agreement) you've signed!

My mother raised me saying, "Treat everything you say as if it'll end up on the front page of the Atlanta Journal-Constitution," and that was her way of saying: Be accountable! Especially when the Internet is forever, choose your words carefully and assume your target buyers will see everything. I have a few really fantastic "good, bad, and ninja" examples of actors using social media to connect with buyers at smfa4.com so please hop over to the site for a little show and tell.

Never confuse "likes" with authentic engagement—comments, sign-ups on your mailing list, building a fanbase of buyers (as evidenced by repeat requests for you to come into their space and show them your work). The latter is far more valuable than a high number of followers who never connect with you. It's the *quality* of the connection that makes a difference in your career, long-haul. If you are *going to* have a social networking profile, be sure to use it meaningfully.

Deadline Hollywood Daily once featured an article on how actors are using the Internet to commit career suicide. I don't see it exactly like that. I remember Jessica Biel trash-talking her show, *7th Heaven*, in a *TV Guide* interview in the mid-'90s and thinking, "Oh! She wants out of her contract. She's trying to rebrand herself. She doesn't want to play 'good, wholesome girl' in network storylines on a Christian-focused show her whole life," and sure enough, that's exactly what she was engineering through that interview. Mission accomplished. Just because the Internet helps it happen faster these days doesn't mean this is new territory. Grabbing the harness on your career trajectory *early* is nothing but a good idea.

Remember, your web presence—your personal website, your social networking accounts, your profiles at casting submission sites, your IMDb page—is your 24/7 brand ambassador. Your web presence is out there working for you *all the time*. Take care to make sure it's doing the job you *want* it to do so you can let it hum along in the background while you hustle out in the real world. Your site doesn't have to be the most technologically-advanced website ever created! It just needs to be professional, simple, effective at making buyers feel as though they're hanging out with you. This is all within your control.

PART FOUR: PEOPLE

Agents are like cell phone service. No one is really happy with theirs and everyone always asks how happy everyone else is with theirs.
—Kelly Wagner, casting director

16: Agents and Managers

This chapter is a biggie. We're gonna take the whole targeting buyers concept to the next level (tracking *their* primary talent providers—AKA the agents and managers), we'll touch on taking the meeting (more on that in the **Working It** chapter), and even get into the "being dumped" element of being represented (it's a reality to face). Nothing here is hard science, but it's a bit of statistical analysis that gets us pretty close to applying a bit of math to this crazy industry. While we'll use episodic television as a means of doing most of the rep targeting research, you absolutely can track films, webseries, commercials, and stage work for the same purpose. Once you've mastered what's covered here, visit smfa4.com for ideas about taking it to the next level.

The Difference Between Agents and Managers

What's the difference between an agent and a manager? Well, according to "E" on *Entourage*, that's simple: "The manager is the one who cares." Of course, that's the joke answer. The serious answer is more complex than that.

In order to get an idea of how agents and managers differ, here's an overview of what managers and agents *do*. Please note that I am referring to talent managers (not business managers) and licensed talent agents (for theatrical and commercial work, typically union), in the generalizations below. While talent managers are big business in Los Angeles, minor markets are only beginning to see managers popping up. But, "as goes LA, so go the minor markets," and that means we can expect to see management complementing and supplementing agency representation more and more, worldwide.

Managers are largely unregulated, but can elect to be members of the Talent Managers' Association—TMA or National Conference of Personal Managers—NCOPM (both of which have specific codes of conduct for members); generally earn 10% to 15% commission on all work you book, regardless of their role in helping you get any particular audition; ask you to sign a three-year contract, as their role is far more long-term and personal than an agent's, and they often work for you for quite some time before seeing any return on their investment in the form of commissions; advise you on your image, headshots, resumé format and content, acting classes, reel, website, personal appearances, and general career direction; make sure you're accurately listed at IMDb, Actors Access, and Casting Networks, and that your membership is current with SAG-AFTRA and AEA; help determine your most marketable type and the projects on which your brand is most likely to find work; help you target appropriate agencies when the time is right; invest a great deal of their time and energy into your *potential* as a working actor before you have a consistent track record of paid bookings.

Agents are state-licensed, are bonded, and either operate under the (currently fractured) union franchise agreement or are members of the ATA— Association of Talent Agents; earn 10% commission on work you book that is a direct result of their submission, pitch, or meeting with the casting director or producer; ask you to sign a one-year contract with a 90-day performance-based out clause; may have input on your headshots, but rarely would want to sit with you and look at all 400 digital proofs from your session; submit, pitch, and hustle to get you in the room with casting directors; negotiate deals when you book the part, including getting you a bigger trailer, better billing, a higher rate quote, paid ads, your name in the opening credits, etc.; work to bring you to the level of "offer only," at which time their team will read scripts on your behalf and recommend your course of action; generally sign you based on your track record as a working actor and may drop you when you can't seem to get a callback on anything anymore.

There is plenty of room for overlap, and even more room for a partnership. Of course, partnerships can be problematic. Many agents and managers work together every day to create the best possible team-based approach to success for their mutual clients. But more than likely, you've heard the horror stories about the agents and managers that refuse to work together, that force the actor to choose sides in an argument, or that flat-out ignore that the other rep exists. It's like having divorced parents. Both still have a stake in your well-being, but they may not necessarily get along. Of course, some families do very well after divorce. Others, not so much.

When You Need a Manager

The axiom goes: "An actor needs a manager when no one wants to cast him and when everyone wants to cast him." I've also heard "at the beginning of his career and when he's at the top." Same difference. Okay, but do I buy that? Somewhat, yes.

At the beginning, you may be an actor who cannot get an agent to sign you. Perhaps you can't even get through the door to meet with an agent on your own. Since agents are in the business of working with actors who already have momentum, it can sometimes be easier to get a manager to take a look at you at the beginning of your career as a professional actor. Now, this doesn't mean you should attempt to get a manager right out of the gate. It means that *after* you've successfully built up your resumé with credits you can get on your own (See: **Become a Booking Machine**) and you've reached the top of that tier, perhaps a manager will sign you and help get you to the next one.

Do you dump your manager once he gets you signed with the "hot agency" you've dreamed of getting? No way! You hang in there for a good year or so, as your manager can help smooth over any kinks in the transition phase or early bumps in the road. Besides, what happens if the new agent drops you right after you've dropped your manager? Oops. Suddenly, the person to whom you've always turned for help in dealing with points of transition in your career is no longer there.

Once you're a household name and you have a staff working for you—personal assistants, trainers, chefs, therapists—the type of manager you may decide you need is a business manager. That's someone who makes sure you've incorporated correctly, your money is invested well, and your "people" are all getting paid. You'll have your publicist on board, and his monthly fee will likely be quite high. Sometimes, actors at this stage choose to leave their agent in favor of an attorney, since that person can both field casting offers *and* handle all of the actor's legal affairs, including endorsement deals, spokesperson offers, licensing the use of your physical likeness, etc. Of course, if you're with one of the "Big 10" agencies, you already have a dozen attorneys on staff for you through their offices.

Great Expectations

Someone asks how old you are. The answer is attached to a certain set of expectations about what should have been accomplished by a person of that age (career benchmarks, marriage, family, home ownership). Someone asks what agency you're with. Based on the answer, there are certain things folks believe you should have accomplished, right? You should be in guest-star land, having left your co-star days behind. You should be earning overscale pay. You should have access to all the casting offices someone repped by a "lesser agency" does not. *Eesh.* Expectations—not so great, are they?

I get that it's handy to attach achievements and goals to certain benchmarks (age, geography, any sort of social status), but just because it's handy doesn't make it healthy. And if I have to choose, I'd always prefer a healthy pursuit in this life than one filled with any sort of pain or struggle. I'd love for us to be kinder to one another by checking our agenda in asking anyone their age, their union status, their representation status, or anything else. "Am I asking how long you've lived in LA because I want to determine how much I should've accomplished by now, based on your answer?" "Am I asking who your agent is because I'm impressed with your recent bookings and want to know which agent has access to such projects?"

You're almost always asking these types of questions so that you can either judge the person with the information or, worse, beat yourself up for being the same age (or older), having as good an agent (or better), or having been in town as long (or longer) and *not* having accomplished what that person accomplished. Instead, take a breath, say, "Wow. Good for you, accomplishing all of that. To what do you credit your success?" You'll be amazed the types of things—unrelated to age, union status, agency representation, geography, or time spent on the journey—that the successful person mentions. Be open to learning like that. It'll go better than you might expect! Landing an agent can be awesome, but it is *not* the key to a blissful career as an actor.

Representation Targeting

Ready to target some agents and managers to help you make your next tier jump? Awesome! Even if you're in a market smaller than Los Angeles, this technique for tracking reps who have direct access to the buyers who need to know you exist will serve you well. Learn it now and use it throughout your career.

First, consider that we're looking at approximately 250 agencies subscribing to Breakdown Services in Los Angeles, and another 700 managers on top of that. When actors say, "Hey, I need an agent. Suggest one," they're failing to acknowledge that matchmaking doesn't work that way. Just like we wouldn't say, "Hey, you're a female and you like males, so here's a male. Get married!" without considering issues of personality type, vibe, age, geography, sexual chemistry, common interests, religion, sense of humor, and a zillion other factors that make up a successful pairing, we cannot say, "You're an actor, that's an agent. Go! Work together," and expect success. Even in a smaller market with fewer reps in the pool, not every option is the right fit for every actor.

Good news! This targeting homework will get you so clear on what you *want* out of representation that you'll know exactly who that "right fit" rep is, when that moment of intersection happens (whether you engineer that intersection or it happens organically). How do we drop breadcrumbs down the path to make that happen? You're going to build on the work you did as a part of the chapters called **Your Bullseye** and **Targeting Buyers** to help map out the best targets for representation.

Remember, you can continue to use these tools for a lifetime in this industry. Use this method to align with the right rep for your very next tier, then use it again when you're looking to leap higher. With very rare exceptions, agents and managers expect you to leave them for "The Bigs," if they are able to help you build beyond their reach. Of course, you'll make any career transition with grace, so there's no unnecessary drama, and you'll always thank those who believed in you *first*, when you're up there holding something gold and shiny.

Many actors ask me, "I just met with *so-and-so* and he wants to represent me. Have you heard anything about him? Is he a good agent?" *thud* Are you *kidding* me? Why would you even take a meeting with someone on whom you've done no preliminary research? Why would you even submit your headshot and resumé to an office you know nothing about? Do you take your career that casually? Sadly, some actors—a lot of actors—do. Not you, of course. You rock.

Instead of tracking which agents and managers *consistently* get clients booked on target projects cast by the "personal shoppers" (casting directors) on behalf of the ultimate "buyers" (producers, directors, showrunners), *most* actors simply buy an agency guide and start blindly mailing headshots and resumés with boring, generic cover letters that start off with, "Hi. My name is *so-and-so* and I'm looking for representation." Please know, no one who opens a headshot and resumé envelope in any office *ever* asks himself, "Hmm. I wonder why this actor has mailed these things to me!"

Don't Lead with Need

There's this gross "lead with need" vibe that happens in this business—I think it's because there are some seedy folks who love the power trip of making actors feel small—and it puts people in positions of authority not because they actually have earned that position but because there's so much fear swirling around actors who are starting out. Heck, even after starting out, you may find yourself feeling desperate to sign with a crappy agent because so many others are frantic to get signed. A clearer sense of how much work exists for you *before* you sign with an agent is a great way to create a healthier mindset about reps. (See: **Become a Booking Machine**.)

Many actors look at agents and managers as a secret weapon that will magically unlock all their dreams when the reality is that a *great* rep (and let's be honest, they're not *all* great) can only help a *great* actor (and let's be honest, there are some *whactors* out there—not you, of course) get into better rooms and then have deals close at better terms. It will always be *your* hustle, *your* relationships, and your work in and out of the room that builds your career the most. That's why your relationship with the person who is representing you is so very important. Sadly, most actors treat it way too casually, signing with agents who've never even seen their work. Think about that! If an agent's goal is to get a CD on the phone, pitching as if his rent money depended on it, he needs to be *crazy* about you. He needs to see dollar signs when he looks at you.

Here's how we use targeting to make that happen. We're going down the IMDb-Pro rabbit hole to really explore the space you need to occupy, as a storyteller. Review those two shows you selected for your target list in the **Targeting Buyers** chapter. Using the "episodes" link for each show, look up every episode from the past season or two. The reason for that is important: Tracking an actor who booked a co-star five years ago will only show you whose agency roster they're on *today*. Maybe they're with that fancy agency now because of a few tier jumps unrelated to this particular booking. Looking at the most current seasons will ensure you are tracking agents and managers who specialize in actors at—or just above—your current tier *and who regularly help populate your target shows* without having to guess whether this is the representative who helped make those bookings happen.

It's the smartest way to approach this totally unscientific process, since there's no data at IMDb-Pro, in terms of representation *history*. (Um, wouldn't that be ninja? If we could see a list of all the agents and managers with whom actors have worked, over the course of their careers? The closest you'll come to this, at present, is through historical data you log in your show bible and watching agents' resumé history at LinkedIn, tracking bookings bragged out via Kabookit, and watching the industry trades like a hawk, since "ankling" is an oft-written-about activity in those rags.)

So, let's go through your target shows' episodes' cast lists to look for the co-stars (if that's your level, guest-stars, if that's your level). At IMDb-Pro, within the show's "episodes" link, you'll see everyone—not just the series regulars, recurring players, and top-of-show guest-stars—for each episode. Assuming you're looking to get a co-star on that show, identify the co-stars. Generally, these are going to be the characters with first names only or job titles as character names (waiter, bike messenger, mom, etc.) and they'll only have been in one episode. Their names were in the closing credits on a shared card, not opening credits on a single card. Ignore those actors whose credits are listed as "uncredited" at IMDb-Pro. You're not targeting uncredited work, are you? No. You're looking for your first co-star booking on this target show.

Next, use the "tabbed browsing" option in your web browser to click through to these actors' pages on IMDb-Pro. Skim their credits. Are they in your neighborhood, except they're booking network co-stars on the shows you need to be on? Otherwise, about the same, in terms of indie film work? Cool. Stick with 'em. (If it looks like this co-star was one in a very long line of guest-stars and series regular gigs and big roles in studio films, instead, close this actor's tab. Stick with actors who are a tier above where you currently sit, basically.) In addition to these actors being around (or just above) your credits-level, hopefully they're around (or just above) your StarMeter ranking. Now, I'm not a fan of living and dying by IMDb's StarMeter. I'm just suggesting you take a look at it, because an agency that specializes in actors with StarMeter rankings of 1 to 5000 when you're somewhere in the 100,000 range is not gonna be a smart starting point.

When you're looking at these actors' profile pages on IMDb-Pro, you'll expand the "contacts" section. Find out who reps these bookers. Oh, and if no one reps 'em, good news! You just found a casting office that is open to seeing unrepped people, probably through generals, workshops, showcases, or files they keep. That data goes in your show bible immediately!

As you poke around IMDb-Pro—noting all this rep data for co-stars on your target shows—you'll start to notice trends. We're loyal critters, casting directors. Especially when we're short on time—when there's been some last-minute rewrite and there's no time to release a new breakdown—we'll go to our favorite agencies and management firms, in search of best-matched actors to the roles we're looking to cast. When you begin to see that your targeted shows consistently book actors (just above your credits level) repped by the same few agencies and management firms (and a disproportionate number of bookings are coming from a few key reps), your target list for representation gets ninja clear.

This is important, so let me say it again: Through this process, you're going to begin to see a pattern of agents and managers who consistently populate shows cast by specific casting offices. That's a sure sign that when there's no time for a breakdown to go out and a casting director needs to cast an episode that's been rewritten, right away, she contacts a handful of agencies and management firms who have at the ready clients who populate those projects, consistently. This is the web of trust at work!

The goal is for you to get in with those agencies because *you* solve a problem they already have, regularly, because they're used to getting that call from that office when there's a last-minute rewrite and if you help them solve the problem one week, that's a commission check for them. Reps are much more likely to want to meet with you when you submit your on-brand materials for consideration, fully displaying your bullseye, which aligns with shows whose casting offices rely on them as suppliers of actors. You've dropped breadcrumbs down the path. All the other actors are submitting without such specificity. Good. Good for *you*.

Once you have a list of agencies and management firms you want to examine closer, you're going to look at these agents' and managers' full rosters. At IMDb-Pro, open each company's client list and sort by StarMeter to see if you "fit" in that neighborhood. Again, you're not going to live and die by the StarMeter, you'll use it as a handy guideline. Just like with real estate, you don't want to be the crappiest house in a nice neighborhood nor the best house in a crappy neighborhood. Also, be sure the agency or management firm doesn't rep *too many* of your exact type. A few? Okay for agencies (not for management firms—unless they're the *big* ones, but you probably shouldn't be shopping in those neighborhoods just yet), and especially if the actors are of your exact type but *older* by a hair, as you can now book the roles they've aged out of, or if they're booking bigger roles, you can swoop in and get their old co-stars.

Feel free to do this targeting homework for as many shows as you like, once you get comfortable with the flow of the research—just know that you'll get an email from IMDb-Pro if you spend many, many, many hours on this project (as some actors certainly can do, because the patterns are fascinating and the information is so empowering) because they'll be sure you're sharing your password with others, since no one person could *possibly* be spending so much time down the rabbit hole. Just reply to them that you're doing Bonnie Gillespie's *SMFA* homework. They know me. They're used to seeing this level of use among *SMFA* ninjas!

As you refine your list, toss out "The Bigs" because, in general, they come get you when they're ready for you. Who are "The Bigs"? So glad you asked! Since this list sees changes more frequently than books get printed, I have your current *SMFA* Hot List of "The Bigs" at smfa4.com. Basically, any of the huge bicoastal agencies with rosters that include full-on, no-doubt-about-it, 100% celebrities are generally not looking to sign "developmental" clients, even though occasionally you'll hear about an actor getting "tapped" by one of "the bigs" early in his career. Good for him. And good for you, when you get tapped. But 'til that happens, your targeting work is better spent a tier or two below these guys. There are plenty of ridiculously fantastic agencies out there—and some dogs, of course—so keep tabs on everyone for your show bible, but don't bother submitting to "The Bigs" when you're still trying to conquer the co-star or guest-star tier.

You don't want someone to sign you just so you can be shelved internally to remove competition from their top-booking client of the exact same type. (The agents may see you as chum in the water for their high-earning shark, so they'll remove you from the ocean altogether by "signing and shelving" you.) But looking for companies whose actor of your type has *just* aged out of your roles is ninja. They're gonna be looking for someone your age to pick up that slack. Keep in mind that there could be clients represented by an agency that don't yet have IMDb pages, so add to the number of clients you're seeing on the roster, especially if most of the clients that agency does have are low on credits and near 1M in StarMeter ranking. Is theirs a good agent-to-client ratio or does this agency rep so many actors that the company is clearly playing a numbers game?

What numbers are good numbers? In general, it's 20 actors per manager, 100 actors per theatrical agent, and 250 actors per commercial agent. If you're looking at an agent with hundreds of clients repped theatrically, please know you may be seeing a spaghetti slinger. And when you track web of trust between agents like that and your target casting directors, you're not seeing *hell yes* rep (more on that, below), you're seeing bookings that happen for the same reason that a broken clock is right twice a day. They're playing a numbers game. You don't want to be a number.

Note whether the representation you're tracking through this process is commercial representation (or hosting or voiceover or personal appearance, etc.), because tracking *theatrical* representation—also known as "legit" or "on-camera" in various markets—is where the power is, for a self-managing actor. In markets like Los Angeles, you will potentially have different agents for commercial and theatrical representation. This will be *exclusive* representation for the market. In minor markets, it's common practice to sign with multiple agencies for the same coverage in the same market. This tends to require a gear-shift for actors who move to LA: You're used to paying commission to the agent who got you in first and not paying commission for gigs you got yourself. In the Super Bowl of Acting, you'll pay commission on pretty much everything you book, as you've chosen a single business partner or a rockstar team.

When you're not down the IMDb-Pro rabbit hole, peruse the sign-in sheets at the auditions you get. What agencies are listed by the names of the other actors coming in for the projects? If you're at a commercial facility with a lot of auditions going on at once, do a lap around the waiting area to quickly skim all of the sign-in sheets and get an idea of which agents have actors out there, daily. This, of course, doesn't indicate how many submissions are being made, but it does give you an idea of whose actors different casting directors are bringing in.

Back to IMDb-Pro, once you've done your homework for several episodes of your *top* target shows, you'll have a good idea of which agencies are regularly servicing the casting offices *you* need to be in. That's your list of target agents for this next tier of your career. Using this technique, you'll refine your list over time and learn which companies are out of reach and which are below where you want to be. This takes time—and research of course—but it's totally worth it because when you *do* meet with an agent on your meticulously-researched target list, you know you are potentially helping *them* and the meeting becomes much more relaxed and happy than when you are needy and not sure whether you're the solution to their problems.

Data Tracking

Your next mission is to create Google Alerts on all of the people whose names you've listed in this process. You'll start having data come to your inbox about the reps who need to know you exist. Revisit the chapter on **Your Show Bible** to be sure you're tracking every bit of information about these targets that could possibly help you understand where your brand best aligns. Every chance to get information that gives you an edge, *take it*.

As you continue to build up credits, training, and on-brand reel footage that showcases the fact that you're meant to be in the offices of those target casting directors with whom your target agents and managers have verifiable relationships, this information will keep filling in your show bible. You will not strike until you see things lining up beautifully—hopefully with a really wonderful referral that helps make it happen—because it's not about *rushing* to grab a meeting before it's time for you to close the deal. Your goal is to have your goodies come across their desk when the timing is right for you to get signed and start making money with your new team immediately!

Once you're nearing that time, you'll begin to put together a submission package so stellar it can't help but grab their attention. That's not because you do anything gimmicky! It's because you're confident in showcasing your bullseye in a way that shows reps that you solve a problem one of the casting directors that is verifiably within their web of trust has regularly. They'll be so quick to say, "Wow! I know a casting office that would *love* to know you exist," and you'll be filled with grace when they say that, during your meeting with them. You'll never let on that you reverse-engineered this whole thing, you ninja badass! Let it be *their* brilliant idea and then be ready to rock it out when you get that first shot in the room you've been targeting all along.

Referrals

Referrals can range from valuable to useless in your submission process. An actor friend of mine was talking about a referral she had been offered by a guy who comes into the restaurant where her survival job takes place. This guy was seated with a group of other suits when he called my friend over and proceeded to talk about how she needed to call *so-and-so*, the personal assistant to *big-name-producer*. After going on and on about it, he gave her a phone number and made her promise in front of his group of friends that she would call *so-and-so* so that she could get set up with *big-name-producer* and have a report to share, the next time he visited her restaurant.

This is what Nancy Wolfson calls the "hero of the moment." It's an epidemic in Hollywood. Someone wants to be cock of the walk, to be some big player, to show off how much power he has (almost always in front of others), and to enjoy the thrill of making you feel as though you've been given a hand in a business that sometimes feels all about connections. It may be as simple as, "Oh! You have a meeting with that power agent? Cool! Tell him I said hi," or as convoluted as the giving out of contact information, coupled with encouragement that you reach out and drop the hero of the moment's name.

Here's how you know for sure you're dealing with a hero of the moment: If the promise is made—"Oh! I have a friend in casting who will do a general with you. I'll make a call"—and the call never happens, that was a hero of the moment who made the promise. If you hear, "Oh! You should be with my friend the agent. I'll give you a referral," and you never get a meeting, that absolutely could've been a hero of the moment in action (or a well-intentioned gesture from someone who has zero pull with the agent in question).

Because a *true* referral, a *true* favor, a *true* offer from a *real* hero goes more like this: "Oh! I have a friend in casting who will do a general with you. Let me shoot her an email *right now*. I'll give her your contact information. Call me in a week if it hasn't happened and I'll give her a nudge." Or, "Oh! You should be with my friend the agent. I'll give you a referral. When you submit your package to the office, include my name in your cover letter. Then shoot me an email to let me know you've sent the package over. I'll fire off a quick email to let him know to be on the lookout for your materials," and then you *do* your part and are CC'd on the email that the *real* hero sends to the agent, after your package is on its way. See the difference?

I'm not suggesting you assume everyone who offers a connection is playing the hero of the moment game, but I am hopeful that you'll recognize when someone isn't truly offering a favor. When that happens, invite them to make it real (to do the connecting *for you* rather than just passing off a number; to explain what it is they hope will come from the connection rather than keeping it vague). If they balk, you know they weren't offering anything of substance from the beginning. Good to know! Now, let it go.

Rank 'Em

After you've come up with a list of about 20 agents and managers (with any of whom you'd happily sign, if offered a good contract), you now know to whom you'll submit (and hopefully meet). The next step is ranking them. You rank these agents and managers so that if two companies offer you representation—*Yay, you!*—you'll know which one is the better match. It's important to have these rankings done before you begin taking the meetings, as your data combined with the vibe you get when you're in the office will be important. The time to decide which of two equally enthusiastic agents is the better agent for you is not in the heat of the moment and excitement over being offered two contracts when a week ago you couldn't get seen.

When I work with private coaching clients, I can show them how their target reps submit their clients on my casting projects and whether they're spaghetti slingers or very selective, thoughtful pitchers. To see where you'd fit in with your future home is incredibly powerful, as you're creating your rankings. Promise me you'll create those rankings with detached professionalism, okay?

It's very easy to get swept up in fits of glee over someone *wanting to sign you* and lose sight of which agent or manager is going to be the better one for your long-term career needs.

Get Your Mind Right

You will transition up and up and up, right? Wouldn't you rather learn *now* the discipline it takes to know your buyers and attract them at *any level* you may reach at any time, so you can use that muscle as you level up over time? Of course you would.

You're going to see a lot of other actors running around doing busy work, sending off mass mailings, slinging spaghetti and hoping something sticks so that they can have an agent—any agent—because they so fear that they will not get opportunities otherwise. Let them do that crazymaking dance that rarely leads to a meaningful relationship with a representative. You? You're going for a *hell yes*, rather than a *ho-hum*.

When you have the choice between an agent about whom you're ho-hum or an agent about whom you're hell yes, which will you choose? More importantly, when you have the choice between an agent who is ho-hum or hell yes about *you*, which will you choose?

So many actors get into the mindset of, "I've gotta get an agent" that they miss the point that a ho-hum agent (in either direction) is basically useless. Just like a ho-hum meeting with a casting director, a director, a producer, a showrunner, a writer, anyone in a position to eventually cast that actor is a waste of time.

That doesn't mean those encounters don't happen, daily. They do. And that's because actors tend to operate from a place of lack, a place of need. They believe it's better to meet with *someone* (regardless of enthusiasm level) than to spend that same time hustling, researching, working toward a better long-term approach to success in this business.

Imagine, if you've gone to the trouble to meet with a ho-hum rep then to sign with a ho-hum rep (and then—at best—get submitted by that ho-hum rep with a ho-hum attitude, from time to time), you're then living at a ho-hum *level*. Worst of all, you've tied yourself up at the ho-hum level when you could've left yourself open for a *hell yes*, and isn't that better? Isn't that what you'd prefer? Isn't that what the buyers you'll eventually meet would prefer? Hell yes!

Commercial vs. Theatrical Representation

Some agencies are strictly commercial. Others (very few) are exclusively theatrical (film and episodic television). Most are full-service agencies, meaning they represent talent commercially and theatrically—and perhaps also represent writers, directors, and producers. What happens if you are offered representation in one department and not the other? What happens if you only want to sign with an agency "across the board," but that isn't the offer you've been given?

Should you sign commercially when you aren't offered across-the-board representation? Well, there *is* a way to make that situation work for you. A friend of mine who was represented commercially only at a full-service agency was tired of getting all his own TV and film auditions and having his commercial agent tell him there was just no way to get him sent out on theatrical jobs "at his level" through their agency.

He put together his two-look postcards and sent one—with a personal note based on his show bible data—to each of his targeted feature film and TV episodic casting directors, providing his commercial agent's contact information only. The agent started getting calls from theatrical casting directors, ready to see him for this role and that role. The agent called my buddy and said, "Well, you've got guts, going around me, but you got yourself some work and kept me in on it, so, we'll sign you across-the-board." Ninja!

Taking the Meeting

After you've done all your targeting homework, scored meaningful referrals, submitted your on-brand materials, and scored meetings, it's time to celebrate! When you meet with your potential agent or manager, it's important to tour the space and learn who does what for whom. If you're going to be repped across-the-board, who is your contact for commercial negotiations? What about print jobs? Promotional appearances? Are you covered there? These are all questions to ask before signing. It's best to know everyone right up front so that when you get the call for an audition from someone other than your main agent, you at least have an idea who you're dealing with.

Is everyone reachable? Can you get through to your agent or manager or are you assigned to intern-only status when you call? Is everything channeled through one point person? What happens if that agent leaves the company? Do you go with him or suddenly lose your point person at the agency? Get these questions answered up front. What if the agency only wants to sign you commercially or what if the manager refuses to work with the agent you're considering? What if no one sees you playing the roles your research shows are *made* for you? What if the agent wants you to work off the card or go FiCore? What if they won't sign you but are willing to hip-pocket you? Are you okay with such a loose commitment? (That's like getting engaged to sleep around.)

Be prepared to do a cold read, as some agents will hand you sides right there in the office. Often, it will be commercial copy you're given (obviously, if this is the theatrical department of an agency you're meeting with, that's not as likely to happen), so you should prep for doing commercial cold reads by transcribing existing ads and rehearsing at home. Very few agents and managers ask actors to do monologues in the office these days, but you should always have one or two ready, just in case. If you sing, have your 16 bars ready!

Whether or not you end up signing on with the agent or manager, once you're in the room having a meeting you should take advantage of the opportunity to learn how they see your type, how they would market you, what types of roles for which they'd submit you. This can inform your self-management tactics from here on out, regardless of what happens! Remember that the *best* part of having an agent or manager on your team is the fact that his belief in your abilities, the risk he takes, that passion with which he is willing to help get you through the door elevates your career to the next tier. Bottom line: If an agent or manager doesn't *get* you, how well will he pitch you?

Some agencies in minor markets charge "admin fees" for copies, FedEx expenses, long distance phone calls, messenger services, subscription to Breakdown Services, etc. This is appalling! Think about it: What incentive does an agent or manager have to hustle, pitch you, or help you get through the door if he is already being paid a monthly amount just for *having* you on the roster? The more actors on the roster, the less actual work required, on the part of the agent or manager. A roster of 100 actors each paying a monthly $20 admin fee yields $24,000 per year before the agent or manager picks up the phone on behalf of a single client. Yikes! What is the value of such rep, if your monthly payment—not your talent—is the criteria for getting on the roster?

Does your potential agent or manager leave town to scout? Be concerned with an agent's frequent trips to scout new talent for a couple of reasons. One, the agent is out looking for more people to add to the roster and you are considering signing with the agent based on several factors, one of which is the number of actors on his roster. Two, if an agent or manager is "doing the circuit" and earning a healthy honorarium with each trip to "scout," where is this person's incentive to hustle for you as a client? Since agents and managers earn money only on a commission basis with their current clients, any *major* source of income outside of those commissions becomes a little suspicious. That includes going on scouting trips, teaching classes, running a headshot photography referral service, charging for having a profile up on their company's website, getting you into red carpet events, and other such "advance fee" territory issues (illegal in the State of California).

If you're leaving an existing agency or management relationship, be prepared to talk about why you feel that partnership is ending, but don't be gossipy! Be articulate and accurate, but not at all negative. This is a very small town and you plan to be a part of its population for many years. To that end, if you are taking meetings with several agents over a few weeks, it is absolutely fine to mention that fact (but you don't need to reveal which agents, in particular). Assuming you are offered a contract at the end of your meeting, ask if you may take it with you and make your decision after speaking with your manager, your acting coach, your attorney, or a union rep. Is the contract union-approved? A widely-accepted GSA (General Service Agreement)?

If we're talking about a manager, is it a TMA or NCOPM contract of record? Is there an "out" clause? How much notice must be given before the contract is considered terminated? Are commissions due long after termination? What exactly is commissionable? What is the commission percentage? How soon after the gig should you expect a check (minus commissions)? Is your image commissionable, should a character you portray be turned into an action figure? This is important! You may only be thinking about how you're up to be the next big star of an action franchise, but somewhere down the line, there's a stocking stuffer crafted in your image, and your reps may be entitled to commission on that sucker forever.

Of course, no one wants to enter an agreement thinking about how it will end. That's the same reason young lovers get engaged and are appalled at the idea of signing a prenuptial agreement. Get over that. This is business. Absolutely, you expect that you will be in a blissful partnership forever, but you *must* protect your business interests. The good news is, if the relationship never goes bad, it was all protection put in place for "no reason." The *better* news is, if the relationship goes bad, you are protected! No one can fault you for building details into your initial contract.

Timing for Targeting

During pilot season (loosely defined as the period of time from late January to early April—when actors are auditioning for and shooting pilots in anticipation of the fall TV season), agents and managers are focused on serving their current clients. April is the go-ahead time for rep submissions as agents are cleaning house of actors who were duds during pilot season or who have different needs than when initially signed. After drop notices start going out, agents and managers will meet with new talent. By mid-July, agents and managers are generally set with their adjusted roster. They'll be moving forward with getting actors in front of casting directors for the many series shooting for the new fall season. This is episodic season.

Another good time to seek representation—though it's a smaller window—is from late October to mid-December. Agents are then looking for fresh faces to present during pilot season, after having dropped episodic season's non-bookers. There will be little time to sign anyone in late December or early January, as vacations are at a premium from mid-December through the start of awards season and the film festival rush in January. Once everyone is back to Los Angeles in late January, well, we're back into pilot season again.

Don't let these drop windows restrict you. Agents have been known to sign new actors to their rosters in pilot season; it's just not as likely, if you're looking at the odds. Heck, I signed with my first LA agent over Thanksgiving dinner, at a non-industry mutual friend's home! You just *never* know. Whatever you do, don't put a timeline on this important bit of relationship-building. Saying, "I'm gonna sign with an agent in X weeks" is like saying, "I'm gonna get married in X weeks" when you're not even dating anyone. Find the *right* one, in *whatever* amount of time it takes.

What to Expect from Your New Relationship

Here's the basic guideline: You're only going to get a few more appointments with new agency representation than you were getting before you signed with this new agent. "A few" can be defined by anywhere from 3 to 300 more appointments. I know that's not terribly helpful, and the reason the range is so very broad is because, *for some people*, signing with a new agent really can light a fire under a stalled career. Most actors, however, will get out just about as often as they ever did, after signing with a new agent.

Agents usually help with bumps in quote, upping your billing, or getting you seen in offices that otherwise have been closed to you. Your number of bookings shouldn't be looked at in an agent vs. actor frame of mind. If you regularly book (or get callbacks), you're doing everything right. It's only *not* getting into the room at all that should have you wondering whether your agent is doing his job.

If you have so much free time that you are constantly lamenting the fact that you do not have an agent, trust me when I say that you will use that same free time to lament the fact that your agent is doing nothing for you, once you get one. *It is up to you* to drive your career forward. Once you're standing on the threshold of doors only an agent can get you through, there will be an agent eager to sign you. Then you'll be on to the next tier of your showbiz career.

Transitions in Representation

If you have an agent, but they're not getting you out, you don't have an agent.

—Joe Lambie, actor

There will come a time when you will face a transition in representation. Your reps will drop you. You'll fire your reps. You'll upgrade. You'll shift to a smaller, more hands-on firm. Whatever. It's gonna happen. The likelihood that your very first manager or agent will be with you for your entire career is low.

Of course, saying goodbye to an agent or manager who helped get you to this point in your career is never easy. Assuming your relationship has thus far been positive, an agent or manager who knows that he doesn't have the powerful connections to help launch your career to the next level should understand that you need to move on. Some agents will even help you transition to "The Bigs." But since most representatives would prefer that you, in your poised-for-major-success position, help *them* reach another tier of relationships by being their "calling card" for bigger casting directors, it's more likely that this decision will be met with significant disappointment. Be prepared for this. Take good care of those who have taken such good care of you, back when you were having a tough time even getting in front of casting directors. And, know that everyone loves a "thank you," come acceptance speech time.

Many actors feel as though their agent deserves a pink slip when they're not getting out enough. Depending on where you are in your career (just starting out, only recently joined the union, working regularly as a co-star, beginning to get guest-star roles on TV and going out for leads in feature films, appearing as a recurring character or series regular and hoping to have your own movie produced at a major studio), the level of importance of "getting out" for auditions varies. At some levels of your career, you will book work without having auditioned at all, or by going straight to producer callbacks. So, the fact that your number of prereads drops could have nothing to do with your agent and everything to do with where you are in your career.

What if your rate quote is not improving? What if your billing has remained the same on the last few projects you've booked, despite an increase in the size of the roles and the buzz for your appearances? These are certainly decent reasons to consider dismissing an agent, but they're probably even better reasons to have a face-to-face with your agent about goals, priorities, and a timeline for achieving the prioritized goals.

Remember, your agent or manager is your employee. So, just as you would meet with an employee of yours in any other business in order to strategize better job performance, you should do that with your agent or manager and then provide a timeline for assessing progress, specifying as many benchmarks for success as possible.

If that restructuring meeting yields no positive outcome, be sure you're ready to fire your agent and that the relationship is irretrievably broken. Make sure you've made a thorough list and have information to back up your claims of what's not working (dates, logs of phone conversations on specific issues). If you've kept a record of what's unsatisfactory about the relationship (saved emails, notes, lists of attempts you've made to address the issues), have that well-organized and handy, in case you need to consult it during the "breakup."

A certain amount of advance notice of termination may be required by the contract you signed. With management contracts, there is often no termination clause. That means you're bound by the term of the contract (usually three years) and even if you are dissatisfied, you cannot break the contract, but instead must wait until you're approaching the end of the contract term and, in writing, request that the contract not be renewed. Make sure you've reviewed your existing contract before you broach the subject of ending it.

Make a list of your projects that are in flux and know which deals may close after you fire your agent or manager. Also make sure you know what is commissionable, both from previously-booked work and those last few deals that may come through. Be sure to discuss the issue of your soon-to-be-ex-agent acting as the "agent of record" for any deals that are closed within the period for which you're giving notice. Generally, any gig you booked under the old agent is commissionable by that same agent. Be sure, though, to write up terms that are more specific than that (addressing issues such as future residuals on projects that were booked through that agent, future DVD or foreign market sales of feature films in which you starred, spin-off rights, etc.).

Ask for copies of any existing contracts. These can be sent over to your new agent or, if you have a manager, the manager should have been CC'd on each of these contracts as they closed. Either way, it won't hurt for you to have copies of these contracts for your own reference.

When you've fired an agent, follow up with a letter to the unions. They will need to adjust their records and, whenever they collect payments for you, send the checks on to your new agency. If you are working a regular acting job, you may also wish to speak with the payroll department to remove any check authorization that was in place with the old agency. Redirect your payments either to your new agent or to yourself. Also take the time to notify the online services that house your headshot and resumé, IMDb, and your webmaster so that your proper contact information is on your website as well.

Should you choose to fire your agent in writing, definitely use the US Postal Service and get delivery confirmation for your letter. That way, even if your agent provides no acknowledgment of the split, you have proof that the termination letter was received. Keep any written reply from the agent in case any issues creep in and you need proof that the relationship is over in your ex-agent's eyes.

Email is okay if you have the type of relationship with your agent that dictates such communication. Meaning, if your agent informs you about auditions via email and you reply with confirmation of audition appointment times via email (and email is your primary mode of communication in both directions), you could justify firing your agent via email. I would still suggest following up with an old-fashioned letter. Another option would be firing the agent in person or on the phone and then following up with an email that spells everything out, just as backup.

If you choose to fire your agent in person, be sure to select the best location for such a conversation. Steer clear of meeting at the agent's office unless you're hoping to be wooed back into the relationship. Their home turf isn't the best place to end things. They have tools to make you change your mind right there at their fingertips ("Oh, look at this breakdown! I was just pitching you for this project!" "I know it's been slow, but we just hired a new office manager and that's going to really help us focus more of our energy on your career. Here, come meet him!" "Do you see the bins of headshots from actors who *want* to be signed by us? Are you an idiot?!?") and they will use them! The Coffee Bean may be a favorite meeting place, but if it's busy and the firing gets emotional, you could find yourself in that hellish lunchtime firing scene from *Jerry Maguire*.

Be professional. You are ending a relationship for career-centered reasons and that should be the focus of the conversation. Even if you have personal problems with the agent, leave those issues out of this talk. This isn't personal. It's a business decision and by the time you're firing your agent, the decision has already been made. There shouldn't be room for negotiation. Get right to the point, stay focused, and thank the agent or manager for all of the hard work he has done on your behalf.

Let me stress the importance of your mindset, throughout this whole process. Remember that this won't be the only agent you fire, and you aren't the first actor who has ever fired this agent. Don't let anyone try to make you feel as though that's the case.

One of the tactics your soon-to-be-ex-rep may use in an attempt to keep you from jumping ship (or in a petty reaction to the ego blow) is making the firing personal when we all know it's a business decision. Whatever you do, don't go there with him. You take the high road and keep your dignity intact. When you find yourself being "hit below the belt" by someone who is upset he's just been fired, imagine this person being on the phone with a casting director and behaving so badly. You *know* this type of thing can't be good for your career. Be glad to know you made the right decision. His poor response to your letting him go is proof that he's not the type of person you want on your team.

When Your Reps Drop You

The first order of business is accepting that being dumped, being cut out of the final project, not being cast after having been told you were *the best* actor at the audition, losing a connection with someone you were sure would be with you through the good times and bad is simply a part of life in this industry. Accept that it's going to happen, soak it all in, and move on quickly. Speed of recovery from painful life experiences is what we're looking for, not the absence of pain.

One of the things that keeps us stuck in emotional pain of any kind is the need to remain in the moment for longer than that moment itself. It's like we believe, by staying in pain, we're honoring the experience and justifying our emotion over it in the first place. One of the best gifts you can give yourself—as someone who has been hurt by another person—is *moving on*. One of my favorite quotes comes from Cindy Clabough: "Resentment is like drinking poison and waiting for the other person to die." Right on. Sure, feel the feelings, but move on. You're not getting over it any sooner by holding on. Get in the habit of saying, "Wow. That wasn't fun. Oh well. *Next!*"

Interpret this "bad news" as something similar to a gardener pruning back a healthy plant. It's only gonna grow stronger because of this cut. What comes next has way more potential for greatness, since there's not so much clutter through which to thrive.

I have an actor friend who makes a deal with himself, when bad news comes around. He gives himself exactly 24 hours to wallow in it. He acknowledges that there are negative feelings bubbling up over the experience, and he allows them to happen, but only for a day. A day later, if he's still grousing about the drop, if he's still mourning the released avail, if he's still mulling over what he could've done differently to keep this whole big, bad thing from happening, his friends have the right to smack him. His accountability partners will tell him to "man up." His acting coach reminds him of the deal he has made with himself. The time for sorrow is over. Now it's time to take action toward the next tier.

Never take it personally, even if it is personal (but usually, it's not personal, even when it *feels* personal). You have to learn how to not take business personally, lest you wish to lose valuable energy and mental stability over it.

Another of my favorite quotes is from Deepak Chopra: "Energy is currency. How do you wish to spend it?" When I first heard that, I visualized every thought I "spent" on an issue as money flowing out of my hands. Believe me, I was very quick to change my "energy flow" after imagining a literal expense with each resentful thought. And truly, an expense of mindset and emotions is more steep a cost than money any day.

Cultivate a business model that includes gratitude and grace. In the end, you are the one who is responsible for the "face" you put on your business. No matter what you experience, the grace with which you handle it becomes what people remember about you. If you can shift your perspective from how to endure the struggle to how you want to be thought of, in the long term, you'll usually make the more grace-filled choice. Gratitude complements grace quite nicely, as your willingness to be grateful for all of the good that came from a relationship, prior to the "dump," is important. In a few weeks, months, or years, no one will even remember this particular break. What they will remember is how you handled yourself when you wanted to rail against someone for doing you wrong. If you stay grateful for all that they did while you were on the same team, you'll come off looking much better. And *that's* a castable vibe!

If I had known how popular going into casting would make me, I would've done it in high school.

—Bonnie Gillespie

17: THE CASTING OFFICE

Before I break down the folks you'll encounter in casting offices, let me first give a strong recommendation that you volunteer your services as an intern. Many actors find that working in a casting office is not only a nice inroad to building relationships but also an amazing learning experience. The demystifying of submissions and sessions alone will up your game. Plus, the only way to really understand the hectic nature of a casting office is to spend time in one. There are several ways to do that—and, hey, some of these experiences have led actors to change careers and go into casting.

Getting in good with any busy casting director is a good thing. While no one would advise you to become a reader, intern, or assistant with the goal of getting seen as an actor, most everyone would recommend that you have one of those experiences—even if you just volunteer one week of your services to a casting director friend of yours.

Remember—whether it's for a week or for one day a week for a year—you are there as an intern. Do *that* job. Let your professionalism shine through and wait until your internship is over to assert yourself as an actor. Use this opportunity to learn and trust that—if the casting director really has exhausted all of her options—she absolutely will look to you as an actor. Don't push the timing on that. We have long memories and we will remember you when we need your type in the future. Trust that!

Has it happened that a reader or intern or assistant just happened to be perfect for a role a casting director was casting and got pulled across the line? Sure. Does it happen often? Nope. And if you go in thinking it might happen, you're missing out on what is really the best part of working in a casting office: learning.

How should you approach a casting director about interning, reading, or assisting? If you have good relationships with casting directors, ask us to recommend you to other casting directors who may need in-office help. If you aren't "in" with many casting directors already, then send a non-acting resumé and cover letter to a casting director, announcing your intention to help us. Don't play up the fact that you're also an actor. That won't help you convince us you don't have ulterior motives. But don't lie, either. We'll know.

The Casting Crew

Interns—While some casting directors hold permanent office space, others hop around to various offices. Therefore, a key intern at a particular facility will get the opportunity to work with many busy casting directors. If you intern for one specific casting director, you may get college credit for the term of your internship or just volunteer your time for the experience of learning casting from the inside. At major studios, indie interns are rare, as almost all interns come from college programs and receive academic credit for their work. Interns mostly sort mail, open envelopes, and copy sides. Regardless of the office, interns are generally not in the room during sessions.

Readers—Most casting directors employ readers, others read with actors themselves. A good reader is someone who has acting skills, but who has no perceived interest in booking a role through that casting director's office at that time. A great reader will know how to give and take and play with other actors without ever outshining the auditioning actors. To become a reader, you'll probably have to work as an intern to establish your reliability, personality, and professionalism, and then get invited to read with actors on occasion.

Assistants—Casting assistants will do everything from covering phones to making copies, from writing breakdowns to opening mail, from signing in actors to reading with them during auditions, from operating cameras to analyzing contracts. The range is pretty broad from casting office to casting office. Assistants are paid (not a lot) and generally hope to move up to casting associate rapidly by showing off their professionalism and responsibility.

Associates—Casting associates typically field agency pitch calls, perform session runner duties, run preread sessions, draft offers, and help casting directors prep deal memos and contracts for the actors who end up being cast. Many associates take side gigs casting grad students' thesis films, low-budget webseries, or small indie films as they build up their relationships, planning to eventually move into the role of casting director. Casting associates tend to have a decent amount of input on the casting process, although this varies from office to office. When actors are creating their own content, I strongly recommend you contact a casting associate about coming on as a casting director. You'll reap the rewards of the casting associate's relationships with talent reps and bring in a higher tier of actors for auditions, due to the legitimacy that a casting director adds to an indie project from a first-time director.

Casting Directors—The casting director is either solo or in partnership and will make offers to name actors' representatives, cast small roles on her own, and bring top choices to producers on every role in between. Most casting directors work freelance and go from gig to gig. A few will be on contract at studios or networks in more of a supervisory role to the CDs who work on a project-by-project basis. You'll often hear casting directors correct people who call us "casting agents." Here's why: There's legal weight to the word "agent" in California (and in other states). There's state licensing, fingerprinting, and bonding to become an agent, which makes the person legally allowed to negotiate deals on another party's behalf. Since casting directors don't have that level of responsibility (even though we do initiate the negotiation process with talent agents before passing off the deals to the production attorneys to finalize them), the title—just like in real estate—creates a burden where one doesn't exist, legally.

Some casting directors are members of the Casting Society of America (CSA). The CSA is a labor union that evolved out of a professional organization and it's a branch of the Teamsters. Some casting directors who specialize in commercials are members of the Commercial Casting Directors Association (CCDA). Both organizations offer benefits to their members ranging from minimum salaries to health care to performance-based awards. Neither is a required membership for a casting director to have in order to work in the industry at a professional level.

Casting is a relatively new profession in our beloved industry. It evolved out of the holding area for actors back in the days of the studio system. All the contract players would sit in holding and wait for the call to come in that it was time for each of them to head to set. The secretary who sat at the ready, manning the list of actors in holding, would take the call from the set, see whose name was next on the list, and send that actor up for his close-up. One day, one of those ladies—yes, this is why casting evolved as a female-dominated sector of show business—looked at the list and instead of sending up the next actor on the list, looked around the room and chose the actor who was a better fit for what the director had asked for, on the set. Casting was born.

Risk Assessment

One of the casting director's primary duties is assessing risk on behalf of producers. Yes, we have this really cool job that involves reading a script, making a list of actors who are best-matched for each role (and that list includes our "wildest dreams" cast and goes all the way down to the new kid in town who sent in a headshot last week that just happened to click for some reason), putting out a breakdown, receiving pitches and submissions, scheduling auditions, weeding through to the final callback level, and then excitedly making offers to the actors the producers choose to cast (followed by the painstaking process of finalizing contract points that cover sometimes obnoxiously minute details, right down to the fraction of the butt cheek we'll see in that one not-quite-nude scene). Truly, our job is about risk assessment. Producers hire casting directors not only to help them find the best-matched actor for each role creatively but also to help them predict the level of risk involved in each casting decision.

We're going to look at your resumé to get an idea of the work you've done in the past, your training, and your special skills, of course. It's the *work you've done* that is going to be most successful in helping us assess risk. If we are casting a film with a lot of green screen special effects and there's work on your reel that shows us you worked extensively with green screen technology, you're a lower risk than someone who hasn't done any green screen work. Casting directors working on multi-camera, live-audience sitcoms are looking for multi-camera, live-audience sitcom work. Does a class in this stuff count? It's not bad, but it's not as good as *experience*. Our risk is lower if someone else has already hired you to do what we're looking to hire you to do.

If you have only ever worked at the co-star level on episodic television, getting that first top-of-show guest-star role is going to be tough. The producer who hires you to do that gig is taking a bigger risk on you than the *next* producer who hires you to do that. If you've never been the lead in a feature film, the first filmmaker to cast you in a leading role will help with your future risk assessment for roles of that size.

When you enter the room for an audition, the casting director is assessing the risk involved in casting you based on how performance-ready you are. Do you appear to need a lot of direction? Are you coming off as high-maintenance? Or did you show up ready to rock? If we're casting a film with a very tight shooting schedule and we've been told that there will be no time for rehearsal, it's going to be important that you show us at your audition that you've already done all of the rehearsing you're going to need to do for this project.

How do you come off in public? Yeah, you may think you're below the tabloid radar and paparazzi might not shout your name when you dash for your car, but you're probably rocking some social networking action, right? Are all of the photos of you ones in which you're semi-conscious after doing body shots? Do all of your blog entries begin, "I was so wasted..."? Are you going to make us worry that you won't make it to set on time if you had to get your party on the night before? Even if your profile is set to "private," there are Internet archive services and cached pages that leave a trail of your online footprints.

Once, a producer emailed me to say she liked an actor for prereads but, after going home and doing a web search on him, she became certain she didn't want to work with him. Turns out he had blogged a pretty negative experience he had had on set once before (and even if he is 100% in the right in everything he blogged, it was enough to scare off this producer). What if she were to be his next target? She wasn't going to risk her reputation on it.

Heck, I'm one of the most open bloggers out there and I still play my industry relationship cards very close to the vest. It's just good business sense! Assume that part of the risk assessment that's going on these days (in any potential employment situation) includes a good Googling.

Much of this brings up the whole catch-22 actors face: trying to get that shot when no one will consider them until they've been given a shot. Personally, I get very excited when I convince a producer to take a risk, cast an unknown, and then have it pay off big. But think about the scale on which we're dealing. Recommending a book to someone is easy. It's an inexpensive purchase or free trip to the library and if the friend hates the book, no biggie. Recommending an expensive colorist who botches a hairstyle beyond repair and costs someone a booking is a bigger risk. Imagine if you recommended an accountant who ended up embezzling your friend's $10,000. You'd be mortified! Okay, so what if you recommended someone for a role in a $20M feature film and that actor ended up shutting down production for a month while in jail or rehab? Uh-oh. Build on the little risks casting directors are already taking on you by celebrating those one-day co-star bookings as you build to the next tier.

In the end, a casting director's word is only worth as much weight as the relationship between the casting director and producer will carry. There are some producers to whom I can say, "Cast this actor," and it's a done deal. There are others to whom I can provide every possible bit of evidence that a particular actor is the right one to cast without it making any difference whatsoever in what the producers choose to do. Just like actors, casting directors build a reputation by having done a great job on the last gig (and all the ones before that). The more often we are "right" in our risk assessment and recommendations, the more weight our opinion will carry. If we've gotten to this point and decided that you absolutely are worth the risk, we'll go to bat for you in a way that's more passionate than even your own agent may be willing to pitch you.

Going Through Submissions

I'm going to share an overview of how I handle incoming submissions on an average breakdown, to help you fully understand the importance of a great, on-brand headshot at this stage of the casting process. There's much more on the art of submitting in the chapter called **Become a Booking Machine**.

I never put out a breakdown without first knowing that I have a good 10 hours stretched out before me to go through submissions as they come in. Probably 90% of all submissions we'll get on any project come in within the first 48 hours of the breakdown's release, so I want to stay on top of the submissions rather than logging on a day later and having an overwhelming number of headshots through which to sort all at once.

My first click, about 10 minutes after the breakdown has gone live, is on the agent or manager that's my favorite of those who've submitted thus far. Lemme back up. One of the sorting mechanisms we have in the Breakdown Services interface is "by submitter." I always start with my favorite agents and managers, rather than going role by role. Here's why: I know I love dealing with these favorite reps. So, as I see who they've submitted, I can mark the actors as "selects," knowing I already have "in the bank" these actors as repped by the person I *most* want to deal with.

As I go through submission groups from other agents and managers over the course of the day, I continue to start with the people who are my favorites, and then work through to the agents and managers with whom I have less of a relationship (or none at all). Let's say your headshot came in via a favorite agent, very early on. Awesome. You're already marked as a "select." Then your manager submits you. If I don't happen to remember you're already in the mix, I'll again go to rank you and the system will pop up an alert to tell me I already have you selected, as repped by agent so-and-so. At this point, I can decide to stick with the agent or switch to the manager, and this will be based on—again—where I have the strongest relationship. (See: **The Web of Trust**.)

Never worry about being submitted by both your agent and manager and then again, a third time when you submit at Actors Access, because we're always going to call you in via whatever "path" we like best, *if* you were someone we were going to call in anyway. It's not like—if you were a frontrunner—you'll be someone we take *out* of the running, if you're suddenly in front of us via multiple submitters.

This sorting method also allows me to discern which agents and managers become my *A*-list folks. I can see with one click who is very picky about submissions—no "the little boy who cried wolf" or behaving as if every client is right for every role—compared with which agents and managers just sling their whole damn roster at me and expect me to be their filter for best fit. No, thank you. That's your job, spaghetti-slinging rep!

While this stuff may not be all that important while I'm casting, it's vitally important when I'm asked by an actor what I think about this agent or that agent. I can safely say something like, "I like their roster, but they rep at least 30 of your type, and submit all 30 of them on every project, every role," and that helps actors know what their experience with that rep might be, should they sign with them. The agents and managers I love are picky! They're selective of who they sign and they're selective of who they submit. I build a lot of trust with folks who treat breakdowns that way, rather than signing hundreds of actors and submitting their entire roster, every project, hoping something will stick.

After I've chosen selects via rep submissions, I'll open up *all* of the Actors Access submissions for all roles, sorted alphabetically, all at once. This allows me to see an actor who chooses a headshot for one role that makes him look very young, then another headshot for another role that makes him look much older. That right there helps me know that this actor—if I don't know him—could show up at the audition looking anywhere from 15 to 35 in age, and that's not going to help me. He won't get called in. Because no matter what you've been told, you do *not* have a 20-year age range. Even if you do have an age range wider than four years, in Hollywood, you'd better zero in on those "best four" within your range and target those roles most. We're a town of specialists and we don't believe you if you tell us you can do everything. In other markets, you can be broader in type range and age range, but not here. Until we know you, there's way too much risk involved for us to give up a valuable session slot for an unknown when we see he may have no concept of his actual age or best-fit type.

Of course, if I know the actor submitting, an off-the-mark headshot is less troubling, because I know your *work*. That means, once you're a known commodity, suddenly, your headshot is less important. What?!? Yep. In casting offices where you're established, your headshot becomes a placeholder, a bookmark, a reminder of the whole experience of *brand you*. So after all this fuss about getting the best headshot, eventually, there will be a time when its job is less about teaching us how to see you and more about reminding us what we dig about you.

A note about submitting early: Do it. Here's why. If you're the first balding, middle-age, ethnically ambiguous male who submits on a role, you've got a much better shot at being selected than if you're the 347th. Basically, you're trying to knock someone else's dart out of that position on the dartboard, when you submit late. If we already have our top twenty selects for that role, you've got to convince us to *unselect* one of the existing selects because you're so much more awesome. It's harder to make us *change* a select than to be an early one who gets selected.

Take advantage of all the tools at your disposal. Have an Actors Access account, have great headshots, have a resumé (even a very brief one, if you're a beginner), have a reel as soon as you can get that together, read the submission instructions, and if you're given the chance to leave a note with your submission, do so if the specificity you share will help you stay in the mix a bit longer. Don't stress about trying to figure out what each casting director's system is. Just know that there are tools you can use to stay "selected" longer and that is a huge part of the battle in a business where the numbers can be overwhelming.

Good to Know

The number in parentheses at the end of each character listed in a breakdown is the page number corresponding with the place in the script where the character is introduced. When a breakdown says "overscale for names," that means there's a budget for paying "name" actors (bankable actors whose attachment can trigger overseas sales of the film before a frame is shot) more than union scale for the same roles. That means there's lower likelihood that not-yet-name-level actors will be considered for those particular roles.

When we list names in the breakdown, suggesting those are the types of actors we're going for, often times we're "going fishing." We're planting names in the breakdown that will make agents or managers call us to pitch those exact actors—or their slightly-lower-tier version—and that's exactly what we want. See, if we call an agency and ask whether a name actor is available during our shoot and if there's any interest in reading the script (before we're ready to make a financial offer), we're coming from the position of need. If the rep calls us to pitch the actor, or just to say, "I saw you're seeking a *so-and-so* type. Would you like to make an offer to us on *so-and-so* himself?" we're not begging them to do coverage on the script. We're already in their system. We're talking.

Cool, huh? Now, let's get you closer to the tier at which *your* name shows up in the breakdown, shall we?

18: PUBLICISTS

There will be a time when you need to hire a publicist to do your promotion for you. To get perspective on that timing, cost, and exactly what to expect, I've brought together some contributions from industry pros, including a few thoughts gleaned from a panel discussion on publicists sponsored by the Talent Managers Association.

When to Hire a Publicist

"Actors need to know that the time to hire a publicist is when you have a story to tell," Kenneth R. Reynolds, president and CEO of Public Relations+, began.

Maryann Ridini Spencer, president of Ridini Entertainment Corporation, added that an entertainer should hire a publicist "several months before the film, the TV show, the record comes out. The campaign has to be put together and planned. There's the writing of the press kit, collection of materials, schedule of releases. If the actor is in a film, I want to have a six-month lead time to put the media list together and tailor it to the target audience. So often, I have people come to me just one month prior to their project, which really limits us."

Don't hire a publicist until there is something worth publicizing. Anne Henry, co-founder of the BizParentz Foundation, said, "I would think it would be a necessity if you were being hounded by the media a lot and needed to manage them, or you were traveling for a music tour (because you don't know the media in each city), or you'd done a big movie where you need to do press junkets. If you have a significant booking, it can be important. A publicist can make sure your face is out there, that you get out there to premieres (not just your own), and that you get photographed in public (assuming you have something to publicize). This sort of tactic *might* help create buzz around your name and thus encourage producers to feel that you are hot property or that you are a *name*. Maybe."

What a Publicist Costs

Henry relayed that actors can be expected to pay $3000 per month for publicists, and that fee may be locked for a six-month minimum. "Considering that after taxes, agents, managers, and basic expenses, you might have 15%

left, well, it's just hard to justify spending that. At least not until there's a series or a major movie coming out—and then you could utilize the publicist attached to the show or network for free. They will get you into events, usually with more success than a personal publicist," Henry said.

"A publicist costs from $2500 to $7500 per month," Reynolds offered, noting that some actors receive PR as part of their latest major booking. Of course, when you're operating as a mouthpiece of a new series, the publicist the network provides is working in service of the show, and not necessarily aligning you with the events and media coverage that's right for *brand you*. There *is* a price to "free" publicity.

Deborah Mellman, partner at Mindful Media Group, concurred on the dollar amounts. "Roughly the same range. The higher end is more corporate or more handholding, more travel. The lower end is more maintenance. Maybe they're not in need of major publicity but they want to attend a premiere, they want to attend a party, they want to attend a fashion event. With entertainers, we're generally paid up front, rather than on commission like with corporate clients. We have a lot to prove by having already earned our money. We prove our relationships. That's our forte. Keep in mind, our monthly fee is plus expenses. Always."

"Oh, yes, that's important to note," Reynolds agreed. "So often, the client thinks expenses are included. It's like the contract is signed, but not read, because it's in there. There's the photographer payment, there's the FedEx bill, there's postage, there's supplies, and they think I should assume those costs. No, I am paid for what I *know*. If you are paying me a fee, and then I pay the photographer out of my fee, and then I pay for reproductions, and I pay the writers to write your bio, and I pay for copies of the bio, where do I get paid for what I know?"

"The range depends on what we do for the client," Spencer clarified. "If they want national press, international press, doing a book tour in certain cities, it varies. Blanket statements are difficult to make, but I'd say from $2500 for actors to $10,000 for corporate clients, monthly." And what if money is too tight for an actor to secure a publicist on a monthly retainer? "They should choose consultation over a retainer," Spencer advised. Many publicists offer *à la carte* services for short-term needs and some offer media training, which is worth its weight in gold for an actor who has a premiere, junkets, or a festival run coming up. For ninja tips on DIY media training options, see the chapter on **Working It**.

Nelson Aspen is the show business editor and on-camera host for Australia's *Sunrise*, he authored *Hollywood Insider: Exposed*, and he offers private coaching in multi-media essentials. "Why I do media training is because there is this question of *when* publicity begins. Media training is money well spent. You spend money on your acting classes, your headshots, and you should also spend on knowing when and how to promote yourself."

What Publicists Do

According to Henry, they'll "seek and arrange charity appearances and attendance at red carpet events (not the ones you are performing in—other movies, awards events); develop a press packet that might include a couple of glossy photos, bio, listing of work done, interesting articles to be sent to potential media outlets; send press releases and use their connections to get blurbs printed; aggressively seek magazine articles and layouts; try to get interviews on TV shows (creating something interesting or just jumping on the trend of the day); train you on how to do interviews and how to be interesting; manage the media; make the judgment calls of what *not* to do and where *not* to be seen or what *not* to talk about. If you screw something up, publicists will make the public statement that fixes everything; usually accompany you to red carpet events or to press junkets to introduce you to the *right* media outlets and help you avoid getting stuck with a *C*-level newspaper; handle fanmail, websites, and message boards (but those are not job-makers—that is catering to the fans—who don't hire you). It is important to note that some *managers* will do some of the above things."

Publicists also get their "must lists" to entertainment magazines and plant stories, scandals, and rumors on fan-driven message boards. Because magazines and online publications want access to publicists' top stars, often they'll profile an up-and-coming actor, calling him a *bona fide* star when no one outside the 30-mile zone ("TMZ," Hollywood's studio zone) has heard of him. When buzz is well-timed, it's perfect career strategy. When it's too soon or too late to take full advantage of a wave, it's a waste of money and—worse—a waste of momentum an actor really could've used some other time.

Reynolds cautioned, "I cannot promise you'll be in a certain publication. But I can promise I'll do my best to make it happen. I'll use every bit of knowledge and creativity at my disposal to make it happen."

Publicists can also help actors keep momentum from a gig that goes away. "If the series got on the air, even if it's quickly cancelled, at least it got on the air. A lead should have a publicist to take advantage of the time it's out there," Spencer noted. "The press kit alone could get them their next job," Aspen agreed, underscoring the value of the professional tools a publicist creates for their clients.

Mistakes People Make in Dealing with Publicists

Aspen began, "Actors—unless they're very experienced—treat publicity like a luxury. It is not a luxury. It has the same import as all the other ingredients to your career. Publicity is not a perk."

"I find that some people don't believe in publicity," Mellman added. "It's another person in the mix; it's another cost. That comes from a power and control factor. Actors have an agent, they have a manager, they have a business manager, they have an attorney, and you're another person in the mix, advising them and working their public image. Many times, an actor's desire to get publicity is overshadowed by network involvement. The actors want to wait to see how that PR is going before investing in publicity."

How Actors Can Make a Publicist's Job Easier

"Make sure you sit down with your publicist and get an understanding of what the relationship is, what the publicist's job is. Know that I am not a marketing director," Reynolds listed.

"Take your publicist's advice on how to deal with the media," Spencer suggested. "You hired us for our expertise."

"Return calls in a timely manner," Mellman requested. "Our job is time-sensitive. We're on a deadline and we can't say, 'I'm sorry, she's with her shrink right now, so I can't get you that headshot.' Also, don't forget your interviews. If I've scheduled an interview for you, show up for it!"

Whether you're ready for a publicist or not, understanding the vital role these folks play in actors' careers is important, now. Study up. Read press releases. Understand spin. That's how you can master it, and become your future publicist's dream client.

PART FIVE: PRACTICE

If you don't love the process, the product will be a problem.
—Justine Musk, author

19: BECOME A BOOKING MACHINE

Because looking like a booker will allow you to enter the game at a higher tier, I want to help you book as much work on your own as possible. I want you to create a career that inspires the *right* reps to jump at the chance to pitch you. As writer-director-producer Reginald Hudlin says about hopping on board with a brand we can back, "No one wants to be first; everyone wants to be second." The goal is to be perceived as low-risk so the buyers get excited to jam with you.

What do agents look for in an actor? *Dollar signs.* Don't hate them for that truth. They work on commission. They're working for free, for you, 'til the first day you book. Let's make that day happen sooner. Here are some sources for legitimate work—paid work—for the days before you're at the next tier.

Actors Access

Of course, I'm going to recommend Actors Access first. No, not just because the fine folks at Breakdown Services and Showfax started hosting my weekly column in 2004, but because even before I started writing The Actors Voice, I was a brand-new casting director listing SAG micro-budget feature film breakdowns on this "new" thing called Actors Access. There was no electronic submitting at first. It was just a PDF of my breakdown that subscribing actors could see, free, and my mailing address for hard copy submissions. Within a few months of my first breakdown in 2003, electronic submissions were introduced and my casting life was forever changed. Never again would I *have to* open headshot envelopes to preview actor submissions on specific roles. Awesome!

I had been casting 11 months when I released my first electronic submission breakdown at Actors Access. I received 179 submissions on one role from seven agents and two managers, plus Actors Access direct-from-actors submissions. This was in January of 2004. Cut to my record-holder role, 3076 electronic submissions from 374 agents and managers (from California, New York, New Jersey, British Columbia, Florida, Texas, and Nevada) and actors submitting directly via Actors Access. (Note: I received those submissions within 48 hours of the breakdown being released.)

I specialize in low-budget indie films, webseries, and the occasional pilot, promo, or play, so you will always see my breakdowns go out on Actors Access.

Not every casting director will list her breakdowns on Actors Access. In fact, the majority of the "big projects" won't go out directly to actors *anywhere* unless the casting director is seeking someone very specific and needs to do more outreach than just to agents and managers who subscribe to Breakdown Services (the parent company to Actors Access).

Still, you can find a *lot* of good, legitimate, paying projects on Actors Access and I recommend that you make it a daily practice to check in and submit yourself early on projects for which you're a good fit. When I learned about the hoops that Breakdowns puts casting directors through before allowing them to post their first project at the site, I knew we were dealing with professionals who have actors' safety and professional dignity in mind. Some sites do no vetting whatsoever to list breakdowns and then charge actors to see them. Not only can you see the breakdowns at Actors Access for *free*, but the folks posting the breakdown have been vetted, and scammy types are not welcomed.

Casting Networks

Casting Networks (AKA LA Casting, in Los Angeles; NY Casting, in New York; etc.) is the leading site for commercial breakdowns, even though Actors Access lists commercials too (and Casting Networks lists theatrical breakdowns as well. Each site has its area of specialty, it seems). Same as above, you should check the site frequently and submit immediately on any project for which you're a good match. With any online submission site, your submission is going to have the most impact when it is submitted *right away* (because it's far easier to get on our radar when we don't have loads of other options than it is to *displace* someone from our short list if you're submitting after we already have our top choices in place for sessions). This is especially true for commercial casting notices, which is Casting Networks' dominant area.

Another tip has to do with video. Casting Networks offers "skill clips" which show your ability to do some of the things listed on the special skills area of your resumé. Whether at Casting Networks or any other online profile and submission site, have footage available. We'll usually save a few slots each session for actors whose work we don't yet know, and you can increase the likelihood that one of those slots will be yours if you lower the risk factor. Meaning, if all we have is your headshot, we can't know for sure that this is exactly how you will look when you walk in the room, nor do we know how you sound or how you connect with other actors when you're acting. Reel footage helps immensely with this!

Now Casting

Now Casting specializes in the nonunion, copy-credit-meals, spec projects, and student films territory, with the occasional available-to-actors bigger project in the mix. The more beginner-focused breakdowns at *any* of these casting websites are fantastic for actors looking to get their first credits, build relationships, compile a reel, and create a resumé that will turn the heads of folks on the larger projects later, *but*, be sure you check out these producers on IMDb (or with a good Google), as not every site screens those who post casting notices!

Something I really want to stress about submitting on breakdowns at any of these sites is this: Check your messages! I'll speak with actors who are shocked when I tell them I've had them scheduled for an audition, when they ask, "Why don't you ever call me in?" I'll ask them to log in and check their on-site messages (C-Mail at Actors Access) and, sure enough, there sits a backlog of audition notifications they never happened to check. What's with that? Part of the beauty of electronic submissions is the whole *electronic scheduling* component. Since we don't have to call you to schedule you, we might not call! So, check your messages, *confirm* your appointments, and break a leg!

Backstage

Backstage lists loads of breakdowns by independent and student filmmakers; producers of theatre, nonunion, spec, and copy-credit-meals projects; bookers offering modeling opportunities; and casting directors holding open calls. You can preview their breakdowns at the backstage.com website, but you must be a paid subscriber to get much deeper than that. If you're a theatre lover, I strongly recommend you hit open calls and auditions for the ton of stage stuff taking place in Los Angeles and New York to exercise that auditioning muscle and get better at the whole process. Same with student films: Get out there and connect with folks who are learning how to do this while you're learning how to do this. Better still, mentor the producers out there who may have less experience than you do! Show 'em how the pros do it so they learn how to be professional. Build relationships, long haul.

The Unions

Both SAG-AFTRA and AEA list auditions on their members-only sites. It's a perk of union membership to have a basic profile up at these sites, so please do so. iActor (SAG-AFTRA's profile site) was late to the online submission party, so most casting directors had already built up history at other sites by the time iActor launched. Still, there are opportunities for you within your union's websites, so take advantage of them.

Craigslist

Proceed with caution! Well, that's true no matter what the site, no matter what the project. Look up principals on IMDb-Pro and if no producers, no director, no casting director has verifiable credits, run away screaming like your hair is on fire! It's just too risky. *Possibly*, if there's a production company listed and you can track a history of legitimate productions from that company, that *might* be okay, but truly, in this business, who's out there trying *not* to get name recognition for their successes in producing? Think about it. If the project looks too good to be true *and* no one is verifiably churning out successful projects, move on.

Never attend an audition that takes place at a private residence. Never disrobe during prereads, even if nudity is required in the project itself. Never ignore your spidey sense where your safety is involved. I've heard horror stories about actors who have encountered everything from being told they have to come up with money to see the project actually completed to truly unsafe propositions masquerading as casting opportunities. Be careful out there! Revisit the chapter on **The Costs of Acting** for my list of red flags.

Various Sites that Sell "Real, Hollywood Breakdowns"

Some people out there steal breakdowns that are meant for agents and managers only. They then sell these breakdowns to newbie actors and add information like a mailing address for submissions while deleting information like submission deadlines and qualifiers like "name actors only." It's gross. And newbie actors fall for it like crazy. It infuriates me. It not only costs actors money to see these doctored breakdowns but to submit on something they have no shot at booking (since often times the project has already wrapped).

Worst of all, it costs "dream points." I hate that actors think they actually have a chance on the breakdown of a project they paid to see and may feel like a failure when nothing comes of it. Same goes for clearinghouse blogs by folks who have no business sharing "leads" from major studios or networks. They're skeevy. They're not authorized to repost the info they're sharing and they're misleading wannabes all over the world—even though they're not charging money for the information. Dream points stolen. Gross.

In minor markets there may be other sites that are used for direct-to-actors breakdowns—and legitimately so—but in Los Angeles, the biggies are Actors Access and Casting Networks. Do you want to be on other sites too? Up to you. But between those two, you're going to see 95% of everything that is intended for actors' eyes, in the current casting landscape on any given day.

Pirated Breakdowns

If you won't heed my warning and decide to see breakdowns that were never meant for actors' eyes, I can't stop you. It's like shooting guerrilla style or speeding on the freeway. Good luck to you and just be smart about it. Being smart about looking at breakdowns that are meant for agents and managers means this: Read 'em. Digest who is casting what and when. Track trends and log details in your show bible. Get to know which offices are active so you can plan your networking activities with personnel in those offices appropriately. And if you're *really* right for something that's casting right now, *maybe* do a mailing or a dropoff or a taped audition using sides posted on Showfax. But don't ever think that this is *the* way in.

Sure, it could happen: You could pick a series of winning lottery numbers by submitting yourself on a role you were never meant to know about, getting called in, and booking it. But know that that's what it is: a winning lottery ticket. Odds are, it's not going to happen, and in some offices, you run the risk of rubbing folks the wrong way for trying to work around their filtering system.

That said, I'm generally a fan of the taped audition but usually as a matter of watching sides go up on Showfax rather than by pinching stolen breakdowns. I know an actor who saw sides go up on a show he was targeting, downloaded the sides, taped himself, dropped the footage off at the casting office with nothing more than a quick thank you, and then got a producer session out of it. It can happen. But it's all about the attitude of professionalism and the lack of expectation that anything may come of it.

Please keep in mind that receiving pirated breakdowns is a crime. Breakdowns are copyrighted material and they are sold to legitimate agents and managers specifically because casting directors like having actors pre-screened prior to submission on specific roles. Should you choose to receive and use pirated breakdowns, know that there are bogus listings created specifically to catch people who are getting them by illegitimate means.

Gary Marsh—owner of Breakdown Services and the creator of the method of using character breakdowns as a means of conveying casting information to reps and actors—has told me that he would, of course, prefer to include actors among subscribers to *all* of Breakdown Services. That would increase his subscription base by a hundred thousand people. And reps pay *much* more per month to access these breakdowns than actors pay in a full year! Of course, giving actors access to the highest-tier breakdowns would cause many casting directors to stop working with Marsh. They would simply contact agents directly to ask to see actors at a particular tier for particular roles. Casting directors already do plenty of this as it is, depending on how much time they have to cast a certain role.

Bottom line on pirated breakdowns: There will always be little start-up companies that exist just to try and separate actors from their money. I am always reluctant to do business with anyone who, out of the blue, solicits me—especially when there's no disclosure of how they got my contact information. Always be careful. Deal with people you know and trust, or people who run businesses whose services you need and seek out through reputable channels.

Other Submission Websites

This will feel like a catch-all paragraph, and that's because online submission services come and go—the "biggies" that endure, I've already covered above—and as of this printing, Actor Cast (an actor-submission interface off castit.biz—a popular studio-level casting site), Let It Cast (an international site through which actors can upload audition footage to open calls), Casting Frontier (a commercial actor bar code system that evolved into a submission interface), and CAZT (an LA-based casting facility that offers audition space to producers of micro-budget projects free in exchange for requiring the auditioning actors to share their email addresses, so they can be offered the opportunity to watch their audition footage for a fee and get feedback on their auditions) are just a few worth mentioning. Of course, at smfa4.com, we have an updated list of newer submission sites, as well as the latest information on any covered here. Further, we have a few favorite regional and international sites on our *SMFA* Hot List at the website.

Tracking Production

As you know from the chapter on **Targeting Buyers**, I am a huge fan of tracking production and updating your show bible using sites like CastingAbout, IMDb-Pro in Production, Production Weekly, The Futon Critic's Devwatch, Cinematic Happenings Under Development (CHUD), Jeff Gund's Info List, Cynopsis, *Deadline Hollywood Daily*, Baseline Research, *The Wrap*'s Power Grid, the Black List, the Paley Center, Kabookit, Who Represents, Actor Genie, *Hollywood Reporter*, *Daily Variety*, *Studio System News*, your local film commission's website, and the sides posted at Showfax as well as the scripts posted at Screenplay Online. Check smfa4.com for updates in our *SMFA* Hot Sheets.

Not only does this tracking work provide you with a really good overview of exactly how much is in production, regularly, it adds to your knowledge base of who's working, who's working on what, and the ebb and flow of production "seasons." Could any of that tracking lead to auditions? Sure! If you've done a great job of connecting people to projects and connecting your type to trends affecting your type and logged all of this in your show bible while refining your web of trust, you'll be able to lean on relationships that could lead to auditions.

Check with your friends and other actors, starting with your ninja community at the smfa4.com website. What are they going out for? What are they hearing about? What markets are experiencing boosts due to tax incentives? Which of the sites and services out there is everyone most excited to use? Poke around. You'll learn a lot about what's happening just by staying informally plugged in.

Old-School Methods

So, do general submissions (not about any roles in particular) help actors without agents get auditions? How about dropoffs? Well, as more and more casting goes electronic for its first wave, there's very little going on that is a direct result of general mailings or dropoffs, but that doesn't mean they don't or can't work.

Services exist to bulk mail or drop off headshots for actors and that seems like a silly option to me. Sure, you can pay someone else to submit your headshots in a big stack with hundreds of other unvetted actors who have paid for this service, but the whole point is targeting and providing that personal touch. Building relationships is more difficult through a middleman. Don't waste your money.

Actor Stephon Fuller is known for saying: "Nobody is casting anything in my living room!" I love this sentiment because it encapsulates the *action* required to survive a creative career. Of course, the last time I saw him—at a union event on self-taping auditions at home—Fuller said, "Well, maybe they *will* be casting me in my living room next time." As always, there's history from which we can learn while remaining nimble so we can handle the next shift in this gorgeous industry.

Living in Los Angeles, the Super Bowl of Entertainment, we are surrounded by a tremendous amount of all kinds of production. As an actor, it's highly unlikely you will get seen for every role you're right for, even if you have solid representation. There are too many projects and too many variables.

My method of minimizing what I miss out on is to get in my car and drive to the casting facilities and see for myself what is happening. I am extremely careful about doing this because the last thing I want to do is embarrass myself, upset my agents, or become a nuisance to the casting community. I have a lot of respect for the work they do. After so many years of being proactive in pursuing my career, I can sniff out an opportunity with stealth-like precision. I have to help my agents help me. We have much more control over our destiny than we believe.

—Stephon Fuller

Bringing This Around to Bookings

As you know I love to say: *It's not the one thing you do; it's all the things you do.* Don't focus too much on any one element to your self-submitting plan. Of course, keep getting out there and creating your own work, and you'll find the process of submitting to just be part of your routine rather than another big *thing* you have to conquer in this biz.

If you're doing all of this good stuff *and* you have agents and managers submitting you (yay, you), always pay commission on work you book, even if you "got the audition yourself." You're a part of a team and you need to pay your teammates as contracted. You may be *sure* that it's your submission that got you in the room, but it could be that it was your submission after a year of pitch calls on other projects from your team that tipped the scales. Pay 'em for that. It's good karma, if nothing else. Remember, you're becoming a booking *machine.* Paying commission is what pros do!

Negotiating a Deal

Until you have your *hell yes* agent, you'll be negotiating some deals on your own. As you know, your billing can help with the perception of your tier, so let's get you asking for the right stuff when you book your own work. Heck, even if you have a complete team, you are the one whose interests are at stake. Staying aware of deal-making is your business!

First, everything is negotiable. Obviously, producers—usually speaking through casting directors—will tell you that terms are set and there is no wiggle room, but there almost always is. There will be some actors for whom producers will relent on every point. Other actors will be considered "high-maintenance" for trying to negotiate, causing producers to change their minds altogether about the casting decision. Problem is, actors don't usually have the advantage of knowing whether they're the actors for whom producers will bend or the actors producers would just as soon replace. So, until you're in a position to know you're not a "never mind" actor, you're likely gonna want to play it safe in your requests for terms too far outside of the standard deal.

If you're a union member, good news! Your union rep will look over any contract if you have questions about its terms. And on union contracts, the union has already done a lot of the heavy lifting for you. There are minimums in place (standard scale rate of pay, paid rehearsals, private space on set, number of rest hours between shoot days, etc.) and those vary from contract to contract. But you're already protected, here. Hooray!

Meanwhile—especially on the lower-budget projects—ask for things that don't cost producers money but that help you out somehow. For example, your position in the order of credits doesn't change your rate of pay, but by getting "top billing" in this film, you may get paid more on your *next* indie film. Or—more importantly—you may be perceived as a hotter commodity by studio-level producers, leading you to bigger gigs more quickly.

Always include a clause that requires producers to provide you with a copy of your work. This is important to spell out because the footage helps you and because it is really easy for them *not* to provide footage, should they not be contractually obligated to do so. I also advise actors to include—at bare minimum—notification of acceptance into all film festivals (and sometimes we negotiate that the actors will be flown to key festivals, receive accommodations while there, bring a plus-one, etc.) as well as award wins. This information is something the producers keep up with and should inform their cast and crew about, even if they don't always do it. Still, set up a Google Alert to be *sure* to hear about all the good news about a project on which you've worked.

On Solidarity

The actors on *Friends* were smart. They had a contract, but when they started to understand how much the producers, the studios, and the sponsors were benefiting from their work, they wanted their fair share. They weren't getting it. They all stuck together! Which is really the only power they had: the same deal for one and all. Solidarity made them strong. Very smart people.

On *Seinfeld*, Jerry Seinfeld was a producer; his paycheck grew as the show's audience did. He really had no alliance to the other cast members, except as it worked in his interest. The others were on their own. They negotiated individually and did not do as well as the *Friends* gang did.

The difference between the *Friends* cast and the *Seinfeld* cast clearly shows the benefit to solidarity. Both shows made into the billions of dollars (yes, with a *B*). However, the *Friends* cast made about nine times what the *Seinfeld* cast made (except for Jerry, who exec produced as well). Sticking together as they did, the *Friends* cast's move was a perfectly designed and executed lesson for us all. It shows very clearly how sticking together is key in negotiation concepts for actors, and I think it points to a bigger picture of how, without solidarity for actors within our union, we would all have little leverage.

—Brad Blaisdell, actor

The Back-End Deal

There are already distribution residuals in place for all feature-length films shot under the union's low-budget agreements, but what if you want to ask for more? It is absolutely your right as an actor to request a better deal, an increase in your rate upon a certain level of profit returned for the producers, or even a performance-based bonus. I've been able to craft some pretty wonderful back-end deals for actors on the films I've cast. During the negotiation process with agents on one film, I received a call from an actor who had no agent, no manager, no one to help her get back-end language added to her contract. She meekly asked, "Should I be asking for a better deal?"

I loved this question! I was so proud of this actor for being brave and asking whether she could see more than the union's daily rate. I said, "I'll go back to the producers with a request for the same level back-end deal we were able to put together for another actor who is working the same number of days as you in a similar-level role. The worst they can do is say no, right?" Of course, they didn't say no. I think actors worry they'll get a response of, "You don't like the deal we're offering? Fine. We've changed our minds. We're not casting you. We're casting the next guy." That's just not likely.

Sure, if you're actor number 23 out of 25 on the cast list, you're working one day, your role isn't terribly essential to the overall story, and your credits don't warrant the modified contract with bumps, you might be better off saving the back-end deal request for a bigger gig. But if you're one of four leads, you're going to be working for all 21 days of the indie shoot, and you've got a healthy resumé and track record of great work, you'd be crazy not to ask for some back-end participation! Do you walk away from the gig if you don't get it? That's up to you. Producers on low-budget projects know everyone is working way below quote and they are usually open to discussing coming back with more money for the actors when the film does well. It costs them nothing up front to agree to this and, as long as the requests for back-end compensation are reasonable enough that the project doesn't risk *not* getting picked up for distribution due to the bleed-out that would follow such a purchase, the requests for back-end are usually met.

I once participated in a panel discussion with actor and filmmaker DB Sweeney, producer Matthew Greenfield, AGVA rep Lon Huber, and then-SAG Indie head Paul Bales. One of the major components of our discussion involved the back-end deal. After Huber provided a wonderful overview of the various union low-budget contract terms, Greenfield advised actors as follows: "These are *minimums*. It's up to you to negotiate your best deal."

Bales crunched some numbers for us. "The average amount of time between the last day of principal photography on a low-budget feature film and its sale into distribution is 2.7 years." Wow! Oh, and beyond it taking a long time for that to happen (*if* it happens at all) is the fact that most low-budget films that are sold into distribution won't earn back the money it cost to produce them. "Only 0.1% of SAG low-budget feature films actually make back their money, theatrically," Bales said. When you know these truths, it becomes even more essential that you get involved in low-budget indies for non-monetary reasons (good footage, investment in relationships, credits on your resumé, possible film festival screenings).

Sweeney made perhaps my favorite statement at the panel discussion when he stressed the importance of relationship-building on indie films. "Actors need to see it as an investment in the extended repertory company that the director is creating and which he'll continue to use in project after project."

Huber made a great point when he said, "None of you got into show business for the *business* part of it, but we all know you have to get good at that part in order to do the rest of it."

Sweeney warned that the language in actors' back-end deals has to be specific and non-threatening to potential distributors. "The first question every distributor has asked me about my film is, 'What's against it?' They want to know what we've agreed to in payouts and profit participation because that all comes out of their end." This is important to an actor (or agent) because what you ask for in your back-end deal could potentially scare off a distributor, nixing a distribution deal entirely.

This is where I chimed in. Having created some great back-end deals for actors on low-budget indies, I was able to suggest some specific wording that I've used to make both producers and actors (or their agents) satisfied. Remember that this is *sample* language and that you will need to work with your agent, your manager, or the casting director herself to craft the deal that is most appropriate for your specific situation on each individual project.

Award Win Bumps: If Player appears in the completed Picture which is bought for theatrical distribution in the United States for which the Producer's share of the United States domestic box office equals or exceeds $1,000,000 and Player is not in material default of the SAG-AFTRA Employment of Performer Contract, Player shall be entitled to a one-time bonus payment of $5000 per win in the Best Actor category for each of the following: Independent Spirit Awards, Sundance, Cannes, Venice, TriBeCa, and Toronto film festivals.

Back-End Bump: If Player appears in the completed Picture which is bought for theatrical distribution in the United States and Player is not in material default of the SAG-AFTRA Employment of Performer Contract, Player shall be entitled to a one-time bump to SAG-AFTRA Basic Codified Agreement Scale (less payments already received).

Contingent Compensation: If Player appears in the completed Picture which is bought for theatrical distribution in the United States and Player is not in material default of the SAG-AFTRA Employment of Performer Contract, Player shall be entitled to a one-time bonus payment of $25,000 if the Producer's share of the United States domestic box office equals or exceeds $1,000,000 (less payments and Back-End Bump already received).

It's less common for me to complete a casting deal that includes points (a percentage of profits) for the actor on the back end. That's not to say it can't happen on low-budget indies, it's just that most filmmakers I've worked with seem to prefer the locked-in amount of the one-time bonus payment. This gives producers a little more control when it comes down to the conversation they'll ultimately have with potential distributors. If they can provide a flat dollar amount as the "pool of deferments" rather than a percentage of all future profits, distribution deals are more attractive and the deals are more likely to go through.

Deals Gone Bad

We hope that all deals will be good ones. You'll sign, they'll sign. You'll show up on set, do good work, and get exactly what your contract said you'd get. But sometimes that doesn't happen. Sometimes you show up on set and there's been a major change. Your private space no longer exists. Your break time is non-existent. Your wardrobe is now pasties and a *G*-string. *Eek!* Well, if you're a union member, you call your union rep from the set. No question. And if you've got an agent or manager or attorney, you call that person and he gets going on making things right. If you're on your own, you're not totally out of luck!

Contract law is simple, in that any contract in which there is no meeting of the minds is unenforceable. So, let's say you agree to star in a film based on your interest in the script as it existed as of a particular date. Great. You sign a contract in which you state you'll perform the services of an actor in the designated role in the project of a particular title based on that script and your meetings with the principals involved (producers, director, writer, other actors). In the contract, there is no mention of nudity and in the script you're holding, there is no nudity for your character (implied or explicit). But you show up to set one day and are asked to drop *trou*.

This is where the script comes into play. If nudity is not spelled out in your contract and there is no nudity in the script upon which you made your decision to participate, there shouldn't be any nudity asked of you on set. This is why it's important to keep the version of the script that existed as of your contract date, since revisions could suddenly cause you to be topless (all the more reason to be sure your contract spells out that you're agreeing to do a role based on a script that existed as of a certain date). If nothing in your contract or the script says otherwise, you can assume that you signed on to do a fully-clothed role.

Can you be sued if you refuse to do work on set that isn't in line with the contract you signed? Sure, you can be sued. Will the filmmaker win? Not likely, if your contract and the script support the fact that conditions on set were not those upon which you had agreed. Even if the film is nonunion, there are labor laws to protect you. Don't ever let someone's lack of knowledge—or worse, his willful lack of knowledge and interest in exploiting eager actors looking for a break—prevent you from getting the bare minimums you are assured by law.

Also, never let a producer tell you that there's no worry about labor laws—especially child labor laws—since the project is nonunion. Um, these are *laws* that have nothing to do with union status. Safe working conditions, breaks, and minimum wage are your rights as an employee, period.

Always get someone to look over your contract, whether an entertainment attorney, small business legal aid, or a manager friend who isn't representing you but is willing to help. Check into the resources at nolo.com if you're a do-it-yourselfer. And, hey, if it's a great project and a large role, you may be able to call up an agent who expressed interest in you previously but wasn't able to sign you at the time. Let him know you've got a deal pending and that you'd gladly pay him commission on it if he'd look over the contract. I know quite a few actors who have scored agents this way! You just never know.

Tier-Jumping

As I often say: *Anytime I see someone succeed, I am happy, for it reminds me that I live in a world where success is possible.* There is something really beautiful about seeing success all around us. It means we're success-adjacent. And if we're not using the success of others as a way to feel bad about what's not working for us, we're happy for the proximity to success. We're aware that means we're in a network of successful people. That means ours is on its way.

As an actor, you may sometimes reach for gigs that are many tiers above yours. For example, you don't yet have your union status but you submit for a recurring top-of-show guest-star on a top network show. You don't yet have an agent but you get a copy of the breakdowns, decide you're perfect for the lead, and submit your own audition tape to Debra Zane on Soderbergh's next blockbuster. You feel you have to do this stuff because you never know. But you should't do these things to the exclusion of cultivating the relationships at—and just above—your tier.

Seeing actors with no representation booking their first co-star on a show you're targeting? That's great news! It means the casting office on that show is open to un-represented actors, and now your mission becomes figuring out smart points of intersection, networking, workshopping, self-taping so you can work smarter, toward your next tier.

What's your tier? Are your most-accessible projects student films? Spec pilots? Webseries? Micro-budget indies? Contest-related spec commercials? I'm not talking about choosing only to pursue those goals which are most easily attained. That's not challenging and it's an efficient way to stay stuck below your "real" tier (and it leads to bitterness). What I am talking about is really connecting with those folks who are coming up at the same time you are. Investing in the future Soderberghs, the future Zanes, just as you're asking them to invest in the future whatever-awesome-working-actor you are.

Just like casting directors crave "finding" that actor who will go on to be a major star someday, part of your job as an actor involves seeking out the filmmakers and producers and screenwriters and casting directors who will be tomorrow's legends. Your "picker" needs to be good. Just like we hope when we're starting out in casting that we're picking projects that will go on to win major festivals and score worldwide distribution, you need to spend some of your energy focused on who your instincts tell you will be around in a decade. Or four. I mean, you plan to be doing this at least that long, don't you?

The "big gets" at several tiers above you are the easy submissions. You know you want to be on that hit show. You know you want to be in the next blockbuster by that major director. You know you need to be in the casting office that casts eight different shows for networks. Those are easy targets for you. But who is winning the top fellowship at AFI? Whose script just won the Nicholls? Who's making waves at the Streamys? Which producer nabbed the John Cassavetes Award at the Independent Spirits? Whose work is on the Black List? Don't care about these things? Well, then you'd better already be a few tiers *way* above "working actor." Because if you are looking to build a brand and create a name in this industry, cultivating those relationships at the ground level is very important.

Booking breeds confidence. Confidence is castable. It's a lovely loop that feeds itself but many actors start too many tiers above for their first goals. It's why they grouse about rejection—they set themselves up to fail. Not you. You'll use the *SMFA* tools to self-assess, research your network of co-conspirators, create content that showcases your bullseye, and look like a booker, sooner.

Never make "getting an agent" your primary goal. I advise a long-haul approach to this career—knowing that relationships take time to build. Work on building a resumé that *attracts* the right representation, rather than busting ass to sign *anywhere* then having no relationships on which to build forward. Let's work toward building the kind of career the *right* agent or manager wants to be a part of! Remember, building relationships takes time. Whether you have *patience* about that process is up to you. *Psst*—being a booking machine makes the patience thing no big deal. Ninja!

Dying is easy, comedy is easy too, but getting a parking spot near a commercial casting office is hard.

—Shon Little, actor

20: Auditions

Scoring an audition for a project you've targeted is always reason to celebrate. Your hard work is paying off! Now what?

Of course, you want to be prepared with the copy (lines you'll be required to recite at your audition, provided in advance at Showfax or waiting for you at the audition location). If you cannot get a copy of the entire script, try downloading the sides for all characters from showfax.com, to see if other characters deliver key information about your character in their scenes. If you didn't do research *before* self-submitting, research the project. What is the tone? Style? Pacing? If you didn't self-submit at all, ask your rep for a copy of the character breakdown that was created for the role. If the audition is for a role in an existing series and you have enough prep time, DVR or go online to watch an episode or two to establish the tone, the feel, the vibe of the environment in which these characters exist from week to week.

Remove stresses over which you have control: your outfit (make sure you've pre-selected what you'll wear, have it clean and ready to go), your transportation (have plenty of gas in the car so that you don't have to stop on the way, have your route mapped out, and know what the parking situation is at your destination—including having coins for meters, if necessary), and your marketing kit (headshots and resumes, already assembled and trimmed, copies of your bio, thumb drives of your reel). If you leave for any audition having taken care of the elements that are in your control, you remove stresses, and that makes your audition go more smoothly.

Arrive in plenty of time to get signed in and to prepare for any last-minute changes that may exist once you're at the casting office (new sides, sudden addition of a scene partner, request for five copies of your headshot and resume for an entire committee of execs—there is *no* excuse for attending an audition without many copies of your headshot with you). Use your extra time to get "in the zone" while you're in the waiting area and know, as you look over your sides one last time, that you are as prepared and relaxed as you can be. Do *not* get sucked in if there are any "waiting room games" going on. Chatter in the holding area can range from harmless to flat-out evil. Pop in your earbuds and focus on your breathing. If you're the type who gets spooked by being around other actors before your read, make sure you inform the assistant of your intended whereabouts before you step out into the hall or outside to wait. You certainly don't want anyone to think you've bailed on your audition just because you're at the water fountain!

> *Don't be late, don't stink up our office with your overabundance of*
> *cologne, and don't have your cell phone ringing.*
>
> —Matthew Barry

Do You Have Any Questions?

You're in the room; you've reviewed your sides; you did your research ahead of time about the character, the writer, the director, the casting director; you've made choices that you feel comfortable with; and you've prepared yourself for this very moment. Before your audition, the casting director asks, "Do you have any questions?" You freeze. Why?

Possibly you've heard so many different things about what to do in that moment that you don't have an opinion of your own about what to do. So, what should you do? As is the ninja way, you do what feels right in that moment. If you've done your preparation for this audition and you still have a question, it is absolutely fine to ask that question before you begin, when given the opportunity to do so.

Do you *have* to have a question, in order to make the most of this moment in the room? Absolutely not! Some acting coaches actually advise actors to have a "fake question" ready so that they take advantage of the "discussion time" available to them, when asked if they have a question. Bad advice, for sure—especially if the casting office has provided detailed information before the audition *and* the session runner asked if you had any questions before you entered the room. I've provided every possible bit of information I have about a project, its crew, the script, shoot dates, locations, rate of pay, contract details, everything and still had an actor ask, in that, "Do you have any questions?" moment, "Yeah. When does this shoot?" or "Is this guy like his brother or something?" Wow. That is *not* good use of that moment!

What *is* good use of that moment? Actually getting a question that you really do have answered before you begin. Of course, if the question is about how you should approach the material and I give you a piece of information that changes everything you've prepared for that read, you've got some quick adjustments to make and that's probably not going to work out well for you at all. So, choose wisely the question you ask. We'd rather see your choices and redirect than have you attempt an on-the-spot self-redirect due to new information.

Why do casting directors ask if you have any questions if we fully expect that you should have no questions, based on the details we've provided prior to the audition? Of course, we want you to feel that, if you *do* have questions, we are open to hearing them and ready to answer them. If having a question answered before you read would help you feel more comfortable in your audition, taking the time to answer that question helps us all out.

Note that we often use the phrase, "Do you have any questions?" as the buffer for the official beginning of the audition. You've walked in and done a little chitchat, now it's time for the real audition to begin. We pose a question that serves as the, "on your mark, get set, *go*," for your read. Sure, we could simply ask, "Are you ready to begin?" and some casting directors certainly do that. But in case you have questions, most of us use that lead-in. Then your audition begins. It's the same code language as, at the end of the audition, "That was great. Thanks!" We all know that line is code for, "Now leave."

The Top of the Casting Director's Head

People get into this business because they are searching for validation. People survive this business by learning that if they do their job right, they don't need it.

—Tom Lommel, actor

You walk into a room, ready to do your thing, hoping to connect with the casting director and anyone else in the room and you're met with the view of the casting director's roots instead of a pair of intently-interested eyes. Sure, that can be troubling. But let's explore the casting director's perspective.

By the time you've walked through the door, the casting director has seen dozens of people for the role (or other roles) and most likely has a notepad filled with scribbles about what and who she's seen so far. She also has a pile of headshots and resumés that actors have brought along with them and she's probably made notes on those as well. She may even have a copy of the day's schedule in front of her and need to keep tabs on how behind schedule they've run or which actors have no-showed (and which agents will need to hear about that). If she has other projects casting simultaneously, she may also have notes about those projects and schedules and be juggling calls and emails to make sure that the next day's meetings get planned in time.

Obviously, none of that has anything to do with you, the actor auditioning at that moment. Of course, you want the moment you are in the room to be *all* about you! You've worked hard to get to this moment and you want to be sure that the casting director is as into you and your performance as possible. You don't want her to miss a beat of your subtle choices and great timing.

I get that. I really do. But by the time a casting director has worked in this town for even a handful of projects, she's seen *thousands* of actors. She knows what's clicking and what's not. She has welcomed you into the room and has developed an opinion of you before you've even opened your mouth. She is looking at your headshot and resumé and making notes about *you* while you are performing. If she is taping your audition, she doesn't necessarily need to watch you "live," as she may be heading right back to the footage after that day's sessions to see how each actor did *on-camera*, which is where it may count the most for that particular project.

"I really needed her to give me something!" you may complain. No. Need nothing. Walk into that audition ready to show us what you've got. You don't need a dang thing from anyone. If you've done your prep and are ready to nail the read, there is little anyone in that room can do to help you *do better*. All anyone in that room can do is throw you off. It is in *your* power to make sure that doesn't happen.

Don't let the fact that the reader is male (when the character with whom you're supposed to be interacting is female), the camera is on your "bad side," the room is too cold, the session is running late, the sides have been changed, or the top of the casting director's head is all you see affect you *at all*. Those things truly have nothing to do with you.

The Three C's

What are we looking for, once you're in the room? I call it The Three C's. That's Character, Choice, and Commitment.

Character is what got you called in for an audition in the first place. Your type matched the character description enough that you were asked to audition. When we reviewed the submissions, we saw something in your headshot that made us believe you could nail a portrayal of this character. Show up dressed in such a way as to suggest the character. Don't go over the top or do any costuming (unless the casting director has specifically requested it—which often happens for commercial auditions), just look like you could, indeed, inhabit this character.

Like Marc Hirschfeld, CSA, said, "It's okay to indicate with clothing, but you don't want to wear scrubs coming in for a doctor audition. Also, I totally discourage the use of props in an audition. I just think it's a crutch that people use when they haven't put a lot of energy into the character." Mark Paladini, CSA, agreed: "I don't recommend wearing a costume, because it sends a message that the actor doesn't fully trust that we'll recognize their talent unless they have a nurse's outfit on. It's even worse when it's worn for the director and producer who have already hired a professional costume designer. A director once told me, 'I always know the actor dressed like a cop won't get the job. The costume is in place of something that is missing in the talent department.'"

The next C is **Choice**. You hear a lot about "making choices" in acting. In watching actors audition, we'll sometimes say, "He was married to his choices," or, "He didn't make a choice." Both are sins and both are avoidable. Make specific, committed choices about your character, the scene, and the world in which your character lives before you enter the room. There's no wrong choice. Just *make one*. The difference between knowing why a character does or says a certain thing and being unaware of what makes the character tick leads to confidence.

Absolutely, be flexible enough to handle a redirect, but if you're not showing us that you've made choices from the beginning, we may not have interest in having you do the read again with our direction. At the time you're in the room, auditioning, that role is *yours* and no one else's. So, own it. Show us how you bullseye it. Be specific, be confident, and show us how you interpret this character. When it's done right, we see a character coming to life right in front of us and we may not ever know exactly *why* we loved your take on the character.

Commitment is my favorite C because it relates not only to your individual auditions but to your career as a whole. You're either in or you're out. Think about watching an ice skater leading into a triple toe-loop, then falling during the landing. When the announcers go back and review the footage in slow-motion, they'll say things like, "Oh! You can see on her face as she's headed into that jump that she knows she's not going to land it. She's lacking confidence before she even starts. She really didn't commit and that's why she fell." I see auditions in the same way. We *love* watching actors come in, commit, approach the jump, and nail it. We don't so much love watching actors *try*.

Beyond auditions, if you're not committed to your career, it will look exactly like that "uh-oh, I'm not going to land this jump" face the underconfident skater makes. And since people love to back winners, your confidence is an important element to success. You know that feeling of not quite committing to it. It's like the way you drive your car the first time out after having been in an accident. It's timid. It's dangerous. So, when you have that "maybe I'm not quite committed" feeling, stop. Breathe. Shake it off. And start again, committed.

Those Physical Scenes

Jane Jenkins, CSA, who—along with partner and CSA member Janet Hirshenson—casts blockbuster feature films, told me about what could have been an overly-physical audition session with Vincent D'Onofrio. "I have vivid memories of Vincent's audition for *Mystic Pizza*," she began.

The sides called for the character to roll around on the floor with Lili Taylor's character in a heavy makeout scene, followed by an abrupt confrontation with her father. "Most actors felt the need to grope me, grab me, or roll around on the floor by themselves," Jenkins explained. "Vincent got down on one knee and did the whole scene as if it were his close up." This tactic impressed Jenkins, as she shares this successful audition choice whenever she speaks to actors at seminars. "When you have one of those physically-demanding, complicated scenes that is impossible to do in an office, do your close-up," she advised.

The Audition Redirect

Sometimes after your first read, you're given adjustments. Some actors do everything right in this moment. Others fail miserably for a variety of reasons, effectively blowing their chances at getting a callback. Here are some pitfalls to avoid.

Being Married to Your Choices. Of course, we want you committed to the choices you've made about the character, the script, and your overall presentation in the room. This does *not* mean that we want to see you locked into those choices so completely that you cannot adjust, when asked to do so. I've seen actors—upon being given direction—turn stubborn, inflexible, and insulted in attitude. It's as though they've been told, "You're wrong. Every instinct you have sucks. Do it this way." When, in fact, what they've been told is, "I like you enough to ask you to try it another way."

Inability to Understand the Direction. This is probably more common than we'd like to admit, on either side of the casting process. Miscommunication is always a possibility, especially in the high-stress environment of an audition. If this happens in your audition the fix is simple: Ask a clarifying question. I know you may feel silly in that instant, asking someone to re-state (using different words) exactly what has already been said, but believe me, an instant of feeling silly is worth the payoff of getting the accurate information so that you can nail the audition on redirect.

In One Ear and Out the Other. This is when the actor hears and understands the direction given but ends up doing *exactly* the same thing anyway. This is different from being married to the choices, as there's no attitude coming from the actor as though he has been offended. In this situation, you'll interact with the casting director in a way that indicates you really *get* what we want to see. But in the second read, you provide us with a carbon copy of the first read. Perhaps it's simply a case of habit winning out. Anyone who has ever tried to stop a bad habit knows how powerful existing patterns can be, no matter how great the will to change the behavior. Spend some time during your prep for every audition doing improvisation in character. Throw yourself some direction and see what changes you can bring into the read without rewriting the scene.

Note that you've been given a gift when you get redirected. You have an opportunity to do the scene again, and in a different way. Use this to your advantage so that the decision-makers get to see your flexibility. Whether this role is the one you book or not, the grace with which you handle the redirect could help you get invited back into that room next time. As the saying goes, "You're always auditioning for your *next* audition." Make it count so you know you've done your best.

Letting It Go

> *Sometimes, you don't hear anything for a long, long time—and then, a project you auditioned for months ago is ready to cast you. So just keep workin' it, "drop it" after the audition, and remember that you never know how close you came, so just keep on keeping on—it'll happen when it's supposed to.*

—Deborah Cresswell, actor-coach

One of my least favorite things that actors do upon leaving the audition room is recreate every moment in their minds over and over and over again, constantly reworking the audition, the scene, the reactions, the choices, the small talk, the *everything*. Okay, let's run a parallel that may prove, once and for all, how ridiculous this bit of actor mind taffy is.

Imagine you are a grocery-bagger at the local market. That's your job. You do a fine job and sometimes you do such a fine job consistently that you get a raise. Ooh, more good work! A promotion! Bonuses! Until eventually you've become manager of the store and, later, the whole chain of stores. You put in your time, you did good work, and you lived a full life outside of your job each day.

As an actor, your *job* is getting auditions and auditioning. Every time you have an audition, you are putting in a day of work. You show up on time, prepared to do a good job, and, when you leave, you clock out and go home, living your life, trusting that your consistent good work will result in a raise (getting hired to act), a promotion (getting hired to act consistently), or a bonus (getting a long-standing contract to act consistently), until you "manage the store" (run your own production company, develop your own franchise, whatever your ultimate hyphenate goal may be).

Now, if you leave every audition reworking all the choices you made, that is just as if you—in the grocery-bagger analogy—leave work and spend the next five hours re-bagging every sack of groceries from that shift. You take out and put back in all the food and drinks, you reorganize the bags in the cart, you change the way you interact with the customers. You are doing nothing but playing mind games with yourself, remaining attached to something that has already happened and over which you have no control: the work you just did. It's over. Go live your life.

Make it a *habit* of living your life and letting go, otherwise, when you show up to do your job (audition), you will second-guess each choice you make, doubt yourself, lose confidence, and end up "getting fired." Yup. Keep overthinking the auditions you do and you'll stop being asked to do them. Casting directors bring in people we love to watch. Who wants to watch someone who has job anxiety? Buyers, consumers, and fans like to watch people who love what they do and are elated to share in their joy. That's what success is about. Every time you are asked to audition, you are being told, "I agree. You are an actor!" And every callback is an indication that you are castable. After that, it's just a matter of which way we decide to go.

Just like you wouldn't have an attachment over what shoppers do with their groceries when they get home from the market (What dish will they make? What salad dressing will they use? Did they open the pack of gum on the way home?), have no attachment to the outcome of your auditions. Have fun; don't suck. Let it go.

Callbacks: Don't Go Changin'

I wish I knew why some actors make adjustments after getting called back from a preread. I have a theory that it's about wanting to show a *deeper* understanding of the material, having had more time with it. Or perhaps it's about wanting to try something different, in order to show the casting director some range. Maybe it's a case of nerves (the stakes are higher at the callback and the nervousness turns into some other take on the material). Who knows? But if you've ever been a part of the audition process from inside the room you've seen this happen: The actor who was the front-runner before callbacks walks in the room and shoots himself in the foot by having changed things up. It's really sad to watch.

It's so important that you not set up *more* obstacles to winning the role than may already be there. Everyone knows how hard it is to get cast. As we've already discussed, being cast is the ultimate conspiracy of so many events happening a certain way at once. So, it's essential to stack the deck in your favor on those few things you do control. If wearing the same thing at callbacks that you wore to prereads is a way to do that, then do it. But most importantly, don't change your *work*. If you were given notes after the preread, by all means incorporate them into your next read, but don't throw out what it was that got you that callback in the process.

Auditions are an invitation to the party. Don't show up feeling "less than." You've been invited!

—Lesly Kahn

Every time you walk into an audition room, the role *is* yours. It's just a matter of showing the casting director that fact. If you've been asked to come audition, there hasn't been another person cast yet. Sure, there may be a front-runner from an earlier session, but your job is to come in and make everyone in the room forget about anyone else they saw (or will see) in that role. Make it yours and own it while you're there. Cast yourself in the role and take the pressure off feeling that you're going up for a job. Come in that room and *have* that job. We'll believe you.

Booking the Room

In our *SMFA* master class, an actor shared some good news. She had just come from a fantastic audition. As she gushed about all the prep work she had done and how excited she was for having gotten into this office (since it was one she had been targeting—and marketing to—for months), I suspected the punchline was going to be amazing. She was going to end this story with news of a booking! I just knew it.

But no. And yes. She didn't book the job, but, in her words, "I booked the room." I had to pause a second and really take in the awesomeosity that was this moment. An actor I adore was telling me that she did something far more important and long-term focused than booking a role (although that would've been great too, of course); she booked the room.

She made fans out of those people. She got 'em acutely aware of her abilities as an actor, her brand, her type, her vibe, her bullseye, her smarts, her chemistry and personality, and they liked all of that. And the *next time* they bring her in (and they will), it'll be on a role even better-suited for the *whole* actor she is. It'll be one she's more likely to book, possibly even a bigger role than the one on which they were willing to take a risk with her, that first time in the office. Now she can count the folks at this huge, busy TV casting office among her fans and they can—and will—call her in more appropriately and for an even cooler role on an even better project next time.

Most importantly, perhaps, this lovely mindset of hers is one that makes the stress of auditioning far less acute, I'd imagine. There's never the goal of "get in that room and book the role! Show 'em you want the part, desperately. Get in there and don't let go of how *hard* you are working," but instead just a very simple, very easygoing, very cool goal of, "book the room."

Have fun. Show off your work at its best. Let us get to know who you are, how talented you are, and what we can expect from you, every time we invite you in. And then let it go. That is how you book the room!

From a Director's POV

Casting is one of my absolute favorite parts of the filmmaking process. Before this stage of the game, the film, show, or project is still all talk. Yes, you've made a shot list. Yes, you've discussed costume ideas. Yes, you've diagramed blocking. But these are all still intangible pieces of a big puzzle—nothing exists yet, and a little piece of you still wonders if it ever will.

Then you start auditioning, and the heart and soul of the project starts to show up in the audition room: Actors! You hear the dialogue you've only read. You see the moments you've only imagined. You discover layers you didn't know existed. The project becomes tangible—you can see and hear the characters that will guide the audience through the journey that you've so painstakingly planned. A new level has been reached—the project is alive!

In prereads, I ask three questions of the candidates: Is she or he the character I'm casting? Is she or he memorable? Do I like this person?

My job during casting is not to find the best actor and put them in my film. My job is to find the actor who can create my story's specific character. I am seeking an actor who can believably realize a character's essence and appear to effortlessly live in that character's skin.

After a long day of auditions, the giant pile of headshots in front of me never daunts me. The actors that are going to linger in my audience's minds days after seeing my film are the same candidates that stick out in my mind even after a day of seeing 100 actors back-to-back.

When an actor comes in and does something I didn't expect but that is completely appropriate and perfect for the scene or character or project, I see that an actor has done their homework and prepared by truly spending time thinking about the project, the script, the sides, and the character. If an actor can do that in an audition, I want him on my cast.

I'm seeking actors who are smart and capable enough to make themselves memorable before I give one word of direction, whether through a humorous beat or a moment beyond the page an actor created. These are the actors that I want to collaborate with because they make the work better and they make me better. These are the actors I want to bring to callbacks.

When a person walks in the room, they bring energy with them. Instinctually, if I can dig your energy, we're in business. If not, all I can think is: "I'm going to spend countless hours with you on set but I already feel unsettled around you."

Ninety-nine percent of the time, that "unsettled feeling" is emanating from the actor because they are so desperate or nervous. I want to work with people who believe in themselves and love their work. Unfortunately, when an actor doubts himself and hopelessly hungers for validation from others, it's visible from 100 yards back and is not the energy I want to bring on set, expose to the rest of my cast, or inject into my project.

At callbacks, I like to give direction. Sometimes the direction may not even make that much literal sense when matched up with the scene or overall project. That's okay—go with it. I'm not trying to "work out" the scene with you in preparation for shooting it. I'm figuring out if you listen.

I'm also trying to determine how an actor works and what's the best way to communicate with *him*. If he's made it to callbacks, I'm seriously considering working with him. I'm doing my own prep work—if I can start to connect with him at callbacks, I'm one step closer to having a great connection with him on set.

Now for the basic question of most human existence: Do I like this person? The *few* times I've gone against my gut and cast the seemingly "stronger" actor even though he or she was not positive, self-assured, or grounded, I regretted it every day on set and every day in post.

I find that if I ask these questions and have a trusting producer and talented casting director by my side, casting is not only my favorite part of the process but one of the most successful parts!

—Anna Christopher, director

Asking for Feedback

If you have a good relationship with the casting director, her associate, assistant, or intern, find out before your audition if it would be okay to ask for feedback. Don't just ask for feedback outright; ask whether her office is open to *providing* feedback first.

Many casting directors won't give feedback simply because what actors are really looking for is the answer to the question, "Why didn't you pick me?" The answer to that question has very little to do with your performance as an actor and is really about your type, the director's choices, interpretation of the role (yours and theirs), availability, directability, nepotism, and a zillion other little unnamable things.

If you truly want feedback on your audition and you've been given the go-ahead to ask for it from a friendly casting director or her staff, know how to accept the comments you are given gratefully, graciously, and without *any* need to defend—even if the feedback seems totally off-target from how you felt the audition went! The last thing anyone in casting wants to do is to defend her choices to an actor. She already has to defend her choices to the director, the producer, and all of her friends and relatives who have asked her to let them read for roles.

Thank the casting director for the feedback and then tuck that information away. Only focus on what you can learn and apply to the next audition. If you need help deciphering the feedback, that's what your craft coach is for. Don't turn the casting director into your teacher. Best of all, learn that a callback is your best feedback! And always remember, feedback is not for the purpose of bargaining your way into that role. That one's gone. On to the next!

Be a Lovely Guest

Actor Crista Flanagan said this, about the casting directors, producers, and directors she meets: "My job is to make them look great. It's not about getting the job. Turning in a performance that I love and that I'm proud of, that's what's important. I see casting directors as friends who've invited me to a party and my goal is to be a lovely guest."

I think it was commercial casting director Beverly Long, in 2001, who first said to me in an interview for *Casting Qs*, that casting is like throwing a party, and you must invite guests (actors) into the room, and learn who needs to be invited back over time. I so love the analogy of what we do as a party-related endeavor, because, in the end, we really are having a marvelous time and it's on us to *keep* having a marvelous time while "expanding our circle" as Flanagan said, about the web of trust in this business.

Auditioning for Pilots

Pilot auditions are a different animal from ongoing episodic, film, and web-based castings, and they're entire worlds away from commercials and stage auditions. With that in mind, here's some advice for when the magical invitation to audition for a pilot comes along.

Download sides from Showfax and practice them. Obviously, once you start seeing sides go up for a pilot you're targeting, use those. Fire up the webcam and practice, practice, practice. Until you see those, use similar material. Of course, you'll be approximating what is "similar" until you have unearthed some juicy details about the pilot. Once you start piecing together some sense of tone, vibe, pacing, and flow of the dialogue, you'll be strengthening your muscle for succeeding at an audition for that material as soon as you land one.

Now, here's an important note about TV material—and especially pilots—*do not change a word* of the script. Don't add a comma where there is none. Don't throw in an "um." Seriously. By the time a TV script has made it to the point you're getting to see it, as an actor, it has been written, rewritten, and wrung through the notes process so many times that you have to trust what is on the page. Sure, you may have an idea that would make that one line so much funnier, but you had better not roll that out during the audition (or if you must, it had better be after you've done one take exactly as written, and have gotten a sense of whether the room is warm to such a thing).

As famously stated by one of my favorite acting coaches: "The script already got paid. *You* are attempting to earn the right to be paid. Don't act like you know better than the thing that's already been paid to show up that day."

If you advance through the process—from preread to callback to director session to studio test to network test (and there can be several of those)—stay consistent. You will be closer and closer to the role with each read, but the room will likely be progressively colder. The suits are business people and they're looking at the bottom line. The creatives are less involved and even if they're crazy about you, once the room is filled with network execs and you've spent the past hour in a waiting room with your direct competition, there's a different energy. But you cannot let that shift in energy change the quality of your work. Consistency is your best friend as you advance through the audition process for a pilot.

Practice now by setting up scenarios—use your fellow actors and workshop these environments—that mimic a preread, a callback, all the way up through a network test. Have fellow actors be rude to you in the "waiting room." Have one play a horribly cliché network exec who wants to ridicule your last project or your weight or your choices, and then try and do the same level of audition you did "last round." Really challenge yourself with this, because no matter how prepared you are, it's gonna be rattling at some point, and your muscle for rolling with it and always being able to perform, well, it can never be too strong.

Read great books like Steven Priggé's *Created By...* and *Small Screen, Big Picture* by Chad Gervich to learn about the creation of television series. Study interviews with showrunners. Those creatives who happen to make themselves accessible via social networking sites and their own blogs or vlogs—holy cow—get to studying their every word about the process *they* go through as creators of programming. Everything you learn about their *how* will help you connect with them, when you get your magic moment in the room. It's such a great time to be an actor, because so many people are putting their process out there for us all to study. How awesome!

The best news? Most people won't bother doing this much work. So, you get the edge you're seeking just by doing it. Heck, that's what *Self-Management for Actors* is all about. It's not easy, but it's work that *works*, so you might as well start doing it. You'll thank me when you hold up something gold and shiny. Can't wait!

Tips from the Other Side of the Desk

As you know, once upon a time, I interviewed 250 or so casting directors for what was then called *Back Stage West* and for my first book, *Casting Qs: A Collection of Casting Director Interviews*. A frequent topic was pilot season and how actors can best survive it. Here are a few of my favorite bits of pilot season advice among some top CDs.

> We get busy. I will add a casting director to our office for pilot season. The stakes are very high. Actors become overwhelmed and their priorities are skewed out of line. Be fully prepared. Your agent can help by not scheduling 12 appointments in one day. Don't be so attached to the outcome that you are depleted and your energy is gone, and you're not present for your auditions. That just adds tension. The hardest thing is to stay present. That's a hard process. There's whispering, there's note-taking. Keep your focus. Connect to your reader. Remember who you are, not who they want you to be. Have integrity and fill the room with your energy. Take the space. Know you're a contribution to the project. The right thing will happen. Know that casting directors are nervous at those meetings too. Be clear on your technique and focus on the task. It's not about getting the job.
>
> —April Webster

> Try to be as prepared as possible during pilot season. It is about the only time of year that a script should be readily available in the casting director's office, so there's no excuse for not having read and prepared the script as much as possible. Ask questions of your agent or of the assistant in the casting director's office. Know the tone of the show. Is it similar to something already on the air? There's no such thing as too much information. All of this will be helpful during an audition.
>
> —Lisa Miller Katz

> You may be the single best thing since sliced bread, the director loves you, the casting director wants to marry you, and the producer is about to call his real estate broker for that $11 million house in the hills but sometimes the *creative executive* doesn't "get you" and the casting director has to start all over again. The lousiest actor in your acting class—the one with acne, bad hair, horrid breath, who won't even make his own funeral on time—will get the job because the same *creative executive* thinks that he's "it." So, you go home and cry and want to move back to the city from which you came and become an assistant manger at your local Home Depot. But you can't. Because as an actor,

you have to keep trying. You have to understand that even if you didn't get the job, the casting director will remember you and push you and insist that smart people hire you because you have talent.

—Matthew Barry

Defining Pilot Season Success

I recommend that actors not feel as though pilot season has passed them by, if they don't have a stack of drive-on passes from the studio lots and clearance badges from the network security gates to show for it, come April.

Remember, it's a long-haul process, and that means relationship-building, booking the room, and enhancing your brand with the buyers who will be at this for decades to come. Being the hero to CDs who need amazing actors—no matter what the project—is the fastest way in on network tests, believe it or not. Lay the groundwork, plant the seeds, do the ninja work.

While pilot season is a high-stress time for almost everyone (fellow actors, agents, managers, casting directors, writers, producers, directors, even your acting coach), you can choose to keep your wits about you and make *everyone's* experience more pleasant. Because being perceived as a solution to a problem is always the most castable thing you can do, pilot season is a *great* time to make that your goal. Yeah, the odds are against us all during pilot season, but as I like to say: If you play the odds, there is no reason to ever attempt a career in show business. If you live your dreams, there's no excuse not to.

Self-Taped Auditions

More and more frequently, actors are being asked to self-tape. Great! Not busy, otherwise? Cool. Self-tape. Do it well. Make it great. When you're given the opportunity to guarantee that you're showing buyers your best take (and not doing your best take in the car on the way home from the audition, after having gotten a parking ticket for how far behind they were running, and playing waiting room games with all the other actors who want to screw with your head), *do it*.

Take the "just do it" attitude about self-taping, rather than trying to figure out what it all means, whether your agent couldn't get you in or the casting director is actually looking at self-tapes or whether they've exhausted all repped talent from sessions and are now opening the search wider or whatever. None of that really matters. An attitude of, "Yay! Another chance to self-tape!" should become your mantra, since self-taped opportunities aren't going away. Building the muscle that says, "Ooh! A chance to tape! Great! Let's make it amazing!" will serve you very, very well.

Work out this muscle on your own, with loads of support in our free 30-day self-tape challenge group, or take it to another level altogether by training with us to **Get in Gear for the Next Tier.** More information awaits you at smfa4.com of course.

Your Home Studio

Before you decide that it's just way too expensive to have your own home studio, keep in mind that technology is cheaper, daily, and the quality of affordable technology is on the rise. Thanks to online reviews of equipment and free tutorials for using most gadgets, the power is in actors' hands like never before! What follows is a rudimentary list of basics, as technology changes *fast*. Please visit smfa4.com for my current *SMFA* Hot List of favorite tools for creating a home studio that rocks (and that doesn't break the bank).

Camera—Yup. You need one. Sure, some folks use their webcam or smart phone camera, and that's an option—especially because the current-era webcam and smart phone camera are finer cameras than what used to cost $1000 in "standalone camera" land—but if you're self-taping more than once in a blue moon, investing in a better camera than what lives within your laptop or phone is smart money. You'll look better, have more control over the output, and you'll just feel like a pro because you have a real camera for running your career like the business it is. Also, using your webcam can sometimes trip on a fan in your computer that drowns out your sound. So, even if you look great, you may be sacrificing your sound by sticking with a webcam.

Look at cameras that record onto SD cards rather than on any sort of tape. Having an external mic is not required but is definitely encouraged (see below). If you're down with running an app like Screenflow and using an external mic (again, see below) to capture audio, there are loads of options that use your USB port and provide HD-level quality (not that that's a requirement for self-taped auditions, of course). If you're given the option of aspect ratio, go for 16x9. 4x3 is also okay. If you're not prompted for these settings, don't stress. They're probably what's already being chosen for you, based on the camera you're using.

Tripod—Assuming you're not running your webcam or the camera in your smart phone, you'll need a tripod for your camera (heck, even if you *are* using your smart phone, you need something to steady the gadget).

Microphone—Okay, so if you're using a camera with an on-board microphone, you're cool without having an external mic. But if you're in a "ponies for everyone" money situation and you think you may expand your empire into podcasting and such, external mics are the bomb. Again, for my current list of favorites, visit smfa4.com.

Lighting—While bad sound is the biggest sin among self-taping, bad lighting is pretty distracting too. You want us focused on your acting, so that means you want to be shot in flattering conditions. Do a Google Image search for "three-point lighting." Boom. There's your layout for some affordable lights you can buy at Lowe's or Home Depot, along with a few little clamps. Heck, you could even use existing lamps in your home, if you point 'em in the right direction. The best light source I've ever used for self-taped *anything* is the sun. A great window with the curtains pulled back will flatter you like nothing else.

Backdrop—I've heard about folks running out and buying backdrops, photo studio paper, blue sheets, and all that jazz. Really, as long as what's behind you isn't in focus and isn't distracting, you're almost always okay, even in your home. Sure, you can hang a sheet (no patterns, please) behind you, or even shoot in front of your shower curtain (be sure your acoustics aren't distracting in that echo-y bathroom, though), but you can also find a blank wall that isn't too stark white or filled with windows that back-light you and you'll be fine. You're not trying to show us how well you can dress a set. You're just showing us the *one* thing we can't take care of via some other department, on this shoot: The acting! As long as we're not distracted by things you include in your shot composition, our eyes and ears are on your acting, and that's what you want.

Editing—Be careful here. If your audition looks over-edited, we'll wonder what you left out. We'll wonder how well you can do in a single take. We'll be distracted from your acting because we're watching your editing. A single take uploaded for us to watch start to finish is sufficient and leaves us asking no questions about why editing needed to take place. However, if you want to add a title card with your name and contact information (a *great* idea, since the info can never be misplaced), getting down with your computer's free editing software is a good idea. I love the free tutorials on using these tools at YouTube. Seriously, Google whatever it is you want to learn to do on your computer; you'll almost always find a vid tutorial to walk you through the whole dang thing!

File Format—As of this printing, the standard file formats (because they're generally what can be uploaded easily to YouTube—check your favorite upload space for the latest on file formats, of course) are .mov, .mp4, .avi, .wmv, .flv, and .m4v (check smfa4.com for updates). Is it safe to send raw files via email to the casting directors requesting your self-taped audition? Not always. If you send me an .flv, I have to use a converter to watch it, because I'm on a Mac. If the buyer doesn't tell you what format she prefers, your best bet is to upload to YouTube—unlisted; not private with a password unless that's what was requested by casting—or Vimeo, as both sites will take care of the conversion and allow the buyers to watch via link. That's cool, because you can track how many times your vid has been viewed.

If you're doing a lot of uploading of confidential audition footage, you may consider investing in an Amazon S3 account, which is charged on a sliding scale based on bandwidth. This way, you're in total control of your footage and there is zero chance that you're falling into the trap of "the price of free," which exists with sites like YouTube and Vimeo, at the non-pro (free) levels, and which could mean your footage is out there beyond the scope of where you'd like to see it available. This also fills producers with confidence that their material (as acted out by you) is not "out there" on the web, where they may not want it. Of course, the same is true for uploads to Actors Access' EcoCast system or any other casting site platform at which you're able to attach footage from your read to your casting profile. At these closed sites, you're exactly where the casting folks have invited you to show up. You've given everyone less work by making sure you're in the mix at the place they're hoping to see most contenders, and your footage cannot be accessed by random folks surfing by.

Your Taped Read

I want you to remember the *only* thing we're hoping to discern, in watching your self-taped audition: Are you *right* for the role and are you *talented* enough to pull it off? That has nothing to do with your lighting, sound, backdrop, or file format. But all of that stuff could distract us, if you let it. Please put what is within your control in its best shape, so that we can stay totally engaged with your acting, your work, your type, and your talent. *That* is what we want to see.

Dress for success, just like you would at the audition if you were invited into the room. That means no bright colors, patterns, or logos that distract us. Be in character without going into full costume. Seriously, treat this just like you were going in for a preread.

Should you slate? If the casting director asked you to do so, then yes. Should you give us more than one take? Only if asked to do so. Frame yourself fully in the shot, i.e., don't put your head in the center of the frame. Keep your reader off-camera but be sure your mic is set to pick *you* up, and whatever you do, do *not* have your camera mic doing the work for sound with the camera option turned to "auto focus," as that will cause the focus of the camera to go *off* you as it tries to find your reader, during his cue lines.

If you are meant to interact with two different characters in your read, or reference someone or something other than the reader, choose sight lines that are off to the side of the camera. Just like when you come in to read for us, live, you'll agree with an audition partner on "where the artwork is" when you're supposed to reference the work of art on the wall in the museum during the scene, you should plan this sort of thing out before you start self-taping your audition. Cheat out and be sure we can see your face for most of your scene. Keep your hair out of your face (unless that's *sooo* on-brand).

Include a beat or two before and after you start and finish the read so you can edit as needed or so we can feel the impact of the button you add and then we can read your edited-in title card in which you remind us your name and contact information. Again, it's just like you're in the room with us. Give your audition space to land. We love that!

Do several takes as you're playing with the material and then send in your best one. Be sure you've had someone test out your footage after you've emailed a link to them. If casting cannot watch what you've sent in, we're not likely to reach out to you to let you know. Whether you've set the file on "private" at YouTube and not sent in the password or you've sent a file type that is unwatchable, we'll just move on to the next actor's footage. So, please, until you're a ninja at self-taping, make *sure* others can view the goods you've created.

You look like a booker in self-taped auditions the same way you look like a booker in the room. You've prepared, you're confident in what you're delivering, you've done your homework, you've made your choices, and you trust that we will redirect you (by inviting you in for a read based on your awesome taped read) if there's something else we want to see.

Your confidence *will* read in your taped audition. Really enjoy this process and be excited that you've been invited in this way. If you have *any* stress about self-taping, practice, practice, practice so that you become as good at self-taped auditions as you are at in-person auditions. It's just a muscle to build. The stronger you are, the more like a booker you look. Of course, you still have to be right for the role, but at least you can control that you are happy with the work you're presenting to the buyers. And hey, if you're *not* happy with what you've created, *do not* send it off! Just because you've been asked to self-tape doesn't mean you're required to turn in what you've created. Just like with in-person auditions, you don't have to be there if you wake up sick and know you're not on your game. This is *not* an excuse to flake out, of course!

No matter how you're auditioning, remember my four-word advice (to replace "break a leg," basically): *Have fun; don't suck!*

Get noticed by the work you do, not the work you want to do.
　　　　　　　　　　　　　—Vinny Guastaferro, actor-coach

21 : ON THE SET

There is no such thing as a typical day on the set. Each set is unique and each actor's experience will vary somewhat. That said, I reached out to some of my favorite working actors to ask about life on the set—everything from the experience for sitcom co-stars to recurring episodic guest-stars, from indie film small supporting to studio feature lead—and they graciously shared their experiences to rock out some *SMFA* action.

Honeywagon is the name for the trailer or dressing room you have been assigned to—a trailer that is composed of several small rooms—depending on the budget, the provider, the size of your role, etc. There can be anywhere from two to eight rooms in the trailer. Generally, they are about 6x8 feet or thereabouts, and have a bench or bed, a small bathroom with toilet and sink (or sometimes the toilet is the only thing in the bathroom and the sink is in the main room), a TV and stereo, a mirror with a counter, a *small* space to hang costumes and clothing (roughly like a motel room would have), sometimes some cabinets or shelves.

There is a metal staircase leading up to the door, which usually has a window with blinds or shades, and there is usually one small window on the opposite side of the trailer (but not always) also with blinds or shades. However you look at it, the basic comforts are there. The honeywagons are powered by generators, so you always have A/C or heat (which you can control separately in your own room). On some occasions, a co-star honeywagon may have four or five rooms, and one or two additional bathrooms that crew can use. (The original term honeywagon stems from the wagon that *empties* portable bathrooms—and somehow came to mean the dressing room trailer.)

If you did not have a pre-scheduled wardrobe fitting, your call time is inclusive of your wardrobe fitting, and the PA will tell you to report to wardrobe as soon as you are settled in. She will also tell you that they will pick up the contract later, so sign it (all copies) and leave it on the counter. Trot over to the wardrobe trailer, get the fitting, and they tell you to go have a cup of coffee and they'll put everything in your room. If you had a wardrobe fitting prior to your shoot date, then your wardrobe will already be hanging on the little closet rod, accessories (earrings, cufflinks, tie tacks) pinned or tied to the hanger in a plastic bag. Ladies' stockings (brand new) will be provided, and are usually on a visible area of one of the counters or shelves.

The PA will come tap on your door if a shuttle or van needs to take you from the honeywagon to set. Sometimes, you are simply within walking distance, but they may still give you a five-minute tap when they're ready for you.

Between quick takes, unless you are dismissed for some reason, you will have an area to wait, and everyone from stars to gaffers will be drinking coffee, working crossword puzzles, playing cards, any number of things. For breaks between scenes, you are usually sent back to the honeywagon, as major setups have to be done, and there is no need to sit around the set—in fact, you will probably be underfoot if you stick around.

There is a natural camaraderie amongst people who work together constantly, of course, but you will *usually* find that everyone is very friendly and welcoming from the PA to the wardrobe folks to the makeup and hair teams. They immediately try to make you feel at home. Of course, people are people, people have bad days, shooting can be running behind schedule—anything.

—Deborah Cresswell

Your first day on a set, huh? A pretty fun, exciting, nerve-wracking, and memorable experience. First things first: Congratulate yourself. One of the hardest steps to take in this industry is that first job!

When you get the job, you will get a call from someone in the production office. They will just introduce themselves and most likely confirm your address so they can send a script. These people are swamped, so make sure you get their name and phone number so you can call them, should anything pop up before shooting. After that, usually wardrobe will call to check your sizes. Sometimes a fitting is needed, but sometimes not. Give them your exact sizes. It's okay if that waist has grown a bit—they don't care—but they *do* care if you are trying to hide your real size and then get to set and nothing they got fits right.

Be ready to fill out your paperwork (contracts, tax forms, etc.). Then just chill. You will do more sitting around and waiting than for any other job in the world, so bring a book, magazine, cell phone—something to keep you busy and active.

Don't expect anyone to introduce themselves. They have too much to do most of the time. So when you see the director, take the initiative to say hello and then just do what you are told to do. When other actors arrive, some are nice and some are not. Be prepared either way. I usually opt for saying hello and introducing myself. Do not be a *fan!* You are a *pro.* You *belong* here, so don't be a fan. Act as if you do this all the time. Relax.

Treat it like you have been invited into a large family's home for the day (or week) and this family is really close. Be polite and respect that this is their home and they live here and you are just a visitor. Respect their rules and their processes, as it is their home.

Be nice to *everyone!* From the PAs to the makeup, from the caterer to the transportation person. *Everyone!* This is you on your best day and believe me if you think that being shitty to a PA or the wardrobe person won't get back to someone and prevent you from working on the show again, you are wrong. These people are family. They respect each other. Not to mention, being nice to people might cause the makeup person to take a little extra time with you in the morning or in between takes to remove some shine before the next shot. *If* you are not so nice, then they might just let that go.

Bottom line: Have fun, be professional, listen, and be prepared for anything! And, if it's your first job, bring a camera. When no one is looking, take a picture of your name on the trailer door.

—Mitchell Fink, actor

The newer the show, the less smoothly it'll go. If a show has been around for 10 years, they've got it down. Also the first episodes of a season are bumpier than later-in-the-year episodes (bad teammates have been fired by then).

Your call time is given to you the day before—possibly very late the night before, because they can't call you with call times until they wrap the day before (that's part of how call times are determined). Make sure you have the phone number of someone you can reach on set—for that once-in-a-lifetime emergency, or even to let them know you'll be five minutes late if it happens (and it should never happen).

Someone will bring you sides (the script pieces that are being shot that day) with a cover sheet with everyone on the set's name and job description— valuable and worth saving for so many reasons—and the order in which stuff is *intended* to be shot (*this changes* for too many reasons to go into, but it's good for you to know the original plan). Behind that cover sheet are the sides—your lines!

About this time you'll get your contract. Make sure it's what you thought. If not, ask. Call your agent or manager. The contract on TV is almost always a boilerplate contract that tells you how much money you'll get, where they'll send your pay (c/o your agent, perhaps), how you will be billed on the episode.

They will give you a quick idea of how soon they'll need you in hair and makeup. There's almost always a meal going on in TV land—if not there's always craft services—my advice is pace yourself on the food. Most likely it's going to be a long day.

We don't get paid to act; we get paid to wait (get used to it). Be ready to act and be brilliant when they are ready for you. This is the difference between a professional and someone who is not: Almost anyone can act well, given a perfect set of circumstances. A pro can act well *regardless* of the circumstances.

So you've waited and waited and you've gone through the works (hair and makeup). Sometimes they want you in wardrobe before you go through hair and makeup (it affects how they'll do your hair and makeup). Also it's less likely you'll stain your wardrobe putting it on after hair and makeup. Usually wardrobe will enter your room and hang your clothes. Once you put these clothes on, you are responsible for how they look. Don't spill your lunch on them! If those clothes don't magically appear in your room in what feels like a reasonable amount of time, gently mention to your PA or 2nd AD friend (after all, you memorized his name) that you don't see your wardrobe. Don't go ask for it yourself. Film sets have protocols and chains of communication.

Know where to sit on set. The PA or 2nd should show you where guest cast sits. (Don't move your chair. They picked that spot specifically. The other chairs are for people that can fire you!) Very discreetly (unless invited), try to spend some time watching the monitors and sort of always give yourself an apprenticeship in TV directing and writing and acting.

Know your lines *cold!* Inside and out, backward and forward. There will be so many things to distract, confuse, baffle you. Don't let that screw with your ability to remember your lines. It will help you give a much better performance and get rehired. *Know your lines!* Can I say it any clearer? People get on set and can't remember their freakin' lines all the time. Leave that to the series regulars! They've got many more lines to remember and many more obligations to the show that would cause them to not know their lines. You don't! So, *know your lines*.

They hired you based on your audition. That's what they paid for. So let that inform what you do on set. I've seen many actors just throw out what they did in the audition for some brilliance they've since discovered. Well, that wasn't the audition that was hired! Directors on these shows have been hired too. They tend to direct co-stars and guest-stars very differently than they do the series regulars. Series regulars can make sure those directors never work on that show again. Also if you work well with a TV director, it can lead to many more jobs over the course of a lifetime.

Feel the energy. Is everyone uptight? Are they running late? Is it loose and fun? Don't have the wrong energy for the set. Be a pro, walk around like you belong there, and deliver a great performance based on what you did in the audition but now dealing with the other actors and some great direction, and the energy of doing it for real—you know, that performance energy that kicks in.

Coverage is all the footage the director thinks he needs to assemble that scene in the editing room. It consists of wide shots (sometimes the master shot), close-ups, push-ins, tight shots, inserts (shots of the actor picking up the gun). Every show has its own look and feel—handheld look, lots of cuts, very few cuts—that will give you an idea of the coverage you can expect. I have had diva actors not act with me when the camera isn't on them, but the best actors tend to be there for everything. Usually the director works wide to tight and the closer we get to the performer's face, the less forgiving it is if you're not giving the best performance. Working wide to tight helps warm the actor up, but always be ready for the curveball on a set because decisions usually have to be made according to what they think will cost the least amount of money to get the show in the can.

When you're done with your work, you will sign out with production. Don't leave set without signing out! Big mistake. If you've signed out and then it turns out that they still needed you, it will fall on the person who signed you out. Otherwise, your head will roll.

This is a relational business, but it is a *business*. Don't get too chatty or presumptuous. Let your work be the first thing people think of when they think of you as an actor, not some silly thing that you did on set.

—Blake Robbins, hyphenate

When we're guesting on shows, our job is just to go on the set and do the best work and not be the pain in the ass. These actors who want to discuss character for three hours, it's like, "That's homework, folks. Do it at home and don't waste our time." There's nothing more boring to me than watching an actor come on a set and want to talk to the director. You're a guest actor. You were hired for a job because you did the job well in the audition. Do what you have to do before you get on the set.

My mother was on a show and I was teasing her once because I had come to the set to get something. It was a Monday morning and the guest actor was walking on the set and my mom went up and introduced herself. She said, "Now, the stage manager is over there. He can answer any questions. Craft service is over there. Let me take you over."

I said, "Hey, Cruise Director Julie McCoy, what are you doing here?"

She said, "You mark my words. When you have a guest on a show, if you're a series regular on that show, Tara, treat them as if they're a guest in your home for a week."

I will tell you, Tony Danza was that way. The lead on the first job I did stood up when we walked into the room. He introduced us to each of the cast members. Friday night taping, there were flowers in all of our dressing rooms from him. He was an absolute gentleman. How wonderful for that to be my first job! This is how it should be.

—Tara Karsian, actor

There's never a problem knowing whom to see. If you're not asked by three 22 year-olds in jeans and headsets what your name is, then find someone with a headset, tell him or her your name, and ask where you should go.

Be pleasant to *everyone*—from craft service to stand-ins to gaffers. They are a family and word gets around quickly if someone acts like an a-hole. Be very nice to hair and makeup (especially if you're vain, like most actors congenitally are). Be prepared that you are a cog in the wheel. Don't expect series regulars to give you the time of day—even though they should because you are a human being, you are a fellow artist, and it is only by the grace of God (or good representation or a good hair day or that their step-uncle is Spielberg) that they are not in your shoes—because most won't.

Know your lines and give it your best shot every take. You don't get to ask to do it again. If you hear no feedback, then you're fine. Don't ask: "Was that okay?"

Just chill out. It's really no big deal. The hard part was getting cast. Show up, be nice, reciprocate behavior (if someone is chatty with you, then chat back; if people keep to themselves, then do the same). And don't be nice to everyone because you think that down the line, the PA will be showrunning *CSI: Des Moines* someday. Do it because it's the thing to do. Oh, and hang up your wardrobe at the end of the day. It's good karma.

I've been a series regular, recurring character, guest-star, and co-star. For better or for worse, getting a series regular gig is outside legitimacy. The funny thing about having any sort of success is it just means you've climbed a mountain and then you have a view of all the mountains around you. If you had told me before *Significant Others*, "You're going to be a lead on a TV series," I would've thought, "Oh, my life's going to be amazing! I'm going to have a house in the Palisades and I'm going to be on *The Tonight Show* every night." But all it means is going to the set every week.

—Faith Salie, Emmy-winning commentator-actor

Arrive early. If you have a 6am call for a drama or a 10am call for a half-hour, it will still take you time to get through the gate and find the place you are supposed to park. It can take up to 20 minutes to get in and walk to your stage. If you have trouble getting on the lot—this happens more than you'd care to know—it's usually that the computers don't have your name, or they have it spelled incorrectly, or the gate man can't read. When you got your call time from the AD the night before, he left a phone number with you. It's his cell. Keep that number with you. If it's not 6am, you can call your agent and they can call the production office. If any problem arises—poor behavior by someone, a shoot situation you don't feel comfortable with regarding safety or dress—call your agent first.

On a half-hour, if this is the first day of the shoot there will probably be a table read. Dress somewhat in character. By that I mean don't wear shorts and a halter-top if you are playing a nun or a suit and tie if you're playing a homeless bum. Keep in mind that the table read is your last audition. It will be the first time the writers get to hear you say their words. The regular cast may not give the reading their all, and may just be reading... but don't you *just read!* Give it the same as you did in the audition.

On a one-hour show, the days can be very long. A really heavy ensemble show, like *The West Wing*, meant most everyone who was a reg was there every day. On something a little less ensemble, you are off some days, or work part of the day. Whether or not you have any input into your character, lines, appearance, etc., depends on the relationship between you and the exec producer who is usually a writer-director.

Your life becomes less your own and very much more beholden to a schedule dictated by the show. Here's a perfect example: On *Desperate Housewives*, we were given a calendar for the year. There were two hiatus periods for the year. Four days off—but each with a table read right in the middle and the leads had to be there. As a series regular, you are expected to participate in PR events and photo events on your days off. You may or may not get two days off in a row each week. Sure, you get a really nice trailer, some get a decorating budget for the trailer, and other special perks (parking your car at the set, etc.), but the hours can be brutal. If you are a *name*, salary can be $100,000 to $300,000 a show. For an unknown (to the general public but not to the networks), a starting salary can be $35,000 to $50,000 a show.

—Kathryn Joosten, Emmy-winning actor

Life as a Series Regular

How is life different for series regulars? Well, it's all about long hours, steady work, and a lack of some measure of control. The best hours going seem to be in the half-hour, live-audience sitcom gig. The amount of time spent on the set seems to grow with fewer spectators and fewer cameras, regardless of the style (comedy, drama, dramedy) or destination (network, cable, Internet). Pilots are a whole different ballgame—almost like little films, but with more pressure.

Several series regulars I spoke with had to check with their network representative, their show's publicist, or their production company's point-person before speaking with me. "All interviews must be cleared" is the rule, for many series regulars. So, while it's a bonus that you have a built-in publicist through which to run many things, it's also quite restricting, if you're used to being your own *SMFA* hype machine and you've got a strong muscle for the hustle.

One of my network sitcom series regular friends who could only speak to me without attribution, per the network, mentioned that her first order of business was buying a house. "You don't know when that series regular money is going to go away, so you have to invest during that first season (but not to such an extent that you can't afford the mortgage if the show gets cancelled or you get written out)."

She also told me about power struggles and tension-filled days, "everyone is scared for their job and making the show 'work.' Honestly, I don't think it lends itself to creativity, productivity, or success. I think that's why so many pilots turn out crappy, 'cause everyone is too scared to go wrong and is wondering what will be successful rather than working on a good product."

Think you're gonna have plenty of time to prep your lines before being judged by someone? Think again. "You have to be funny at the table read, otherwise they start changing your jokes and butchering everything. Every night, we get a new script at 2am, so the script is constantly evolving," my sitcom series reg friend told me.

Some sitcoms do a day of pre-taping "in front of laughers, which are people who are paid to laugh in the audience. Day five, we have a full audience. You still get a script at 2am. There are new jokes. You have to learn to think on your feet and be flexible. You have to learn to land the jokes," she said.

Another few notes from my friend: "The writers and producers are completely in charge. Everyone has an opinion on things and then there are censors. It's constantly evolving. You may have an awesome joke on the first day and then it's completely gone on the second day. It's all about being flexible. They change jokes. You always have to be on your toes. A sitcom is constantly changing. It's not like a play. It's kind of intimidating at first when you are not used to that format."

I was a series regular on two television shows and both were filmed, not taped. I loved it. The hours are longer, but it's worth it. You have a lot more locations and set-ups to dress and a cinematographer that is working hard to light them. When you get to set, the first AD takes you to the set where they are setting up the first shot. You rehearse in your own clothes (don't wear turtlenecks or anything you can't take off easily since you are in hair and makeup with your own clothes). After you rehearse, you go back to your trailer and get into your outfit, shoes, and jewelry. Perhaps a touch-up of hair and makeup. Then you go back to the set on time and do your scene.

Sometimes your scenes are spread out. You do one in the morning then another at 6pm. By then, your makeup is making the pores in your face so deep you could plant shrubs. You'll get a touch-up, do your scene, and then come home and take a hot bath. Hang up your clothes and leave them the way you found them. This enables the costume designer's assistants to get home earlier and they really appreciate it.

Life on the set as a series regular is much like life. You have to be a mensch. When I'm in the makeup room with one of the stars when I am a guest, and not a regular, I don't talk to them until they speak to me. When I'm a series regular, I introduce myself and try to make every actor coming in welcomed and comfortable. I love being a series regular. It's a family. When I did *Clueless* and *Fast Times*, the cast and crew always had close relationships. The crew are the people I depended on.

There is nothing better than being a series regular *in town!* Even with long hours, you sleep in your own bed at night and get your mail on time and can talk with your friends. When you're finished shooting for a season, you can't wait for it to be over... and when it's over you can't wait for it to start.

If I am on the set for a day, I keep a low profile. I don't complain about anything, even if I think I need more makeup or a different style. I'm a hired hand and I just do as they say, learn my lines, and try to figure out how to turn the air conditioning off in my trailer!

—Twink Caplan, actor

You can't beat the sitcom schedule. The first day is a table read and usually that's it. Next day read, rehearse, and then a producer's run-through. Day three is read, rehearse, and network run-through. Day four is camera blocking and day five is some fine-tuning, camera blocking, and then studio audience. The schedule is embarrassingly easy time-wise, but the run-throughs can be stressful—if you don't nail a moment, it will be gone, gone, gone the next day—and constant rewrites can be frustrating to some. Some actors love a studio audience and some don't.

On hour-long episodics, supporting series regs, you can be blessed with several days off, but days on can be extremely long. You will also work with a wide array of directors, which can be good and bad.

I was a series reg on a half-hour largely improvised comedy on TBS called *10 Items or Less*. This was unlike any show I've worked on, although the format has increased in popularity over the last few years. We shot in a working supermarket and shot each episode in three days. We had a four-day work week (most Fridays off) and due to the deal with the supermarket, we were on a very regular schedule of 6:30am to 7pm. Because the show was improvised, we often had no idea what the scene would be until we arrived on set and the director gave us an overview. We learned what plot points we needed to know and what information we needed to get out in the course of the scene and then within minutes someone was slating. We shot with three cameras and within a few takes the scene started to take shape, although very rarely was any dialogue locked. Personally I loved, loved, loved the job, but I know many actors for whom this routine would be maddening. I was called almost every day, but there were plenty of breaks throughout.

For me, one of the greatest pluses of being a regular is that you develop a real rapport with not only the other cast but also the crew and director. It really becomes like family (however dysfunctional).

In today's landscape, there are so many types of product being shot that there are no rules anymore. But I still think that getting a series reg is really the golden ring and every actor who does should remember how lucky they are to have grabbed it.

—Bob Clendenin, actor

The first thing that happens the night before is you get a callsheet and calltime. It normally arrives 12 hours before your calltime. *Prom Queen* was shot like a feature film. We didn't shoot on a studio lot; we shot at several different locations. We never knew if the next season would be greenlit. I didn't know if it would be greenlit but my character would die in the first episode. Being a regular comes with a false sense of security.

I would wake up, take a shower, brush my teeth, and drive to location. You don't have to do anything to your appearance. Girls (and guys) arrive with no makeup and looking pretty rough, seeing that they are beautiful on screen. Half the magic happens in makeup. During that process, the stylist is picking wardrobe and checking her continuity book and giving out revisions. I am a quick study, so it is not a huge deal for me, but one thing to keep in mind is: "Memorize but keep it flexible." I would get made-up and dressed, and I'd find my first scene partner. If they were working, I would run the scene. I wouldn't want to be thinking about lines during the scene, so going over it a few times without emotion would get the lines to set in and become second nature. Since we shot like a movie, we shot several partial episodes in one day. This meant our director could change hour to hour or stay the same all day.

At this point, I would usually be asked to do a vlog or photo session. Since our show was on the Internet, we were constantly asked to grab a partner, grab a camera, and go off during the downtime. We'd create histories for our characters at all times. Not only were we documenting our character lives at all time, but an "off-duty" director would be looming around with still photography snapping away, capturing natural moments.

Lunch was always good, but better with less people. If they were only shooting two actors all day, they'd break out the really good menus. I tend not to have any food in my fridge at home when I am shooting. All my food comes from craft service on set.

At wrap, we'd get callsheets for the next day. Sometimes we'd go out and decompress from the day and sometimes we'd each go straight home to hit the hay. After shooting the prom sequence into the wee hours of the morning, we still went out and drank. We needed it! I was still emotional and it was amazing to have such a supportive cast and crew (family) there to help me deal with its after effects.

After wrapping, it's back to the grindstone. Auditioning when you can get the auditions. Hope that your work is getting noticed, and hope that it will help secure the next job. All and all, *Prom Queen* took me out of the state, out of the country, to my hometown, etc., so I am very grateful. The show getting nominated for an Emmy, a Teen Choice Award, and a TV Guide Award just made it that much cooler and exciting to be a part of.

—Sean Hankinson, actor

Your constant presence on the same sets will give you both an extreme level of comfort and maybe a confusing amount of déjà vu. Practice your new blocking on set. Because though you've entered through that kitchen door 100 times, sometimes you cross to the fridge, sometimes to the table, sometimes to another room, etc.

Working for weeks on a project as opposed to a few days gives you proportionately more downtime. Now, you will need some of this time to learn the new blocking and constantly changing script. And the rest? You'll quickly tire of small talk at crafty which consists entirely of trying to hook up if you're single and trying to get your next job if you're married. I had to learn to stay at least somewhat focused for when I got called back to the set to work. So, in between the endless hours on PlayStation, writing your own screenplay, and surfing the 'net, you might want throw in a little stretching or meditation for balance. You'll be in your dressing room or trailer for weeks at a time so you can bring in more personal items to make you more comfortable and inspire you. I travel with lots of pix of my wife.

Learn everyone's name! It is hard because there are so many people involved. But it's common decency and a sign of respect to the crew who also work very hard.

The day-in, day-out familiarity with everyone from the EPs to the interns may embolden you to suggest new lines, actions, and even plot lines for your character. I've found that writers and producers either are genuinely receptive to this or will at least humor you. Everyone is keen to make every character as strong as possible. But don't abuse this. If the bulk of your suggestions include you jockeying for more sex scenes with hot leads, you'll quickly earn the reputation of one to be ignored (not that I know from experience).

—Brian Palermo, actor-author

My second series regular role was for a single-camera comedy for VH-1 called *Free Radio*. I played a morning talkshow DJ and the foil to my co-star (and creator) Lance Krall's charming moron character. We shot the first eight episodes in five weeks. The radio talkshow was fictional and we had celeb guests on as themselves promoting in real time what they had going on in their careers. The episodes were outlined, but the dialogue was improvised.

It was the most fun I'd had on a show and every day was completely different. I usually worked daily from 8am to 6:30pm, but that's really a pretty easy schedule compared to my friends who are regularly called at 5am or on night schedules or on location in a place like San Pedro.

Every night, I prepped like crazy, reading everything I could about our guests so I could interview them without a snag. Then when the interview happened, I was freed up to have fun with the person and improvise a fun interview. At the end of the day, I was exhausted, not realizing that I'd used all my energy to be on.

Our show had a tight budget, so I was always mindful of where I could help speed things along. My hair was the same style the entire first eight episodes since we didn't have time to spare on huge hair and makeup changes. We always needed to get the shots off quickly and move on, and I never wanted to be the one to blow a take.

With any new show, you look forward to seeing how it will be received. Once you're done shooting, the rest of the process is out of your hands, so watching how a show is marketed and publicized—plus seeing how the ratings are—is much like having to let an audition go when you walk out the door. I do the best job I can, and the rest is out of my control!

—Anna Vocino

Life of a series regular: Hurry! Hurry! Wait. When I worked on *The King of Queens*, there was a *lot* of downtime. One of the reasons I miss theatre so much is because on stage—with the exception of tech rehearsal—it is all about the actor. You spend every minute rehearsing. In film and television, it is much more about the technical aspect. It's about the lighting, the cameras, the blue screen, the green screen, the rewrites, the producers, the network, and—finally—the actor.

There is a *ton* of waiting, while your crew is busting their collective asses to set up the perfect shot. But when you're called to set after sitting around for an hour, you have to be *on* and ready to go. Then you're done with that shot and you sit around and wait some more. So the challenge is to stay ready, stay focused, and avoid craft services. Personally, I suck at avoiding craft services!

—Victor Williams, actor

As you can see from these awesome, firsthand experiences, there's no such thing as an average day on set, but you can count on having fun, waiting around a lot, and being offered up lots of temptations at the craft services table! Make the most of your time on set! Get to know people without being in the way. Remember every person you meet—those names all go in your show bible, right? And after you wrap, shoot another thank-you note to the casting director, your agent, your manager, your coach, and anyone else who helped build the bridge to that set! No one is in this journey alone.

You want to make something of yourself? Make something yourself.
— Dom Hughes, Rockwood Films

22: CONTENT CREATION

Why do I think self-producing is so important? Dangit, it's the key to the only "true" shortcut in this industry. Show the industry what you're capable of. Build your audience as you refine your brand. Learn the true power of producing so that you better understand every step of the process as you continue to work as an actor. No, you may not turn into a power-producer. You may only make that first project and learn enough to know that you really want to let others do the producing from here on out. But I can promise you that the experience will be one you'll never forget. And because it *could* be something that lands you on our radar faster than the ol' "submit, workshop, and pray" routine, it's something you've just gotta try.

No, you don't have to fill every crew position yourself or even write your own script. All you have to do is be so aware of your brand, so clear on your targets, and so surrounded by fellow creatives who want to collaborate and create content that the "hey, let's put on a show" vibe fills your life in such a way that you can't *not* do it.

This is not a terribly popular topic with actors, because so many folks don't want to go through all the heavy lifting involved in self-producing. I get that (I really do), but when any actor whines about not having footage that showcases them doing their bullseye best in front of their target buyers, I shake my head and point 'em right back here: Producing your own content *is* the solution to the "no one *gets* me" problem. It's the solution to the "I can't get in the room to show them my work" problem. It's the solution to the "no one will rep me because I have no footage" problem.

More importantly, producing your own content puts the power in your hands in the most important ways: You suddenly understand the industry in a way that you didn't before you created content. You *get* the storytelling process from a 10,000-foot view. You show up to every audition with renewed confidence, because if you don't book this one-line co-star, okay, that's more time to work on your next festival-bound project. You transition from being one of those needy actors who throbs like a toothache to being a power player in this industry we all adore.

As Blake Robbins advises, "Pursue the work, not the people." It's inspiring to know that you control a whole lot more about your career and your profile among the buyers in this industry than you may have ever realized. No more excuses.

The paradigm shift—of bringing your craft directly to your fans, your targets, your potential buyers—needs to occur with the artists first. If we see ourselves as both creators and *suppliers* of content, it's only a matter of time before the buyers see us that way too. They'll learn to come to us for the goods. Talk about cementing a brand in the industry! Get known for not only your type and what you deliver in the room, every time, but also for being able to serve it right up to the audience who demands it, no middleman! How cool is that?

For so long, we've seen artists as creators and suits as the business-savvy sharks who make it possible for our work to get to the masses. Why? Because that's the way it has always been. But clearly, things are shifting. It started with bands leaving behind their record labels and delivering their music directly to their fans, but on-camera performers are joining the movement. See Louis CK, Zach Braff, Joseph Gordon-Levitt, et. al. If the "big guys" are taking their business directly to the consumers, it's only going to become easier for the "little guys" to *get to* "big guy" status using the direct-to-customer business model.

Sure, we may not get access to *as many* people on our own as the corporations do, but if we do point-to-point connections, aren't we more likely to have our message understood? Aren't we more likely to reach our core audience? Aren't we more likely to create a loyal fanbase that sticks with us for decades to come?

Creative control is beautiful. Identifying your core audience and getting your goods directly to those people is way fun. And knowing that your intended message is reaching its intended audience in the exact way you've created it and crafted it is really cool.

It's the "small but loyal" vs. "large but fickle" fanbase issue. Which would you rather have: A small group of buyers (whether those "buyers" are actual consumers of your work who buy tickets at the megaplex or are casting directors or agents who are eager to consume your work and call you again and again, rep you, etc.) who can say that they *get you* or a very large, fanatical then forgetful, fickle group of kathousands of people who worship you today and ignore you tomorrow?

Do you want to be the flavor of the month whom everyone needs to sample right this moment—but may spit out the next—or the acquired taste that fans understand and that, eventually, even the not-yet-fans want to try? Nothing wrong with wanting to be wildly famous and hugely popular, but it's almost impossible for an artist to reach the mighty masses, instantly. So, it's important to know your message, know your customers, and know your limitations of reach. If your goal is to hit as many potential viewers as possible, you might want the help of the big-time content providers—and be willing to lose some of the creative control—in order to make it big. I'm not suggesting that actors eschew the traditional Hollywood business model to jump on the good ship DIY, but instead that everyone be open to all potential avenues of reaching the buyers.

Let's Do Research!

The more viable it becomes for the film industry to provide content directly to consumers, the more essential it becomes for the creators of the content to learn how to be the *distributors* of the content. Buy your video camera, learn how to use iMovie, set up your YouTube channel, and figure out what your first message to the masses will be. Work out the technical kinks before you put yourself all the way out there (and work with a partner if you're more of an idea person than a technician, but I advise you to learn how to be a little bit of both) and use that time to identify your target audience too. Research, research, research.

The big musical artists who are dumping their record labels have the advantage of having decades of sales figures to analyze, allowing them to calculate exactly who might buy their direct-to-consumer offerings. They know their listeners download content and they aren't worried about losing customers because there's suddenly nothing for them to buy in a brick-and-mortar record store. You, on the other hand, will have to do your research based on what is *already* out there in the spaces you want your message to hit as well as of the vibe you plan to present. Are people visiting websites to view short films like those you want to create? Are those websites ad-based or membership-driven? Are the short films part of a larger storyline, available one chapter at a time? Or are they longform content and available less frequently than you might be able to churn 'em out if you really got rollin'?

Does your audience turn out to a comedy club or anywhere else there are adult beverages to be had during the entertainment? Is your target audience made up of people who love the theatre—especially obscure black-box spaces where people are mounting original works or even doing script-in-hand readings of works-in-progress? Or, is your true fanbase that group who never leaves home, only ever watches network TV, and somehow makes it so that the most ridiculous series end up on the air for years and years?

Do your research and map out your plan for getting in front of your buyers. And if that first level of those buyers is comprised of casting directors and your goal is to get into as many offices as possible—not at all concerned with creating and delivering content directly to the masses—that's okay too. The research still needs to happen, as these are all potential buyers, consumers, audience members who will ultimately lead to your ability to have that greater reach you're hoping for.

Your best course of action is to learn not only how to create your best, most on-type bullseye character, but also how to present it to multiple audiences: the audience of one in a casting room, the audience of dozens in a black box theatre, the audience of hundreds at an indie film festival, or even the audience of thousands who might click on a link from your website. Learn *now* how to create, package, and distribute your gifts to the widest potential audience that you hope to reach someday.

Get Started

Your first step needs to be *taking a step*. Often, actors who think they may want to self-produce will let inertia keep them from moving forward. They'll stick with the habits of submitting and mailing and workshopping and hoping someone sees something somewhere and brings them in someday because that's *easier*. Easier, but not necessarily more effective.

It's actually not that terrifying to take one little step. Don't let your fear of "I'm not a writer" keep you from putting pen to paper. Open a Word doc. Start typing. Brainstorm with fellow creatives and come up with something! Don't worry "what if it sucks." It might! But get started. Get that first thing done so you can get your next thing done. Make all your mistakes with that first thing. Don't make it your pet project, because you don't want to learn all the mistakes you're going to make with the one you care most about. Learn the mistakes on the test project. You'll learn a *lot* of things that currently, you don't even know you need to learn.

Trust that you have a zillion stories to tell. Keep a file of your best lines that may find better homes in future scripts someday. And know that your dearest friend—if he isn't a good fit for the story you're telling right now—will actually *hurt* your project, if you try to force it to happen. A dear friend who knows you have a zillion stories to tell will be happy to hold the boom on your first project, because he knows you have a leading role available in the second one.

Shorter Is Better

I know you think it's funny as-is. I know you love watching the idea develop on screen, remembering how much fun it was when the idea developed on paper (or live, if improvised). And you not only love seeing it in playback, but you love giving it that moment—that moment it so richly deserves—to be appreciated for the brilliance that it is.

Dude. It's not that brilliant. Edit it down. We don't need you to hit everything with a sledgehammer. We don't need a full 10 seconds to recover from the fits of laughter your joke has sent us into. We get it. It was cute. Move on.

The Best Vids Cement Your Brand

When done right, actors who self-produce have gotten very clear on their brand before roughing out an idea, before scripting a concept, before storyboarding a short, before shooting a single frame. When done wrong, actors who self-produce figure, "What the heck? Let's roll!" And it may be after spending a ton of money that they realize they probably should've had a blueprint before attempting to build a house.

Since the whole point of self-producing includes building a fanbase and getting on the radar of the buyers as exactly what you sell best, doesn't it stand to reason that you should do a good amount of research on *that* part of things *before* you start rolling? You'd think so. I've seen way too many self-produced clips that are a starring ingénue vehicle for someone who could start booking right now, today, as "the best friend." And I think, "Wow. What a missed opportunity to cement *that* brand!" Know yourself. Know your targets. Use self-producing as a means to get from one to the other.

Shorter Is Better

Yeah, Bon. You said that. Got it. Really? Do you? Really, really, really? Because I'm willing to bet you still keep a bit of the scrapbook syndrome happening in your work. Heck, I do it in writing for you! I'm sure I've made my point, but I go on about it a sentence or two more, just to be sure. Why do we do this? We either don't trust our audience to be smart enough to "get it" or we know that there are folks who *won't* get it, so we figure let's give a little more in case it makes a difference.

I've learned this well: It doesn't. Those who aren't going to "get it" are never going to get it, no matter how much we repeat ourselves. So, let's all agree to serve the audience that's smart enough to get it in the first place, knowing that those who won't get it weren't going to get it with one or two or even eight more laps around that joke or that bit or that brilliant analogy.

Be Ready to Move

If you're calling what you've produced "the first episode of a webseries," you'd better have five other episodes in post before you launch. If you're calling what you've produced "the trailer to a feature," you'd better have a feature script written and partially financed. If you're calling what you've produced "a weekly feature" at your blog, you'd better be going up weekly. If you're going to open to an audience eager to see what's next, you'd better have "what's next" ready. Because if you aren't ready to move, your ever-fickle audience will surely be ready to *move on*.

Shorter Is Better

You guessed it, I have one last plea that you check out whatever you've created *at each stage* of the process (rough outline, script, storyboards, each individual shot, edited scenes, the whole project itself) with an eye toward, "What can I lose?" I promise you, there's almost always something you could spare, and in doing so, you wouldn't make the story worse (you'd make it better), you wouldn't sacrifice the point (you'd make it clearer), you wouldn't miss a thing (and if you really did, you could always release that goodness as "deleted scenes" and "outtakes" and thrill your fans that much more).

Screenplay Without a Crew

So, let's say you've scripted a fantastic story but you want to explore something like screenplay contests, to help your material find a life at a much higher tier than you could access if you were to push through on your own. Luckily, there are a lot of options for you, wherever you live! Some contests offer monetary awards, others provide coverage on the material (which can be even more valuable than money, depending on who's providing that coverage and script notes), and some lead to staffing deals at networks. As you shop around, always check the fine print to see which might be the right fit for your needs.

Paperwork

Your first self-produced project may be a total "run and gun" guerrilla project (no permits, no insurance, no union contracts) or it may be by the books, with all the proper paperwork in place. I'm not going to tell you which road you need to choose, because you may be looking at a $35 short, like *Girl's Night Out* (YouTube), or you may be considering a $10,000 short, like *The List* (Vimeo). Come to smfa4.com to check out these badass self-produced clips, plus others we're most excited about today! You know what your list of resources looks like. You know what vibe your project needs to have, as it showcases your bullseye. You know your budget. And only you know if it can happen at the amateur or professional level.

My favorite part about the union contracts for self-produced projects is how very producer-friendly they are. You're not suddenly asked to jump through crazy hoops; you're walked through the process of jumping through hoops you may not have even realized exist, since you're a first-time producer! Yes, paperwork can be tedious and unglamorous, but having your shoot— after you've pulled together so many favors to have so many collaborators show up for free to help out at this donated location—*shut down* because you have no permit will teach you that it's very difficult to get all those favors to line up the next time you ask. (See: **The Web of Trust**.)

Because you want to enjoy the production process, because you want to be a success at it, because you want to tell many stories for decades to come, I want to encourage you to "go pro" and get the deck stacked in your favor for success by utilizing the many indie resources available to you from the start. Visit smfa4.com for your *SMFA* Hot List of a bunch o' sites we love to recommend regarding contracts, getting your indie project up on IMDb, filling out union paperwork, entering screenplay contests, and jamming with fellow ninjas to make your story a reality!

Ready to Crew Up!

You're ready to bring your crew together and start rolling. Awesome! You've written something on-brand (or collaborated to bring something together), you're saving every penny or running a crowdfunding campaign to raise the money needed to get shooting. Well, who's on your team? Here's a quick list.

> This is a minimal list of jobs and it is geared toward smallish, indie productions. The full list of descriptions for each job is available at smfa4.com with details about duties as well. All of these duties are critical for the success of any movie, even yours. If it's just you and another person doing a project together, you still have to cover all of these jobs. When you're working on a studio or network project, there are varying degrees of specialization in the jobs I've listed here: writer, producer, line producer, associate producer, executive producer, unit production manager, 1st assistant director, director, script supervisor, DP, grips and gaffers, sound mixer, boom operator, production designer, costume designer, hair and makeup, 2nd AD, 2nd 2nd AD, PA, casting director, editor, sound editor, composer, craft services.
>
> —Keith Johnson

Hit smfa4.com for juicy job descriptions of each of those positions, because no matter how few people you have on your crew, each of those jobs must be covered!

Beware the Island

I used to say that I work with a lot of first-time filmmakers. But technically, that's not true. I work with a lot of *second-time* filmmakers, because first-time filmmakers cast their films on their own and then realize they'd rather pay someone to cast for them, because the filtering process is so much work, and they need to focus on about a zillion other things in pre-production. They can visit the casting issue well after submissions and prereads to make some decisions, saving themselves loads of stress.

That said, I have met—and worked with—a few filmmakers who are, unfortunately, hyphenates. Wait. *I am* a hyphenate, so I *can't* use such a sweeping generalization as a negative. It's fine to do many, many things in this industry. In fact, Hollywood thrives on those who live the hyphenate lifestyle. So, let's say it's the *über-hyphenate* who becomes an island that I'm talking about, here. You've met the type: "I am the writer, director, producer, star, camera operator, makeup artist, composer, singer of the soundtrack, caterer of this project and this baby is mine." There's something that happens when someone assumes *all roles* in his project. It's a form of tunnel vision, and it's ugly.

A producer's fingerprints are *already* all over the finished product. A director has placed his stamp of approval (or taken a stand against a certain producer's choice) on each shot. The script exists in the writer's voice. Every character is living the hyphenate's POV. So, when the finished product is all about this *one* person, there is often very little that is relatable to those in the audience who do not share that particular person's POV (and that's most members of the audience).

Surround yourself with creative collaborators and run your big decisions through a group filtering process (not to say that *every* decision must be made by committee) to be sure you're creating something that's island-free.

Distribution

Choosing an on-brand showcase of your material is just as important as the content itself. Some shorts "feel" better on Funny Or Die than they "feel" on Vimeo. Some series are made for Blip TV, while others have a more Strike TV vibe. Some projects are made for Crackle and others rock on Comedy Central Studios. Still others may be gold for a deal with Hulu+ or direct-to-airline distribution at Virgin. Poke around. And don't upload your piece *everywhere*. Pick the most on-brand place.

Also, for the love of all that is holy, if you plan on entering your work into a film festival, make *sure* you have not uploaded the footage *anywhere* until after you're notified of your project's status. You may think nothing of submitting your short to Sundance and then uploading it to Facebook, but that last action just voided your submission, as Sundance wants nothing to do with footage that isn't "premiere status" for their festival.

Read the fine print. Be smart. You don't want to get this far with something you're really excited about and then not be able to take it all the way to the finish line at the highest tier available to you! Check the IMDb-Pro festival calendar. Read up on TubeFilter and track the history of projects produced by IAWTV members. Stay plugged in at smfa4.com to start tracking what *you* like to watch, and where, so that when it's your time to distribute, you can choose the right space. And, hey, if "the right space" is simply on your existing demo reel? That's badass! You've taken control. You've crafted content to show the buyers what you're capable of, as a performer *and* a producer. No more excuses! You've showcased your bullseye in a totally on-brand way. Ninja!

Kicking It Live

I had been auditioning for films but not yet really booking anything. So, here's my advice: Go out with your friends, rent a space, pick a play, pay the copyright, make posters, go out at midnight and put your posters up where you're not supposed to put 'em, and then put on your show. Feel great! Talk to your friends afterward in the lobby and do all of the fun theatre things that come with it and then see what comes from there. They weren't always great plays, but we felt they were great because they were ours. We were supporting each other and this was our clubhouse.

—Tom Everett Scott, actor

A great example of putting a showcase on for free (at much cost to yourself, at first) comes from the best one-woman show I have ever seen. Jonna Tamases performed *Jonna's Body, Please Hold* for over 10 years throughout Los Angeles. Her willingness to put on this show—about her numerous bouts with cancer and her ability to kick its ass—repeatedly at no charge to attendees is what led to its award-winning six-week, fully-produced and completely-funded run. Her free shows during the development process allowed her to invite potential investors—as well as industry—to see the work-in-progress. She believed so strongly in this show that she sunk every penny she had into it, so that she could share it with others. Her personal investment paid off, as members of the industry—and cancer survivors all over the world—rallied around her and brought this show to its highest production values thus far. In fact, her pet project evolved into a film, and she's living proof: Your showcase is in your own hands.

The only thing I wish I'd done differently is start self-producing earlier. It was not easy, and I can't even say it was always fun, but I learned a ton and I grew a ton. It's given me confidence as an actor because I know now what kinds of things the producers are going through when I walk in the room to audition. And best of all I've ended up with starring roles in movies I'm very proud of.

There is sooo much under-used talent in this town, and many of those people are happy to work on low low low budget projects (for fun, for their reel, 'cuz they like you). Form a group with your friends; help each other. Find or write a script you like, earn some money to put toward production (you'd be surprised how little you need), reach out and invite people to help, and make your own work.

Ready? Go!

—Jonna Tamases

You just never know what the reaction to your creation will turn out to be! Therefore, you must get involved with something you *really love* and cultivate its reputation. That pays off on the most important level: It feeds your soul!

23: SELF-PROMOTION

All publicity begins with you. Don't think you need to wait until you reach the level at which one would normally hire a publicist to begin learning the art of publicity and promotion. It's all part of marketing, and you're getting very well-versed on that art just by rocking *SMFA!*

Promoting a Show

If you are in a *good* play, you should plan to invite press and industry to attend. If the play is really only *okay* or your role is tiny, perhaps wait to invite industry to a bigger, better showcase of your talent. Make sure it is a strong production with professional lighting, sound, costumes, and production values of all kinds. Make sure that you and your castmates are strong in your performances. "Do as much local theatre as you can. Send a postcard and tell me you're in something, even if I haven't met you. I do tend to see a play with a larger cast," Marnie Saitta, CSA, specified, since a one-person show may be amazing, but it doesn't let us scout a bunch of actors at once.

Put together a press release announcing the run well before opening week and send it to blogs and papers for your local area. Your press release should include the where, when, who, what, why, of course. Include a phone number for reservations and industry comps. Shows are more likely to be reviewed if they will be running for one month, minimum. It just doesn't make sense for a reviewer to see a show in its opening week, have the review come out in the show's second week, and have the show close in week three. So, make sure you have at least a month of a run scheduled, to maximize the chances that your show will be reviewed.

Once the blogs and papers get your press release, reviewers will be assigned to cover the play, and they get in for free. You still want the cost and public reservation line included in your press release, so that this information can go in the paper's calendar listing. Always have one person listed as the industry contact and make sure there's a *professional* outgoing message attached to the number you're giving out—none of that insipid "please listen to the following song while we connect you to your party" or "please state your name at the tone" prompt nonsense.

Set up a separate industry comp RSVP phone line so that you will know who is coming to your show and when. Request a business card from industry reps and reviewers when they show up. This allows you to properly identify who gets industry kits and press kits as well as providing you with current contact information so that you can easily follow up with thank-you notes after the show, update your show bible, and keep folks posted on future events. You are always building a mailing list for future promotional pushes!

Call the reps at blogs and papers two weeks after they've received your press release. Ask if they'd like a press kit or stills from previews of the show to run with the review you're hoping they'll do. Be ready to provide those if that offer is accepted. Make sure you're on their "to review" list and, if you can, find out who's doing the review, so you'll have someone ready to meet and greet that person the night of the show.

Of course, the best way to get a review is to have good buzz about your show out there. So, don't just focus on getting the blogs and papers out. Do a little more legwork, if possible. Create postcards, flyers, and a professional-looking website. Whatever your design is, make it clean and easy to read. Include the pertinent information here as well, and get the postcard, flyer, and link *everywhere*. Have cast, crew, classmates, and friends help paper the town, stack flyers or postcards in every performance space, rehearsal space, casting studio, and industry hangout you know of. Ask each cast member to include the show's URL in their email's signature file and to share the link frequently via social media.

If you can spare the funds, put your flyer in Breakdown Services' announcement section. They will include it with the breakdowns that go out to hundreds of subscribing agents and managers. Again, provide lots of contact information and have a clean, professional look. If a Facebook ad is within your budget, consider that as well. Be very specific about how you target the news feeds in which your ad will appear. Shoot promo vids and post 'em at YouTube to drive Google spiders to your project.

About two weeks before the opening, send out more postcards inviting everyone already on your ever-growing mailing list to come see the show. Make sure that you have a phone number on the postcards for industry comps. "It's really random, but postcards are still the best way to get a casting director to come see you in a play," Cathy Reinking, CSA, explained. Even so, send an email to your mailing list as well. As always, if you're doing this from your own email account, use BCC to protect addresses. Better still, use a service like MailChimp to keep your fans and friends informed.

Keep in mind that industry folks get invited to every show going on in town every day (and there are plenty of them). Make your invitation stand out by having the most professional presentation you can afford. Make sure the industry kits and press kits—available upon request and at the ticket window—match the theme and design of the website you've created and the postcards you sent out. Kits include headshots and resumés, bios, programs, flyers, and any press you've already received. Make them look good!

These kits are what the casting people will take away with them, along with notes they make during your performance. And if they no-show, offer to get kits to them anyway. Many will accept that gesture and call actors in directly off the professional kit and the show's good buzz! CSA member Richard Hicks stressed, "Be in a *good* play. I read the papers. I know what's getting a good review. If you're in a good play, you'll get seen. Believe me."

As with anything like this, it's hard to know exactly what impact a mailing has on actual attendance. View the mailing as more of an investment in your reputation as a working actor than a way to drive attendance up. Sending show invitations reminds casting directors that you are *out there working* and keeps them informed of it.

Some theatres will do special industry nights in which casting directors, agents, managers, producers, and directors are invited to a catered affair with valet parking and an open bar. Are you bribing people to come to the show? No. You are presenting a special night just for us, knowing we won't have time to get dinner between leaving the office and coming to your show, knowing we'll be in a rush to find parking, and knowing—upon seeing our colleagues—we will most likely want to have a cocktail and schmooze a bit. Industry standard for these events is Tuesday, Wednesday, and Thursday nights with a start time of 8pm.

Read Chris Brogan and Julien Smith's *Trust Agents* or Malcolm Gladwell's *The Tipping Point* and it'll become abundantly clear that one of your best assets is a big-mouthed well-plugged-in supporter! Making your event feel as though it's a *must-check-out* show is a great approach, to get butts in seats *or* to benefit from the buzz even for those who don't show up to see your work. If you can point out *any* buzz you've gotten, press you've already done, words from plugged-in folks, etc., and get that on the radar of your target people, you could get a few of 'em to come out!

A great source of press is from your hometown. Contact reps from your alumni newsletter, hometown paper, a local radio show, even the morning news. Especially if you've moved to a larger market, your story could be an example of "local kid gone bigtime" and they love to feature lifestyle stories to round out all the hard-hitting news. A cover story in the college paper may not seem like a big deal, but that press goes into your collection of coverage and adds to the perception of you as lower-risk and on-the-rise, by buyers worldwide.

A multi-tiered approach to marketing is the best way to get (and keep) the attention of casting directors and agents you want to attend your shows. I know you don't want to know this, but return on investment for all this publicity is actually pretty low, unless you're involved in something that we were planning to attend already. That's why you shouldn't look at the cost-benefit ratio on publicity. It has a cumulative impact. And remember, you are in this for the long haul!

Postcards

I mentioned postcards for show promo already, but let's talk about postcards of your own, for your ongoing promotional efforts. These are just like "wish you were here" vacation postcards, but the photo you're showcasing on the front is of you. Some actors will use two headshots and a bit of text, others will stick with one, larger headshot and use stickers to promote the news of the moment, rather than printing up new cards for each new bit of career progress they're hoping to get out into the world. Of course, include your contact information on your postcards—at the very least, your website's URL.

It's important to note that you're not looking for instant gratification from sending postcards. It's like a billboard on the side of the road. You see the huge ad for Coca-Cola as you're driving along and hopefully the next time you're in the mood for a tasty beverage, you'll grab a Coke. Coca-Cola doesn't put up billboards hoping that you'll see a billboard, slam on the brakes, and pull a U-turn into the nearest 7-11 in order to buy a Coke right that second. Instant results are not what billboards—or postcards—are about.

> A memorable experience we had was when my son Chris was tracked down by a casting director from Los Angeles. We were living in New York City at the time while Chris was performing in a show. The casting director remembered Chris from a show he had seen him in five months earlier in the Los Angeles area, for which we had sent out postcards. He wanted him to audition for a pilot while we were still in New York. The casting director had kept the postcard with the agency information on it, which made it easy for him to locate my son for the audition.
>
> —Denise Winsor, parent to a young actor

Actor Blake Robbins told me about how he promotes shows using postcards. "I know mailing labels are fast and easy, but the message you're sending to the person who receives it is that they are as important as the thousand other people who might get this postcard. I highly recommend not doing that! Handwrite those addresses. The recipient then has a very different impression of that postcard. Next to the handwritten address, I wrote something very specific to my relationship with the recipient and a request for what I would like to see happen next. The only reason to send a postcard is if you know what you want to have happen when it gets there. It should be short, sweet and to the point."

Great Reviews

Have you gotten a great review? Share with the world! When you're trying to get people to invest in you as a performer, you want them to see how easy you are to sell, work with, and promote. If you were in a show with a great review (and the *entire* review was outstanding), consider reproducing the review with the masthead, date, and reviewer's name, then send out the entire one-page mock-up of that day's paper to people in the industry with the bits about you highlighted.

If the review for the production itself was so-so or the publication isn't one of the "biggies," instead use the best line about *you* at the bottom of your cover letter, somewhere on your resumé, or on your postcards. Remember my *LA Weekly* review? That whole "Bonnie Gillespie is excellent" thing? Doesn't get much better than that! They weren't crazy about the play, but you betcha that tagline became a part of my promotional materials.

Don't know if you've been reviewed? Set up a Google Alert for your name. You'll be emailed every time your name appears online. If your name is frequently misspelled, sign up for Google Alerts for those variations too. If you have a too-common name, add +actor or the name of the show to the Google Alert to narrow your results. Remember, you earned the review. Share it!

DIY Publicity

If you don't have a publicist on retainer (they're very expensive), how do you get on a red carpet? Well, if you aren't a movie star yet, maybe you've been in an indie film that got accepted into a film festival or two. Find out if this festival will have an opening night gala or red carpet event and do whatever you can to get yourself invited.

Have your agent or manager call the festival to get you two tickets to the red carpet. Don't have representation? Have your buddy call the festival, pretending to be your manager, and have him persuade them to invite you. Have that same buddy there with a camera to take shots of you on the carpet in case you don't see your pictures later on wireimage.com. It's good to have these.

Now, you might be saying that all this red carpet silliness is nonsense, pure vanity, and has nothing to do with acting. Well, you're right. But this is a business and a huge part of the business is marketing. Red carpet events lend to an air of mystique and excitement. There's something about a shot of you looking oh-so-dapper and gorgeous on the red carpet—with cameras flashing—that makes people wonder who you are. Why are people taking pictures of you? Are you the next big thing? It's almost ridiculous, I know, but I swear people think like this. Important people. People who can hire you.

Think I'm exaggerating here? Think again. My first four years in Los Angeles, I temped at a major film studio, in just about every department, as an executive assistant. I picked up phones, scheduled appointments, made all kinds of reservations and lunch plans for at least 70 executives, from a young manager in the facilities department to the head of the studio. Guess what. There really are people in the publicity departments leafing through magazines like *People* and *US Weekly* to see who's currently "hot" and getting attention. These very people will then make lists of the photographed actors and see if they can be fit into the studio's current roster of films in pre-production and development. It's sick and wrong and has nothing to do with acting, but it's true. It can't be ignored.

When the time is right, you'll want to have a good publicist on your team. Until then, be your own damn publicist and work hard for yourself.

—Assaf Cohen

Create Your Own Press

One of my favorite ninja moves came from an actor who had a small recurring role on a very highly critically-acclaimed (but low-rated) show. She knew the show wasn't going to stay on the air, and that meant she'd be looking for another series soon. She also knew that the only way she'd get considered at the next tier was to be sure everyone—even those who had never seen an episode of this brilliant show—knew she was low-risk for similar work. She created an interview.

Basically, she hired a team to write a profile about her, put her on the "cover page" of a magazine that doesn't really exist, and take photos of her being totally on-brand. Then she created a mailing and targeted everyone who needed to know she was thrilled to be a part of this show (that we all knew was about to be cancelled) and that she was absolutely smart enough about this business and her position in it to be given the opportunity to at least test at network, the following pilot season. So, let's reverse-engineer this whole thing.

She started with her targets. You know how to map out and pursue a meaningful list of target buyers thanks to the chapter on **Targeting Buyers**. Just that simply, she chose *not* to reach out to everyone in casting, but to those who stood the best chance of needing her on a pilot the following season. That cut the number of recipients of this mailing way down. Were she to target agents, she'd be looking a tier above her existing rep. There's no point in blanketing the town with even the most gorgeous of marketing materials. Even in tiny markets, not everyone on the buying side needs to know you exist in order for you to make a living as an artist.

What next? She hired a stylist, a photographer, a graphic designer, and a writer. Not cheap, but also nowhere near as expensive as hiring a publicist and media trainer. She outlined her goals for this piece of advertising—let's be honest, that's exactly what it is—and she talked with the writer to get all the salient points across, succinctly. No spin on the part of the network, the talkshow host, the stringer trying to get a story picked up by the wire services, or some random blogger. Nope. This was all manufactured to align with her brand *and* her goals for the following pilot season.

After creating a cover photo for this "magazine," and a three-page "interview" to feature within it, she created a kit to mail out. Using nothing more sophisticated than a three-ring binder sheet-protector sleeve and a piece of clear tape, she put these documents—printed on high-quality bond—into something she could mail without an envelope! The sheet protector went straight through the mail, with a stamp and mailing address label and her return address label all strategically placed after she consulted with the graphic designer on layout of the "cover." Even if no one were to open the mailing, it was doing its job, because you couldn't *miss* the point.

The "cover" was her face and some "WOW! POW! YAY!" type words just like you'd see if any celeb were gracing the cover of the 'zine. Printed on the back of that page was the beginning of the interview, but you'd never see it unless you took the piece of tape off the mailing and pulled everything out to explore more. The goal was not to get people to read the whole interview. This was basically a high-priced postcard, to help her buyers perceive her as upper-tier. The second piece of card-stock paper in this mailing was the rest of the "interview." Also two-sided, with the really *important* stuff on the page that faced in the other outwardly direction, in this clear-sleeve mailer. All the best sales language about *where she was headed* after wrapping this amazing show that was so highly critically-acclaimed was on that back page, as well as a few other on-brand photos, just like you'd see in any magazine feature, profiling a famous actor.

But this actor wasn't (yet) famous. She had read for me a few times in my first few years of casting, then she got this show after doing the usual one-line co-star up to one-scene co-star up to first-time guest-star on up to this particular recurring guest role on this hot-in-the-industry (but underappreciated in the rest of the world) TV show. So, when I received this mailing, I knew she was telling me, "Look at my tier-jump! Don't you think I'm ready for my series regular, next pilot season?"

Sure enough, this actor booked a small but memorable role in the pilot of a series that ran for five years. She was named a series regular by episode six of season one, when her little recurring character had hit so well with the fanbase that there was no question they needed to lock her in, rather than risk losing her the following pilot season, as she would have been able to test elsewhere, had they not committed to her (and therefore vice-versa) right then.

So, let's say she invested a couple grand into this particular marketing strategy, once you tally up the pros she hired to help execute it, the printing costs, and the mailing supplies (including postage and address labels). When did that pay off? Before the first commercial break of the pilot episode of the series that would go on to pay her very, very well (and continues to do so, thanks to residuals).

Did anyone on the receiving end say, "Ooh! Yes! I remember this edition of 'Not a Real Magazine' quarterly?" No. Of course not. She didn't mock up a cover of *People* magazine. She *got* interviewed. That she paid to make that happen? Irrelevant. Yes, you could have the same thing happen via a "real" interview, if you're lucky enough to have connected with a journalist from a small paper back home, or an up-and-coming blogger looking to profile up-and-coming actors. But do you have quality control that way? Nope. And at some point in your career, the investment could make the difference.

Obviously, this actor was already on the rise. She was having as close to "linear success" as is possible in this industry, going from co-star to guest-star to recurring, and then she pounced on the opportunity to get considered for the next tier. Would she have booked the pilot without the mailing? We can't know. As I've said from the very beginning of my time writing for actors: It's not the one thing you do; it's all the things you do.

Should you put out full-page ads in the trades, congratulating yourself on getting cast in a studio feature film or signing with a fancy agency? You could do that. It's guaranteed exposure (for a *lot* of money) with an audience of the biggest power players in this industry. Is that your next target? The top agent at the top agency whose clients are all *name* actors? The network exec who's looking for his next 10-year top-10 sitcom star? Maybe not yet. Certainly, people at tiers below these folks see the ad too, but this is where the research you've done on your target buyers will help you choose what investment is worth it, at this stage.

Make a quick list about what career experiences you've had that would be (or could be) considered newsworthy. Maybe that student film you did five years ago didn't turn out great, but did you notice that the director went on to win a Streamy last year? Maybe that low-budget indie from which you never got footage is a black hole in your mind, but hey, didn't the writer of that script just win the Nicholl Fellowship? You don't know? It's your *job* to know. "Starred in a feature by the latest Nicholl Fellowship winner," is newsworthy. Really look at everything you've ever done—and the people with whom you did it all—and see if there's good spin out there, somewhere.

Armed with that heat, consider creating a press release. A simple three-paragraph notice at prlog.org could be smart, if well-timed. But before you take a stab at that, make sure you've studied up on what press releases look like (that same link is a great place to poke around; you'll soon learn what's standard and what's not), follow the formula (don't get cute), and be prepared that a placement could lead to a news organization looking to do a story based on your press release. Send that press release around to your hometown paper, along with your bio, press photo (it doesn't have to be the same as your headshot), and some convenient times for a follow-up interview, if they'd like to run a story. And then, keep that story (PDF the webpage, if it ran online only) to add to your press kit, going forward.

By far, the most important element of *allllll* this type of work is that everything be ridiculously on-brand and in service of where you're headed. If you're mysterious? Having a social media presence at all could take away that enigmatic quality that makes you castable. Creating postcards, show flyers, a website, a media kit, a press release, a social networking profile that doesn't show us how to cast you next or that doesn't leave us feeling as though we *get you* will not help you. On the contrary, it could hurt you.

The key to charisma is public self-acceptance.
　　　　　　　—America's Next Top Model season one

24: Working It

Like it or not, developing relationships is one of the most important elements of getting work in Hollywood. For most actors, working the room is the scariest part of the game. I hear actors say they'd like to avoid networking, hoping to "be a recluse" à la Johnny Depp. Well, I hate to break it to you, but you don't get to skip schmoozefests, avoid the press, and live abroad until *after* you're famous. Before that happens, you *must* work the room. Johnny Depp earned the right to indulge his natural desire to stay out of the Hollywood hype machine by becoming a bankable commodity. Before he landed *Nightmare on Elm Street* or *21 Jump Street* (or the indie projects he did before those gigs), he had to work the room just like everyone else.

You cannot master the game without some measure of networking. But as with most things in this business, getting good at "working it" has everything to do with setting yourself up for success, creating a plan of action, building strength through practice, and following through. So, let's get to it, shall we? Here's how to work the room.

First off, put yourself at ease by realizing that no one is at a *legitimate* networking event because he has been *paid* to be there. Of course, there are networking events at which professionals are paid for their time, but even then, the high-profile people who might've lined their pockets in exchange for an hour or two don't *have to* stick around and chat with you unless they want to. Therefore, the biggest misconception of networking—that no one really *wants* to meet you or spend time with you—is exactly that: a misconception. If the casting director, the agent, the manager, the producer, the director, the writer, is *there*, talking to you, it's because she wants to be there, talking to you.

If you're at a networking event that takes place after a play or a showcase, you know that these fine folks have experienced your work and want to chat with you to get to know more about who *you* are outside of that work they just saw you do. If you're at an event that begins with a Q&A or panel discussion by the industry pros and then ends with a mixer, well, then these folks may not know anything about you other than the fact that you belong to this group and you've enjoyed the presentation. Start from there.

Your job is *not* to sidle up next to someone in the industry and begin spouting off an oral resumé. Honestly, the best opening line you can give to anyone is very simply: "Thank you so much for being here." If that is met with a reply of, "It's great to be here," you're given the greenlight for continuing communication. (If you get a polite smile and nod, just move along.) Wanna set yourself up for the best possible connections as you build your web of trust? Let's start with a few fundamentals.

Choose the right scene. Make sure you're not opting in for failure by showing up at a place that is too cool for you (or an event that's not cool enough for you). The mismatch will be what we see and feel in you and it'll be what you remember about the event.

Back when I was an actor, I had been led to believe that I needed to "see and be seen" at trendy Hollywood parties in order to tier jump. Most of that sort of networking is purely social. Do deals get made in that scene sometimes? Sure! But more deals happen over lunch, in offices, over the phone, or via email. So, connect with folks at trendy gatherings if you're the type who cares to go to such things, then follow through. And, if you're the type who prefers non-Hollywood schmoozefests, take heart! There's plenty of networking going on in your style.

There are far too many networking events and random industry parties out there to make it *easy* to know which one is going to be the best investment of your time and energy. Until you've experienced all types of events, you might not know for sure which ones are your speed. (This is not permission to find your speed and then stay only within your comfort zone, of course.) But when you are *learning* how to network, it is vitally important that you find the types of events that suit you best. Targeting the right scene is going to put you in a room with others who may share your general vibe and business style, and that'll be a good start, even if you're a wee bit uncomfortable at first.

De-stress. Alleviate any stress you might have over the fact that you're about to talk with someone who could "do something for your career." That anxiety bleeds through your chitchat and makes everyone uncomfortable. It's like a bad date with a desperate person we'd otherwise find attractive, if it weren't for that cloak of *needy*. The spin on this that works for me is: "This producer and I are at the same event *not* because he can do something for my career, but because we obviously share a common interest or else we wouldn't be at the same place at the same time, having the opportunity to have this conversation. Maybe there's some synergy to experience here. Let's chat!" Approach the interaction as an opportunity to connect and then be open to what that might mean. Open. Not attached to anything going any particular way.

Get over the whole "fake" issue. Yes, networking is going to occasionally feel "fake" (and by "fake," I mean "surface-y"). But it's actually good news that our industry operates so close to the surface. My husband says he loves the shallowness precisely because it means that a very casual introduction over a round of drinks can lead to feelings of deep connection. That level of instant intimacy—when properly harnessed and then maintained with professionalism—can yield many future career advancements. A meeting at a showcase doesn't have to conclude with an audition scheduled for the next day. Once I've seen your work and schmoozed with you enough to know that you're someone I'd love to put on a set someday, you might not hear from me for a year or more. But you can bet that when the right role comes along, I'll be calling you, since we have that "shallow" personal relationship that you've maintained, ninja style.

One of the biggest obstacles actors set up for themselves in networking is this feeling that they're going to be required to let strangers in too far and too quickly. Nope. No one really wants to get intimate. Most folks want to talk about themselves. Accepting the shallowness of Hollywood relationships clears that right up. You can spend an entire evening bonding with someone over the topic of *Beverly Hills, 90210: The Brenda Years* and come away feeling totally connected with your new best friend (me), all the while keeping your soft underbelly safe from sharp pointy things.

Do your homework. If there's anything you can figure out about the people you're meeting, do it up front. Google folks. Don't come up, shake someone's hand, and ask, "So how do I get in on projects you're casting?" Most casting directors who are out in the world, networking, are also sharing their journeys online. Research them before you show up! Better yet, revisit your show bible, since you've long ago done research. Don't waste facetime with a buyer asking about something you could've learned elsewhere. That only makes sure the impression you make is not about *you*, but about what you didn't bother to look into ahead of time. Not ninja.

Build your networking skills. Confidence is attractive. We like being around people who feel comfortable in their own skin. Fake it if you have to. Talk about *things*, not people. Things are better topics, safer topics, easier topics. If someone insists on bringing the convo around to *people*, find a way to compliment others; never gossip.

If you're struggling with remembering names, employ kinesthetic remembering and repetition to help with that. The simple act of physically connecting with someone else while saying their name does wonders for cementing that person's name in your memory. Handshakes, touches of the arm, hugs (when appropriate, of course) all work. And if you're in an environment where that's not possible, repeat the person's name a few times within a few moments (once or twice aloud, early in the conversation; the rest of the time in your head, as the conversation is just getting started and you're unlikely to miss more than early pleasantries). Text it to yourself, if you can!

If you still forget names, let yourself off the hook when you do. Think about how you feel when someone forgets your name. It's no big deal, right? The *anxiety* is the obstacle—not your ability to remember someone's name. So once you remove the stress over "how bad you are" at remembering names, you'll find it's actually a lot easier to get better at it! Meanwhile, be okay with saying, "I know we've met, but I've suddenly forgotten your name." While introducing your contact to someone else, it's a great time to get this admission off your chest. Since the person is now focused on meeting the other new person, they're not troubled by the fact that you've temporarily forgotten their name. Your flub will be glossed over and you'll get a chance to hear their name again and employ a memory tactic that can help you seal their name into your mind.

Use a wingman. The buddy system worked for grade school field trips and it works for networking. Have an ally and check in with each other. This helps with meeting folks you don't already know, remembering names, taking the pressure off when you feel the need to carry a conversation, and for getting "tapped out" when you say or drink too much. I remember a Hollywood Happy Hour event at which we had a few folks who *way* overindulged. It's not pretty when I have to say to a producer, "I'd love to introduce you to that awesome actor over there, but she's falling down drunk, so let's do it another time." A good wingman keeps that from getting so ugly. A good wingman also helps you from being vulnerable if someone skeevy is on the prowl, rather than actually looking to do authentic connecting with fellow professionals.

Any time you're attending an event with someone you know (which I strongly recommend), have a plan in place to help one another through the schmoozefest. If you are shy, you should avoid teaming up with another shy person. You'll just stand off in a corner *together* instead of alone. Don't network with the same wingman every time. If the only association someone has of you is that you're "that guy's wingman," you may be losing out on strengthening your individual relationships within the industry. When my husband and I attend functions together, we are rarely found near one another. It's far better use of our networking skills to have him talking me up to a producer who may want to hire me to cast a project while I'm across the room talking my husband up to a theatrical agent who may want to sign him.

Play host. It's one of the most effective ways to survive networking, if you're filled with anxiety about it. Introduce folks who don't know one another. This takes the pressure off you as "the new one" and gives you the comfort of a familiar face standing next to you as you muster up the courage to meet someone you've been targeting. Don't play host the whole night, just long enough to loosen up about meeting that next new person. You'll see—by introducing others—it's no big deal.

This is one of the primary reasons my networking skills began to flourish. I made it a goal to constantly surround myself with the best people I knew, whether they knew one another or not. And then any time I stood in a room where two of the best people I knew didn't know each other, I'd make sure to introduce them and get them talking. It may seem as though I'm being a good host, by behaving this way. That's happening. But what is *also* happening is: I am networking. Suddenly, I'm the one who hooked up two people who may happen to go on to work together in the future. "Gosh, we've been working together for a while now. How did we first get together? Oh, right! Bonnie Gillespie introduced us," becomes a refrain. And if you think that kind of conversation going on when I'm not around is not helping with *my* web of trust, you're missing the point.

> *The value of networking is not measured by the number of people we meet but by the number of people we introduce to others.*
>
> —Simon Sinek

Be ready for the tough questions ("How long have you been in town?" "How old are you?" "What are you working on?") and the easy ones ("How do you know so-and-so?" "Who is your agent?" "Where are you from?") but try not to ask the tough ones of anyone. You know it hurts to be asked what you're working on when the answer is, "Nothing." And you know it's tough to spin that you're "new in town" when asked, directly, how long you've been here. So don't put others through that, either. If you're new to town, be new! Talking about what excites and confounds you about your new home is a very safe networking topic.

Producers, directors, writers, casting directors, etc., can get really tired of being asked what we're working on. At some point, we feel like just grabbing a mic and announcing the list to the entire venue, once and for all, because having to repeat it all so many times becomes tedious. Shouldn't we—the most creative people on the planet—find a way to have a little more fun with this topic? It's simple. Pitch coach Dyana Valentine asks, "What are you good at?" I love to ask, "What makes your heart sing?"

The answers to those questions are far more interesting, revealing, and fun to hear! Better yet, the answers may be more in-line with your bullseye, your pitch, your brand, your logline than you may ever imagine possible! Won't that be fun to bring together, organically?

How NOT to Work It

Sometimes the way to get good at working it is by knowing what behaviors don't help you. Because what doesn't work is often pretty easily identifiable, here are a few biggies to avoid.

Being too vague. Of course there are projects you might be working on that have elements not yet open to the public. Got it. But when you say too little about anything, we wonder if it's actually "for real" or if it's fictional action going on. It's like mentioning a boyfriend no one ever meets. At least give the guy a name.

Being cliché. Just like no one wants to read in your bio that you began acting "at the tender age of five" or that "Hollywood was calling," no one wants to hear you *speaking* in Hollywood clichés. Come up with actual, meaningful, not-overused words and phrases that help cement your brand and let us get to know you.

Being all about the business cards. I'm sure somewhere, some well-meaning career coach thought it would be brilliant to tell actors, "never leave an encounter without a person's business card." *yawn* If you're obsessed with getting or giving out business cards, you're missing the whole point of an in-person networking event. It's to *get* one another. It's to *connect* as people. Let paperwork happen organically.

Complaining. No one wants to hear you grouse about how much the economy sucks, how crappy your little apartment is, how much you hate Los Angeles, how you're dropping your "useless agent," or anything else you need to go to therapy about. Chronic complainers are like that Peanuts character Pig Pen. The cloud of ick stays around far too long. Don't be that actor.

Dressing poorly. Now, I have to be careful on this one, as I am never going to be accused of being a fashion plate. I have one or two things I like to wear and that's what I wear *all the time*. But when I see an actor show up at a networking event in gym gear, I'm kind of shocked. This isn't yoga class. Put on a bra for cryin' out loud! And please, run a comb through your hair and swish some mouthwash around. Finally, for the love of all that is holy, do not *bathe* in cologne. Thank you.

Ingratiating yourself into conversations. I get that this one is a tougher balance, especially if you're not so good at reading signals from others. (But, you're an actor. Get good at reading people. Please!) When you pop over to say goodbye—interrupting the conversation to do so—make it quick and then go. Don't turn it into an opportunity to launch into a story, now that you have someone's attention. Unless you're given the physical or verbal signal to join in, be careful. Whatever you do, don't join in and then make it *all about you*. Be interested, not interesting.

Being needy. Needy throbs like a toothache. Find a way to turn that stuff *off*. Don't think about how, among these people, could be your next agent or someone who could cast you in something or anyone who may "change your life" in any way. That's like going on a first date thinking up baby names. Don't do it. We all feel it. Relax and enjoy getting to know people. Take the pressure off yourself and off us!

***

You don't have to get good at networking, of course, but it sure does help! Considering the fact that those of us in the business of filtering talent will use any excuse to remove someone from a list, that you were *bad* at networking when we last encountered you could be enough to keep you from advancing on a project or staying on a list at an agency. The numbers are huge, and we'll use whatever help we can to thin them sometimes. Increase your odds that it's not your "bad networking" that got you excluded from the room.

Directional Networking

There's the kind of networking that's beneficial for everyone to some degree. People come together to build relationships that could pay off in several different directions. Producers connect with directors whose vision they find inspiring. Directors need financial backing from people who believe in them. Agents connect with casting directors on whose projects they want their up-and-coming clients seen. Casting directors connect with filmmakers whose work they enjoy. It all feeds into itself.

And actors network to connect with everyone. They meet writers who want to create vehicles for them (or at least who want to recommend the actors, on projects they've created). They need to connect with agents or managers who cannot wait to help them to the next tier. They need to build trust among filmmakers and showrunners and producers and casting directors. Actors need to find a way to spark some sort of motivation in each of us to *think of them* when we need an actor of their type. But when actors network, must it always be one-directional?

When a new-to-town actor reaches out to a casting director or agent and says, "Let me take you to coffee," there's a whole lot of potential upside for the actor getting this meeting, and a whole lot of potential downside for the industry pro, which is why this sort of invitation isn't often accepted. You maximize your chance for making it happen by bringing something to the table other than your sparse resumé, out-of-market headshots, determination to succeed, and new-to-town enthusiasm. Obviously, the greater the chance that we might be scooping the rest of the town on tomorrow's "hot new star," the greater the chance that we're gonna see that meeting as filled with upside for us too.

That's what you want to create: a win-win meeting. It's good for you. It's good for us. Your ability to sell us on why it's good for us is key. It's one thing to say that you've worked with the hot young filmmaker everyone's trying to score a meeting with at Sundance. But to say that you *and* the hot young filmmaker are meeting up for coffee and you'd love to have a particular agent join both of you to see if there's possible synergy in the relationships is to present a whole different level of opportunity. Now the agent might not only be meeting with a great future client (you) but perhaps meeting with someone (the hot young filmmaker) who will potentially be a long-term source of work for everyone on that agent's roster, should they hit it off and become besties.

Whenever you can add incentives for a meeting to take place by introducing a third party to whom the industry pro would love exposure *or* even by being a powerful hyphenate yourself, you're far more likely to be met with anything other than that painful "don't call us, we'll call you" vibe, after you've taken the risk to reach out.

How often do you network in the direction you're asking us to network? How often do you meet with green, enthusiastic, completely-clueless-to-the-biz actors upon whose lives you could make a positive impact, just by showing them how to format their resumé or where to download sides? How often do you share your toys, offering advice at actors' message boards, in local schools, or via your blog? Do a little mentoring. Pay it forward. Invest in a relationship with someone who offers you absolutely nothing whatsoever in return.

Let two things wash over you, here. One: Agents, managers, casting directors, producers, writers, showrunners, and directors are asked to do exactly this type of thing *every day* by *many* actors. You do it a few times and consider the ridiculous volume of requests to do it we're fielding and you'll understand why it's both rare that we engage in it and a huge deal when we do. Two: Mentoring can be a wonderful way to remind yourself of how far you've come. It can allow you to get a different perspective on the day-to-day stuff you're facing. It could even connect you with someone whose career will skyrocket long before yours does, and that person might be so grateful to you for the early support that you'll benefit in ways you never imagined possible.

Networking is often seen as an "all about me" venture. That simply doesn't have to be the case. We can change the direction of networking right now.

Get Invited and Go

One of the bizarrely more important elements to the "actor on the rise" formula is the "being out there" of it all. Not just networking and going to parties, but also hitting red carpet events, getting invited to gifting suites, or being photographed in front of a charity auction's step-and-repeat. Having your photos up at Getty Images or on WireImage or coursing through IMDb-Pro will make a difference, when you're at the right tier to take advantage of these elements.

Make a daily visit to the sites that feature red carpet photos and browse through all the people whose names you don't yet know. Better yet, go through the archives of these websites and check out actors whose names you know today, but didn't know a year ago, because they're *that* new. Of course, looking at their IMDb profile, you know they're not new—not by a longshot—but they're new to this tier, and that's usually not by accident. They probably "did the scene" a bit. If you're in a minor market, that means attending the film festivals that come to your town or to towns nearby. It means hitting premieres or any industry events that come close to where you live. It's going to those opening nights of plays at the bigger theatres, taking advantage of being seen at any event that is industry-like anywhere nearby. It will help cement your reputation as one of the folks *in* the industry, even in a non-industry town.

For those in Los Angeles, piece of cake! You are able to attend something daily, in Hollywood. Of course, that adds its own wrinkle, because you have "option overload" and you have to be smart about the events you choose to attend. Run everything through the brand filter. Which events reinforce your brand and which ones make people scratch their heads about why you're there? Pore through online photo banks and start making a list of what *feels* like a *you* event. Read through the PR calendars of events to determine *what* is going on out there, and whether you need an invitation to attend. Visit smfa4.com for your *SMFA* Hot List of resources for industry events and to discuss ninja tips for getting "on the list" to attend.

If you'd like to hire a publicist for a short-term purpose, several folks in PR do à la carte offerings that are way more affordable than keeping a publicist on retainer. If you're frugal but smart about it, you could hire someone for a few weeks, hit the circuit, get a little media training, and then use that foundation to do it yourself when you cannot afford having the extra person on your team. No, I'm not saying you'll be able to get yourself into *all* of the events that a well-connected publicist can get you into (the *R* in PR stands for relations, which means, we're trading on relationships, here, and publicists have more relationships than probably anyone else in this business), but you *can* get started. At certain tiers, that's more than enough to get a little leverage!

Networking as "Yes, and..."

Consider looking at networking as an opportunity to improvise! That's always fun, right? Use the improvisational staple of "yes, and...." It's that wonderful way that every question is answered, in which every line of dialogue is met. Never deny. Always build. You know how to "yes, and..." when you're acting. Let's look at networking as a great opportunity to do even more of that.

Never tell someone they're wrong for having enjoyed your work by saying, "Oh, no. I was only okay." That's a very bad actor habit, and one that's easy to overcome with practice. If you're someone who would ordinarily deflect compliments in the way Wonder Woman deflects bullets with her bracelets, you can turn every bit of the conversation into an opportunity to "yes, and..." while not feeling like an egomaniac or a denial-driven actor. Find ways to say,

"Wow. Thanks. This was a really fun role," when you're told your work was awesome.

What about audition room chitchat? Is that a form of networking? Absolutely! Is it a sign that you're more likely to book or less likely to book, if it happens or doesn't happen, after your audition? Nah. I've seen actors asked to stay in for a chat and be the absolute last choice in producers' minds; they're just fascinated by something on the actors' resumés or want a date or something. Many times, the chitchat has *nothing* to do with whether you're close to booking the role. Booking the room, though? Definitely, this is a factor.

Can bombing that small talk keep you from booking when your audition was otherwise strong? Well, yeah. Let's say you're totally right for the role and you did a great job at the audition. But the director has another actor in mind who he knows really well in person. He knows, based on this relationship and the subtleties of the non-work-environment interactions, that the other actor is a great fit for the role. And if you can both be a better actor than that other actor who is on his mind *and* hit those subtle levels of personality that come out in chitchat, the role could be yours. If instead you choke and give really bad "room," you're less likely to book, simply because these folks know they're investing in days or weeks on set with you, and they have to "get you." No one wants to spend a ton of time around someone with whom they're feeling no connection.

Taking the Meeting

Between the days of "submitting and hoping for a preread" and reaching "offer only" status, actors do something called "taking the meeting" in order to get cast. This is when you aren't yet a *name* actor but certainly have enough credits that your work speaks for itself. Perhaps you're a "qualified name," which means a grandma in a Red State doesn't know you beyond, "Hey it's *that* guy," but the industry knows exactly what you add to a project in terms of bankability. Once you're at this stage, the questions become: "Is this actor right for the role?" and "Is the actor interested and available?" and "Do we all want to work together?" In order to get those questions answered, you've got to take the meeting.

Meeting Prep Work

Find out who will be there. Your agent should be able to nail this information down for you. Ask others who have met with this casting director, this showrunner, this producer, this director, this writer, what their experiences were like. This is not to put yourself in some "other-focused" state of mind before the meeting; it's *just* to get clear on anything that might throw you off (and knowing about it up front can take the edge off). For instance, "Jamie" is a female, and you thought you were meeting with a man. Or they have a dog in the office, and you're afraid of dogs and would've totally become freaked out upon encountering the critter. Or every single general this casting director has ever conducted has started a half-hour late. Knowing these things before the meeting puts you at ease about "what it all means" and keeps you from turning anything into "all about *you*."

Revisit the chapter on **Your Show Bible** for tips on studying your targets ahead of time. Now, some folks are going to be tougher to research, because they like keeping an air of mystique. They may not *do* interviews or appear on panels at film festivals. They may not *have* a Facebook page or a LinkedIn account, where you can at least get the scoop on their path to their current position, up from the mailroom 10 years before. But at least you tried! Knowing they're not "out there" is *also* intel. If you've searched thoroughly and asked your fellow ninjas to check their show bibles as well, your lack of info isn't coming from lack of effort, so you're okay.

Read the script. Read it twice. And if you don't have time to read it, ask your agent to send you the coverage that was done (by someone on staff at the agency, usually) on the script, when the agency was determining whether this script would be a good fit for you. Ask an assistant at the agency to flag a couple of scenes that are key for your potential character. At the very least, read those. Be ready to read from the script. It won't always happen, but be prepared. You'll likely talk about the script, the storyline, and the character you're hoping to play.

Don't try to impress anyone. You're not being asked for a meeting because you *aren't* what we're looking for. You're someone we like for this project and now we just need to see if we want to work together at this time. If you're a working actor who has taken a break to go to college, raise a family, or do theatre somewhere out of town, we may just want to meet with you face to face to see what you look like these days. While your reel may look fabulous and your headshot is stunning, if we can see the injection points from your last Botox treatment, we may be very glad we took the meeting before casting you outright to do those extreme close-ups in HD!

Meetings 101

Sometimes your meeting will take place in a room at the production office or on the studio lot. Sometimes, in a conference room or at the casting director's office. And sometimes the meeting will be held over a meal. You can assume if it's a meal meeting that lunch is on us. Don't order anything too outrageous and don't booze it up. Keep your desire to work the room with other movers and shakers to a minimum. This is the type of party where you dance with the one that brung ya. Obviously, be polite and say hi to others, but stay focused, even if Bruckheimer is at the next table in the commissary.

Don't have anything scheduled for a couple of hours after the meeting. Of course, it's fine to be busy and have other things going on (auditions, table reads for current projects, fittings, shoots, etc.), but when you're doing the Hollywood meeting, you never know how long it's gonna last. If a busy day is the only option for the meeting, make sure your agent has communicated your time restrictions with the producers ahead of time.

Whatever you do, don't be results-oriented. If you're able to wrap your mind around the concept that your only mission in taking the meeting is to learn more about this person with whom you're meeting, let this person get to know more about you, and strengthen (or begin) a relationship that will last for decades, you can relax more fully. But if you show up with the stakes high, feeling like it's make-or-break, like this is *the* role you have to book, guess what "reads" in the room? None of your professionalism, none of your authenticity, none of your gloriously-prepared talking points, none of your relaxed vibe, none of your brand awareness, none of your bookability. Nope. All that shows when you're results-oriented is your need for a certain result. All that shows when you're driven by what you hope will happen is that you hope something will happen. And that feels like desperation on the receiving end.

When your only goal is to authentically connect—just like you do with your scripted material as an actor—you shine. Anything else that comes from the meeting is a bonus.

In the Room

Don't make it all about you. Don't make it all about us either. Be prepared to talk about the work of those you respect, coaches under whom you've learned the most, plays you've seen, your thoughts on the award-winners at recent festivals, viability of various shows presented at the upfronts, anything that shows you're keeping up with the industry *and* that shares your POV about it all.

Often the meeting is as much about stroking the egos of the guys in the room as it is about the director, producers, casting director, or execs getting to know you as a person. If you've done your prep work and know enough about the background of the people who will meet you in the room, you will easily be able to have a conversation about their work and your thoughts about what their strengths are. Y'know how good it feels when someone says to you, "Oh, I saw you in that film! You were *excellent!*" Well, we love hearing that sort of thing too. Share the love. As long as you know what you're talking about and genuinely mean what you're saying, that sort of thing can't hurt.

Consider this a great opportunity to pitch yourself as a viable commodity. Talk about your existing fanbase and the types of marketing your publicist will do on your behalf, as a cast member on this project. Make it clear that you love doing junkets and interviews. That sort of thing really makes the number crunchers happy, in terms of knowing you won't have to be paid outrageous bonuses in order to do press tours or to show up at film festivals, since you enjoy doing it.

Ignore verbal commitments. I know that in "real life" a verbal *yes* feels like a done deal, but you need to prepare yourself for the Hollywood truth: Producers and directors will say things in the meeting that they have no intention (or perhaps no ability) to carry out. All formal casting offers come—in writing—from the casting office. We email over an offer and then spend hours (or days, or weeks) hammering out the details of the deal memo with the agent. Certainly, there are cases in which verbal contracts have been found binding, even between talent and production companies in Hollywood, but the majority of the time, until you have a contract in front of you with a producer's signature on it, you shouldn't assume you've been cast, no matter what the director or producer has said during the meeting.

Following Up

Have your agent make contact the day after the meeting to relay any thoughts you were left with about the project, shoot dates, possible conflicts, your enthusiasm for being a part of the project, etc. That phone call from your agent will also serve as a temperature check on the producers. When an agent calls me after we've done a talent meeting, I can let the agent know the disposition of the producers, director, and anyone else who was at the meeting. I can let your agent know if we'll be moving forward with a formal offer or if we have more meetings to get through. I'll share a bit about our timeline for making decisions and also come up with a date by which we should talk again.

Your Pitch

Every time you open your mouth, you're conducting your own personal PR campaign. What brand are you putting out there?
—Kara DeFrias, writer-brand manager

You won't often be asked to pitch yourself or a project on which you're working at networking events or in meetings, but when you *are* prompted with, "So, tell me about yourself," the ninja move is to have a pitch ready. Ideally, it doesn't sound rehearsed, it hits your bullseye, it touches on your *why* as an artist, it demonstrates the castability or bankability you posses, and it gets listeners jazzed about being in the "you" business.

The reason we want to get very comfortable with the process of talking about ourselves in a meaningful way is because it helps our potential buyers, our potential representatives, our potential fans *easily* understand what it is we do, who we are, and how they can benefit from getting on board.

Lead off with how you want the industry to see you. And if you want to be seen as, "I can do anything and everything," let me remind you that the "Jack of All Trades" is usually the "Master of None." Sure, you may be masterful at several things. Save that nugget 'til they've bought and paid for your services in the one thing for which you are primarily associated. Trust me, this specificity is the shortest distance between two points—those points being wherever you are right now and where you ultimately want to be in this industry.

Being clear on who you are is your first step to a good pitch. This comes down to knowing your bullseye and being really clear on not just your type, but also the vibe of the stories you like to tell, as a creative. Being authentic, speaking about yourself on-brand, and talking about projects that inspire you will help others understand who you are and where it is that you may intersect, profitably.

Your passion is a beautiful thing to have humming in the background, but don't lead with it. Stuff like, "I got into this business because I am driven to tell stories that help people come to a better understanding of the human condition," or, "I saw a performance when I was a child and was so moved that I forgot I was watching a play. I was transported to another world, right there in the theatre. My life would never be the same," these are gorgeous *whys*. But people on the buying end rarely want to know about those motives until you're on *Inside the Actors Studio*.

Take advantage of family dinners to test out your pitch. Practice networking at non-entertainment-industry events. Practice shaking hands, schmoozing, and entering and leaving ongoing conversations with a safe group of friends and colleagues 'til you get more confident. Don't strive for perfection, just "better than last time" each time. Fire up your webcam and shoot a pitch to test out your wording and presentation, even your wardrobe. Practice now will benefit you later, when that golden opportunity comes along. The time to get ninja at pitching is *not* the day you've received the invitation to do so!

Have a few *short* stories at the ready—something from your childhood; your craziest audition; your favorite shoot; the best play you ever saw; your "boring" day-to-day life that proves you're pretty dang normal, even if your brand is wacky, goofy, or creepy. Be able to make your point without rambling and keep people engaged. Keep your stories short and watch yourself for tics and "ums" and places where even you get bored. The goal is to have some talking points available at all times that make your face light up when you go into them!

What makes a great pitch? I use my logline as a starting point: "I'm living my dreams by helping others figure out how to live theirs." Then, I elaborate that whether I'm writing, casting, producing, speaking to large groups, leading seminars in person or online, or coaching one-on-one, the core is that by helping others refine the tools that empower them to get to the next tier, I'm in my bliss. Your pitch may have examples of the types of roles you play, the kinds of stories you tend to tell, the names of actors to whom you're often compared, etc.

Keep in mind that a pitch does not *have to* include a logline, nor does it have to include a hybrid-cross type blend of known actors. *Only* if these things serve your pitch—by making it *easier* for the folks on the receiving end of the pitch to *get you*—should you include them. But no matter what, your pitch should flow organically and easily. Even the words you choose to use in your self-description should be on-brand. For instance, I'll always have a "y'all" in my pitch, at some point. I'm folksy. Using the word "y'all" makes sense for me, and it is not only on-brand, but it's a very efficient way of conveying my folksiness!

If you do have a logline that describes "brand you" beautifully, have it ready. Industry hyphenate Jeff Bollow says a logline is something we must learn to love. (Note: In his original list, Bollow is talking about loglines for pitching scripts, but I find these concepts to work quite well for creatives talking about themselves.)

> ➤It saves everyone time. It's not a judgment statement; it's a time-saver.

> ➤It demonstrates the marketing angle, which buyers need to *get*, before they get on board.

> ➤It pulls them in. We all want to experience exciting concepts, not vague ones.

> ➤Pros are great with words and self-assessment. Your ability to embrace—and use—your logline with ease puts you in the professional category, quickly.

If you've ever found yourself feeling stuck when someone asks how they might best cast you or what you're best at, as an actor, developing a personal logline is going to do nothing but help you. It'll also drive your focus when you're submitting on breakdowns. Sure, you're "allowed" to just go ahead and click submit *every* time you see your gender, ethnicity, and age range mentioned in the online breakdowns, but isn't it far better use of your energy, your optimism over whether you're going to hear from casting, and your *focus* to submit only when the role is absolutely within your brand?

Brandprov

During our first-ever online offering of the *Self-Management for Actors* course, I was in the middle of recording a lesson about pitching and "living on-brand" when I started talking about comic Greg Benson's *Excellent Questions* vid (now titled *Trolling the Red Carpet* at YouTube) and what a great example it is of actors who are brilliant at the art of Brandprov. As I *said* the word "Brandprov," I realized there was a reason I created that mash-up. It's ninja! There's being on-brand, and then there's being *so* on-brand that you can be caught off-guard with questions that make NO sense and still represent your brand well, as you improvise. For the direct link to this vid and other good (and bad) examples of Brandprov in action, visit smfa4.com now.

Of course, you can watch for this art on any latenight talkshow, daytime talkshow, red carpet event, paparazzi-covered moments, upfronts, or junket footage that's not terribly well-edited. The more "live and raw" it is, the better the chance you're going to see whether a celeb is excellent at Brandprov or better suited for interviews that are scripted by a publicist.

Head down the rabbit hole on YouTube and see the difference between someone who has had media training and someone who has not strengthened the muscle for handling questions with grace. Media training involves speed drills on all the various questions you'll encounter. Prep yourself now by rehearsing responses to all sorts of questions: the ones they always ask, the ones they never ask, the ones you hope they never ask, and the ones that make no sense but that help you clarify "brand you," just by practicing your answers.

It's not a job requirement that you be fantastic at improvising on-brand. But the more you rehearse talking points on-brand, the stronger that muscle for Brandprov becomes. Brandprov is simply on-brand improvisation. Try it. Drill yourself using some examples we have available at smfa4.com and make this a part of your business plan. Take every opportunity to test your ability to keep teaching the buyers how to cast you next.

Working the Red Carpet

So, you've had a tier-jump. You're building momentum. You're feeling good about where you're headed, as you live your dreams and deal with some of those "quality problems" that you always hoped would come your way. Awesome! Now what?

Now you either pony up thousands of dollars per month to retain a publicist and hire a media trainer, or you rock the *Self-Management for Actors* way: Do for yourself what you can do for yourself, 'til you're at a point where paying someone to book your print interviews, escort you down the red carpet, or get you seated on the best latenight show sofa—all the while teaching you how to be ninja with your ability to stay on-brand as the interviewer flings random questions your way—is a no-brainer. How do we do that?

You've already mapped out which events might be right for *brand you*. You've worked your own relationships to get invited to at least one event that fits. You've studied wardrobe choices and accessories and hairstyles and poses that have made waves in previous incarnations of events like this, thanks to the archives of those red carpet galleries. You know what to wear if you want to fly under the radar. You know what to wear if you want to make a splash. You've spent hours on YouTube watching junket and red carpet footage to get clear on how reporters and interviewers operate, what questions they're asking of anyone who gets in front of them, and what makes the interviewee look smart and castable vs. nervous and non-pro. You've majored in Bravo's *Watch What Happens Live* as well as the more traditional latenight and daytime talkshows to see the difference between stars who are media trained and those who let the interviewer drive the interview.

You've fired up your own webcam and interviewed yourself, played back the footage, watched for your own tics and *uhms* and other bad on-camera behavior and you've continued to shoot yourself to improve with every take. You know how to deliver a soundbite. You've mastered Brandprov. You know how to charm the interviewer (if it's on-brand of you to do). And you know how to answer the questions the interviewer should've asked, using the sometimes less wonderful questions as jumping-off points. How do you know how to do this? You've *watched* the masters. Just like athletes study game tapes and run plays that the greats ran before them, your work of watching all those clips and interviews and junkets—combined with the on-camera crash course you're giving yourself—will absolutely have you ready.

Whether it's the opening of a film you were in, a festival screening of a film you helped produce, previews for a play, the opening of a new facility at your union's local office, an awards show for webseries, or a launch of a celeb's new liquor line, you'll need to take all your prep, choose a totally on-brand outfit that *photographs* perfectly (test this out ahead of time), and dive in. Don't stress about the people with mics or cameras—they're most likely looking for the most famous person there—but do smile, welcome them with your eyes, and be ready should you be asked to do a quick interview as you arrive. If that never happens, no stress! Study what's going on, just like you did from home, and take in all the ninja moves the highest-profile folks are using.

If you have personal demons, consider being out about those early on, as that prevents anything from being discovered and revealed about you at a crucial career moment. Certainly, we are living in a time when things that would've been career killers a few years ago aren't as damaging, but you can bet that if there's anything that might cause your three-picture deal to die, it's a secret that the press gets ahold of before you can do spin control.

But you have to get out there and *try it* to be sure what's okay to say and how to say it. This is why I recommend that you get interviewed in your hometown paper or by a friendly blogger, early on. Having a few good experiences that are lower-stakes under your belt will help a great deal, when the nerves are really flying.

Also consider some questions that might throw you off, or that you'd prefer were never asked of you (questions ranging from the inappropriate to the unprofessional). I'm not suggesting you feel compelled to answer questions about your real age, your sexual orientation, your religion, or anything else that you'd rather keep to yourself. What I am encouraging you to do, though, is to prepare for how you will field those questions, when asked. Will you clam up, get rude, and change the tone of the encounter altogether by crossing your arms and saying, "You can't ask me that," or will you use your charm and your wit—on-brand—to fire back a clever response that keeps your privacy intact without making the person asking the question feel like you just scolded them?

Always be gracious and professional. Talk about what a joy it is to work with such amazing people. Credit the designer behind the duds you have on. Try not to weigh in on issues of indiscretion regarding your co-stars or people you've never met. Even if you are certain your words can't be taken out of context, believe me, they can be (and they will be, if they can be spun to make a better story). Should you end up being interviewed or photographed, use those Google Alerts you've surely set up on yourself by now and when a photo or story comes out, send that link to your agent and manager right away. If it's really fantastic, tweet it. Facebook it. Add it to the "press" page at your website. Feature it on your IMDb profile. Save it all as a PDF for your press kit. "Yes, and..." that publicity so that it can have a ripple effect with the buyers, when the time is right.

Is a casting director more likely to call you in because you were photographed at an advance screening of a cool new film? Maybe. She is definitely more likely to know your name when you're pitched by your team, though. She's more likely to say, "Fan of your work," when she greets you at your next audition in her office. She'll feel you're lower risk, somehow, because you're in the machine. It's a subtle shift, but it happens. And that you helped make it happen is what's truly ninja, here!

Doing Junkets

Junkets are exhausting. You meet dozens of journalists from big- and small-town media outlets, all of whom have been wooed by the studio (for the price of a lavish trip, a stocked gift bag, and the promise of entire minutes of sit-down time with glamorous stars). There is so little time that these reporters' questions come fast and with very little ramp-up or foreplay of niceties. (Oh, and in case you're wondering, these junket reporters are the ones who love, love, love every movie they see. The studios won't invite them back to do press junkets on the studios' tab if their reviews stink.)

As Patton Oswalt said after having done his first ever press junket, for *Ratatouille*, "How do actual movie stars do it? Will Ferrell puts out 27 major studio movies a year, and he promotes each and every one of them like a champ. How has he not been reduced to bludgeoning stewbums at railroad yards to release the tensions?"

Right. So, you'll need endurance, extra pressed powder and lip balm, breath spray, bottled water, and your best sense of humor and patience for banality. Even then, you can expect to be misquoted, photographed at your worst moment, taped when you're told cameras aren't rolling, and plastered all over YouTube for the world to enjoy. Yippee. (Oh, and you're usually contractually obligated to do these junkets, as a part of starring in this film.)

By now you should have a publicist to help you navigate this world, but the prep you can do now includes knowing how "in charge" your publicist is going to be (like, if you're misinformed about a topic, if you're late for an interview, if you're on a phoner to a radio station whose DJ has been stalking you) and how, in the end, the proverbial buck does stop with you.

Dealing with Paparazzi

Let's say you make it to the *TMZ* level of fame that gets you photographed as you live your life. The part you might not be prepared for is how very ready for you the paparazzi will be. Why? There are informants at every major hot spot in town who know they can earn a *C*-note by making a quick phone call to their favorite photographer (even more money, if they promise it's an "exclusive" call), just to say, "Clooney's here."

Sure, the finer locales will fire someone in a heartbeat for trading on this sort of information, but there are rose-sellers, valets, and even the actors' own publicists who want to churn up buzz on their clients, all willing to make a quick call to get photographers on the scene. And the paps will run redlights to get there if the stars are big enough.

If you're the type of person who loves to pick your nose, smack your gum, suck your teeth, or pluck ear hairs with your fingernails with reckless abandon, get those habits in check, and fast. It's not just about paparazzi anymore. Everyone with a cell phone is selling photos to magazines and websites. And if you're caught snorting cocaine off an illegal underage hooker at your favorite no-tell motel, you'd better believe that mess is gonna lead the next day's entertainment news. Pick your wedgie out in the privacy of your own home. Tape your revealing dress to your nipples. Practice getting in and out of cars in various states of underwear before someone is snapping pictures of your you-know-who-hoo.

Be prepared to be photographed no matter when, no matter where. And if you don't want to be snapped, be prepared to be mocked for choices like wrapping yourself in blankets or fending off photographers with umbrellas. This is where it gets into the whole "you asked for fame" thing. Yeah, you may have only chosen to pursue acting because you love the craft, but if you found success in Los Angeles especially, you can expect the "we own you" bonus that comes with it.

Fielding Offers

Designers will want you to wear their fashions. You'll be asked to do endorsements of products and services. Direct casting offers will come your way (that's right, no auditions). And you'll certainly get loads of meetings out of your new level of notoriety. Hopefully, you'll have a team in place to advise you on which deals to take (the movie with Denzel) and on which ones you should pass (the personal lubricant spokesperson gig in Japan).

There will also be entirely "too good to be true" offers to watch out for. You already know that scams are big for aspiring actors, but they're even bigger business for recognizable actors. Just like winners of the lottery, new-money celebs get targeted by scam artists offering "wonderful investment opportunities." There's always some long-lost family member just hankerin' to connect with you after all these years, once you're "somebody." Perhaps worse, you put your business affairs in the hands of someone you trust and he runs off with all the wealth you've worked so hard to build. *Eesh.* This is one of those times when checks and balances will be your best friend.

Let's not forget the offers of sex, drugs, guns, whatever you might want! There's gonna be someone able to get you whatever you crave, and it's going to seem mighty tempting sometimes. Well, here's what I have to say about that: Finding balance in your life before you're a *name* actor is going to be vitally important. Balance now means balance then. What you struggled with before fame, you'll continue to struggle with after (and that struggle will probably be magnified, depending on what it is). Get your mind right, now.

The Importance of Your Team

Of course by now you'll have the agent, the manager, the publicist, the attorney, the financial advisor, the personal assistant, the stylist, etc. That's a lot of folks counting on "brand you" for their paychecks. They'll want to keep you happy. There will be times that you really want to believe your own hype. If you surround yourself with yes-men, that's going to be easy to do (and the fall from divadom can be harsh). A good team can keep you centered, grounded, and focused. A fractured team can exacerbate issues already tough for an actor to face.

That'd be all of the items of balance I've already mentioned, plus oddities like fans, stalkers, haters. Should you sign autographs? Or create a policy about not doing so from the beginning and then stick to it? How do you know when a fan is just a fan, or when that fan has crossed the line into stalkerdom? And what about those strange people who love to bash successful people? Whatever you do, ignore the chatter, the wannabes, the people who come out of the woodwork to tear you down. The more public you are, the more of those you'll have to face.

> *If you're looking for faith in humanity and stuff,* do not *read YouTube comments.*
>
> —Caroline Timm, actor

Certainly, you have to believe you're pretty dang special to some extent, or else you could never really navigate the ridiculous parts of showbiz in order to get to this career level. But be careful that you don't isolate yourself to such a degree that you lose touch with reality. (And not "showbiz reality." I mean *real* reality.) Whatever you do, don't complain about how hard it is, once you're at the top. These are quality problems you're hoping to have.

What to Do When It All Goes Wrong

What do you do when it all goes wrong, despite your best efforts? You can do all your prep, all your mindset reminders, all your best work to make sure you rock the meeting, and you can bump into your nemesis in the lobby, say the wrong thing at a crucial networking moment, or get home and notice a huge chunk of spinach wedged in your teeth after your industry lunch. Yes, all of that is possible (and so much more). So, what do you do?

First, shake it off. Everyone experiences bad mojo sometimes. The instant you *feel* things going south, you need to find your center and get ninja, quickly. Because as Maya Angelou says, "People will forget what you said, people will forget what you did, but people will never forget how you made them *feel*." That means, when you are turning into the anxious place, when you are losing all control over how things are going, when you are simply sweating and cannot stop the skid, that *feeling* is what rules.

Your most important muscle for surviving any slipup while working it is the one that takes you back to breathing, that gives you a beat during which you can take a sip from your bottled water, that reminds you there are no stakes higher than the ones *you* have created (which means you can reject them, right now, while it feels like they're in control). Simply laughing and saying, "Wow. I'm nervous. Can I take a moment to gather my thoughts?" could be the smartest move, since it's no *secret* that you're nervous. Just letting the other person know you need a moment lets *them* relax about how scattered your energy may feel.

What they'll remember is not that you got nervous, not that you got rattled, not that you needed to take a moment, but that you were a pro who could get things back on track. That ninja move will give them greater confidence in you, as a pro with whom they'll have a relationship for a long time, in this industry. That's a beautiful thing! Remember that working it is *not* about making an impression. Make your goal in setting out on any networking endeavor to create a positive environment. Don't try to impress anyone or to *be* anything in particular. Relax. Breathe. Don't drink too much.

25: MONEY MANAGEMENT

One of the things I would've liked to know when I started the pursuit of a professional acting career in a major market is how much that pursuit was going to cost me. There are many people out there vying for a share of the actor's hard-earned dollar (and actors are so often looking for an edge that they'll pay dearly for something that purports to give them that advantage). What, then, are the *required* expenses to pursuing a career in acting? What is optional?

Photos and Reproductions—Without a doubt, the number-one *must-have* is your headshot. A headshot is an actor's calling card, so a headshot session and the reproduction of prints is not negotiable. An actor's photo session should cost between $300 and $500 (but some spend $1000), with hair and makeup running an additional $150. Child actors get a pass here. They do not absolutely *have to* shoot professional headshots until their look "stabilizes." Even then, they should not spend too much on headshots, since they'll need new ones at least every year. Retouching should be used sparingly and usually runs about $45 per photo. Reproductions are $100 for 100 color repros or $300 for 500.

Online Presence—At bare minimum, take advantage of your IMDb listing as soon as you have one by uploading a photo and reel footage, adding your bio and a link to your official site, and including a list of your other works. The two essential casting submission sites are Actors Access and Casting Networks. Listing a profile on Actors Access is free, so even if you never use it as a submission tool, you should create a profile in case a casting director uses the search function to find actors of your type. Should you wish to use it as a submission service, you can pay per submission or join Showfax for an annual fee, which includes the download of audition sides and emailed updates when sides are changed, as well as unlimited submissions. Casting Networks has one pricing structure for actors with agents and a higher monthly fee for those actors who are unrepresented. Repped actors who don't want to pay the monthly fee can pay per submission. If you maintain memberships at IMDb-Pro, Actors Access, and Casting Networks, you're generally looking at spending $250/yr. Creating your own website is a great idea. (See: **Your Online Presence**.) Even if you don't have it in your budget to maintain a website right now, you should register your domain name so that someone else doesn't nab it and squat.

Classes, Coaching, and Workshops—On average, scene study and ongoing classes range from $125 to $350 per month, with the "gurus" charging up to $600 per month. Actors often work with audition coaches at a rate of $75 to $100 per meeting. Private consultations (with a life coach, business expert, image stylist) fall in the $100 to $300 per hour range. CD workshops are anywhere from $45 to $75 each, or $175 to $225 for intensives. Absolutely, these items are optional and many actors do quite well without ever having taken part in anything outside of a regular scene study class. Other actors rely on these marketing boosts and networking opportunities as a foundation upon which to build their acting career. Can't afford classes? At the very least, transcribe scenes from movies and TV shows, download scripts from websites, and put yourself on tape doing the material. You'll at least know what areas need improvement, just by seeing yourself working.

Union Dues and Professional Memberships—Obviously, once you become a union member and pony up that hefty initiation fee (currently $3000 for SAG-AFTRA and $1100 for AEA), you'd better keep up with your dues (current annual minimums are $198 for SAG-AFTRA with 1.575% of contract earnings up to $500,000 tacked on; $118 for AEA with 2.25% of contract earnings up to $300,000 tacked on). There are also optional professional organizations such as Women In Film, Film Independent (FiND), IAWTV, SAG-AFTRA Conservatory, the Paley Center, Academy of Television Arts and Sciences, Big Vision Empty Wallet, and many more listed at smfa4.com. Membership in a theatre company is generally in the $45 to $75 per month range.

Personal Care—This includes your gym membership ($175 initiation fee with $35 per month dues—but watch for specials), yoga classes ($50 per month), acupuncture ($60 per month), personal trainer ($100 to $300 per session), teeth whitening ($250 first treatment with $100 per year maintenance), and hair color maintenance ($130 to $200 every two months). I'd lump dry cleaning for your audition clothes into this category too (about $20 per month).

Subscriptions, Trades, Books, and Directories—You could spend a lot of money on trade publications, if you chose to subscribe to all of them (*The Hollywood Reporter*, *Daily Variety*, and if you're starting out, *Backstage*). Savvy actors supplement their trades with the free daily subscription to Cynopsis (which is also available in a free podcast format). CastingAbout is the go-to for insider casting information, all the way down to the names of the assistants in temporary casting facilities. Following all of these resources on Twitter is a no-brainer for a steady stream of free updates, if a paid membership is outside your budget. As far as books are concerned, actors regularly purchase books on the craft and business of acting. Many browse at the Samuel French

Bookstore or Drama Book Shop and then buy at a discount on amazon.com. What actors can buy at the specialty stores that they can't find elsewhere are plays, dialect tapes, agency and casting director guides and labels, etc.

Office Supplies and Postage—Just like any other business owner, you must set yourself up for *doing* business. That means having a computer with Internet access and—if you print your own resumés and cover letters—a printer too (be sure to budget for ink cartridges). Also required: a cell phone with voicemail. If you're always trimming your resumés to fit your headshots, get a $20 paper cutter. Budget for envelopes for headshot mailings, paper, staples, labels (if you don't buy pre-printed labels), and Sharpies. Best money-saving tip I can give you for your office setup is to go in with other actors and create a shared workspace. Sure, you'll go through the supplies more quickly when several actors are using them, but you can also buy in bulk and save on the cost per envelope, for example. Even though you've shifted much of your "hard copy mailing" budget to your online subscriptions, you will still need to mail headshots and postcards out from time to time. Leave off the bells and whistles in your postage expenses (no need to overnight a general submission, or pack a headshot with cardboard to keep it from bending). However, if you are dropping your agent, you should invest in a certified, return-receipt letter.

Reels—Actors spend anywhere from $50 to $300 for reel editing, with the average hitting around $150 for the first version of the reel, $30 to $80 per hour for edits, and $5 to $10 per DVD copy including generic packaging.

Agency Commission—It's tough to imagine budgeting for agency commissions before you're repped and booking, but if you have representation, you're contractually obligated to pay a percentage of your bookings for everything you book. There is a significant service you are getting for that commission. And just as your agent or manager doesn't come after you for expenses when you "come close" but don't book the role despite all their pitching, you shouldn't make your rep come after you for commission on work you booked (whether you submitted yourself or not). Budget for these commissions paid to the people who are out there hustling for you every day.

Gifts—Gifts to people in the industry are totally optional, because your real gift is the fact that you did a great job. If you choose to provide your agent and manager with a little something each year for the holidays and send something to the casting director who cast you in the role that got you your union eligibility, that's cool too. Flowers, cookies, giftcards to Starbucks, fruit baskets, wine, etc., are all okay.

Entertainment—Good news! Your human need to see movies, plays, and stand-up comedy can actually be considered an acting expense! Yup, your DVR, cable, and Netflix subscription can all be covered come tax season, but you should check with an actor-friendly tax preparer to be sure you're not sending off "audit flares" with your deductions. Use resources like Goldstar, Big Cheap Theatre, and TKTS, or hit plays on pay-what-you-can and preview nights to save money. Some class tuition comes with bargains for shows by the mainstage group. Theatre company membership offers up ushering in exchange for available show tickets.

Transportation—You're going to have to get to your auditions. That means your car needs to be in good shape, you need gas money, and there's parking to deal with too. Certainly, you can park at a meter far from your audition location and walk, but that's not always appropriate for the amount of time you have to spare, nor is it always safe. Oh, and in LA, you can count on parking tickets at least once a year. It never fails, no matter how sure you are that you've read the signs. Just count on it and consider a ticket earned during an audition a sign of good luck. For NY-based actors, there are subway passes, tolls, and taxi fare. No one rides free.

Incorporating

Every year, I receive thank-you notes from creatives who heard me talk about the value in incorporating, looked into it, did so, and immediately started saving money. Every year, I also hear from folks who lament that they didn't do it sooner, that they're not ready to do it yet, that they're scared, that it can't *possibly* be that easy, that affordable, that good a deal, something.

If you are getting 1099s, if you're paying year-end taxes, if you are paying *into* the system via payroll deductions that come in anywhere *over* $1500 each year, incorporating could save you money, since $800 would be your pay-in for taxes in the State of California as a corporation, Federal taxes don't exist 'til you're into profits, and you need to have money to pay your CPA.

Take a look at your favorite actors on IMDb-Pro. How many of them—when you look at their contact tab, and sift out the agents, managers, publicists, attorneys, and such—are officers of their own corporations? More than a few, right? How about your favorite directors, writers, and producers? These folks may be listed as president of a production company that has no productions produced! They're running their money through their corporations because it's the best deal going, tax-wise. And it's their God-bless-America-given right to do so!

Now, financial advisors will suggest you wait 'til you're clearing $100K to $250K per year before you consider incorporating. I say, why wait for a day that, frankly—for most artists—may never come, when it's precisely when you're below the $50K/yr. mark that saving $2500 to $5000 could make a *huge* difference in your ability to stay in the pursuit another year?

Read *Inc. Yourself* by Judith McQuown immediately. Yes, you can hire someone to do everything for you, but you can also incorporate in the State of California (and in most other states) for a few hundred bucks, today. For Cricket Feet, Inc., we went with the DIY model and followed every step in *Inc. Yourself* and the nolo.com "California Quick-Corp Guide." These days, you don't even need that. You can go online to get your EIN (your company's Social Security Number) and to file your fictious name statement. For our favorite resources and the updated links to start this process, visit smfa4. com, where we also have a breakdown of the various corporate structures (sole proprietorship, joint venture, LLC, S-Corp, and C-Corp). In general, "disposable" companies go the LLC route, because they know they're only in business for a short amount of time. They're producing a movie, then disbanding after the movie sells into distribution (amazingly, just in time to show no profits for paying actors or anyone who agreed to "points" on the back-end). By the way, this is how the majority of Hollywood productions get touted as "money losers." It's book-cooking. Nothing more. Oh, and it's all perfectly legal.

Since you're most likely not looking to set up a disposable corporation, but instead hoping to create a way to save more of your money as you grow your creative career, go ahead and head to C-Corp land, even though that means you'll pay more to get your taxes done each year (no more H&R Block). What you'll save will often be more than worth that choice, and growing into a C-Corp is *much* easier (and more affordable) than starting out as an LLC and then trying to transition into a C-Corp, where officer loans and repayment of officer loans are a huge part of keeping your money flowing in the right direction each year.

Can you keep a survival job outside of acting while you are the officer of a corporation? Absolutely. Your corporation dictates what its officers can and cannot do, in terms of side jobs. I worked the last of my actor-days survival job 'til February 2007 (and only stopped because the company for which I worked got bought out and we were all let go). We just worked the payroll earnings from that company into our best overall tax burden, each year. Many companies are happy to learn you're working as a loan-out, as they have less paperwork to do on you if you are *not* an employee.

Will production companies know what to do with you, if you show up to set and say you're working as a loan-out of your own corporation? You betcha! More people on that set are working as a loan-out of a corporation than those who are working on W4s and I-9s. You just tell 'em you're a loan-out, they'll hand you a W9 instead, and you'll give out your corporation's EIN, not your Social Security Number, and—huge bonus—when the check comes, it's got no deductions of FICA, no withholding, no taxes taken out. Nope! *You,* through your corporation, are responsible for paying into the system as you see fit.

Yeah, you have to be organized as hell. You have to have a *real* CPA who is ninja about balancing out the overall tax burden as best distributed for your specific situation. You have to be able to pay into the system on a schedule or hold your savings in a very safe place to do a lump payment each year, and that's not for everyone. But if being incorporated doesn't scare you, consider making the leap.

Survival Jobs

There are many jobs that can support an actor's creative career. What's important is knowing what each job's requirements are, what sort of money you can expect from doing the job, and what the downside to a creative career might be. I worked a dozen survival jobs at once while pursuing my acting career, and that allowed me to have loads of flexibility and tons of fun. But let's be clear: I'm one of the most organized people on the planet. So, cobbling together a bunch of different jobs worked for me! Here are some gigs common to the world of the working actor, along with a rundown on what to expect from each.

Academic Tutor—*requirements*: intelligence, academic "book smarts," excellent communication skills, patience, must be good with kids, motivational, organized; *perks*: excellent pay, extremely flexible; *downside*: occasional family drama.

Actor Services (headshot retouching, resumé formatting, demo reel editing, designing marketing tools, brand consultations, etc.)—*requirements*: awareness of trends in the industry, design (or editing or marketing or retouching or personal shopping, etc.) skills, excellent communication skills; *perks*: pay can be good if you set your rates right, extremely flexible; *downside*: chasing your payments can be a pain in the butt so be sure to set specs and payment details outlined up front.

Airline Work—*requirements*: varies greatly—depends on the specific job within the airline industry; *perks*: pay can be very good, free travel worldwide, ability to get to auditions in other markets and work as a local hire; *downside*: obviously not flexible in the short-notice arena.

Babysitting—*requirements*: must be great with kids, organized, responsible, excellent in a crisis, have reliable transportation; *perks*: potentially great pay once you've proven yourself with a family and gotten in a rhythm with them, flexibility in general but not once you've committed to the gig; *downside*: loads of responsibility for someone else's most precious angels.

Bartending, Food Service—*requirements*: fit, healthy, charismatic, must be a people person, reliable, friendly; *perks*: can pay very well if you target a great bar or restaurant with consistent customers, flexible due to shift-swapping with co-workers; *downside*: some days are just the pits with bad tips and bad customers and bad attitudes all around, you have to be *on* all the time to make your bank.

Driver for Hire—*requirements*: must have a clean driving record, must be insured, must have reliable transportation, excellent communication skills, personable with strangers (some drunk); *perks*: good pay, loads of flexibility, not required to have a cab license thanks to companies like Lyft entering the scene; *downside*: dealing with tipsy people, future of non-permitted cabbies offering rides is iffy.

Extra Work, Stand-In Work—*requirements*: patience, reliability, punctuality, attention to detail, ability to follow directions with a smile; *perks*: union work pays great and leads to benefits, nonunion is less consistent, build web of trust while learning an incredible amount of information for your show bible; *downside*: no flexibility once you're booked for the day, potentially getting branded as *B*-team rather than an actor.

Fitness Instructor—*requirements*: fit, certified, motivational, personable, reliable; *perks*: pay can be great and you're working out while you're working, if you're at a gym you can sometimes swap shifts with co-workers, if you're a personal trainer you're setting your own rate and schedule; *downside*: may not have a lot of time to get camera-ready for a last-minute audition after a workout.

Freelance Writing—*requirements*: excellent communication skills, flawless grammar and spelling, attention to detail, a clear "voice" as a writer, consistent output; *perks*: varies greatly (10 cents per word is standard for a brand new writer submitting to a major publication, on up to $5/word for writers with an established fanbase), loads of flexibility; *downside*: takes time to build up a consistent voice and a rabid fanbase (but it's worth it).

Fulltime Work—*requirements*: reliability, organization, excellent communication skills; *perks*: potentially great pay, benefits, insurance, ability to create a cushion of savings if you're smart about money management; *downside*: almost zero flexibility for an acting career, "golden handcuffs" are hard to unlock.

Game Show Contestant—*requirements*: huge personality, quick wit, smarts; *perks*: fun way to win cash and fabulous prizes while being on TV; *downside*: you're not an "actor" while you're competing and you can't really count on this for steady income.

Graphic Design—*requirements*: artistry, expertise with latest software trends, tenacious communication, organization; *perks*: excellent pay, very flexible; *downside*: high-pressure demands from clients, constantly-changing technology.

Hotel Work—*requirements*: varies—depends on the specific job within the hospitality industry; *perks*: pay can be very good, flexibility of shifts if you have enough co-workers with whom to swap shifts, can network with some very high-end industry players if you're working in a luxury hotel; *downside*: can get known for your hospitality job and not for your work as an actor among some high-level pros.

Landlord—*requirements*: responsibility, must be handy with tools, able to coordinate workmen with residents' schedules, organized; *perks*: usually the "pay" is free or discounted rent in a unit on-site; *downside*: can be demanding and emergency-based which can cut into acting flexibility.

Market Research—*requirements*: must have willingness to "fit" whatever demographic they need, must be opinionated about the product without having inside knowledge about it; *perks*: good pay, one-time commitment, over quickly; *downside*: need to gauge what they want during the intake interview in order to be chosen, can't do similar studies for six months to a year.

Massage Therapist—*requirements*: organization, certification, your own table and supplies, love for what you do, stamina for standing long hours; *perks*: pay can be great, as you set your rates and get tips if you work through a service, set your own schedule; *downside*: sometimes have to chase your money from clients who cancel last-minute or no-show.

Messenger Service, Delivery Service—*requirements*: must have clean driving record, must be insured, must have reliable transportation, excellent communication skills; *perks*: good pay, generally short shifts, get a great lay of the land and all the best parking spots; *downside*: lots of time on the road, potential tickets, potential accidents.

Mock Jurist—*requirements*: attention to detail, ability to follow an intense (or boring) court case, reliability, excellent communication skills; *perks*: great pay, you're helping attorneys present more compelling arguments on the part of their clients; *downside*: once you're scheduled, you're booked for the day and there's no time off for auditions.

Parts Modeling—*requirements*: flawless skin, gorgeous hair, beautiful parts, perfect proportions; *perks*: excellent pay, extremely flexible; *downside*: meticulous parts upkeep can cut into a normal life.

Pet-Sitting—*requirements*: reliable, good with animals, responsible, good in emergency situations; *perks*: decent pay, moderately flexible; *downside*: unpredictability of critters, dealing with poop.

Production Jobs—*requirements*: awareness of the biz without pushing your acting self on the situation, organization, communication skills, punctuality, responsibility; *perks*: pay varies, as does flexibility, great way to learn about other parts of the industry and build your web of trust; *downside*: risk getting seen as a non-actor, generally long days with no ability to leave for auditions.

Rent Out Your Space—*requirements*: tidy home, minimal clutter, comfortable with strangers being in your space, own your home or have a lease that allows for short-term rentals via companies like Air BNB; *perks*: can be a great source of side income if you're willing to share your living quarters; *downside*: unpredictable unless you live in a place with loads of seasonal tourist traffic due to festivals or conferences.

Retail—*requirements*: punctuality, awareness of what's in stock, good with money, personable, patience for customer service issues; *perks*: decent pay, usually a discount on the merchandise at the store, short shifts, generally flexible due to shift-swapping with co-workers; *downside*: many people end up spending most of their paychecks on the cool clothes or goods they can buy at a discount at their store.

Sales—*requirements*: charismatic, outgoing personality, good communication skills, organization, reliable transportation; *perks*: excellent pay if you're good at what you do, loads of flexibility within your day as long as you hit your sales calls; *downside*: tough to shift gears quickly for an audition and leave the sales-y vibe behind.

Seat-Filler—*requirements*: punctual, well-groomed, with outfits ranging from upscale casual to very formal, ability to smile and clap on cue; *perks*: good pay to sit in empty seats at award shows or decent pay to fill the audience of infomercials; *downside*: not hugely consistent work but fun.

Standardized Patient—*requirements*: attention to detail, acting chops, ability to stick to an outline of medical symptoms while improvising the conversation with the student, reliability; *perks*: great pay, it's acting work, you're helping train the future doctors and police officers on how to gather information; *downside*: once you're scheduled you're booked for the day and there's no time off for auditions.

Studio Admin (at a CD workshop facility or an acting studio)—*requirements*: knowledge of the industry and its players, communication skills, organization, great personality; *perks*: fair pay, free workshops and the constant flow of industry pros, building your show bible and web of trust; *downside*: risk being seen as a workshop admin and not an actor, risk bitterness due to seeing other actors get called in.

Studio Audience—*requirements*: ability to smile and cheer for hours on end, a healthy back, willingness to live off candy and caffeine; *perks*: decent pay, cool behind-the-scenes look at part of the industry, meet cool people; *downside*: long day, no flexibility within the shift, can be mind-numbingly boring.

Substitute Teacher—*requirements*: reliable, must be good with children (and clear a background check in many states), certified, smart; *perks*: pay is generally good, schedule is last-minute so you can decide whether you're free to sub when the call comes in; *downside*: it's a long day and can be really exhausting for an actor who has rehearsal to get to after school.

Temp Work—*requirements*: flexibility, available on a moment's notice, must have a professional wardrobe, be organized, have good communication skills, general office skills, good personality; *perks*: good pay; *downside*: only flexible in that you don't have to work daily, but once you're committed for the day you're booked out from acting, you run the risk of being wooed to fulltime work if you're a great temp.

Third Shift—*requirements*: ability to be awake while everyone else sleeps and vice-versa, focus, patience; *perks*: potentially very good pay depending on your level of responsibility at your overnight job, leaves your days and evenings free for auditions and classes; *downside*: gotta figure out when to sleep in there somewhere, can't be a zombie at your auditions and shows.

Traffic School Instructor—*requirements*: charisma, memorization, administrative abilities, attention to detail, improvisation; *perks*: good pay, performance-related; *downside*: long day, no flexibility within the shift, captive audience not happy to be there.

Transcriptionist—*requirements*: fast and accurate typing, attention to detail, good with jargon; *perks*: good pay, extremely flexible; *downside*: lots of last-minute deadlines and pressure.

Virtual Assistant—*requirements*: organizational skills, excellent communication, flawless writing ability, attention to detail; *perks*: can be fantastic if your skills are exceptional, loads of flexibility as long as you stay on top of your deadlines; *downside*: if you get a client whose communication skills are lacking you could work on a project for which they don't want to pay, very important to get specs and payment details ironed out up front.

Web Design—*requirements*: up-to-the-minute expertise with all the latest coding trends, tenacious communication, graphic design abilities, organization; *perks*: excellent pay, very flexible; *downside*: high-pressure demands from clients, constantly changing trends.

Phew! That's a lot of options, eh? And that's just scratching the surface of the jobs that are most aligned with creatives. The best part of a creative career is the creativity you can apply to the jobs you take to support you in the pursuit of your dreams! Yet so many actors fail to think creatively about this "problem" and simply take "dumb jobs" that end up sucking their soul.

Whatever you do, do *not* stay in a job that crushes your will to live, that bums you out, that leads to bitterness. All that energy will spill over into your auditions and meetings with fellow creatives and it'll brand you as wholly uncastable. Always remember that your "survival job" is meant to feed your dream. Sure, there will be good days and bad days, but if you've found that you've entered into a bad situation—with no sign of getting better—it's time to bail (professionally, of course). For great sources of various jobs, get your hands on the latest UTA Joblist, visit entertainmentcareers.net, and hop on Jeff Gund's Info List.

If you need more guidance in this area, check out the excellent books *Survival Jobs* by Deborah Jacobson and *I Could Do Anything If I Only Knew What It Was* by Barbara Sher. The latter takes you through "scanners" vs. "divers," and those are the types of people who either try a little bit of everything or who go very deeply into each thing they do, respectively. Beyond that, if you're still not quite sure where your strengths lie, take the "Strengths Finder" assessment in *Now, Discover Your Strengths* by Marcus Buckingham and Donald Clifton. Don't worry about fixing your weaknesses, here! Instead, find work that aligns with your assets.

Whatever type of job(s) you take on—just like in your acting career—it's the relationships and your reputation for doing good work that will take you farther faster than anything else. Find work that fulfills you and inspires you to follow your true passion, while never resenting that "survival job" you have. Know your *no* line! Always know the point at which you'll walk away. Some "career temps" advise never staying in a position for more than a few months, because once you're in a gig for a year, you've gotten committed and you may find it very hard to part ways when the right acting opportunity comes along. Getting clear on what you'll do, what you won't do, and where your *no* line is—before the opportunity is presented and money starts to cloud your decision-making—is vitally important.

If you find yourself doing too many things and needing to pare down, I highly recommend that you check out Marie Forleo's vid on profit clarity (visit marietv.com for this and many other inspiring business vids). Profit clarity is a game-changer for those who need to focus their energy on what's really working, rather than running around, scattered, working *hard* but—uh, oh—not all that smart, after all. Just by ranking your revenue streams and learning how much energy you're putting into each of your gigs to yield how much money—sort of like the "Interview Your Bookings" exercise I had you do earlier—you gain clarity on where you're *best* spending your energy, and where you can stop.

Creating a "Thrive Job" Out of a Survival Job

It's been my experience that when I create a quality of life for myself that makes me feel happy and secure, my artistic life improves immensely and the world around me opens up in delicious ways. My first day job upon moving to Los Angeles in pursuit of a career in television was that of a cater waiter. I soon realized though that schlepping around other people's dinner plates, serving thankless people who had the jobs and money that I so desperately wanted wasn't serving me in reaching my greatest potential.

Bound and determined to never go back to catering, I scoured Craigslist daily. One day I came across an ad that read, "Looking for a personal trainer for my overweight eight-year-old girl." The ad caught my attention really because I was appalled by the mere notion. I was moved to respond mostly because I was frustrated with my own failed job search and the outrage of her ad seemed like the perfect target to take it all out on.

I wrote something like this: "Dear Mom, I don't believe children should have personal trainers and I can't imagine any eight year old enjoying having one either. I wouldn't be a personal trainer for your daughter, and I can't guarantee weightloss. But I will find ways to be physically active with her through play and doing things she loves to do based on her own talents and interests. I can focus on self-esteem building and finding joy and empowerment through physical activity with her. If you're interested in something like that, let me know. Oh—and I charge three times what you're offering." And hit send without thinking twice.

An hour later, I got a call from the mom saying, "We have to meet you." Next thing I knew I was pulling up to a huge mansion in Hancock Park. Emmys lined the hearth in the living room where I sat on the largest couch known to man. Across from me was this little round-cheeked brown-eyed girl perched properly on the ottoman staring up at me with this look that screamed, "Somebody play with me!"

Little Leah and I got to talking. She said she liked to dance even though she had no formal training. I made a CD of her favorite songs and soon enough, three days a week I'd go over to her house and make up dances for an hour and a half to her favorite tunes. Eventually we moved on to other games and adventures. But suddenly I was making an impact in a way that felt so good and rewarding. I was setting my own schedule and getting paid what I needed! This one client eventually lead to multiple, which then eventually led me to my own business, Play Coach For Kids! I went on to train and hire other people (mostly actors) to do the same thing. Passive income is our friend.

That is my story about how I got to a point where I didn't need to cater to live. But the message behind the story is the most important for me to convey. And it's this: When I eliminated my sense of struggle, the quality of my being was elevated. People responded to me differently. I wasn't aware of this huge gap between me and "those people"—you know, the ones I used to cater to.

That's when I started booking. That's when I started collaborating with the people I admired. That's when the desperation, the bitterness, the fear melted away and I was coming at everyone and everything from a much different and much more empowered perspective.

Shine the light on areas of struggle and then change it. Let go of your attachment to how it's "supposed" to go. And apply your abilities and talents to creating a full life. Place your focus on being in joy and everything else falls in place. It's like a law of the universe or something. Seriously.

—Zibby Allen, actor

Expenses and Savings

Many people—especially in Los Angeles—live a superstar lifestyle when they can't afford it. And that puts them in very tough positions when credit card payments are hundreds of dollars each month for life. Consider putting limits on dining out (when brown-bagging and eating at home will do, most days), full-package cable television (when so much is available free, online), cell phones with all the bells and whistles (when your agent only calls once a week), gym memberships (when going running is free), Starbucks visits (when you can brew your own at home), salon manicures and haircuts (when at-home paintjobs and Supercuts get the job done).

A studio apartment or roommate situation is fine sometimes! Consolidating your errands and leaving early will conserve gas and give you plenty of time to park and walk (rather than having to pay high parking fees or getting speeding tickets followed by parking tickets for those last-minute red zone choices). An older, reliable car is fine (and, hey, lower insurance). But AAA membership is a must in most cities (and, yay for travel discounts)!

If you have a marketable skill, try to barter it for something that benefits you as an actor. Are you an ace at web design? Find an acting coach with no web presence and offer up a website in exchange for classes. Do you have loads of free time to spare? Work as an intern in a casting office so that you can reap the benefits of seeing thousands of other actors' headshots and learn a bit about the casting process. Are you super-fit? Perhaps you could trade off personal training services to a demo reel editor who will edit your reel in exchange. Get creative!

If you're doing regular mailings of your headshot and resumé to casting offices (and not seeking representation, for which you would submit your most professional packet), consider sending your headshot as an oversized postcard. You can print your resumé directly on the headshot in about 3/4 the usual space, then use the rest of the space to print the recipient's address and place postage. I get these "oversized postcard headshots" quite a bit and they are never worse for the wear than headshots sent in envelopes. Best bit is, they help you save on postage *and* envelopes. Union members should look at the many member perks and discounts listed at the SAG-AFTRA website.

Of course, if you've earned a treat, give it to yourself! But when you're considering *stopping* your craft classes because you "can't afford them," really take a good, hard look at where your money is going. That means actually listing out exactly what you spend—and on what. Some fantastic tools for this terrifying (but essential) process are available from actor-author Miata Edoga's website: abundancebound.com.

Thinkin' Lincoln

The simplest savings plan in the world is called "Thinkin' Lincoln," and I love this so dang much. *Every* time a five-dollar bill comes into your life, put it into a shoebox, a piggybank, something! (Get it? Abraham Lincoln is on the five. "Thinkin' Lincoln!") A five is small enough that you may not miss it in your wallet, but it's big enough that it adds up quicker than if you were squirreling away singles. If you work in a job where a lot of cash runs through your hands, you'll find yourself changing out your bigger bills *for* fives, so that you can add to your savings account. I started "Thinkin' Lincoln" on July 17, 2010. On October 1st—when my best friend asked how much I had saved—I did a count for the first time: $995. She handed me a five to make it an even thousand, and then she started "Thinkin' Lincoln" on that day. By Christmas, she had saved enough to buy a new sofa, and by May, 2011, enough to take her family to Italy. This plan works. I'm still "Thinkin' Lincoln," to this day.

Now, if you don't often handle cash, this may not be as aggressive a savings plan for you as it has been for me. For the check-writing folks in the mix, I recommend something my mother taught me as a kid: "Drop the change." For every check she wrote, she would round up the check to the nearest dollar when subtracting it from her checkbook register, to "hide" anywhere from a penny to 99 cents from every check in her balance. At month's end, she'd have an additional 10 dollars in her account sometimes, depending on how many checks she wrote.

If you're a plastic-only type, get into the habit of overpaying the credit card that has the higher interest rate, so you can get it paid down earlier, thereby saving you money. As you pay off higher interest cards, close them and roll that monthly payment toward the card with the next highest interest rate, since you're already used to spending that money each month. You'll pay off your credit cards faster using this "debt snowball" tactic. If you have your choice of credit cards, try to get one with a cash-back rewards program. While we're on the topic of debts to repay—because they are generally very low interest—don't overpay your student loans, and if you can, see about getting them placed on the income-contingent repayment (ICR) plan, so that your monthly payment is based on your income, rather than a flat rate. This can save you thousands, each year.

Whenever you shop online, Google promo codes to see if you can save a few bucks (or even just get free shipping) by entering the right string of letters and numbers before checking out. If you're a beauty supply junky, get yourself a Birchbox membership to sample products that otherwise would be cost-prohibitive to buy outright, and share with your friends anything that's not your speed. If you can't afford promo postcards, cut up those old headshots you're no longer using and send 'em out just like that. If you want to really go nuts with frugal living, check out any of Amy Dacyczyn's books, especially *The Complete Tightwad Gazette*.

Always decide what's worth doing yourself vs. what you know is better to hire out. (For me, that's food. I burn water, so to go out to dinner is a no-brainer, compared to the mess of energy, frustration, and nonsense that attempting to cook a sub-par meal would be.) Every person will be different, here, because what one person values at $10, another values at $100. Think about what you might be able to create (and perhaps earn passive income from) during those same hours in which you do something that frustrates you. Yeah, you save a few bucks by doing that frustrating thing yourself, but your creation could generate enough money to hire someone to do that thing... and more! *Net* cost is what you need to examine, here.

I'm not asking you to be so strict on yourself that you begin to resent your financial experience. The goal is to have so much space and flow and ease surrounding your relationship with money that there's no question you have the ability to create with passion, and follow your dreams with gusto!

The Prosperity Game

On that note, Esther Hicks of Abraham-Hicks introduced me to a phenomenal game that I love playing with friends. The first time I played it, it taught me that I was not in as much debt as I thought I was, and that I'm not far off from having ridiculous freedom to take care of everything and everyone in my life, with ease.

Using a notebook, a spreadsheet, or ledger of your choice, start on day one with a "balance" of one thousand psychic dollars. How would you spend that thousand bucks? Pay off a credit card? Get ahead on a car payment? Perhaps grab a new high-tech gadget and all the extras that would make it really fun for you to play with? Maybe a spa day with your best friend? Whatever it is—and if you're playing this with a friend, you'll each spend a grand and share your list (usually via email) with one another—write it down and spare no detail.

Day two, you now have $2000 to spend. Rent? Another credit card paid off? A little vacation with your sweetheart? Day three, it's $3000. Initiation fees for the actors' union? Maybe pay off your car altogether so there are no more monthly payments? How about repaying a debt that a family member always said was "no big deal" to repay? Day four, when you have another $4000 to spend, maybe you create a scholarship fund or donate books to your old elementary school's library. Day five, you guessed it, there's five grand to spend, and now your last credit card is paid off. Boom. In just five days, there's only student loans left. By day nine, you've put a down payment on a house. A few weeks later, you've prepaid the mortgage on your house and bought a rental property for passive income. Within a month, you've launched that side business that will make sure you never need another survival job. The next three days in a row get you enough seed money to finance your feature film.

Um, yeah. This is a powerful exercise and if you're just skimming this section, thinking, "Yeah, yeah, yeah, how powerful can it be? It's not real money and in my heart I'll know it's not real money so what's the point?" I can assure you, you'll thank me for having you do this exercise. I want you to do it for at least two solid months before you give up on it. My bestie and I did this together (we've actually done it several times, together and with other partners) one time and got up to the point of having spent *many* millions of dollars, financing all our friends' passion projects, creating endowments, supporting causes, and investing in so much more than silly "debt repayment."

Here's what happens, after a few days: You start waking up excited about what you'll spend that day's money on. You'll walk through your day behaving as if money is no object as you think about how you can have *anything* you want, and help others get what they want too. Suddenly, there's no more, "Oh, that's so cool. I wish I could afford something like that..." with a pang of twisted emotion about money and your powerlessness. Now it's, "Ooh! That's very cool! I can buy five of those tomorrow! I think I will!" You're retraining a very well-developed muscle with this game. If you're trying to replace decades of wondering, "Where's the money gonna come from?" at every turn, you'll love feeling like money is no object. It'll plant the seed for the *flow* you're going to start to feel, regarding money. Financial freedom really gets rooted here.

You're not being held hostage by your financial circumstances. Your debt is more manageable than you think it is. Let the dread begin to fade away. You're bliss-adjacent, and that's a great energy from which to manifest everything you've ever dreamed of having as an artist.

Focus

Once upon a time, Vin Diesel earned *and saved* $47,000 as a telemarketer before he made it big. First, let me say that telemarketing is *hard* work. Next, the most important thing to focus on in that story about *all that money* is this: Not only did Diesel earn $47,000 in his first year in Los Angeles by telemarketing, he saved every penny he could. He said that he watched other aspiring actors buy hot cars, rent big apartments, throw parties, dress nice, and go out all the time. He knew that doing those things would be fun, but would also put him at a greater distance from attaining his dream.

So, he drove his old car, wore the same clothes every other day, and lived in a tiny single while he saved his money to invest it in his self-produced film. That film was what got Steven Spielberg on the phone to him. It's not just the *earning* that makes a difference; it's the *investment* you make in yourself as an actor.

Also consider the story of Jim Carrey—who had been homeless and who was hustling to try and make ends meet in Hollywood. It was 1990. He drove his car to the top of the Hollywood Hills, parked on Mulholland—overlooking the lights—and wrote himself a check for $10M "for acting services rendered." He carried that check with him in his wallet as an affirmation that this level of success was possible—and that it would come. Of course, it did. And then some.

I want you to fully participate in these mindset exercises. Play the prosperity game. Play it with enthusiasm. Write up your purchases in present tense and celebrate with a buddy who is committed to the game too. Write about how it feels to be free of financial stress and pressure. Write about how it feels to audition when you aren't worried about booking the job "or else my agent will drop me," and how it feels to celebrate storytelling regardless of what the payday would be, at that next tier. Write in present tense. Remind yourself that your current beliefs about money do NOT dictate your future level of financial freedom! Put glee in this recipe.

If you see people with "all the money" as greedy, selfish, dishonest, or undeserving, your job is to *rewrite that script* so that you have nothing but love for abundance, and therefore invite more of it in. The universe will not let you become something you abhor, so it is your job to align yourself with openness for what it is you say you want: success as an actor, financial freedom, happiness! Yeah, this is some woo-woo stuff, but balanced with the nuts-and-bolts tips, also in this chapter, you've got a recipe for improving your relationship with money, right now.

Always focus on what you are passionate about. Your acting, of course. That's easy. Let's also find qualities in your survival job—hopefully a combination of things you love doing, that challenge you, that offer you flexibility, and that keep you creatively fueled for your acting—about which you are passionate. Celebrate those qualities. You're closer to financial freedom than ever; just keep building the muscle for success in this *flow*. This freedom will be rewarded.

It's an award for interactive, *almost by definition making it an award for us all.*

—Bernie Su, Emmy-winning showrunner

26: GRATITUDE

Many people have asked me—a good Southern Belle who believes thank-you notes are *always* appropriate—what the best methods of expressing appreciation are in our industry. Send a thank-you note for every audition? Probably not. Send a thank-you note when you've been called in against type or someone has taken a risk on you? Absolutely. Send a thank-you note when you book a role? Without a doubt! Flowers are nice if you've booked a national commercial, a series regular role, your first union gig, or any other tier-jumping job.

Me? The only thing I ever request of people who find my life's work helpful is this: Just give me a ninja shout-out when you accept your Oscar, your Emmy, your Tony, your Golden Globe, your People's Choice Award. Cool? Cool.

As for the more traditional displays of gratitude, nothing beats the thank-you note. Short and sweet is plenty. Send a photo postcard (or even a standard thank-you card with your photo business card inside) saying, "Just wanted to thank you for bringing me in. I really enjoyed meeting you and hope to work with you soon!" If you had a plain, flat-out good audition, say thank you for that. Your goal is to say "thank you," not to kiss butt.

Gifts

Unique gifts are appreciated *when appropriate*. A friend of mine orders custom-made headshot labels for gourmet products, so that gift baskets, wine, and the like are also a means of getting his face out there, just one more time. Casting directors like things we can use (and if that's gourmet coffee and creamer or some packaged goods, that's a good idea). I know that one casting director was very amused by—but not at all interested in hiring—the guy who gave him a coffee mug with his headshot on it. So, expendables with your promotional photo may be a better balance.

> For agents, I'd send an email to one of the assistants asking for gift ideas. They expect clients to ask, so they will have a list ready. A more personalized gift says more, to me. My son has been fortunate to book regularly, so I really want to show our appreciation for his agents' hard work. I feel we should spend money on them since he's making money because of them. Each client's situation is different, of course!

> Some ideas: gift certificates (Sephora, Best Buy, Barnes and Noble, Pier One, Cost Plus World Market, Burke Williams Spa, favorite restaurants, coffee houses, massages); flowers (check for allergies in the office, though); food is always a big hit (especially delusciouscookies.com cookies and milk), but they get so many fruit baskets, chocolates, and such, that they end up in the kitchen at the office for everyone to enjoy. In addition to giving a personal gift to each agent, I like to give each assistant a bag of homemade cookies and brownies to enjoy.
>
> Now, if you're new with the agent or don't have the budget for gifts like these, remember that any gesture is greatly appreciated. A bottle of wine; a self-crafted basket of goodies; scented candles; a photo of you on the set in a slate-frame; a bound, autographed copy of the script from your time on the set; even a card is plenty! Remember, it's all tax-deductible!
>
> —Lori Johnston, parent to a young actor

A dear friend of mine bakes an amazing Coca-Cola cake and she gave mini-cakes to a few casting directors at the winter holiday season one year. One casting director said to me, later, "As much as I like her and am sure this is a fine cake, I cannot accept food from actors." She indicated that the idea of "something slipped in" was just too strong to ignore. I was surprised, but then realized it's not that different from parents discouraging kids from eating unwrapped Halloween candy given out by strangers. So save the baked goods for people with whom you have a more solid relationship.

Don't spend too much money, but make your offering memorable (in a good way). The gifts aren't really necessary, but true gratitude most definitely is. If it's not your way of doing things (meaning, you don't feel comfortable doing anything too gratitude-laden, since it feels *false* to you), then by all means *don't do it!* Err on the side of what feels natural. If it feels phony to you, it'll feel phony to us too.

Mentoring

There will come a time in your career when you have accomplished a little something. You may be so focused on where you want to go next that you neglect to recognize exactly how far you have come. One of the best ways to keep it all in perspective (while recharging yourself at the same time) is to mentor someone newer to the ranks of "actor" than you are.

This is the time to do student films *not* because you need tape but because you can teach a student filmmaker how the pros do it. Participate in a staged reading with an up-and-coming playwright not because you hope to win a role, but because your presence will add credibility to the project. Speak to graduating performance classes at local colleges and high schools to give them an idea of what the biz is like in the real world. Help along someone who is where you were not too long ago. Your perspective will be treasured!

No, none of this looks like anything that's going to help propel you to the next level of your career, but that's what makes it so important. Mentoring is not only essential on a karmic level, it also provides an amazing amount of perspective on how far you've actually come.

Once you've scored union membership, agent representation, bookings upon bookings, and significant relationships within the industry, *now* comes the hard part: sticking with the path while it's kind of flat. This is when most folks will get bored, having accomplished the "easy" stuff. Good. Let them all fall away. You keep doin' what you're doin' so that everyone knows you're still around and those bookings will get bigger and better. Staying the course is sometimes all it takes to hit the next level. I know it gets tough to just "stick it out" sometimes, but it's so important that you do. Unless it's time to quit, it's time to really buckle down.

A Letter to a Young Actor

Below is a letter I sent a year ago to a little girl named Alexis whose grandmother works with my dad. Alexis was having a tough time dealing with her parents' divorce, and her grades were slipping in school. Her grandmother was distraught at learning that her soon-to-be ex-daughter-in-law told Alexis not to worry about school because she could always just grow up to be an actress. Since Alexis has continuously expressed interest in being an actress when she grows up, her grandmother was looking for stronger, sounder advice to give Alexis than that actors could be dumb. Knowing that I was an actress, Alexis' grandmother asked me to please pass on some words of wisdom to encourage her and make her aware that acting is more than lazy art.

Dear Alexis,

Hello there! My name is Tara Platt and I am an actress living in Hollywood, CA. (If you don't know who I am, that is okay, but I am a working actress in film, TV, voiceover, and theatre.) My dad works with your grandmother at the hospital and she mentioned that you want to be an actress when you grow up.

I wanted to let you know that I think that is a wonderful goal and an exciting career choice, but can also be difficult at times. I would like to give you a little advice from one actress to another, which I've learned through working in this profession. Work as hard as you can and learn as much as you can while you pursue your goals, whatever they may be.

Read and write all the time. Become very proficient in your language and communication skills. Because you will need to be able to read scripts and break them down for character motivation, beats, and dramatic arcs, English and grammar classes will focus on these skills and help you become well-read and well-spoken.

Understand history and social behavior. Your knowledge of history will help you put situations into their proper context and, as an actor, better understand the *when*, *what*, *who*, and *where* of your character in present-day situations or in historically accurate (or inaccurate) positions. You want to be able to make creative choices because you are knowledgeable.

Learn math and science. Since much of "being an actor" is about the business of being a self-employed individual on the prowl for more work, one of the best things you can do is to become your own best bookkeeper. Really learn and understand the best way to save and spend your money wisely. You may have a job one day that pays a lot of money, but then not another one for three months. You want to make sure you will have enough to last during the lean times.

The best advice I can give you is: Stay focused, stay determined, and work as hard as you possibly can in school and in life, because being an actor is the best job in the world, but also one of many very difficult professions out there. I worked hard in school and got good grades, which allowed me to attend college at Rutgers University and get a degree in theatre, and then go to London to study at the London Academy of Theatre. These opportunities have helped me create a wonderful and exciting career as a working actress in Hollywood. In fact, I still take classes and learn as much as I can about life, literature, history, people, the world, and myself.

I wish you well whatever you ultimately decide to do with your life. I hope you always have happiness and use your mind (which is really the best and most important thing we each have) to give you the best skill set to make whatever choices you want for yourself.

Be well. Keep in touch.

I didn't get a note back from young Alexis, and I do hope that she's doing well in school. I did however get an extremely enthusiastic response from her grandmother, and a very appreciative thank you delivered to my dad, letting him know how touched she was, and how it was above and beyond her expectations of, "Hey, you should work hard in school, 'cause actors need an education like everyone else," and how impressed she was with how important a working actor considers all aspects of education and how they relate to an acting career.

Acting is a lot more than just being pretty or coasting by. I have the years of working multiple jobs to make ends meet and the piles of no-longer-usable headshots to show for it. I've been blessed—partly by my own determination and work ethic—to make my living solely as an actor and have been a working professional actress since I played Fredrika in *A Little Night Music* at age 14. As I look back on my words to Alexis, I'd also like to include that it is so extremely important to stay true to yourself, to find your own boundaries, to be willing to push them creatively while not sacrificing your humanity, and to surround yourself with supportive and honest friends that you can rely on and be there for in turn.

Never forget that this is a business of people wanting to work with good people, that you never know where someone will be in a year (including yourself), and that every moment is a possibility to discover more about yourself and life. Auditions come and go, roles change and get cut, and jobs will always have an end; but you are *you* your whole life, and it is important to make sure your inner light is ignited so that you can show it and share that light with the world.

—Tara Platt, actor

There are so many ways to mentor someone. Buy copies of your favorite acting books and donate them to your old high school's library. Organize a series of staged readings starring the kids at your local elementary school. Take a small group of people who live in communities without a community theatre to a play in a nearby city. Answer the "annoying, beginner, everyone-knows-the-answer" question someone posts at an actor-centered message board.

Remember that you're giving an awful lot back, just by sharing your firsthand experiences. Since you know how it's done now, you kind of can't go back. You've made progress. Decide now that you're going to help make Hollywood a better place and do something really wonderful, kind, or filled with badassery *today*.

Where the body goes, the spirit follows. Therefore, move thy butt. Put your ass where your heart wants to be.

—Steven Pressfield, author

PART SIX:
DO WHAT
YOU DO

Everything's bigger in Texas, including your bullseye.

—Keith Johnson

27: Mastering Your Market

Whether you're headed to the Super Bowl of Acting (that'd be Los Angeles, where there are more units of entertainment created for the rest of the world to consume than in all other markets combined) or not, there are elements of *SMFA* that will allow you to master your market. There is great benefit to being perceived as the top-tier talent in your minor market. Please remember, "minor market" does not diminish the quality or professionalism of the work that's taking place outside of Los Angeles. It's a description of quantity.

Wherever you choose to live, there's a way to thrive there. In this chapter, I've brought together contributions from actors from various minor markets—some of whom chose LA for a time—sharing their thoughts and feelings about where they live and how they rock it out! There is no one right place to live to have a full, happy life as a creative. It's all about what kind of fish you'd like to be.

Big Fish, Little Fish

Once upon a time, a director whose amazing film I had cast contacted me to let me know we'd been invited to two festivals. The big, fancy one and the small, sweet one. We would have to choose which would be our premiere. Now, you might have an initial reaction like I did: *Big fancy one! Big fancy one!* But wait, there's more.

See, the big, fancy one could find us premiering opposite something huge like Tarantino's latest. Or we could get the 3pm on a Tuesday slot in the smallest theater the festival uses. No guarantees. That small, sweet one offered us the featured slot. There would be a premiere party. They would pay to fly out our cast. They would even give a lifetime achievement award to the film's star.

Big fish, little fish. What did we want to be? What do *you* want to be? If you had to choose between a career in Los Angeles (but a career in which you may only ever play at 3pm on a Tuesday, i.e., do lots of copy-credit-meals projects, maybe book a few co-stars, rock the low-budget indies, and self-produce to a small but loyal fanbase) and a career "back home" (where you could book bigger roles sooner than you may even have access to such roles—if you ever would—in Los Angeles), what would you choose?

If you could be the big fish "back home," would that be more fulfilling? Or do you need to "make it big," even on a small scale, because that small role on a "real, Hollywood project" feels more like success than a much bigger role in something "smaller," out of market? What is it that defines "success" for you?

One of the toughest things about this question is that you will never know whether "the other road" would've been more fulfilling or whether you may have found greater success (or, more importantly, greater happiness) had you chosen that other road. You just *can't* know, because we cannot live two lives simultaneously.

So, the most important thing I can say about choosing is this: Get very confidently behind whatever choice you make. Pick a lane and drive in it. Because as anyone who has navigated traffic knows, it's the jayhole who tries to be in several lanes at once—switching and causing dangerous situations constantly since he's not sure which lane provides the "best" traffic experience for him—who arrives at his final destination annoyed for even having had to experience the journey. Don't be that guy. Enjoy all of the traffic. Pick a lane. Drive in it for a while. Be sure you've made the right choice *for now* and enjoy what happens there. It's all a part of building your life experience, so you might as well enjoy it.

Where do you *want* to live? What level of success do you want to have *the opportunity* to reach? This is important to know because—once you get those two questions answered—you're on your way to knowing exactly what kind of fish you want to be.

So many people complain about living in Los Angeles. They say they hate it. I don't get that. I almost think it's something they think is "cool" to do: Hate LA. How can you hate a place with such a high concentration of creative people living their dreams, spending every moment focused on storytelling and making magic, connecting with one another to come up with ways to create something out of nothing?

Sure, traffic sucks. Sure, smog is not a lovely thing. Sure, earthquakes can rattle your sanity from time to time. But have you seen our sights? Experienced our weather? Simply enjoyed the vast beauty of being in a place that is at once extremely busy and incredibly laid back? I love it. Except for about two other places on the planet, I couldn't imagine myself living anywhere else. But I get that I'm in the minority. Many people hate LA. And they love to say so. It's like the exact opposite of New York, where locals will fight with you if you say anything bad about "The City."

If you are totally anti-LA and would only choose to live here *because* of the opportunities it affords you as an actor, okay. That's good to know. Because now I want to address the second question of the two I asked above: What level of success do you want to have *the opportunity* to reach? Not even considering the number of actors in each market, let's look at how many people exist in service of populating the stories we tell, as an industry. There are 10 times the number of *casting directors* in Los Angeles as there are in New York. There are 200 times the number of CDs in LA as Chicago. Think about that. It's a factory town, plain and simple.

Absolutely, 100%, undeniably, indisputably, without question, the greatest opportunities for the largest and meatiest roles in the biggest and most-expensive projects on the planet happen in LA. Every day. Now, let's get to the bottom line. How many of those will you book? Almost none, unless you're one of the very few, very lucky, very ready, very gorgeous, very charismatic, very well-connected, very right-for-it, very all-stars-aligned actors on the planet. For almost everyone who even gets a *shot* at those biggest roles in the biggest projects, the outcome will be, "Hey, great audition. Good relationship-building. Nice brand-building. Well done. Don't call us, we'll call you." It's just a matter of numbers. *Most* actors will not become *name* actors. Even if very successful and very well-known within the industry, most actors *whose work we all know* can walk around without being stopped for autographs.

Can you be okay with that? Would making a living as an actor whose work is known and respected, but whose name may not be screamed by teens in malls in Middle America be okay with you? Are you so dang charged up—just getting the opportunity to work alongside "name" actors, in small supporting roles in bigger films or in bigger roles in smaller films—that it's still cool with you? Would *that* still be considered "success" for you? If so, great! Being in love with the pursuit is the largest ingredient in any actor's recipe for success. And amazingly, it's those who get in love with the pursuit who somehow seem to book bigger roles in bigger projects than those who detest the pursuit and bitch about it all the time.

Hey, the pursuit is what it is. Even as technology evolves and the process of casting and self-producing provides greater opportunities for those who otherwise would never get a meeting, the pursuit is still the pursuit, and it's not going away.

Whatever you decide, just get behind it and do it. Commit to it and make yourself the happiest *you* you can possibly be, while you live your life. That makes you more fun to be around and therefore more fun to cast, more fun to work with, more fun to have back again and again on bigger sets in bigger roles—whether you're in a fishbowl or an ocean.

I did a play at the Dallas Theatre Center and then for the next year and a half, I got no theatre. As much as I loved it, I was so frustrated I wasn't getting theatre work. I was impatient. In hindsight, it was just a year and a half. But at the same time, I was getting these TV roles and these movie roles and these commercial roles. My whole thing was, "Well, fine. If theatre doesn't love me,

I'll go where I'm respected." It was a business decision but also sort of an emotional decision. I wanted to work. I wanted to feel wanted. And when I looked at the resumé, I was getting some TV, film, and commercial work. So, I needed to move to LA.

—Victor Williams

Because I'm from New York City, I had that sort of "LA is evil" kind of bias. LA has been really kind to me and good to me and I like it so much more than I thought I would. But I went to college on the east coast and I grew up there. I have such deep roots there. After I graduated, for years it was kind of this specter of LA and knowing I probably should just go there and see what it's about, figure it out, and see if I could make a life there that I was comfortable with and happy with. I was sort of afraid but I kind of had this tough girl New York attitude like, "Screw LA. I don't need it. I'm a New Yorker!" My defenses were definitely way up.

—Angela Goethals, actor

New York is what you do either early on when you're totally ready to be a poor, starving artist and you think it's cool or you do it when you've made it and have a nice view of Central Park. I go back and forth. In fact, I'm going to LA next week to pitch a show. It's fun. It's nice to do the back and forth. Initially, I chose LA because, when I left England, it had not been sunny for four months and it was truly depressing. I needed the sun. I went to a college where tons of people went into the business and a lot of them were already in LA. I moved there already having a great network of friends. And then, my career took me to New York.

—Faith Salie

I got out of college and went straight to New York and lived there for four years and couldn't get arrested. I tried everything including the Spanish. It's a much smaller competitive market. I have a beautiful sister who is an actress in LA who said, "Stop it. You need to come to LA. You'll start working immediately." When I got to LA, I started working immediately. I started with Spanish commercials and that has been solid the entire time. Spanish and English, really.

—Ed F. Martin, actor

I've always been in New York. The irony is, my two least favorite places in the world are LA and New York, in that order. But, if you're an actor, you have to be in one or the other. I think, on balance, New York for me is a healthier world. LA, for all of its strengths, is essentially a one-industry town. No matter what you're doing for a living there, it's all focused and dependent on the entertainment industry. New York is not. I think that—for the human soul—is better for me. That's why I've always stayed in New York, and I'm lucky.

—James Rebhorn, actor

The two major things for me that were dilemmas in this career have been: "Do I go to grad school?" and "Do I go to LA?" I chose not to go to grad school because I started getting jobs and I was learning and in class anyway. I'm jealous of people who've been able to go to conservatory and kind of be in a bubble for three years, just really delving into plays. On the other hand, there's something to be said for going out there and scrapping. That's the path that I chose. The LA thing, I always have my little catchphrase: "I'm going to make a name for myself in New York and if something brings me to LA, I'll go."

—Matthew Del Negro, actor

I was on top of the world in Boston. Why would I want to go to New York? New York City is disgusting and it's scary and it's dirty and it's crazy. I meet with a New York agent and she says, "So, when are you moving to New York City?" I said, "I'm not moving to New York City!" As I'm leaving the building, she calls me on my cell phone and says, "Pack your bags. You're moving to New York. It's unanimous. We're signing you." I ended up absolutely loving New York and having the time of my life. I grew so attached to New York; I did *not* want to live in LA. I especially didn't want to live in LA because it was so *yuck!* Instead of having a going-away party when I moved to LA, I had a wake. Everyone had to wear black.

—Suzanne Whang, comic-host

New York is easy. I'm five minutes from where I work. I don't like LA. I can't take that schlepping around constantly. I lived in LA for six months while I was in a TV series called *Baby Boom* with Kate Jackson. I lived in West Hollywood at the bottom of Laurel Canyon in what looked like an old-age home to me. It's not my cup of tea. I'm a ghetto girl. I'm a definite type for a sitcom. I always was. But I wasn't interested in living in LA. I've always managed to have a career that's not as big maybe as it could've been because I insisted on staying in New York.

—Joy Behar, comic-host

What I love about New York is that it's such a small community. You think it's big, but really it's not. Everybody knows each other through someone here. I'm an independent actor. I respect the independent film filmmaker and I respect independent film. I've done movies in LA and been there for three months to do stuff, but it's such a major difference. Everybody always complains all day about LA. You can talk about LA for hours, whether it's the driving and the traffic or whatever. LA is the type of place where it's hard to establish a network of supportive friends. People are really out for self. It's hard to establish a network of friends who aren't in the business because you're surrounded by the business in LA. If you go out to LA with credits and a reel and an agent and a manager, you can make it. If you have all that, by all means, go out there. But bottom line, you have to work twice as hard when you're in LA. You can't just do a couple of rounds and drop headshots off and all the little things that we can do in New York. You can't get on the studio lots in LA like you can get into casting offices in New York. You really have to prove yourself a lot more in LA and separate yourself out a bit more.

—Al Thompson, actor

Portland is hopping. From big Hollywood productions excited about our locations and film incentives; to indie filmmakers wanting to do projects their own way; to the various commercials, infomercials, industrials, and animated films being shot here every year; regional production is in full swing. It doesn't take long for a skilled actor to become known to all the local casting directors when there are only a few offices. When someone's good, it's common for us to read him or her a half-dozen times a week for various projects. Compare that to the number of auditions an LA or NY newcomer gets to attend.

In a regional market, you spend less time commuting and trying to make ends meet, which means more time to devote to your craft *and* to having a life outside of acting, which—in my opinion—makes you a more interesting, well-rounded person. Just as independent filmmakers choose cities like Portland to forge their own paths, so do independent-minded actors. Smaller markets are great places to start your own theatre or production company; write, produce, direct, and star in your own projects; launch a new idea or even start a business to support your craft. The risks are fewer since costs are lower and you can always relocate once your ideas have proven successful. Just think of your regional location as an incubator.

—Lana Veenker, CSA

My academic mind was ashamed to admit that I had no professional experience, but hey, everyone has to start somewhere! I began with what I knew—I studied. I Googled theatre in the area and immediately found Theatre of Puget Sound, a wonderful conglomeration of theatres in Seattle and the PNW. Their callboard listed auditions for plays, commercials, short films, student work, indie features, and voiceovers. So I began auditioning.

Since I was trained in stage technique, I studied books about the business side of the industry and how to translate stage performance to working in front of a camera. One of the first books I bought and devoured was *Self-Management for Actors*, which I found incredibly relevant despite being written primarily for an LA market. And as we all know, Bonnie is a goddess.

Looking back, I came to Seattle very green. But I was incredibly fortunate. Seattle is made up of an *amazing* community of people willing to lend a hand, point you in the right direction, make suggestions, provide guidance, and take a chance on you. I booked roles in student films, webseries, commercials, animated series, music videos, and indies where I was able to explore new media.

I slowly built up knowledge and experience in commercial, film, and television. With the help of acting coaches, casting directors, and peers, I molded my stage training into film performances. I learned how to talk to agents and casting directors. I also gained very valuable insight about how the business side of things work, which I discovered needs to be given just as much attention as the craft. All the while, the wonderful people around me supported me and allowed me to take risks, grow, try new things, gain confidence, and *learn*.

Am I ready to take a leap and move to LA? Yes, I am. But I cannot imagine having done it without the incredible stepping-stone that was and is Seattle. Never could I have fathomed how much there still was to learn when I left college, bright-eyed and ready to take on the world. And I had no idea how well I would be nurtured and supported by people I had yet to meet. I know I would not be entering the LA market with the set of tools or confidence I have now, had I not spent my years in a smaller market, specifically Seattle.

—Sarah J. Eagen, actor

The regional markets have become very savvy and successful. Now, I cast roles regionally that years before would have only been cast in LA or NY. We have all grown. New Mexico offers a 25%-30% rebate on all production expenditures (including New Mexico labor) that are subject to taxation by the State of New Mexico. This is a *refund*, not a credit. That can add up to big bucks—fast. New Mexico is booming with production business. We need more good actors in New Mexico. Maybe your ever-changing dreams will lead you here.

—Jo Edna Boldin, CSA

The Louisiana film industry is thriving. According to *P3 Update Magazine*, Louisiana is one of the top 10 filming locations worldwide. In addition, New Orleans has consistently placed on *MovieMaker Magazine*'s "Top 10 Cities to Be a Moviemaker." And it's not just because of the incentives! A large part of the attraction to Louisiana is our creative filmmaking community. And by community, I mean a strong, supportive group of folks who share a common interest, but who also have created a strong support system for each other. We carpool to auditions, we take collections for those of us who have stumbled upon hard times, we pay our respects when those among us have passed on, and we celebrate our marriages and the births of our babies.

Because of the ease of social networking sites—but mainly because we really want to know how we are all doing—we keep up with one another. We work on one another's projects and we attend each other's screenings or plays. We are a community in a true sense.

—Shanda Quintal, actor

Upon arriving to film their movies in Louisiana, both director Renny Harlin and director Oliver Stone expressed their concerns to me regarding the level of acting our local talent possessed. Both Harlin and Stone wanted to see headshots and resumés for the roles they had in mind that would be cast out of Louisiana. My partner and I brought files and files of actors' headshots to show them, but stressed to them to please refrain from making any remarks until they saw the talent live and in person. They did just this, and after our first round of auditions, both Harlin and Stone had equal reactions.

With a shocked looked on his face, Renny Harlin sat back in his chair and said in his Finnish accent, "I saw 10 to 15 A-list actors in LA for some of these roles, and I think I just cast my entire movie here in this one session with you." Similarly, Oliver Stone turned to me and said, "Where did you find some of this talent? They are terrific and actually have a 'life' besides focusing on acting 24/7."

This wealth of hidden talent, deep down South, is why I wake up every day excited to see which directors' and producers' socks we will knock off next... not to mention the "wealth" I will be keeping in their pocketbooks with our sweet tax incentives! Therefore, it is a win-win situation! There is a reason movie crews can't get enough of Louisiana once they set foot here and, therefore, always come back for more: it's our Louisiana *lagniappe* (all the li'l somethin' extras): southern charm, southern food, southern silver screen sales tax, and most importantly, southern stars!

— Brinkley Maginnis, casting director

If you're an actor in DC, you can actually do film, TV, and video projects during the day and perform in an Equity show at night. And then you can proudly say that you are a working actor. But nothing comes easy. You have to work hard. Get your training. Figure out your market. Build your resumé and most importantly remember that show business is a business. DC is the third largest industrial and the sixth largest commercial market in the nation, and the amazingly talented theatre community here is the second largest Equity market in the nation. I guess the secret is out.

—Carlyn Davis, CSA

Many look at regional markets as a kind of purgatory: a proving ground that leads either to success in a bigger city or to a silent descent into the boundless and overcrowded depths of obscurity. But people do live in other markets. Movies are made in North Carolina, TV series are shot in North Carolina, we have a ton of commercial production, and our strong crew base stays busy most all the time. We are all individuals, so everything is contingent upon your goals, passions, and personal responsibilities (although talent and bravery also factor in there somewhere). You will soon find out if your market can sustain your acting habit, or if you need to broaden your circle. If you are driven by your craft to move to NY or LA, you still need to start somewhere, and there's no place like North Carolina.

—Kristi Stanfill, talent agent

Chicago has a vibrant and rich theatre scene and I am not just talking about landmarks such as the Steppenwolf or the Goodman but there is a huge "store front" independent theatre scene that offers great opportunities for new actors who wish to build credits and sharpen their skills. There are plentiful theatre opportunities for actors at various stages of their career.

Unfortunately this is not the case for film and TV actors. Most of the available on-camera work in Chicago is limited to commercials and industrials. As for film, especially with Columbia College, DePaul, Northwestern University, the Art Institute of Chicago, and most recently Flashpoint Academy to name a few, the opportunities in no-pay student films are in abundance. There are also the occasional low-budget nonunion indie films. However, when big-budget Hollywood studio films come to shoot here, the majority of the roles have already been cast in LA and the one-liner and dayplayer roles are usually given to local actors with heavy theatre credits.

—Ayman Samman, actor

Chicago is a thriving market for actors. Instead of many studios and networks, we have weather! There are few casting directors in Chicago, so it isn't too hard to get known by them (for better or for worse). As for agents that are franchised with the unions, there are about 10 of them. So different from New York and Los Angeles, eh?! We do get *tons* of work in Chicago and the actors generally tend to dip into all forms of the business.

So, one week an actor might be filming an industrial and then get a role in a feature for a large studio followed by a small role on TV and then do a play at night. We have some great training centers and acting classes and, of course, magnificent colleges and universities surround us. Our theatre is world-class. Playwrights and directors come here to work in relative peace—a wonderful opportunity for any actor. Even though our market is small (roughly 9000 professional actors), we still look at the resumés to see if an actor is union, or has training, or has been in some plays. Anything less than *very talented* just will not do.

—Jane Alderman, actor-casting director-coach

I set my sights on the American Conservatory Theatre in San Francisco and fell in love with the San Francisco Bay Area. It seemed to be a place where one could be himself, no matter how freaky. I am a big fish in a smaller pond up north, getting meatier roles in indie films. But the filmmakers who have the money to make indies that can get distribution often cast in LA or get a "name" to carry the film, so naturally there is a better chance of getting the film picked up or sold. I may get better roles, but often the acting and or production is uneven, or I work for the low budget agreement of $100 a day with the balance of my regular day rate deferred to when the project sells.

To make ends meet, I'll do a print ad; a voiceover; a tradeshow; an industrial; party work; fundraisers; educational entertainment; environmental theatre work; historical reenactments; books on tape; proof of concept; coaching or speaking on acting, casting, protocol, or teamwork on the set; teach an improv class; consult with a director trying to find a way out a problem on set; hold private acting lessons; appear at a fan convention; speak at film expos; do a SAG-AFTRA Foundation seminar or a DGA workshop. Some of those pay a little. But all in all, it's not an easy task. Remember, finding this kind of work is a nonstop hunt.

— Jeffrey Weissman, actor-coach

The actor's bread and butter in Colorado are commercials and industrial films. Local, regional, and national commercials shoot regularly in Colorado. I've seen commercial castings for the all of the "big four:" pharmaceuticals, fast food, cars, and beer. Extra work on these commercials can compensate very well.

Major motion pictures and independent films cast a lot of extras, featured, and supporting roles. National cable television production companies producing unscripted television audition and cast hosts for their shows locally. I would be remiss if I didn't at least mention the six-hour drive to nearby Albuquerque. Colorado talent is finding open arms in the booming New Mexico market with many opportunities there in features and on television.

The key to my survival in the Denver market has been to diversify. I've cultivated opportunities within the film and television media but beyond that also lay many other performance prospects. The Denver Center for the Performing Arts is the region's jewel of professional theatre, hosting yearly open auditions for local performers. There is a network of professional regional theatres and local not-for-profit theatres, including summer fringe theatre and the Colorado Shakespeare Festival. And for those of you that are "really, really good looking," there are a fair amount of print jobs out there for commercial and fashion. Stand-up comedy and improv venues with performance options exist all over. Theme parks, cabaret, broadcast, radio, tradeshow, and promotional opportunities round out the diversity of prospects available in the Denver market.

—Maíz Lucero, actor

We do a lot of actor-friendly, multi-platform casting at The Philadelphia Casting Co., Inc. We cast everything. In the bigger markets, casting companies usually only handle one thing. They specialize in voiceover, or theatre, or films, or TV, or commercials, etc. So do the agents. So, you need one agent for each area of coverage and you really have to push yourself in one or maybe two directions to get seen at all. The agents in the Philly area handle it all. So, there are options! And we're aware that principal actors, here, do background work (and we don't judge them negatively for that choice). Unlike casting directors in Los Angeles, we respect actors that accept background work. We figure, at least they are working in their profession, as opposed to waiting tables in between gigs.

—Susan Gish, casting director

In the UK, if you want to be considered a professional actor, you usually need to have studied acting fulltime. There are exceptions of course, but in general you are expected to have trained for the profession. There are several accredited drama schools (what would be known as acting conservatories in the US) and there are other universities, colleges, and private institutions where you can train. In the UK, each school will take 'round about 30 students on its fulltime acting course. Some will take even less. So if you consider that some of those schools have literally thousands of applicants each year for those 30 places, the chances of getting in are slim—not impossible, just slim! I have friends who auditioned once and got in, while others got in on their sixth attempt. Part of the moral is—like any lesson in acting—if you want this hard enough, you will get there, but you have to be prepared to put your time in. Also, in general the schools do like you to have a little life experience before studying post grad.

—Angela Milton, actor

Why Decide?

Here's my take on it. Why decide? Further, why feel like any decision is forever? I chose LA (twice) after having worked in a minor market for many years. I loved both my experience in Atlanta as an actor and hand model, and my experience pursuing an acting career in Hollywood. Obviously, an acting career on a large scale in LA was not to be, for me, but luckily it was that pursuit of acting that led me to the career I now have and love so much. And if I ever get "over" living in Los Angeles, I'll leave it.

I think people like to put a lot of emphasis on the decision-making process, believing that it is of utmost importance to *get it right*. I say, make a decision after having put thought and research into it, of course. And then, if you find you'd like to make another decision later, go for it again! Now, don't give up on one decision before you've given it enough time (18 months is a bare minimum to try out any new venue to be really sure you understand the flow of it all), but don't be afraid to change course either. No one says you have to "choose LA" and then keep that choice chosen *forever*.

28: Moving to Los Angeles

Moving to LA is like saying "I love you" for the first time. You're never sure that it's the *exact* right time, and then you leap.

The best thing you can have going for you when you move to any new city is a connection to a community of wonderful people who will help you avoid missteps and show you the ropes. I am still connected with some of the fine folks who helped me when I arrived at the base of the Hollywood sign in 1993 and again in 1998. Their advice kept me from having a harder road than is necessary. Their support helped me through times when I drove into proverbial ditches despite their best efforts to help me steer clear of them. I am very fortunate to be connected to a community of amazingly generous and genuine people. Survival tip number one for moving to Los Angeles: Plug in!

Luckily, that's even easier to do before you move now, because of the huge community of actors who gather online, worldwide, like we do at smfa4. com every day. Also check out the message boards at Showfax, *Backstage*, or the Delphi forum PARF (especially for parents of young actors). No matter where you go for online support, do the site regulars a favor and perform a *search* of a topic before you post a question. Chances are, it's been discussed before—maybe even very recently—and you can ask a better-informed follow-up question, rather than a general, unresearched one.

It's also very easy to read about LA-based actors' experiences, thanks to the blogosphere and actors' interest in putting their lives "out there" for all to see. Stephon Fuller was one of the first actors to track all of his auditions, meetings, close calls, and bookings via the web. Now, thousands of actors of all levels post about how they Taft-Hartleyed themselves, how they got their first agents, and who shot their best (and worst) headshots. The only caveat I'll mention here is that many people post their experiences anonymously. *Danger!* If someone is unwilling to say who they are—so you can check their credits to know if their advice is even worth believing—beware. There are people who create Twitter accounts, blogs, and Facebook pages saying they are casting directors, agents, managers, publicists, directors, producers, etc., when they are *not*. Be very careful taking advice from anyone whose experiences and credentials you cannot verify. Back in the day of the face-to-face meeting, you could be sure you were getting advice from someone you could trust. Now, anyone with a keyboard and an Internet connection can call himself an expert and advise actors in ways that are irresponsible.

Read everything, yes. But before taking action, be sure you've filtered the advice carefully. As Fuller says, his "Long-Ass Bio" is an account of what steps he took in *his* career, not a prescription for success for anyone else. And if anyone is selling something, keep that in mind as you read any free advice they offer. They may lay out tips that make you feel that the only real key to success is to take their expensive intensive or buy their materials.

People move here every day without a net, without a plan, without a single connection and they do just fine. The great power of the Internet is that now you can tweet, Facebook status update, blog, or post at any message board a quick, "Anyone have firsthand experiences with so-and-so's class?" before plunking down your money. Awesome. Take advantage of that, to avoid unnecessary pitfalls. For my latest *SMFA* Hot List of updated resources for the big move—including recommended reading, watching, and listening— visit smfa4.com.

Of course have your profile up (and updated) at Actors Access and Casting Networks, as those are the two most-used sites for theatrical and commercial casting, respectively, in Los Angeles. Check in *daily* (if not hourly) to see what's actively casting in your soon-to-be new market. Keep in mind that there are significant (high-end) breakdowns *not* available for actors' direct submissions. Keep an eye on the sides at Showfax, and all the production info at sites listed in the **Become a Booking Machine** chapter to develop an overview of the massive amounts of production going on in LA, every day. Don't get overwhelmed. Just start soaking it in.

Reach out to your alumni and hometown buddies. Wherever you're from, there's a posse of folks in LA that are also from there. Whether that's your old acting studio, your college, conservatory, or even high school, there's someone in LA who has that in common with you, and that's someone with whom to connect.

Get clear on your bullseye. Especially if you're from a minor market where you can be less specifically branded, narrowing your type and age range even more will help you. Research LA headshot photographers. Find the ones who shoot your type very well. Prep for LA auditions by grabbing sides from showfax.com for co-star level auditions in episodics and supporting role auditions in films. Fire up your video camera and practice! Use an app like Rehearsal to help you along. Until you're in Los Angeles taking classes from folks who can advise you on how to nail the first auditions you'll experience here, you can teach yourself a lot, just by watching yourself deliver these one-liners.

For international actors, really spend time researching resources for your O-1 visa or green card application and do *not* get wooed by "too good to be true" shady players who have no verifiable track record for helping actors get legal to work in the States. Visit smfa4.com for our favorite referrals and for links to sites to help you "Americanize" your accent, should that be one of your goals.

If you can make a trip to Los Angeles for a visit before your move, that's awesome. A reconnaissance mission to get the lay of the land, the pace of the day-to-day, the flow of it all can make a huge difference in your ability to plan for the move.

The Reconnaissance Mission

People who are from the continental United States tell me that even they felt culture shock upon arrival in Los Angeles. This gave me a certain degree of comfort. Fellow aliens, allow yourself the luxury of acclimating to not only the weather but to the pace of life, the food, the local culture, the traffic, and the currency before you even attempt to get your head around the official business of pavement-pounding.

That's why a reconnaissance mission had real importance for me. When I arrived to "start my new life," I felt less like a tourist because I had spent a few weeks here, drinking in the vibe and researching where I wanted to (and could afford to) live.

For those of you whose natural dialect is what gets you the work, great! Work that uniqueness. For those of you (like me) who will cross over and perfect that American accent, don't forget that your natural accent and expression is what sets you apart and adds flavor to your choices as an actor. Don't get lost in translation. Investigate those qualities that are uniquely yours and allow them to flow into every aspect of your work and preparation, for it will surely make you a more interesting actor. Go forth and be... exactly as you are.

—Elle Newlands, actor-singer

Check out panels put on by *Backstage*, the Paley Center, and SAG-AFTRA (plus SAG-AFTRA Foundation Casting Access Project, LifeRaft, MOVE, Conservatory, and Conversations) as well as anything going on during local film festivals. Without even being a member of SAG-AFTRA, you can check out recorded streamed events at their website. Also check out other groups that mount industry gatherings, panel discussions, or meet-and-greet opportunities (some free, some not). Get plugged in with the many writers' groups that utilize actors for staged readings. This is a great way to connect with higher-tier buyers and content creators even before you have an agent! Shocker—I have a list for you of my favorite reading groups at, you guessed it, smfa4.com.

Set up Google Alerts for high-priority people and groups you want to connect with. The more you know about their history before you arrive, the better shot you'll have at jumping right in without that annoying ramp-up that comes with feeling "new" to a group. Follow key people on Twitter and connect at Facebook. Don't underestimate the power of *smart* social networking. Visit essential sites daily. Yep, your list of our favorite sites is waiting for you at smfa4.com. I'd say a daily visit to our site is a no-brainer. The community is what you make it, y'know?

You might want to take CD workshops. Actors who are new to town, talented, and totally ready to book—both due to talent and business savvy— tend to do very well at CD workshops. Understand the law (See: **Casting Director Workshops**) and really research your workshop targets. Tracking which shows are cast by whom (using IMDb-Pro and CastingAbout) and determining not only which are the best match for your type but also which new shows are most likely to be given time to "find their audience" in the new season is a great use of your energy. Doing it before you're in LA means you'll be even better at it when you are here (when you'll be able to add firsthand information to your show bible). Then when you score that meeting or audition with someone on your target list, you'll be armed not only with your talent, but also with lots of intel that gives you an edge.

> All too often people come here with stars in their eyes believing that they will be "discovered" whilst eating at a small patisserie on Sunset. But let's get to the facts. All of my heroes whom are in this industry had to work their ass off to get where they are now. Also, it took a great deal of focus and discipline to attain their aspirations. Hollywood is not the place to figure it all out once you get here.
>
> Hollywood is simply high school with more scandal, more drugs, and more room for major error. Please be the one who understands the consequences for their actions and will choose to not falter from who they really are. There are many ways to get sidetracked here and it is only those who stay on their road that will get what they have always worked for.
>
> Don't give up. Patience and perseverance really are so vital to anyone who has the goal of going after what they love. Make a deal with yourself about how hard you are going to work and how to deal with the many obstacles that will come in your way. Because here in this business, there is always someone working harder, staying more positive, and learning as much as they possibly can. Are you the person that's working harder than the rest? This business is not easy, but for those who are up for the challenge, I salute you.
>
> —Kendall Toole, actor

Have you saved up enough money? A lot more money than you think you need? Please do! Also, check out reputable moving companies if you're not going to do it yourself. Read the reviews. Ask around. Be sure you're in good hands and that your valuables are insured or 100% within *your* control during the move so there's no drama. Fill out those change of address cards at the post office. If you're going to be moving anywhere near the end of one year or the beginning of the next year, please do whatever you can to avoid paying "partial year taxes" in both places of residence. It's a huge headache, and if you can avoid it by timing your move (or your last paycheck back home) just right, you'll be so glad you did, come tax time.

Be prepared for smogging and registering your car if you're bringing it with you, and of course, for getting your local driver's license (always make an appointment with the DMV online, as it cuts down on wait time drastically). Keep all your pieces of ID together before and during the move, because you'll need access to it all both to close out your world back home and then to open bank accounts and establish utilities, here. Don't forget to register to vote in Los Angeles County!

Pre-move, clear your clutter and review *Backstage*'s articles in their "Welcome to LA" edition. Get the latest updates from the website for Judy Kerr's amazing book *Acting Is Everything*. Check out our exclusive **Six Weeks To LA (6W2LA)** program! Review the neighborhoods of Los Angeles and see where they line up with casting offices. At smfa4.com, we have a map of LA with busy casting offices plotted out, so you can consider neighborhoods based on targeted projects. Of course, LA is huge, so you can expect to be covering a lot of ground for your auditions, wherever you decide to plant yourself.

The best way to get a place to live in Los Angeles is to drive around with a good buddy and a cell phone, going up and down the streets on which you want to live, looking for "For Rent" signs posted in windows. Usually, by the time the best places are up for grabs for even a day, they're already spoken for. So, if you see something you like, call from the driveway and say you'd like to come in and look at the place. Have your checkbook handy, along with paystubs and references, as most places won't hold a unit without a hefty deposit and some words in your favor from past employers or landlords.

Consider a membership at Westside Rentals, check crime stats (if you must), prepare your earthquake safety kit, study the Metro, join AAA, read up on traffic laws, find an honest mechanic, install the HopStop and Waze apps on your smart phone, and bookmark the SigAlert website.

Is it possible to find something not terribly expensive, centrally located, and available? Yes. Absolutely. But, you may have to hit town (perhaps bunk with a friend or find a temporary housing situation) before you can really refine your housing search. There's no amount of online research you can do that will match the experience of getting to LA and discovering where you want to be.

Getting Around in Los Angeles

There is such complexity in the issue of navigating Los Angeles—and you certainly will do that quite a bit as you hit all of your auditions—that I asked actor Robin Gwynne and casting director Steve Lockhart to contribute the following section on getting around.

The riddle of the Sphinx and the mysteries of the Great Pyramid of Cheops pale in comparison to trying to decipher the "logic" of driving in Los Angeles. The first freeway in the nation was a six-mile stretch of what is now The 110 Pasadena Freeway, built in 1940. Not surprisingly, this city also has the dubious honor of being the home of the very first gas station in the country, which opened in 1912. And while we're on the subject of history: Among the oldest human remains ever found in North America were those of Los Angeles Man. He died in the area of West Los Angeles about 25,000 years ago, perhaps from boredom while stuck in a prehistoric traffic jam (though some might argue it was while waiting for a callback or a call from his agent).

Just the size of this city makes driving in it intimidating! There are over 160 miles of complex freeway systems and over 5400 miles of other roadways. The longest of these is Sepulveda Blvd., which within city limits alone runs for 31 *miles* (and yes, it gets its name from the extremely rich and powerful ranch family Sepulveda, the great great grands of Warner Bros. TV's senior VP of casting Tony Sepulveda. And by the way, the accent is on the "u" as in "*pull*" and the other syllables are throwaways. Newbies to this town are instantly recognizable when they say "SepulvEEda").

The shortest road is Powers Street, located Downtown. It extends a mere 13 feet (but since "Nobody Walks in LA," no doubt people complain that they had to park "all the way down at the end of the block," even on Powers Street). In a recent DMV census, there were 7.1 million vehicles registered in Los Angeles with over 24 million peak-hour motor vehicle trips. No statistics as to how many actors were late to auditions on account of traffic, probably because that is the pat excuse even in the rare instance that it isn't true.

Los Angeles covers an area of 465 square miles. If its silhouette on a map were an inkblot test, one might say it resembled a stingray, or, if tilted on its side, a ray gun. A coincidence? Or does somebody up there know something?

To help add confusion to the already complicated equation, Los Angeles has whole cities inside of it, and some cities you *thought* were cities are not. They are only regional names to areas long ago swallowed up by Greater Los Angeles. The difference is not something that can be deciphered intuitively by examining the name of each "city" alone. You would probably have greater success studying tea leaves or the entrails of chickens. Beverly Hills is its own city; Bel-Air is not. West Hollywood is, but North Hollywood is not. Nor is

Hollywood itself for that matter. Culver City is, but Studio City isn't. And Universal City isn't a city at all as it has no residents (though it does have its own fire department).

The corner of First and Main Street is the center of the street and house-numbering system for the City of Los Angeles. *In theory*, street numbers in the city are numbered according to how far they are from that Downtown intersection; however, not all the cities within Los Angeles stick to this scheme, so numbers can jump around wildly when you cross city lines within Los Angeles. The same is true for street names. For example: If you are heading east on Magnolia in Los Angeles, it turns into West Magnolia once it reaches Burbank. Be really careful looking for an address on Robertson or La Cienega as they go through Beverly Hills. Not only do the numbers stop, change to new numbers for a few blocks and then switch back, but the two systems are very similar numerically, so you may think you're close enough to your destination to park and then find you are still a mile away. Are you getting a headache yet?

Now into this mix add the craziest element of all: the people. Over 3.8 million of them within city limits. Their most peculiar habit seems to be rushing up on red lights. No one knows why. Perhaps it gives them more time at the stop so they can admire themselves lovingly in their rear-view mirrors and marvel at what a difference those Botox injections have made. Here's another peculiar behavior: They will often creep slowly into the intersection while the light is red, as if this action might save them a nanosecond of time. They forget that it is Los Angeles *quid pro quo* to run red lights that used to be yellow. So if the last five seconds of a red light are considered pretty green and the first five seconds of the red light are seen as fairly yellow, you can see why our accident rates are sky high.

However, when a Los Angeles driver is waiting to make a left turn, he doesn't creep into the intersection while the light is green, but instead only enters it once the light turns yellow, to the great annoyance of the drivers behind him also waiting to turn left. So, apparently green lights are also open to interpretation. This difficulty in making left turns in Los Angeles is exacerbated by the fact that the city has almost no left turn signal lights. Oh, and of course, no expensive cars seem to have working turn signals. We happen to know a Porsche driver who says she never signals because if she does, people speed up to keep her from making her move. Noted.

So, *huge* city, multiple Cities within the City, and millions of insane drivers: great! But here are some helpful tips and caveats garnered at great personal expense, including bloodshed, to help you deal with this Byzantine system.

"Rush hour" on weekdays is roughly 6am to 10am and 3pm to 7pm. Many freeways also have "rush hours," even on weekends, that seem to fit no discernable time pattern. Think: get to work, lunch hour, leave work, run errands, out for dinner, out to a club or movie, home late. So, what's that? Like, seven rush hours a day? That's about right. And that's not including the traffic composed of people trying to miss rush hour.

It's true: Los Angeles drivers do not know how to drive in the rain. Give plenty of room and move slowly. When possible, stay home.

A Los Angeles freeway exit will not always necessarily have an equal and opposite onramp. This can be very frustrating if you take the wrong exit. So, don't. Especially at night. A bad one is this sudden left lane "Exit Only" into the north side of Downtown off the old part of The 110 South as it curves right. It sneaks up on you if you're in the left lane, and you might end up on a scary dead-end street with only your emergency brake to turn you around and no way back onto the freeway. Pay attention.

Here's a tip few seem to know: If you're on the freeway, driving along in one of the right-hand lanes, and the white dashed line on your left gets thicker, either a double dashed line or a solid line, you're now in an "Exit Only" lane. If you don't intend to exit, this is the early clue to merge left. Los Angeles signs don't allow a lot of time for these decisions, but if you know this little "tell," you'll avoid many-a-last-minute, hair-raising merge that no one seems to want to let you make.

Completely unsubstantiated observation: The middle lane (or the lane just right of the fast lane) on Los Angeles freeways tends to be the best one, averaging fewer stalled cars (they like to pull over one way or the other), fewer last-minute merges, and more in-it-for-the-long-haul drivers.

Some alternate routes one can take instead of the freeway: Sepulveda Blvd. between The Valley and The Westside and to LAX; Coldwater Canyon Drive between The Valley and Beverly Hills-West Hollywood (Coldwater is Beverly Drive in Beverly Hills, a north-south street *not* to be confused with east-west-running Beverly Blvd.); and Laurel Canyon Blvd. between The Valley and Hollywood (Laurel Canyon is Crescent Heights in West Hollywood). Investigate Beverly Glen as another sneak-across to get over "The Hill." They're technically the Santa Monica Mountains, but *puhleez!* Other alternate routes are La Cienega Blvd. between Hollywood-West Hollywood and LAX; Highland Ave. between Hollywood and North Hollywood (which goes to Barham, to get to Burbank, or Lankershim, which leads to NoHo); and Cahuenga Blvd., which is a great Hollywood to Burbank fly-through.

Streets aren't straight in Los Angeles. There is no true grid. This can take you totally out of your way, or you can use it to your advantage. Watch out for San Vicente Blvd., truly the Bermuda Triangle of Los Angeles streets. It's great for a block here or there, or to sneak through Brentwood toward the sea (if you don't mind veering north), but unless you're a seasoned pro, a good rule of thumb is not to count on it for more than, say, three blocks. National Blvd. is a little-known, handy shortcut heading West (and north-ish) from Palms over to West Los Angeles, but it has lots of turns and detours, so get to know it when you're not in a hurry and can pay attention to the faded, not-so-conveniently-placed signs.

Wonder why Santa Monica Blvd. is north of Wilshire in Hollywood but south of Wilshire in Santa Monica? Because the two thoroughfares cross each other just east of Downtown Beverly Hills. Venice Blvd. slants north when you're heading east from Venice (it's only a block south of Pico Blvd. at La Brea, as opposed to a couple miles south at Robertson). It can be a very convenient alternate route to Hollywood from Venice-West Los Angeles (via Culver City and then the La Brea-Highland trick). Olympic Blvd. is also a good east-west alternative, but not once you're east of Western, unless you want to swerve way south. Heading west, Culver Blvd., after it branches off from Venice Blvd., is a low-traffic, straight shot to Marina del Rey. And if you're coming from Beverly Hills, the little-known curvy road called Motor Ave. cuts straight from Fox Studios on Pico to the Sony lot and Culver Studios in Culver City on Washington Blvd., which goes straight to the beach!

Since left-turn lanes at major intersections often don't have left-turn arrows, they become so backed up during peak times that it is actually much faster and less frustrating to drive one block past that intersection and then turn (either left or right) and circle around that block. A great built-in U-turn is at the left from Venice to La Brea heading north. It's there for the police station. Very convenient!

If you are trying to find the nearest branch of a business (such as a bank), keep in mind that in a brochure or ad they will be often be listed according to the "pseudocity" they are in, instead of Los Angeles. If your car or your handheld device is equipped with GPS, use it. Get good at using it. Double-check your most complicated routes using the Internet before you head out the door, just to make sure you're going in the right direction!

Auto insurance rates vary wildly, so you may want to factor that in when deciding where to live. For example: On average, auto insurance is twice as much in the Hollywood area as it is in the East Valley, which can work out to an added cost of $50 to $100 or more a month. Ouch!

When you buy tires, go somewhere that gives a lifetime warranty; they usually include rotations, too. For gas, get a Costco card and fill up there whenever you can; it's about ten cents cheaper per gallon (and food and stuff are cheaper too). And get AAA. It's inexpensive and can be a lifesaver!

Looking for super-duper clothing bargains? The California Mart Sample Sale is on the last Friday of every month. Go to 110 E. Ninth St., 90079 to start out. Parking is expensive, but the clothing deals are amazing! It's a cash-only business (oh, and bring your own shopping bags). Grocery stores (to which you also must bring your own bags) are overly busy on Sunday during the day and during evening rush hour (see above), but are relatively quiet on Saturday nights. Unless you're going to shop at the Farmers' Market, avoid

Santa Monica's Third Street Promenade area on Wednesday and Saturday mornings if you can. Farmers' Market parking is nearly impossible. Of course, there is nowhere in Los Angeles to truly escape crazy traffic. There are cell-phone-talking, organic-fruit-loving, fellow-driver-hating, non-signaling, might-is-right, Namaste-a-minute-ago road-ragers everywhere. Gotta love it!

Now, freeways! The 101 Freeway is a *diagonal* freeway. It runs northwest and southeast. So, if you see an onramp labeled 101 North, when someone told you to take The 101 West, it is the same thing. The freeway heads north in some sections and west in others, but takes a northwest diagonal trend in general. Same thing to note the other way; you may see a sign for The 101 South, when you want to head east. And The 134 West turns into The 101 West (North). If you want to get onto The 101 South from The 134 West, you have to exit where the sign says and then get back on at the appropriate onramp. Oh, and there is no exit for The 10 West off The 101 South. You have to take The 110 South, which is not referred to as that. It is labeled The Harbor Freeway and it connects to The 10 West. This can be a big time-waster and steering wheel-pounder 'til you figure it out! It works in reverse too. (No, not by putting your car in reverse, silly!)

Also, if anyone tells you that The 5 and The 405 are the same thing, don't believe them. This is only true(-ish) way north of Los Angeles, where it is completely useless info, since The 405 disappears. The 405 is far west of The 5. They run basically parallel, but far apart, until they meet somewhere around Pasadena or south of Santa Clarita. Try to avoid The 405, anyway—it's always a parking lot! Coldwater Canyon and Laurel Canyon will save your life if you take the time to get to know them. Even Highland is way better! Cahuenga is a great little thruway, too. Handy tip: The 90 Freeway is a great way to hit The 405 from Mar Vista via La Cienega or from the Marina.

Other freeway standouts: From The 5 South you can get on The 134 East, but not West. From The 101 South (East), you can't get on The 170, but you can if you're on The 101 North (West), but then you can't get on The 134. The 170 South connects to The 101 South (East), but not The 101 North (West), but you *can* get on The 134.

And our personal favorite: If you're taking The Hollywood Freeway (The 101 North-slash-West) out of Downtown, you have to change freeways to The 170 North to stay on The Hollywood Freeway, if you just stay on The 101 North instead, you are actually on The Ventura Freeway. And if you're traveling south (east) on The Ventura Freeway, you have to change from The 101 South (East) to The 134 East to stay on it, if you stay on The 101, you're on The Hollywood Freeway again. Got all that?

If you were to fly over at low altitude and follow the actual *structural* freeway, The 5 South gets renamed as The 10 West, and The 101 South gets renamed as The 5 South. The net result is if you take either The 10 or The 5 in either direction through Downtown, you're actually changing to a different freeway in the process to continue on that same freeway.

Also: Have you ever wondered why everything seems such a mess of merging freeways Southeast of Downtown? That's because none of the through freeways actually goes through. It's a sleight-of-hand trick where they just renumbered the existing freeways, and they feed you "through" using merging onramps.

Always have quarters in your car for meters—you don't want a ticket waiting on your parked car after your audition (though some say that's good luck). Always have headshots-rezzies (stapled!) in your car. Always think twice before getting on The 405 Freeway (and get used to the "The" before freeway names). Always allow *way* too much time to get to meetings and to auditions and to *set!*

Don't give in to road rage. That might be the casting director for your next audition that you're yelling at. Lock your doors. (You *have* seen the highly-televised chases, right? When the bad guy jumps out of his car and into the neighboring pickup or hatchback? Not good for the actor in a hurry. Though you would get on TV!) Watch overhead signs for Amber Alerts and always wear your seatbelt.

Try to primp only at red lights, not while in motion. If you must car-flirt, do so responsibly. Get an earset for your cell phone and use voice activation to dial. It's the law! Texting tickets are very real and very expensive. Oh, and if you call 411 for information about Los Feliz, just forget your high school Spanish class right now. If you pronounce it correctly, they'll never understand you. Here in Tinsel Town, it's either Loss (as in "moss") or Lohs (which is correct) Feeluhss. Feel free to sing in your car; everyone here is used to it. Drive defensively, meaning: Expect the worst and make room for the bastard. Be psychic. Breathe. Signal, for God's sake! And don't pass us in the right-hand turn lane at an intersection. That's just rude.

—Robin Gwynne and Steve Lockhart

Tips from Traffic School

I used to teach traffic school for the Improv (yes, that lovely stand-up comedy traffic school course) and I am going to give you a few tips for getting around citation-free in Los Angeles. Disclaimer: This information is accurate per the California State Vehicle Code. Do not apply these laws to your state unless you have checked your own vehicle code and know for a fact that they are identical. I cannot help you get out of a ticket, nor can I walk you through traffic school, should you get that option when you get a ticket. That said, I can do eight hours of stand-up related to the California vehicle code, and that's just fun!

Only cars that are in the intersection prepared to make a left turn may *complete their turn* after the light changes to red. Anyone who *initiates the turn* (which means entering the intersection) after the light changes to red is risking a ticket. Yes, be prepared for honking. When I first moved to Los Angeles, writer-director-producer Jeff Greenstein told me the following: "Approximately three-and-a-half cars can make a left turn after the light changes. Approximately seven-and-a-half cars will attempt to make a left turn after the light changes during the holidays. The holidays are defined as the period between Halloween and the Sundance Film Festival."

Pedestrians have *curb to curb* right-of-way. That means, if you are in West Hollywood or Santa Monica where there are lovely little island dividers between eastbound and westbound lanes, you *only* must stop for pedestrians entering the crosswalk at *your* curbs. But you *must* stop! Once the pedestrian is in the center island and headed across the other set of lanes, you may continue forward without getting a ticket. Otherwise (and even if they're jaywalking), you must stop for pedestrians as soon as they step off any curb.

Motorcyclists are legally allowed to pass between cars in two lanes of same-direction traffic as long as they are going no more than 5 MPH faster than the flow of traffic (with a limit of 35 MPH). If you are going faster than 35 MPH in your car and a motorcycle goes between you and another car headed in the same direction, that motorcyclist can get a ticket. Otherwise, they are complying with the law to get through traffic. A lot of people move to LA and get mad at bikers for doing exactly what they're allowed to do. It's a safety issue. Bikes are safer at the front of the flow of traffic, in stop-and-go city situations. They are generally in the right, to get to the red light ahead of stopped and slowing cars.

If you are turning right into a driveway and there is a bicycle lane between you and the curb, you must first merge *into* the bike lane and *then* make your turn. When my husband first moved to LA, he (and his bicycle) got creamed by an Escalade turning 90 degrees *across* the bike lane. Merge first, then turn. It's just like another lane of traffic!

Yellow curbs are loading zones from 8am to 6pm Monday through Saturday *only*. All other hours, a yellow-curbed loading zone is *free parking* (unless, of course, there are posted signs about it being a valet zone on certain nights or it is on a street-sweeping restricted block, etc.). The next time you are running late and see a yellow curb *outside of the loading zone times*, impress your friends by parking there. No one believes this tip 'til they take a chance and try it for the first time and hold their breath to see whether they get a ticket. It's fun, though, once you trust you can do it.

It is *illegal* to change lanes in an intersection! This one is my *biggest* LA-driver pet peeve. You are *only* allowed to change lanes within actual *lanes*. Once you enter an intersection, you have *left* the lane and may not *move* to where the "other lane" would be until you are out of the intersection. Cars turning right on red get slammed into all the time by drivers who move from the left to right lane within an intersection.

You may not pass on the right. Passing is defined as moving into that other lane to overtake another car. Now, that said, if someone is pokey in the leftmost lane and you *have* to get into the right lane in order to get past them, the only *legal* way to do this is by staying in the right lane for at least 100 feet. This is true for the highway and the city streets.

U-turns are legal where posted but *never* within 100 feet of an intersection. If you are in a *No U-turn Zone* or are within 100 feet of an intersection, your only option to do a legal turn is a "Three-Point Turn." You turn left into a driveway of some sort, back out into oncoming traffic, and then proceed forward in the new direction. Yes, some lawmaker actually thinks this is a *safer* choice than allowing U-turns 100 feet within intersections in Los Angeles.

If you think you can "cut corners" by going through a gas station's corner lot to make a right turn without waiting for the light at an intersection, just know you can get a ticket for that move. So, you'd better make it look like you were *seriously* considering pulling in to get gas and then changed your mind, and good luck with that.

Parking signs will contradict one another and you *will* get parking tickets by thinking the one sign you thought was the "this sign trumps all" sign was the most restrictive, when actually another sign down the block was. Consider it good luck. A parking ticket on the day of an audition is a sure sign of a callback, I've heard.

If you move to LA from a big city, you think you know what it's like when we say "traffic sucks," because you go on three auditions a week in your current market and you drive an hour each way, every time. So, to you, it seems like LA residents are making too big a deal about traffic. Okay, but you're hoping for the three-auditions-a-day level of work in Los Angeles (totally attainable, by the way). Traffic means something else entirely when you're dealing with so much of it to that extent, daily. And at any hour.

Check sigalert.com before heading out. Tune in to KFWB or KNX for frequent traffic updates as you drive. Keep an "actor bag" in your car with a Tide laundry pen, hairbrush, toothbrush, bottled water, snacks, clean-up wipes, activity books for kids, charging cables for your electronics, change for meters and tolls, even a flashlight, and perhaps mace! Pretend you're a Boy Scout: Be prepared!

Traffic in Los Angeles is like the crossword puzzle in the newspaper: It's easiest on Monday and gets harder as the week goes on. By the weekend, the crossword puzzle (and the traffic) sucks. If I don't finish the Monday crossword puzzle, my self-esteem for the week is crap!

—Jon Hughes, actor

More LA Resources

If you're in need of any specific resources tailored to people with disabilities, PWD resources specifically for actors exist in LA. Same for actors needing support of the 12-step variety. Mental health resources abound too! Creatives need support! LA is great for that. While not my favorite name for a website, I Hate My Life has a ton of free and cheap resources for medical care, housing, and job listings. Check out LA Freecycle and LA Re-Use It to repopulate your decluttered home, once you've made the move.

The UTA Joblist is an awesome resource, if you can get access to it (our best hook-up is, of course, linked at smfa4.com). Check sites like The Hollywood Temp Diaries and Entertainment Careers for some creative ideas, too.

Do some Googling on gyms and fitness classes and churches and synagogues and temples and mentorship groups for giving back (I like Do Good Stuff, as the hyphenate who started it—Annie Wood, Cricket Feet Showcase alumna—is the reason WriteGirl came into my life), but also run 'em all by your community here for good measure. Same with referrals for healthcare, getting your taxes done, headshot photographers, whatever! The community at smfa4.com is ready to help. And, of course, when checking out acting coaches, you'll want to audit if you can, and again, check out those folks' reputations with as many other actors as you can reach. Don't do this to stall out on making a decision of your own, of course.

Pilot Season

Even though pilots are shot all year and in cities outside Los Angeles, because pilot season is such a huge part of LA living, I'm including its overview here. Remember what I've said about premature moves, especially if you're considering making your first LA experience line up with the craziest season of all. During the period from late January to early April, producers are working at breakneck speeds to try and bring pilots (new series, which may or may not ever see the light of day) to life. Characters that have not yet been inhabited by actors are being written and rewritten, writers' deals with various production companies and networks are being negotiated and tweaked, and actors are scurrying all over town in an attempt to read for as many potential new shows for the fall season as possible. It's truly manic, most days!

Crista Flanagan is an amazing actor, writer, and comic whose work I first became aware of during a stand-up showcase at the Comedy Union. Flanagan turned many of her on-stage characters into on-screen characters as a series regular on *MADtv*. This is in addition to her wildly popular recurring character on *Mad Men* and her regular work with the *Epic Movie* spoof film franchise. In addition to building up an IMDb page filled with amazing credits, she's graced the cover of *Playboy*. This busy hyphenate graciously supplied the following journal entry, depicting an average day during pilot season.

Tuesday, March 25th:

It's 7:05pm and my eyes are swollen from fatigue and exhaustion. I worked late last night and worked on my auditions for today when I got home. I had five auditions today, and a job interview. I'm supposed to go see two shows tonight and then perform at the Improv, but I had to cancel my evening. I feel too poorly.

Five auditions... all for pilots. I guess things are coming to an end. This morning, I woke early so I could curl my hair. It looked terrible, so 20 minutes before I left, I got in the shower and washed it. I left with wet hair, packed my car with headshots and resumés, bottled water, and four different outfits for my auditions.

The first was at Fox at 8:30am. Since that means The 405, I left at 7am. Barely made it, but the casting directors were late, so it didn't matter. I changed in my car and headed back to Burbank. This one didn't feel good at all, but oh well. Grab some migraine medicine and change clothes in my tiny Toyota Tercel with the big scratch down the side. Put on pantyhose for this one. Yikes, it's starting to get really hot.

Audition number three. Again, didn't quite feel right, but no time to think too hard. Back in the car to Raleigh Studios. Now it's really hot in the car and I change clothes again. About 40 minutes early, there are signs posted everywhere, "Keep your voices low. Taping auditions in room next door." But, there's a guy sitting here, saying his lines really loud. It's kind of funny. His name's called, he comes out quickly, he looks down, he heads for the elevator. He wasn't in there long. That probably means... what? I go in. Mediocre. There's a picture of an actor I haven't seen in years on the wall. I wonder what he's doing today.

Back in the car, short drive this time. I arrive at Paramount. My name's not on the list. I wait. My appointment's at 2pm and it's only 1:20pm. The security guard says I can't come in until 2pm. I tell him I need to change clothes and work on my script. He doesn't care really, but offers the utility closet for me to change in. I do. The floor's wet, but I don't realize until my shoes are off. My socks are wet. I hope it's not urine. I walk out of the closet and someone turns around, only to accidentally spill his drink on me. I'm soaked. He says, "Sorry. But it's just water." I can tell he feels bad; I say it's okay. This is the outfit I have to audition in. I'm going to producers for this one.

The security guard takes my ID, checks it out, still can't find my name, makes a few calls, goes through my bag, there's a bra in there for a different outfit, the one I have to wear next. Another girl walks up. She's auditioning for the same part. I can tell. She looks familiar. She gives her name. I've done stand-up with her. She doesn't recognize me, and I realize that she's on my email list. I probably shouldn't send emails to people who don't recognize me. I'll take her off the list when I get home. Right?

The guard lets me in. I park my sunny car and take off for the Mae West building. I pass another actress that I know. She just got out of her third callback for the part I auditioned for two auditions ago. I wasn't very good, so I don't feel competitive. She looks nice. I find my room, I sign in. The casting director is late.

Finally! This one goes pretty well. I get some direction. I take it. I feel good. They seem pleased. Great! One more to go! But wait, I need gas. I get some Tofifay candies while I'm at it. I still have my migraine. Am I drinking enough water? I've had two bottles' worth.

Back to Burbank for the next one. I sign in and sit next to a girl who was waiting with me three auditions ago. We smile at each other. I look over my sides. I like this part. I want it. The breakdown says I'm supposed to be plain and plump. I go to the bathroom, change my clothes, take off my earrings, and settle my hair so that I'm plain. Plump? I look kind of "pillowy," but I don't know about plump. Oh, who cares?

A girl walks in. She's in a commercial that I auditioned for. I hate watching that commercial because it plays all the time and I thought I did a good job at the audition. Oh well. She looks plumper than me. Wait a second; she's here for something else. Who cares? Focus. Okay, I feel good. They take us in late, so I feel confident. The casting director gives me some direction. I do it well. She says, "Great." I know she means it. It felt great.

Time to check in. I call my managers; let them know how each one went. Change clothes again, drive far to a job interview. I'm early. I go window-shopping. Wait, a 99-Cent Store. I go in. I buy two clipboards, a calculator, and some curlers for my hair. It's only $3.99. Wow.

I go to my job interview. I'm 15 minutes early. She comes out and says she won't be ready for 15 minutes. When it's time, she welcomes me into her office. It smells bad... like trash. I sit and within five minutes, she tells me I'm not qualified for the job. I know that I am, but why argue at this point? I don't really want to work there. Well, 6pm get back on the freeway, get home by 7pm. My eyes hurt.

It's hard to carry all four pairs of shoes from my car to my apartment. I can feel the remnants of my migraine rattling around in my head. I've got to walk slowly. Apartment: dark. No one's home. I drop my things and try to take a poo. It's somewhat difficult. I guess I'm not hydrated enough. I'll drink some water. I'll watch TV. I wonder if I have any auditions for tomorrow. I feel lucky and tired and hurt and lonely and right. Goodnight.

—Crista Flanagan

Love it or hate it, pilot season is a reality of pursuing an acting career in Los Angeles. It's the three-month period when the stakes are high, the pressure is on, and the rewards can be unfathomably good. Of course—after six trips to producers—being told, "We went another way," can be a crushing blow. As CSA member and coach Patrick Baca once told me: "Pilot season is like Vegas. It's the one time of year when all of a sudden, there are more slot machines available for you to play on. Anyone can hit it big. Even the little old lady sitting next to you can land a pilot. If you don't hit the jackpot this time, you know there is always next year. Hopefully, you'll be a more experienced player by then."

To that end, I'd advise that you go into pilot season hoping to *get great* at managing the stress of the season, because with *that* as the primary goal, you may find some wonderful opportunities to develop self-management skills that will pay off during *all* audition situations. Look, pilot season is intense and insane even for those who've lived and worked in LA for several years. It's just *tough*. And that's not the learning curve you want to be up against, if you're only beginning to build your professional acting career. For LA actors *and* those out-of-towners who refuse to heed my advice regarding premature moves, I'll say this: Spend as much time as you can in preparation for your auditions; really connect with your choices; allow plenty of extra time to commute, park, and find your way to the audition location; and be graciously patient. Remember that pilot season affects everyone in this town, and no one should take any of the stress personally.

Even those of us who do not regularly cast pilots feel the impact of pilot season. It is simply more complicated to do our jobs when everyone is slammed at pilot season, so we all tend to work longer hours, feel more frazzled at the end of the day, and do less scouting (whether it's theatre, showcases, or CD workshops). We all find that it is more difficult to schedule actors for auditions during pilot season, as they are trying to see five or six different CDs a day sometimes.

How frantic is it? As Peter Golden—executive VP of talent and casting for CBS—told me: "Within four to six weeks of getting the script, we're shooting the pilot, so sometimes our casting directors hold auditions with just an outline and one scene. The actor will go from reading for the associate, to the casting director, to the producer, do a callback, maybe read for the director, get to the studio level, and then final choices go to the network, all just in a few weeks."

The biggest mistake newer actors make is thinking they're going to be able to "get in" on pilots during pilot season. What most actors need to focus on is getting into the offices that are casting everything *other than* pilots, because they're going to be having a hard time getting "bigger actors" in, since every agent wants to keep his top clients free for pilots. *Many* agents advise actors otherwise open to doing theatre, commercials, and indie feature films to hold off on auditioning for *and even accepting* other roles in the event that a pilot should come through. Heck, some will even advise against *studio* features and ongoing episodics, since the "pilot booking" is *the* biggie.

See, even if the pilot doesn't go, there's a holding fee, there's the status of having been a series lead in a pilot, and agents know that means there's an even better—more lucrative—season ahead for clients at that level, and that means decades of commissions on bazillions of dollars.

So, for the *name* actor or for the working actor with many guest-star credits on IMDb, pilot season exists as most folks imagine it: Learning about new shows before anyone has ever heard of 'em, reading scripts for pilots that may never shoot, signing NDAs, getting to meet with creatives who will be leading the field of entertainment for decades to come, creating characters and bringing them to life in front of the network suits, and being rewarded with offers that are truly life-changing.

But for most folks in Los Angeles, pilot season is just a busier time, and the ninja actors are doing research on pilots and their players with an eye toward where the industry is headed and how they fit within the future pilot seasons to come *while* going in on all the episodics and indie projects that the pilot level actors are being held back from doing. Yes! While doing all the delicious pilot season research, focus your energy on getting seen for "old" episodics, commercials, stage plays, and feature films. When "bigger actors" are harder to get, these opportunities become *yours!* There are plenty of co-star and guest-star roles—that you wouldn't normally be seen for—during pilot season. If you focus *not* on getting seen for pilots but instead on "being there" for the offices that really need you right now, you actually can have a better pilot season than you may have expected.

And, hey, if you *do* happen to go in on a couple of pilots, *yay!* Just don't *plan* to test for series regular roles on pilots unless you've already had a few pretty high-profile guest-star years under your belt. Yes, *years*. Remember, a pilot is a "maybe" until the upfronts. Unless you can help "sell" the show to advertisers, you're likely not at the top of producers' lists during pilot season. So build toward that.

Other Important Building Blocks

Before you get to LA, whip out your calendar and schedule your first coffee date with a friend you've made online. Schedule your first lunch date with one of your fellow ninjas. Plan to attend your first networking event and take a buddy—to be your networking wingman—if you can. Pick a date to check out your first play or improv match or sketch show. Register to attend your first SAG-AFTRA event or other panel discussion type event at the Paley Center or at a film festival.

Schedule your first trip to the beach, the Santa Monica Pier, the Grove, the Hollywood sign, the Walk of Fame, Griffith Park, Universal Citywalk, and other iconic places that tourists come from all over the world to experience, so you can stay mindful of the fact that this town is bigger than just the crazymaking busywork so many folks do in this industry. Schedule an audit of at least two of the classes you want to consider for your ongoing training. Pull CD workshop calendars from facilities' websites to see how often your targets are doing the rounds. Get a Thirsty Third Thursday on your to-do list, for sure! We go to rockstar karaoke on the third Thursday in any month with five Thursdays to celebrate the collective awesomeosity of *SMFA* alumni.

Learn the "Hollywood NO" (postponing 'til the other party goes away) and begin to buffer yourself against assuming anything is a lock 'til you're in the makeup trailer.

Realize how very lucky we are to be in an era where people who used to pride themselves on being harder to reach, mysterious, protective of anything that helped them get an edge are sharing—usually for free—career notes and tips about their journeys. What a wonderful time to be an actor! You can create your own content, you can figure out how to succeed in a market you've never even visited, and you can give back to others who are coming up after you by mentoring in much the same way. This business is changing for the better every day and we're a part of that shift. Isn't that awesome?

This is the Super Bowl of Acting. Be ready. And 'til you're ready to suit up for the biggest game in the world, train. Prepare. Build a life that is a great foundation for success at the top tier. Find your *happy*, because that will keep you thriving, wherever you live. Stay "new" as long as you can and enjoy the mystery of discovery. It's delicious! Congratulations on your decision to try Los Angeles on for size. It's not easy, by any stretch. But it's a place that is beautiful, warm, and filled with people from all over the world all in pursuit of their creative dreams. What a wonderful place to be! Welcome, ninja. Welcome home!

I am very grateful to be in the group of casting directors who are former actors. I'm very proud of that. Actors are very courageous, very wonderful, sensitive people for whom I have such respect. I am grateful to have that respect for people I get to work with—and hire—every day.
—Kate Brinegar, CSA

29: Casting Director Workshops

My first experience with a CD workshop was as an actor in Atlanta. It was 1992 and my agent told me I should attend this weekend-long event with two casting directors who had flown out from Los Angeles to scout talent and do a workshop in Atlanta. I paid $35 for two five-hour days (lunch and parking included) and met two top casting directors of that era, Jerold Franks and (now manager) Al Onorato. It was awesome. I learned more about what to expect in Hollywood in those 10 hours than I had been able to soak up in reading dozens of books previously. I did some cold reading, did a monologue, got some notes on my work, but most of all got a ton of questions answered. I knew what steps I needed to take to get ready for a career in Los Angeles. I'd heard it right from the mouths of those who'd been doing major casting for decades, that weekend.

I first arrived in Los Angeles in August of 1993. I met a fellow actor at a networking event put on by the *Hollywood Creative Directory* just three days after unpacking the U-Haul and that actor told me I had to get in on some CD workshops he and a group of actor friends did weekly. My new friend and I each spent 10 bucks a week, did a prepared scene for one casting director, and then each of us and the 10 other actors would get one-on-one time with the CD of the week, going over resumés, scene choices, primary types, tips tailor-made for us, etc. The CDs I met via workshops in 1993 and 1994 were *A*-listers. Some still are. They gave great advice, we shared a few laughs, there was a spread of coffee and donuts, and the actors' $10 per week went to rental of the space (a meeting room in the basement of a Unitarian church) and purchasing of the aforementioned coffee and donuts. These CDs did not get paid to show up. They either needed to see actors or wanted to share tips with us. That was the agenda. Period. The business model we now know had not yet been created.

Cut to: 1998. I return to Los Angeles after having gone back east to get a master's degree in journalism. I track down my old gang of workshoppers and am told CD workshops have changed. They're no longer small gatherings costing actors a few dollars. Workshops are now something I'll have to pay 30 bucks to be a part of, and I can't choose my material or my scene partner. I can't prep in advance. It's now called a "cold reading workshop" and I'll be doing sides on the spot in front of 30 other actors and someone who "works in casting." There will be no one-on-one face time with a CD and there will even be a wrangler whose job it is to make sure I don't annoy the casting person with any silly "all about me" questions. The casting assistant or associate I'll see will get $150 and that means the rest of the money ($750 of the $900 collected each night) is going to the facility. They say it's for operating costs, but I can do basic math and realize that the wrangler is an actor whose paycheck is a free slot in tonight's class, the rent on this dump in the Valley isn't exorbitant, and the only one getting rich is the guy who owns the facility, in which sometimes *six* of these workshops are going on every single night (to the tune of over $30K/wk. for the facility owner).

I learn at this time that the Casting Society of America has taken a hard line against workshops and the casting offices that want to participate are intentionally keeping one CD on staff as a non-member of CSA so that there is someone who can go earn an extra $150 a night, shop for talent without having to sit through a boring play or long open mic night or an in-office general, and come back to the office with some folks to pop in the top shows, which need a dozen or so actors each new episode. CSA members are not allowed to do CD workshops at this time. Definitely, things have changed in the four years I've been away. It's getting to the point where full CDs aren't even doing these workshops much anymore. They're almost always conducted by associates and assistants. These folks are underpaid as it is, so they're supplementing their income, seeing actors of vastly disparate talent levels, while helping facility owners get rich. Heck, at this point, there are even people working in casting who have learned they can sell actors' headshots on eBay for a tidy bundle (especially photos of kid actors to suspected child predators in private auctions). It's ugly. And it's about to get uglier.

Another two years in and CSA has relaxed its stance on workshops. I'm no longer an actor, but I'm a columnist for *Back Stage West*, so I'm staying aware of this issue. I'm interviewing CDs weekly for my column "Casting Qs" and I'm asking them about workshops. While top casting execs and the CDs whose projects shaped our industry over the past decades won't *touch* CD workshops, there is a new generation of CDs who think workshops are great. More and more casting directors, associates, and assistants are lobbying for the right to use workshops as a means of finding new talent, efficiently. Actors are clamoring for the "right to workshop," and it's becoming clear that—absolutely—actors who are TV-ready, the right type, and choosing the right workshops (as some are no-audition-required facilities at which CDs do nothing but collect a check, watch scenes without giving feedback, and dump a stack of headshots in the waste bin upon leaving, because they have exclusive deals to call in actors from the "better" workshops) are getting an edge over those who can't afford the same opportunity.

Some actors who can afford the access are getting opportunities they're nowhere near ready for. They have no business being seen by people who cast work at any level above copy-credit-meals gigs or student films as they're building up their craft and their consistency, but because they can buy the opportunity and are *sure* they're right about their readiness, they're keeping workshops in business. Meanwhile, the one or two actors who are *truly ready* to be seen at the level for a network co-star are becoming the major success stories the workshops are using when advertising their companies.

A CSA member who owns a workshop becomes president of the CSA. (Full disclosure: It is former CSA president and former AIA owner Katy Wallin who would go on to hire me for several of my first jobs in casting, as casting coordinator on three shows for Fox and as casting director on a show for E! in 2003 and 2004.) At this point, there is no more CSA-related opposition to workshops, and as the CSA slowly evolves into a union, it welcomes with open arms the casting employees who work at the associate level, and that's the biggest population of folks working in casting who regularly do workshops. They are the most vocal of the casting population who want workshops to continue. Workshops are an efficient means of getting to see actors outside of the office. It seems no one wants to go back to generals or seeing plays or scouting at showcases—not when there's money to be made, using the workshop model.

Workshops are the subject of a story on *20/20* in late 2002. California introduces guidelines about how workshops must be advertised, marketed, and conducted. Within weeks of these guidelines being adopted, they are only occasionally stuck to, and most of the "reading of the disclaimer" portion of the night is done while eyes are rolling, as everyone gets that "we can't call it a job opportunity," but we all know the only reason anyone is plunking down now nearly $50 a night is to get access to a booking from this casting office someday. Casting folks are now getting about $200 per workshop, which means our math now goes to $1500 collected per workshop night, $200 going to the casting person, and $1300 per room in which there's an event happening going to the facilities. Big business!

Cut to: Now. In California, a law exists to protect the "not ready" from spending thousands of dollars on many "too good to be true" opportunities, CD workshops included. "The Krekorian Act," AB1319, The Advance Fee Talent Services Scam Prevention Bill exists in the State of California and similar laws are in the works in other states.

One of the major targets of AB1319 is the "talent convention" model. I was approached in 2003—just three months after my first casting gig—to do one of those "talent conventions" in Florida for a few grand. Yup. An all-expenses-paid trip and five-star resort accommodations, plus a few grand cash in exchange for a few hours of watching several hundred actors (mostly kids, whose parents had paid thousands of dollars for the opportunity) as long as I pledged to "call back" a dozen or so of the kids, so the promoters could say their program works. "No, thank you," I said. And that's when I knew that it was simply my name appearing in the Breakdown Services' *CD Directory* that made me "qualified," in the eyes of this major corporation. They weren't looking for CDs to come demystify the process in their minor market. They didn't care what wisdom I could impart. They didn't even care what I was casting. They were looking for folks they could call "real Hollywood casting directors" in their expensive radio ad campaigns or when they "scouted" kids at the mall. This is why AB1319 exists.

In 2010, I was asked to go undercover for a major international news magazine show, in their exposé of similar "conventions." The most vulnerable population of actors—kids whose parents don't want to deny them an opportunity and may not truly research the legitimacy of it before plunking down thousands of dollars—is being targeted the hardest by these conventions. But it's also happening outside of the United States, and companies change their names frequently to avoid scrutiny or Googleability. At the core of AB1319 is protection against advance-fee talent scams. There is no question that there are seedy, skeevy scam artists out there scheming millions of dollars out of starry-eyed hopefuls (or their parents, in the case of kid actors) while selling promises that simply can never be met.

A source who was instrumental in the development of the law told me, "AB1319 requires CD workshop providers (the ones who are raking in the dough) to post a bond so that if they run with the money—and they have—the actor has some recourse. Posting a bond, by the way, is no big deal if you aren't a criminal to begin with. After looking at dozens of scams (the biggest took about $20M from actors over a six-month period, and he is now in bankruptcy—listing 2500 families as 'creditors'), we identified certain behaviors as 'bad.' Those behaviors were things like false advertising, claiming successes that were not their own, promising jobs, promising job interviews, promising agents or managers, etc., and we set about creating language that defines behaviors. These behaviors are wrong no matter what venue they happen in (if you want to call it a competition, a CD workshop, an acting academy, a talent listing service, whatever). In writing the law, we never intended to make CD workshops illegal. No business model is illegal. It is their *behaviors* that are being regulated."

Why Regulation Is Good

Access is not an actor's *right*. Access to people at a certain tier of any profession is limited with good reason! There are far more actors than roles and that will always be true. Far too many actors are sure the only missing element is that they haven't been seen yet, when truly, they may need loads of training still. If workshops are compliant with AB1319, that actually improves the quality of the workshops and ensures the access is worth something more than it has become in some facilities (the "your check clears so you can be in the advanced group" ones). So, for the best actors in the bunch, the idea of getting into workshops that are compliant with people who will actually have to do a little hoop-jumping to follow up with those they're most inspired to cast later should be exciting! It's like getting signed by one of "The Bigs," when you're hunting for the right agency. There's prestige to being sought out by the best. Reaching that status should feel much better than sitting in a room filled with desperate newbies.

Casting director workshops did not evolve as a means for actors to learn the ins and outs of specific casting offices, discover the dos and don'ts of auditioning for current projects in those offices, or receive craft-oriented feedback on performances. Sure, those things sometimes happen *too*, but it's because doing a scene in front of a person in a position to cast you someday started leading to *getting cast* in that office that CD workshops became big business. The very simple CD workshops I described going on here in the early '90s organically led to actors getting cast. Someone saw a way to monetize that process by *adding a middleman* to the experience. A pimp, let's say, who takes the lion's share of the money that used to exchange hands from John to working girl. When done right (you target like a ninja, you're on-brand, you're *ready*, and your research shows the casting director you'll see actually calls actors in from workshops), workshops can be very powerful opportunities.

Here's what I think, and this is coming from an actor who has had almost *all* of her TV auditions—and has booked work from said auditions—via workshop-met CDs. Workshops rock. And they suck. And because no one stopped the trend in time, they are now an almost-necessary tool for the small-resumé actor. Workshops rock because there truly is the potential for gleaning an audition and perhaps even a booking via that contact with the CD, no matter what the required disclaimers state. And workshops suck because they are yet another way that actors are convinced to part with their money, just to get the sliver of a chance or a tingling of hope that maybe, just maybe, this is the thing that will help. There were a few—very few—people back when workshops really started getting common who were very outspoken against the practice. "You don't pay for a job interview; why would you pay for an audition?" and I'm pretty sure most actors feel that the disclaimers everyone has to issue about it not being "an audition or job interview" are just legal CYA hooey. I feel pretty confident saying that we probably all feel like it's a general audition.

> So why would we pay to audition? Because there weren't enough actors with the confidence to refuse to engage in the practice. This is yet another industry sideline that has taken advantage of the fear and desperation found in most actors (even those who hide it well, especially from themselves). The good news is, there are casting people who actually do use workshops to find new talent *and* actually have the necessary "say" to recommend them to come in for auditions. The bad news is, I'm pretty sure that percentage is very small. I've been luckier than most in this arena, and I still do workshops when I can afford them. But you can bet I do my research, and I am very selective about which ones I do and where I do them. This is a business where one minute with the right person at the right time can change your entire career. I'm still one of those so-called "suckers" that believes it can happen to me. And if it costs me $40 to get that one minute, so be it.
>
> —Kate Rene Gleason, actor

It seems the standard practice in Los Angeles is to take CD workshops while the various casting offices are getting to know you, weaning yourself from them once you've been called in to audition outright. Veteran actors often refer to CD workshops as "something I did when I first got here" or an option "for a very specific purpose" in connecting with a particular casting director.

Be Smart about It

I have always said that if you're going to do workshops, you must do your research. Hell, I say that if you're going to do *anything* in this business, you must do your research (yet every day, countless thousands of actors put absolutely zero thought or time into their business decisions and that's simply disheartening). I suggested years ago that actors create a database in which CDs who do workshops are ranked, rated, and discussed, so there's open information about whose rooms you most *need* to enter, after all. We have some dialogue of this level at smfa4.com, of course. If you're sure you've properly targeted your key shows and the people who cast your type on them, consistently, and you're also *ready* for this level of opportunity, do it. But think about the CD workshops you've attended: Would most folks in 'em say they're at an "expert level" of talent, ready to book top of show if given the chance? Yup. And you know—c'mon, you *really* know—that's just not true. They're not even ready to do a one-line co-star much of the time. But dangit, they want their access and they're gonna pay for it and they know they could book if they could just get seen.

If you decide to do CD workshops, watch out for facilities where you're paying for a consultant to advise you on how to pad your resumé or where to shoot headshots. What are this consultant's credentials? And what is the tie-in between this facility and the businesses its consultants recommend? Buyer beware!

And *of course* the consultants will always recommend the off-season three-week intensive with a casting director. "More exposure is better," they insist. Nope. Not unless that casting professional is a masterful instructor, really giving you something you could consider to be training. If you just need to pop on her radar because she casts a target show, one on-brand exposure is plenty to start building that relationship.

Let's Explore the Alternatives

As much as I adore and support all of the initiatives put together by SAG-AFTRA Foundation, they're just not as well-attended as they should be. Heck, even their super—and free—streaming series usually has live viewership of dozens, not hundreds or thousands like it should. But this supports what one of my sources said is true of actors, "They don't want to learn from anyone. They want to be seen. They'll spend fifty bucks to do a two-minute scene in front of someone who answers phones in a busy TV office, but not attend a free Q&A with a person who cast decades of film and television, to learn about her world. Idiots."

I'd like to celebrate the handful of actors who *do* take advantage of the free Q&A, the panel discussions, the streaming video series, the amazing amount of information that *is* out there and available to them at no cost, rather than focusing on those who would rather pay to play.

The bigger question for me is how we want to be viewed as an acting community. Why is it that we demand for our right to pay for what used to be free? We claim to be a community of creatives, and yet when it comes to the business pursuit of our careers we often become myopic, doing the same things as everyone else. We live in a time where there are more ways than ever to get on the radar of anyone with the ability to hire us. From social media to self-submitting to self-producing to webseries to networking events to more television shows on air than ever before to good ol' fashioned phone calls—there are myriad ways to get ourselves and our work in front of people on the other side of the desk. I worry when there is an uproar over not being able to pay for the privilege.

In a day and age where an email or even a tweet can deliver a reel of our best work to anyone instantaneously, I am reticent to think that actors cannot get their work seen by CDs in any other way than a workshop. Get together the 20 actors who were going to go to the workshop, pool the $40 apiece, and take that $800 to hire a full crew (DPs, writers, editors, the whole nine) for a day to film reel material for everyone. Or take the $800 from everyone's next workshop and produce a showcase, or a webseries, or a play, or whatever—all ways to get your work seen. Or hell, if it really is about the educational experience, then take all that money and hire one of these CDs to come direct scenes for two hours, or see a play, or critique reels, or be filming something and have the CD show up to direct or critique. What better way to get casting directors to know your work than to invite them onto a set to see how people work?

—Ben Whitehair, actor

In the end, actors don't *want* CD workshops, they want *access*. That access is most valuable when it is earned through hard work and discipline over time. Build relationships. Yes, you can start building a relationship with an encounter in a workshop, but it's also possible to start building relationships in many ways that don't cost you a penny (and in many ways that do, like creating your own content, which I also encourage). As CD workshops spring up in other markets, I hope everyone revisits the history of CD workshops in Los Angeles and learns from this journey, so that only the most positive takeaways exist, in every new workshop that springs up around the world.

Do what feels *good* to you because you love it and it's feeding your creative soul while building your business. Don't judge others for what they do that you don't agree with. I could get mad at everyone on the freeway who speeds or I could just enjoy my journey and stay out of their way.

Here's my bottom line, regarding the ways in which I consume actors' work. I want to see actors *coming alive* by performing in an inspiring play or doing an exciting showcase or being a part of a networking event where I can get to know *them* as people and not be asked for the zillionth time, "What are your pet peeves?"—which, as you know from the chapter on **Actor Mind Taffy**, is the most useless question, ever. Seriously. Don't ask casting directors what pisses us off. Ask what *inspires* us. *That's* how you get us happy to engage with you.

I don't ever like seeing actors when they're mired in fear and desperation and resentment. And that is why I personally avoid CD workshops, even though I attended them when I was an actor. There have been only a few rooms I've entered in the CD workshop environment where there's a warm, happy, friendly, excited-to-be-there, can't-wait-to-show-the-work vibe. Life's too short to spend a few hours at a time in a room filled with negative emotions. The positive—if it can cut through the smog of the negativity in the room—*really* pops! So if you're gonna do CD workshops, be happy to be there. You *will* stand out (and hopefully get called in).

If you choose *not* to do CD workshops, know that it doesn't mean you're not going to get opportunities to get cast. Absolutely *no one* (not even the most vocal CD workshop-supporting casting directors out there) is going to *refuse* to see an actor for a role when he is right for the role, just because he didn't come through a workshop environment. Sure, some offices may be *easier* to penetrate if you come in via CD workshop (especially some of the busier TV show offices), but just consider what our job is: To evaluate talent for specific roles and get the best choices in front of the decision-makers. Why would we close off *any* source of discovering the top actors out there? We wouldn't. Our *job* is to know who's out there and what your work is like. We each have our favorite ways of figuring that out. So, don't feel trapped. Don't feel that you *have* to do CD workshops. If you want to do 'em, do 'em. If you don't, don't.

You've got to get to the stage in life where going for it is more important than winning or losing.

—Arthur Ashe, tennis champion

30: Niches

Commercials, hosting, voiceover, looping, theatre companies, sketch comedy groups and improv troupes, showcases, reality TV, soaps, and student films—these are all topics we'll explore, briefly, in this jam-packed chapter. Their classification as "niches" in no way diminishes their value in an actor's career, nor the level of success you may reach in pursuing any of these areas. As always, for in-depth conversation about any of the niches, plug in with your ninja community at smfa4.com today.

Commercials

While students of advertising know there are dozens of types of commercials from the ad agency's point of view—based on everything from the amount of jargon used to the type of spokesperson employed (authority figure, celebrity, "real people") and from the amount of facts and figures used to tactics of emotion (fear of what happens if the product isn't used, quest for status, desire to please)—for actors, there are two far more basic types of commercials: *narrative* (commercials with a storyline, with a product or service being sold as a part of the storyline) and *spokesperson-driven* (commercials with an actor speaking directly to the camera, addressing the viewing audience, speaking about the product or service being offered). Within these types of commercials, there are many variables of style (humorous, realistic, testimonial, expert, slice-of-life, self-improvement, etc.).

Because so many commercials are narrative in tone, the days of a traditional "commercial headshot" are behind us. Your best headshot for a commercial submission is usually an on-brand "cleanest" version of you.

If you are a seven-foot tall Inuit with buckteeth, you can book a commercial. If you're an overweight middle-American woman, you can book a commercial. If you're a 6'1" kinda Jewish-looking goofy guy with brown hair and blue eyes (Hey, that's me!), you can book a commercial. And yes, if you have model looks with a perfect body, you can book a commercial (that's not me). Truth is, truth is in. The days when every ad would feature a perfect family with perfect teeth are gone. These days commercials are mini-movies. They have a story and a point. It's too easy for a viewer to switch the channel, hit mute, or fast forward. The ad agencies want realism. And in life there are a million different types of people. That doesn't mean that our Inuit friend is going to audition as much as the model. But it does mean he will audition and there is work out there for him.

The commercial business ebbs and flows. There are times of the year when I'll audition once a week or less. Then there are times when I'll audition four or five times a week. It's all about what's being cast at any given moment. Don't give up just because there isn't much out there for your type today. Those auditions will come soon and the more specific your type, the less competition you have for roles. As my grandmother used to say: "Commercials may be simple but it doesn't mean they're easy. Now stop slouching."

—Eitan Loewenstein, actor-writer

Commercial Terms

Avail: a sign that you are close to a commercial booking. How close? That depends. Three actors or more may be placed "on avail" for a commercial (meaning it's down to you and a couple of other actors). One of you will book it. Many actors prefer not to know they're on avail. I say, it's a sign you're doing everything right. Keep going.

Buyout: a purchase of your future rights (by flat fee) for the commercial acting gig, resulting in no residuals. This is especially common for nonunion spots, so be really sure you're cool with granting rights to your image in perpetuity.

Conflict: a term reflecting the fact that you have done a commercial for one product, service, or company which would prevent you from doing another commercial for a similar or competing product, service, or company during the term of the conflict.

Conflicts Available Upon Request; No Current Conflicts: phrases commonly on an actor's theatrical resumé indicating that any commercial conflicts will be provided in a list or that no current conflicts exist, respectively.

Holding Fee: a payment to keep you "held" for a commercial that has run one cycle, so that they may run it again. This extends the amount of time you have a conflict, which is why you're paid for it.

Residuals: payments over and above the session fees made to the actor every commercial cycle (or 13 weeks).

Nailing Commercial Auditions

Eat the chip (AKA: Just do what they ask). The audition instructions are to sit at a table and eat a chip. The people making the decisions need to see the actors eating. So they want you to eat a chip and enjoy it. Just eat the chip.

Don't look at chip, think about the chip, contemplate the chip, smell the chip, stare at the chip, study the chip, or lick the chip. Just eat the chip. As you. How you would do it. A human. A real person.

<u>Make the unnatural look natural</u>. Here's where your actor can come out to play. Commercial auditions do very little to make you feel comfortable: Pretending cold corn tortillas are awesome pieces of pizza, Starbursts are Gas-X, and that you can drive the infamous car with the invisible steering wheel. Your imagination skills are vital in auditions. The camera picks up everything and you can't hide. You must make the uncomfortable look comfortable, quick. A pro knows how to hold any product like it belongs in their hand, how to make copy look effortless, and how to interact in the callback room like they are at home. Some actors are just born with the skill (we hate them), or, if you are like me, you have to practice your ass off.

<u>Use your strengths</u>. Know your strengths. What do people depend on you for? What are your best qualities? What seeps out of your pores when you are not looking? If you don't know, start figuring it out. It's your slam-dunk booking tool. Your niche, your essence, your brand. It's what you can fall back on time and time again. Because it's you. And you need to make sure that quality leads you into your audition and stays there. It's you at your best.

—Fawnda McMahan, actor-coach

Commercials: True or False

True or false? You can make $100,000 on a big, popular, national commercial. False. Most advertisers now know how to manipulate the system so that their ads get national airtime without costing them a (SAG-AFTRA Class *A*-Network-level) bundle. By buying time on cable by geographical units (which allows for much more targeted marketing) and adding the occasional wildspot buy, advertisers are able to have a 13-week national while only paying principal talent around $5000 or $6000. That's a session fee ($600 to $1000) plus cable buy ($2500) plus wildspot (up to $2500). Nonunion commercials pay even less, usually under $1000 for a straight buyout.

True or False? The union will collect overtime audition pay on your behalf. True. Some actors worry about "blowing the whistle" on casting sessions that run long, despite the fact that the union assures actors they will remain anonymous. Principal performers are entitled to payment for any time beyond an hour spent at a commercial audition (calculated from the sign-in or appointment time, whichever is later). SAG-AFTRA will pursue payment for all members in this situation, not just the actor who reported the overtime.

True or False? You can write "on file" in the blank for your union ID number on the sign-in sheet. True, you *can*, but according to SAG-AFTRA, you need to write in your union ID number if you are to expect payment for overtime at commercial auditions. Additionally, SAG-AFTRA advises all actors to always sign in *and out* at commercial casting sessions, to document the time spent there.

True or False? You do not have to keep up with where and when your commercials are airing. True, you don't *have to* keep up, but you certainly should. There will be mistakes. There will be misreporting of markets in which your ads air. There will always be cracks for details to slip through. So, get used to tracking your commercials by using services like ispot.tv, clipland. com, and nielsenmedia.com (visit smfa4.com for our updated *SMFA* Hot List of resources).

True or False? Improv training is required to book commercial work. Well, this is murkier than "true or false." While your improvisational abilities are treasured at commercial auditions, the union requires that you not improvise, as that makes you a writer and you should be paid for writing commercial copy. Many actors have seen their brilliant audition "buttons" being landed by other actors, after having "yes, and..."-ed the goods in an audition but not booking the part. Of course, *your* ability to land that button could make the difference in your ability to book, so it's a tough call. But should you take improv and commercial technique classes? Yes. The work *and* the networking you do in those classes can pay off.

Hosting

To be a good host, watch game shows. See what the timing is like and how people interact with one another. Look at the interaction and the ability the host has to think quickly. So much of that work is not scripted. Actors need to know that.

—Carol Elizabeth Barlow, casting director

Host work is a wonderful option for actors whose style is less aligned with scripted fiction and more aligned with improvisational jamming with panelists, with products, with athletes on the sidelines, with stars on the red carpet. Kristyn Burtt, who has worked as an on-camera host since 1998, has a few simple guidelines to rocking a hosting career.

Hosting is one of the best-kept secrets in the entertainment industry. There are so many different genres that need hosts: game shows, entertainment shows, reality shows, industrial films, home shopping shows, variety shows, and children's programming... the list goes on and on. First, ask yourself: Are you in the business to be an actor or a host? If your answer is "actor," then go out there and be the best darn actor you can be. Why are you taking time away from your acting career to host? Is it an easier way into the industry? Not necessarily. Focus on your true passion because that is when your dreams are realized. Should hosting be for you, here are the basics.

Training—Hosting is truly about showing different colors of your own personality—the fun side, the serious side, or the informative version of you. Like with acting, it is so important to understand who you are to be a good host. A way to discover those aspects of your personality is to take a host class. For a current list of top host coaches in major markets, visit smfa4.com.

People with news backgrounds are often trained to use the IFB (the earpiece that allows the producer or director to talk to talent while on the air) and have extensive experience with live broadcasts. In the journalism category, interviewing is an area that will always be a part of your host career. A TelePrompTer allows the script to be posted in front of the lens of the television camera. The trick is to make your read as natural-looking as possible. An ear-prompter allows you to record the script in your own voice on a digital recorder. This recording is then piped into your ear, where you hear the script about two seconds before you recite it. TelePrompTer skills are crucial to hosting on camera, but ear-prompter proficiency has only broadened my job prospects.

Another type of class I would recommend is improvisation. So many host auditions include ad-libbing the script. You have to be able to deliver information in a clear, concise way, but in your own words.

Headshots, Resumés, Reels—As Bonnie has emphasized—so many casting directors will tell you that the people who walk through their doors do not often resemble their pictures. In essence, you want your photo to capture your energy. This will be a part of your entire PR package. You want the personality of your photo to carry over to your reel, which carries over to your bio. It is really that important to understand who you are as a host.

Your resumé should resemble an acting resumé in organization and setup. There are certain items that I highlight on my resumé that I think are important for a casting director or producer to know. For instance, my TelePrompTer, IFB, and ear-prompter proficiency tells the casting director that I can give the crew options on how to deliver the information through me to the viewing audience. My live television experience shows a director I can handle split-second changes without having an on-air meltdown.

You will use your reel all the time. Unlike an actor's demo reel, your host reel will almost *always* be submitted along with your headshot. It is often the first thing casting directors ask for, and they may prescreen who they will call in based on the reels. In fact, I have noticed a trend where more jobs are booking directly off of reels versus even holding auditions. This should really inspire you to keep an up-to-date reel on hand. And again, you want your reel to reflect your personality.

If you are just starting out, you probably do not have footage. Write some copy, choose your locations, and go shoot with a crew. If you want to do entertainment shows, go stand outside a movie premiere and cover it. You will not get access to the stars, but you will be able to use the action in the background to your advantage. If you are an extreme sports fanatic, interview snowboarders at an event, go to a skateboard park, or even jump into the action yourself. MTV-style editing is preferable in the hosting world. Remember, this is your calling card. Deliver a reel that you are proud to show to everyone. It should be updated regularly once you begin working. I update mine as often as three times a year to help keep it fresh for casting directors.

Agents and the Trades—There are agencies that specialize in hosts, or there are big agencies that have host departments. As with landing a theatrical agent, it can be difficult to get a host agent. In fact, a host manager represented me before I got a host agent.

Please do not ignore the power of Actors Access especially if you are in New York or LA. Actors Access has a comprehensive list of auditions for hosts in the world of infomercials, industrial films, websites, and network shows. Get a list of current cable networks. Read up on who is creating new shows. Stay updated on the latest news in the entertainment industry. Read the trades, scan the Internet, and follow up with leads. You never know where some simple little tip will take your career.

Tradeshows—Why am I including this in my host preparation tips? Well, it is how I got my start in this industry, and I believe it is a great stepping-stone to a career as an on-camera host. There will always be a need for spokespeople on the tradeshow floor. The tradeshow industry is a great place to network. It is a wonderful way to get those ear-prompter skills up to par. You will have many distractions and interruptions on the tradeshow floor, so it helps with that "live" element, should you ever do a live show on TV. Often, you have to do a PowerPoint presentation or interact with a video screen using an IFB. These are skills that I honed from within the tradeshow industry that are serving me well today as an on-camera host.

Remember that hosting is a journey. Results do not happen overnight. I still live by my own suggestions listed above. I still market myself, I still work the tradeshow circuit, and I still update my PR package. So, keep at it... because success happens when preparation meets opportunity!

—Kristyn Burtt

Voiceover

You hear about people making a great living in voiceovers and you want to get involved. You hear about actors working from studios in their own homes, sending their voiceover work across the Internet to clients all over the world and you think that's really cool. You've been told you have an amazing voice and should really look into doing voiceovers. "Sign me up!" Right? Well, not so fast. There's a lot more to becoming a working voiceover artist than you might think. Just like actors, voiceover artists have to train, identify their type, and market accordingly.

Anna Vocino is one of the busiest voiceover artists out there. In addition to having a thriving on-camera career, she does everything from British phone-on-hold prompts to celebrity voice matching for the trailers of some very popular films. She even voiced a soap opera's life-sized chipmunk in one of the hottest daytime storylines out there. Here she shares her top tips for launching a career in voiceover (and she shares more at smfa4.com).

Training—Train with the best. Go to voiceoverresourceguide.com to find the best coaches and demo producers. I recommend you use the same person for both. Voiceover is unlike on-camera coaching and reel editing in this regard. Do your research to find the right person that you gel with.

Demo—Start with your commercial demo. Always. Even if you think you rock the funny voices, do the commercial demo first, then you can make money while the animation ball gets rolling. Important: no demos longer than one minute! In addition to having a fully-produced demo, have your demo split in chunks by your producer, with each snippet as its own MP3. These will help you pitch specific jobs.

More Demos—You can produce your own audiobook, IVR (interactive voice response), corporate narration, and industrial demos to post on online VO casting sites to start making money immediately.

Home Studio—You must have a home studio, and you must know how to use it. The AT2020 USB mic, a pop filter, and Audacity will get you started for around $130 until you can build up to nicer equipment. Visit smfa4.com for updated equipment tips. Practice auditioning from home like a mo-fo on this equipment. Email these auditions to your coach and get feedback. Auditioning on your own is the lifeblood of the voiceover business. *Make sure the sound quality in your home studio is fantastic* (no room noise, outside noises, or hums), or else your audition goes in the trash. No excuses. Hire an engineer to come to your house if you can't figure out your best home studio setup.

Website—Get a one-page website with your VO demo and some appropriately-branded artwork. Use lots of keywords that are on-brand. Sound like Mike Rowe? Put that in your site's meta-tags. People are looking for a Mike Rowe voice right this very moment, but they can't afford the actual Mike Rowe!

Agents—When you have that kickass commercial demo, your website, and that home studio fired up, email regional agents for representation. Book jobs. Make money. Get to know more people in the VO industry. Then you can get that hallowed referral to an LA or NY agent. When you have a major market agent, you can still audition from your home studio for your regional agents. We love agents! They are the gatekeepers to the high-paying gigs and they are your biggest allies in voiceover.

Even More Demos—Make promo, radio imaging, movie trailer, animation, and foreign language demos when you are ready.

Online Casting Sites—Self-submitting through legitimate casting sites that list voiceover opportunities is a great way to get your foot in the door, develop long-term repeat clients, and start recouping your expenses through mostly IVR and narration jobs. I always recommend people getting started commit to one of the online casting sites for a year simply to practice auditioning daily. Did I mention that auditioning by yourself in your studio is the lifeblood of getting jobs in voiceover? Even if you go into your agent's office a few times a week to read, you still need to perfect the skill of auditioning from home, thereby becoming not just a voice talent but your own director and your own engineer.

—Anna Vocino

I'm going to underscore Vocino's first tip. So many actors believe they don't need to train to have a career in voiceover. They figure, "Why do I need training? I already have a great voice." You simply *must* train before you can compete in the voiceover market. When you train, you learn how to analyze copy, you create a "signature" or "voiceprint" (jargon for "type" in the voiceover market), you learn how to work with the equipment you'll encounter (how far to stand from the mic, not to touch the equipment, what sort of volume you'll need to use, how to work in group situations based on the equipment provided, what breath sounds or mouth noises are picked up on the mic that you would never know about until playback, etc.), you work out the kinks on sibilant and popping consonants, you learn how to support your voice from your abdomen (and know when to shift into your head voice), and—perhaps most importantly—you get a regular workout, just as a professional athlete does, even when not working every day. You have to stay in top condition, as a voiceover artist. Regular training is key for that. For the *SMFA* Hot List of our favorite voiceover coaches in major markets, visit smfa4.com.

Looping

Looping (also known as "walla" and, most correctly, as ADR: Automated Dialogue Replacement or Additional Dialogue Recording) is a post-production process conducted for almost every on-camera production out there. You've experienced the results of looping as a consumer of films, television programs, and commercials all your life. So, why is this very essential part of our industry's output cloaked in such mystery? Basically, it's because it is a seriously cushy gig! Where else can you earn union scale (yes, at the same rate of the on-camera dayplayers, including residuals) in your jammies?!?

Loopers voice pretty much everything. A small group of actors (no more than 10 people, usually) will produce the voices of on-camera featured extras, assigned faces in the crowd, radio or television broadcasts within the scene, drive-thru restaurant speaker boxes, the other side of telephone conversations, and more. Most loop groups are run by a looping coordinator who sets a call time. The day's work is anywhere from four to eight hours. In that amount of time, a loop group can complete ADR on a one-hour television show. Feature films tend to take two days.

If folks on-screen are walking by the principal performers, the loopers will be asked to walk around and do "pass-bys" during ADR. They'll talk while walking around (or jogging, running, whatever the scene requires) in the studio, passing the mic in order to get the necessary audio tracks. Sometimes, loopers are recording the general crowd sounds. That's pretty much exactly what you think it is. Loopers are chatting about whatever folks in the background would be chatting about in a situation as depicted on the screen in the recording studio. Depending on how identifiable certain people are, loopers are sometimes assigned on-screen actors to match, during the looping session. Loopers will also do "call-outs," which are the lines that tend to stick out among the murmur of the crowd. Crowd sounds, call-outs, and pass-bys will all be blended (or "mixed") by the sound editor later, creating what is called a "soundscape" to match the on-camera scene.

ADR work is quite lucrative and enjoyable, however it is not so easy to break in and join 'em. Loop group coordinators typically organize sessions, cast the actors, and maintain a pool of loopers from which to pull at all times. Many looping coordinators also work as actors in theatre, film, and television (rarely revealing that they are, in fact, running loop groups). When these folks hear a voice they like (or need, due to the fact that a similar voice isn't already in their stable), they'll invite the actor with that voice to join in the loop group. It's seriously *that* simple—yet that "invitation only" in nature. For a current list of our favorite loop groups, visit smfa4.com.

Theatre Companies

> *Actors should do theatre for the love of it, not because they want to be seen. Sometimes, even if the play is not very good, there are good people in the play. We remember them.*
> —Cathy Reinking, casting director-author-coach

Becoming involved in theatre is good practice. You will perform on stage; get seen in regular work; benefit from workshop and lab performances, staged readings, the community you are a part of, and the relationships you are building. If you are in LA, know that theatre is made up of more "black box" than Equity houses, by a long shot. Many LA theatres fall under the Equity 99-Seat Agreement (visit actorsequity.org for information on this agreement). Still others are not covered by any Equity Agreement and operate as nonunion houses or rental facilities. In a market like New York, rich with Equity houses, the need for black-box theatre companies doesn't exist to the same extent. Actors who are not performing on Broadway still have many other AEA contracts under which they can choose to perform in New York, including at much smaller venues.

Watch out for companies that require a hefty initiation fee and charge a very low monthly membership fee. Typically, "companies" like that will always find ways to recruit from outside the company—even when there are existing company members who could fill the roles for the next play in the season—because they earn more money from initiation fees. Why would the leaders of this group ever cast from within the company, if they stand to gain $100 a pop for each new recruit? With a steady flow of newbies into LA, they just keep alienating their old members and bringing in new ones.

Membership should be in the neighborhood of $45 to $75 per month at most companies. Benefits (outside of being in the pool from which all plays are cast) include workshopping works-in-progress with professional directors, using the space for your own works without having to pay rental fees or hiring a crew, ongoing classes, and participation in company-level industry showcases. Do your homework, see shows, ask questions, and find the place you'd be most proud to call your on-stage home.

Outside of LA, theatre can be a much larger part of an actor's life. Agents in LA will sometimes discourage their clients from doing plays because the rehearsal and performance schedule may make the actors unavailable for location shoots or lucrative TV bookings. But in markets where the number of on-camera opportunities are less plentiful, stage work is often a much larger part of an actor's life. Like CSA casting director April Webster says, "Actors have to work harder to make LA a theatre town because of the time commitment in getting to and from the theatre for rehearsals—you can't just hop the subway a few stops like in New York—but there is excellent work going on here."

Sketch Comedy Groups and Improv Troupes

Sketch comedy groups and improv troupes can create some of the most fun an actor can have on stage, while providing a wild ride for the audiences. Many actors find their most close-knit "family" away from home by being a part of these teams. Check out shows produced by each group you're considering before auditioning or getting into the class structure that leads to performances. Also find out about their writing labs for members.

"Sketch groups are extremely Darwinian," explained Bruce Smith, of Omnipop Talent Group. "The Groundlings' program is based on surviving the system. But thinking on your feet is never a bad skill. In this business, you're thrown against the wall very hard. If you stick, great. If you don't, no one worries about your concussion. It's an ostracizing process. When you fail, you must retreat, regroup, and come back with a vengeance. One way to do that is by writing. Do what it takes to get writing so that your entire ego isn't wrapped around the performance end of the experience."

A huge advantage to sketch comedy group membership is the *writing* muscle it develops among its actors. No, you may not always get hired for being the "package deal" that you are, but if your writing is top-notch *and* you're out there performing with a group you love (and letting others perform your work even more brilliantly than you may have done so), you increase the likelihood that producers and development execs will find something intriguing about what you're doing.

As for improv, obviously, there's no structured writing happening before the shows, but you're basically writing on your feet all show long, which is an invaluable skill in auditioning, networking, and life! Casting directors often scout sketch and improv performances because we can see many actors at once, the pace is fast and fun, and glimmers of brilliance really do shine through. But the bottom line for all stage work is this: Do it because it feeds your soul and keeps you sharp. The people it puts you in front of? Bonus!

Showcases

Let's start by defining the term "showcase," which is often used interchangeably (and incorrectly) with the term "workshop." To complicate matters further, consider that in New York, the term "showcase" refers to an Equity contract similar to the LA Equity 99-Seat Agreement. For our purposes, "showcases" are defined as rehearsed, planned, promoted, catered presentations of scenes. Many theatres rent space to performance groups and others sponsor their own company members' performances. Most big acting degree programs and some private acting classes culminate in seasonal industry showcase performances. No one is paid to attend these showcases. These buyers come for the chance to scout new talent, eat a little food, schmooze, and take home an industry kit filled with headshots and resumés.

Many casting director workshop companies will use the term "showcase" in promoting some of their workshops. Some acting coaches will provide incentives to industry (stipends, swag bags, gift certificates), hoping that such perks will result in higher attendance. Generally, these showcases are held in lower regard, since talent isn't the *only* motivating factor in casting directors being there. The higher-status (non-incentivized) showcases can boost an actor's reputation, even if the buyer cannot attend the show.

Some showcases are outright pay-to-participate events. Your money goes toward rental of the facility, catering, bartending (supplies and staff), industry kits, promotional materials (flyers, letters, postcards, listings in the trades, website), and tech crew. Remember, you are not showcasing in order to line the pockets of the showcase producers. You are presenting your talent to the industry and paying for their producer services.

Other showcases are the final event after participation in an ongoing class or program. Usually your tuition covers the above-mentioned costs, although I have been to some "graduation showcases" for which the actors paid an additional fee.

There are showcases produced by management companies. These are produced in an attempt to promote an entire client roster. Some managers lay out the funds in order to improve the likelihood that their clients will book work on which they will earn a commission; others require their clients to pay for this service.

Theatre companies occasionally produce member showcases to the industry. Your membership dues go toward this benefit.

Some regularly-produced plays or sketch shows will culminate in an industry night. Generally, the cast will present a version of the show that has been cut to a more showcase-friendly run-time and serve food and drinks to invitation-only guests. Whether actors chip in for this special production's extra costs or the theatre itself covers this sort of thing varies.

Actors' unions, television networks, and production companies frequently offer casting incentive showcases for under-represented performers. That includes people of color, senior citizens, and actors with physical disabilities. These are almost always mounted at no charge to the participants. While most studios and networks hold regular diversity showcases, they aren't very well publicized to the general population. Most networks have someone who is in charge of *scouting* for diversity showcases. That person (or her team) goes to clubs to see stand-ups, checks out sketch comedy and improv groups, and takes suggestions from agents who have signed hot new talent. Occasionally, the top grads from certain conservatory training programs are invited to participate as well.

While the above paragraphs describe several major categories of industry showcases, some events actually fall into two or three categories at once. Do your homework on any showcase you're thinking of becoming a part of, in order to know what you're getting into and what the industry's perception may be. Best bet: Attend the showcases produced by the groups you're considering so that all of your questions are answered. Talk with actors currently participating in each showcase and then decide which might be the right fit for your needs.

A few quick words of caution about showcasing too soon: "One of the biggest problems," explained Comedy Central's VP of development and original programming Zoe Friedman, "is that people are seen too soon out here. You really need to wait until you're ready."

Reality TV

As an actor, I really don't like reality shows. As a hypocrite, I watch a couple of them.

—Bill Lippincott, actor

Many people perceive reality shows as taking jobs away from actors. Having worked briefly in reality TV casting, I can assure you, there are as many actors working on reality shows as there are "real people," and some actors have tried to take advantage of the trend in order to boost their acting careers. Of course, like with all parts of a self-managed acting career, it takes *research* to make the most of these opportunities.

"Reality television" is probably the most popular oxymoron out there. By now, everyone is clear that there are characters, stories, and arcs produced for maximum oomph, just like with scripted programming. The difference is, you don't need union membership in order to be nationally televised on reality shows. In fact, being perceived as an actor can ruin your chances of getting cast in this environment.

If your goal is to be famous, get on any reality show you can, right now. If your goal is to have a career as a working actor, either don't do a reality show or choose to do the reality show that will cause the least amount of damage to your career. Make sure, if you agree to be on a reality show, that you sign a release with a clause stating that you are appearing as *yourself* and not performing. Note that actors who appear on reality shows are rarely depicted as actors (since reality show producers don't want their shows to be seen as fictional or manipulated in any way, even though all of them *are* to some degree). Should you apply to be a participant on a reality show, it's likely that you'll be asked to call yourself a "teacher," "waiter," or "tutor." (I can't begin to tell you how many people I've seen on reality shows whose headshots are in my files!) For most reality show participants, once the show airs, you'll be perceived as a personality rather than an actor.

When you attend an open call in an attempt to get cast, remember that the cast is often pre-selected and that the recruiting tours in cities other than Los Angeles and New York are actually promotional in nature. Think about it! Casting calls are cheaper than as many days of constant advertising the show itself would be. During the casting calls, recruiters get locals excited about the show and there will be tons of free coverage in the local news media. Sure, if a hometown favorite does make it past the initial open call, that's a bonus (with a built-in audience). But for reality shows, finding a cast is usually secondary to gathering gag-reel footage and generating buzz via "worldwide searches."

Risk management is a funny part of the whole reality show culture. Risk management experts know your background and all of your secrets *before* you're on the air and only act like the info is "news to them" when it "breaks." Of course, it only breaks after they've leaked it, usually in conjunction with the need for a spike in viewership during sweeps. Believe me, I know how much of a background search goes on in reality TV casting. A candidate won't "fail" the background check due to "issues," but the producers sure as heck will know when and how to leak those "issues," should the press threaten to expose them. It's risk *management*, not risk *elimination*.

Note that in reality show contracts, you agree to being manipulated by producers, since there may be elements of the show that they cannot fully reveal to you during production (including the true nature of the show itself). Yep! There is a deception clause built right into the 60-page contract, which includes a confidentiality and non-disclosure agreement with penalties of millions of dollars built in for revealing pretty much anything about the show and the contract itself. If you're on a performance program (*American Idol, Project Runway, The Voice*), you also surrender all rights to any original material! That explains why we hear so much "cover music," eh?

You also waive rights to your safety and even agree that your family is not permitted to sue the network or production company if you die during the show's stunts or challenges. Further, you sign away the rights to your life story. Yep! Even if you were well on your way to having a great story brought to life on the big screen (or in a book), you owe the network and production company the right of first refusal on any pitch (and they can block you from going elsewhere for several years, while they decide whether they'd like to produce your story). All press you do for any reason must first go through these folks too. While this may not seem like such a big deal to an aspiring actor (Hey! Free publicist! Cool!), if you turn out to be the next major reality show personality, their need to "contain" your image could prevent you from benefiting to the max. Remember, it's the producers' needs that will be met first and foremost.

Editing is tricky. You're not a character, you're *you*, but you're also *you-as-edited* by the producers and their agenda for the show. One of my actor friends who participated in a reality show told me, "It's a good exercise in *self-PR*. It can be surprisingly hard to go out there as 'yourself,' not knowing how you will be edited. After seeing yourself being taken out of context, you learn to edit yourself in the best light (which can come in *very* handy down the road when facing media or being interviewed)." Viewers feel that they know you intimately and will interact with you as though they have every right to do so (and that feels very different than having a fan react strongly to a series of characters you've played).

If you're considering going out for a reality show, make sure you do your research. Know the types of shows (dating shows, social experiments, documentary, makeovers, prank shows, and contests) and know which type is the best fit for your overall goals. A note about contests: Some don't actually deliver the full extent of what is promised to the winner. We all know the scandal behind the first season of *America's Next Top Model* and Adrianne Curry's fight to get the Revlon contract that was promised (and the omission of her image from any opening footage of future seasons of *ANTM* after she began to fight Tyra Banks for her due). What about winners of the show *Fight for Fame* or *The Starlet* and how those who "won" endorsement deals never got those big national campaigns? Or worse, how about the actor who signed on the dotted line of that big juicy agency contract and then never got a return phone call? Shelving hurts for any actor. When you've been promised a happy agency relationship on national television and *then* you're shelved, that's publicly harsh.

Soaps

I strongly recommend that you do some extra work on a soap if you've never experienced a soap set. As extra work goes, soap sets have some of the best working conditions in the industry! While there are stories of soap extras who have made it in good with the AD and gotten bumped up to speaking roles, don't count on that happening. Just go to that set ready to learn, be professional, and have fun. Most soaps have hotlines set up for extras, so make sure you call in regularly to state your availability, once you're on their radar. The major benefits to doing soap work are that it's fun, it's a relatively short day, and the pay is very good. In general, the casting directors for extras are not the same as the casting directors for contract roles. Should you wish to pursue principal work on soaps, target those CDs just like you would target the buyers for any episodic show. (See: **Targeting Buyers**.)

Student Films

> *Remember that student films don't just pay in copy, credit, and meals. You should also be paid respect. Give as much as you can, and demand the same in return.*

—David Bronfman, actor

We've already talked about the benefit to doing student films: You're contributing to the experience of the future filmmakers of our industry, you're investing in relationships, you're amassing footage for your reel, and you're building your brand. Some schools enroll students who churn out higher-quality projects than others, of course, so visit smfa4.com for our current list of top programs in major markets.

Terminology that's specific to student films includes *sync-sound* (which means that you'll be recorded on audio at the same time as video or film) and *non-sync-sound* (which means that your video or film performance will be set against audio recorded at a later time). Don't shy away from the latter just because that technique isn't mainstream. Those films come off more like voiceover narration projects, so, if you're the lead actor and also the narrator, that's a huge role. If you're just the lead actor, and someone else does the narration, it's more like acting in a music video.

Note that union members can only do student films at institutions with blanket union agreements or, in some cases, at non-approved institutions when an individual student producer has secured a union agreement. If you have any question about your ability to work on a particular student film, call SAG-AFTRA with the name of the project, producer, and academic institution.

Make sure you take a blank contract from copyprovided.com with you to set, so you can have documentation that you will receive your footage! Be sure to get the professor's name before the shoot, so if you don't receive your footage, you can make a call to the school, as the student filmmaker's grade depends on having completed the assignment (and providing promised footage is part of that assignment).

31: Union Membership

There are currently more than 160,000 members of SAG-AFTRA (Screen Actors Guild-American Federation of Television and Radio Artists) and nearly 50,000 members of AEA (Actors Equity Association). To join SAG-AFTRA (the union covering on-camera actors, journalists, and hosts—among many others), you must show proof of employment on a SAG-AFTRA project at a qualifying contract level, complete three days of voucher-qualifying background work, or be a member of a sister union (ACTRA, AEA, AGMA, AGVA) for one year *and* have worked under a qualifying principal contract level for that union.

AEA membership comes from employment under a qualifying Equity contract, principal work in a qualifying contract from a sister union (SAG-AFTRA, AGMA, AGVA) along with partial initiation fee and a letter from your parent union, or the EMC (Equity Membership Candidate) Program. EMC work requires 50 weeks' employment at participating theatres.

Must you be a member of a union in order to get seen by casting directors? No. In fact, the act of Taft-Hartleying specific actors in order to turn them into union members is simple and very commonly done. If you are Taft-Hartleyed, the casting director or producer has written a letter explaining why she has hired you for the job, rather than hiring a current union member. She must justify your inclusion in the union with documentation that you are, in fact, pursuing a professional acting career or that you meet some specific criteria that she was not able to find in the group of union members she auditioned. Actors younger than 18 or older than 60 can be Taft-Hartleyed with the least amount of trouble.

Unless you have some extraordinary skill that simply cannot be found in union actors of your type, the production may be fined for using you. Even so, the fine is generally much lower than most producers would have you believe. Don't let producers tell you otherwise. Your little Taft-Hartley fine would never break the bank!

When casting directors go on and on about how they can't consider you until you're in the union, it's really because that's an "easy no." What's an "easy no"? That's something you can't bargain your way out of. It's a "stopper."

➤"Your hair is too long." "No problem! I'll cut it." (Easy to bargain your way out of.)

➤"You look too young." "We can age me using makeup." (Easy to bargain your way out of.)

➤"You're not in the union." "True." (Can't bargain your way out of that one.)

What I've seen, over and over again, is actors being told that it's their union status that's keeping them from getting into the room. And then they join the union and—guess what—there's a *new* reason they're not getting in: headshots, training, reel, whatever. I've found, when excuses come quickly as to why you're not getting into the room to begin with, they're simply easy stoppers that have nothing to do with your union status.

Of course, you can Taft-Hartley yourself if you're producing your own project under a qualifying union contract. Important: Remember what you read in the chapter on **Premature Moves** to be sure you're ready to Taft-Hartley yourself! Because once you're a member of the union, you're barred from doing nonunion work—even if it's under the jurisdiction of a sister union—and that's true even in a right-to-work state (see Wikipedia for a current list of RTW states). While you aren't required to join the union to *work* on union projects in RTW states, once you do join the union, your nonunion days are over.

Staying Union-Eligible

Union-eligible is one of the best statuses to have in this town. Before you're union-eligible, you're nonunion. That means, of course, that you cannot be hired to work on union projects without getting Taft-Hartleyed, earning union vouchers as an extra on union projects, or working under one of the low budget agreements that allow for nonunion performers (which doesn't get you any closer to being a union member). Visit sagindie.org for more information on these agreements.

Once you're union-eligible, you may work on union *and* nonunion projects. Suddenly, you have the best of both worlds! Should a producer choose to hire you on a union project, he will not risk the fine that comes with a rejected Taft-Hartley letter (since you're already eligible and he will not be doing a Taft-Hartley letter on your behalf). You simply must go to the membership office and pay your initiation fee and first dues prior to the Station-12 clearance date for shooting the union project on which you've been hired.

While union-eligible, you can continue to work nonunion, meaning there are more (albeit usually lower-paying) options available to you, while you're building your resumé and your reel. This is the time when most people become union-eligible: when they have built a few good credits and are getting their first professional reel together, approaching agents and managers for representation, and are about to leave the non-pro acting world behind in favor of risking less-frequent, but much higher-paying work in the industry. Please note: After your first day of SAG-AFTRA eligibility, a clock starts ticking. You have 30 days to work all the union jobs you can score without having to plunk down initiation fees. On day 31, you are what's called a "must join" and cannot accept any other union work on qualifying contracts without paying your initiation fees. Be sure you're ready to start that clock!

"SAG-AFTRA-eligible" on your resumé tells buyers that you are available to do on-camera union work without costing them much hassle or potential fees *and* that you are available to do nonunion work without violating union rules. A caveat: Do *not* put "SAG-AFTRA-eligible" on your resumé unless you have at least a few grand put away in savings to put toward your initiation fees. You don't want to earn the opportunity and then not have the ability to seal the deal!

Realities of Union Membership

About 80% of all members do *not* earn enough in any given year to qualify for health coverage. In a recent census of union members, for example, just over 10,000 members earned over $25,000 and only 1500 members earned over $200,000. In contrast, just under 38,000 members earned *zero dollars*.

There will never be enough union jobs to keep all its members employed fulltime and that is precisely why I caution against premature moves involving union membership. Because you don't get married so that you can sleep around, I say joining the union should put you into your healthiest monogamous relationship. Of course, not everyone chooses monogamy.

Financial Core (or FiCore) is your right as a union member (it's federal law), but it's a state that weakens the union, and you know I'm all about actor empowerment and building an industry we're all proud to be a part of, daily. FiCore was created to protect union members in industries where workers could not earn a living wage within the union, and (for example) these steel workers' families would go hungry without the union member's ability to take nonunion work when union steel mills weren't hiring.

Well, the entertainment industry—though unionized—has never, can never, and will never be able to assure its members a living wage due to the number of jobs vs. the number of actors aspiring to fill them. Even *working* actors often subsidize their acting work with survival jobs. Therefore, while "going FiCore" and working as a fee-paying non-member is an option, it's one that deteriorates the union's bargaining strength for better contracts, gives more power to producers (who already have plenty), and puts actors in a position of begging for work rather than being empowered by their creative careers.

Most of the time, actors who choose to go FiCore do so from a place of fear (and you know how I feel about making business decisions from a place of fear, right?) and not from an awareness of who it is they hope to be in the world long term. See yourself as a leader of this industry. You've reached your highest goals. You're being interviewed about "those dark days." Do you brag about how you brazenly went FiCore while others kept survival jobs a little longer or do you talk about how you held true to your commitment to the union that protects you now that you're making more money than you ever imagined possible? What does next-tier you think about FiCore?

My favorite source for information on FiCore comes from BizParentz Foundation, a nonprofit organization for parents of young actors (who are often faced with this dilemma). Please visit the bizparentz.org website for the complete overview of FiCore and performers' unions in particular.

If you're not ready to be *in* the union, I say *don't join the union yet*. Get union-eligible and stay that way as long as possible. Then, you won't even have to consider going FiCore, since you'll have reached the level at which joining the union was a good idea, once and for all. As with everything in this business, get informed and make your decisions based on having all of the facts available to you.

32: *SMFA* FOR YOUNG ACTORS

Several times in my casting career, I've been hired to cast children in indie projects. I have found that it is frequently up to me to educate producers and indie filmmakers on issues regarding hiring young actors. Since the specifics of *many* issues facing the young actor aren't covered in film school, it may come down to you (the performer or parent of a young performer) to educate folks about your rights! I've brought together contributions from some fantastic parents of young actors, here, and I'm excited to be sure we're all speaking the same language, as we bring young actors into our projects.

18 to Play Younger (18 TPY)—Often, this phrase appears on a breakdown to indicate that the filmmaker would like to see an actor age 18 or older to play a younger character. What "counts" as 18, in this case? Being 18 obviously counts. Also, being 16 and having passed the CHSPE (California High School Proficiency Exam) counts. Why? Once you are 16 and have taken the CHSPE (and received the certificate of completion), you no longer need an on-set studio teacher (an expense for the production) and you can work "adult" hours. An actor need only be a second-semester sophomore to *take* the CHSPE, although many will tell you "being 16" is the requirement. Nope. See California Labor Code 1391.2(a) for the nitty-gritty. Because this saves producers money, producers looking for "18 to Play Younger" usually want actors who are clear of both on-set studio teacher needs *and* child labor laws. The certificate of completion of the CHSPE accomplishes that. However, many studios require a parent on set for anyone under the age of 16 (or even 18 in some cases) due to insurance issues. So, "True 18" is really the best deal going for producers on a budget.

Emancipated—Typically, this is on a breakdown *incorrectly*. A young actor needn't be emancipated in order to work as an adult on the set. Emancipation is a severe court process involving a legal divorce between child and parents! What emancipation does for an actor is allow him to sign legally-binding contracts without a parent and to work without a parent on set. Emancipation alone does not impact the need for an on-set studio teacher, requirement of a work permit, or the work hours required under child labor laws. Since it is assumed that a production would indicate wanting to work with an emancipated child actor to save money, it becomes clear that what the producers likely mean to say is that they want actors who are cleared to work as adults, not necessarily ones who have become emancipated, live on their own, have their own source of steady income, etc.

GED-CHSPE-Legal 18—This phrase indicates that the producer knows that one of these things (General Educational Development test, California High School Proficiency Exam, or being 18) helps save him money on set. Since he isn't sure exactly *what* it is he needs you to have done, he simply asks for it all. The GED is a high school equivalency exam for people within 60 days of age 18 and over. Some parents, agents, and managers will mistakenly believe that their young actors need to have a GED, since producers sometimes ask for that. Some may also mistakenly pursue the CHSEE (California High School Exit Exam), which isn't what you need either.

Early Graduation—One of the things that helps producers is early graduation. According to Marie Watkins, director of Romawat Academy: "Early graduation is exactly that: the student has graduated, is Legal 18, does not have to do school on set, has no age minimum for being a grad, nor is a work permit needed."

School Absences—For young actors attending public school in California, AB776 requires that a maximum of five absences of five days each be considered excused absences if the young actors are on set with a state-certified studio teacher those days. Now, this does not equal 25 individual absences! It's five bookings, each up to five days in one school year. Schoolwork completed on set must be accepted by the public school when the young actor returns from set.

If you are a young actor (or the parent of one), be prepared to become the authority on these issues and find a succinct way to explain the facts to those around you. While a producer may only ever do *one* film with children in the cast (and therefore never feel the need to educate himself on the child labor laws, young actor work permits, educational requirements, etc.), you have a longer-term need for having the most accurate information available.

An essential site filled with descriptions of various child actor issues as well as resources on all things families of young actors may face is run by the BizParentz Foundation. Among many other topics, bizparentz.org covers the pros and cons of having the CHSPE certificate of completion. The official website for the CHSPE (with test dates, registration fee, and information about test format) is chspe.net. BizParentz's site also has an Emancipation Grid that is worth printing out and taking to set!

Work Permits

If you are under the age of 18 and planning to work in California, you must obtain an Entertainment Work Permit. The application form needs to be signed by both your parent and your school principal, vice-principal, or registrar. Be sure the official that signs the form also prints or types his name and position under his signature. The application must also include the school stamp or seal. If you are homeschooled, the permit must be signed either by a representative of the school district you are living in, or by the homeschool administrator of the program with which you are affiliated. This varies from state to state (check with your local labor office).

For California, the form can be obtained through the Division of Labor Standards Enforcement office. The application can be completed online at permits.dir.ca.gov/ewp and must include an upload of a certified copy of your birth certificate. Be sure to follow all the directions on the form very carefully. Your grades must be certified as "satisfactory" by the school (usually Cs or better). Getting a work permit should be taken care of as soon as possible, before booking your first job. Once you have booked a job, you must always have your original work permit (not a copy) with you at any job location for the studio teacher to sign. As of this printing, work permits are to be renewed every six months.

What if you suddenly book a job before obtaining your permit? If this is the case, you and one of your parents can go to the labor office taking your original, certified birth certificate, the required application form signed by your parent and school official including the school's stamp or seal, and a Letter of Intent to Employ by the production company with whom you've just booked the job. Call the labor office ahead of time to confirm this procedure.

—Denise Winsor

According to Anne Henry, co-founder of BizParentz Foundation, California also offers a 10-Day Emergency Permit, "once in a lifetime, for those in a hurry for a first-time permit. The beauty of this is that out-of-state actors need not get a CA work permit 'just in case'. They can get one very quickly at permits.dir.ca.gov/tewp online."

In New York, a minor's work hours, trust accounts, etc. are regulated by NYCRR Part 186. They require a permit similar to the one required in California but NY requires a physical for the actor as well. In terms of work permits and legal requirements in other states, "there really is no national database that is reliable. There are a few databases out there, but we—at BizParentz Foundation—have found them to be inaccurate, and laws are always changing. A parent's best bet is to look for 'entertainment laws for minors' in their State Department of Labor website, or their State Film Commission office," according to Henry.

For the latest information on California and New York child performer laws—as well as resources for verifying your rights in other markets—visit bizparentz.org.

Coogan and Trust Accounts

You will be required to open a Coogan Blocked Trust Account (in CA) or an UTMA-UGMA Trust Account (in NY), which is a special trust account for actors who are minors. This is in compliance with the Coogan Law that was revised in 2000 (SB1162), in 2004 (SB210), and in 2013 (AB533) in California, that requires a minimum 15% of a principal actor's gross wages to be withheld and deposited into your trust account by the payroll company of any production company you work for. Other states (including New York, Louisiana, and New Mexico) have also enacted similar versions. Since CA law is the most restrictive and its accounts are acceptable in other states, consider opening an account that satisfies CA law, to keep it simple.

These Coogan trust accounts can be opened at a bank, credit union, or financial investment firm. If you choose a bank it is helpful, but not necessary, to open the account in a bank that is nationwide. This is suggested as a matter of convenience in the event you are working in various cities for extended periods of time and would like to be able to make additional deposits into your trust account while you are working outside of your hometown.

In California and New York, the Entertainment Work Permit states that the Coogan account must be established within 10 business days from the date the work permit is issued. This is important and should be taken care of as soon as possible. It is advisable to always have copies of these documents with you at every audition, in addition to multiple headshots and resumés. Always be prepared! No excuses!

—Denise Winsor

According to Henry, "It is easier to find an entertainment-friendly credit union to open a Coogan account, since many banks will not open them anymore. Examples of those are Entertainment Federal Credit Union, Actors Federal Credit Union, and AFTRA-SAG Federal Credit Union."

She continued: "The Coogan system is not perfect. In fact, many millions of dollars have not made their way to child actor bank accounts. Managing your child's trust account takes a bit of diligence on the parent's part, including checking every paycheck for a deposit *and* making sure it actually made it to the account. It is highly recommended that parents regularly check for missing Coogan money. Check your state Unclaimed Funds Department, as well as the departments where your child might have worked, or where the employer might be based. In other words, check California if you worked for Disney, since the company is based there, even if you worked in Texas. Visit unclaimedcoogan.org, The Actors Fund, where more than three million dollars currently resides."

Homeschooling

Before we get into the complexities of homeschooling, let me recommend that you visit hslda.org/laws to check your state's homeschooling laws, in their current form. You'll be glad you got informed!

There are so many educational options available that the choices can be a bit overwhelming. Start by checking out the laws in your state regarding compulsory education and homeschooling. A family might choose to do an independent study contract with the existing school, or try a hybrid onsite-offsite program from their district, or an online public charter school, or a for-profit private school, or homeschool, or even choose concurrent or dual enrollment at a community college.

If a family wants to homeschool independently in the state of California, they need to file a private school affidavit (PSA) or enroll in a private school satellite (PSP) program. Filing a PSA is a fairly straightforward process but it does require the willingness to keep good records, get a school seal made for stamping work permits and other official documents, and register with the state once a year. Some families don't feel comfortable signing their own child's Entertainment Work Permit so they enroll in the PSP option so that someone else's name is on forms.

Regardless of the option chosen, it's important to have a frank discussion with the school or program to find out what their requirements are for seat time and testing, especially if you chose a virtual school, because sometimes you will be on a set with limited or non-existent Internet access for weeks at a time and won't be able to log in at all. What happens then? Does schooling stop and do grades drop? Is the curriculum available in paper form or just online? Does the student have to be online for video classes and chats at certain times of day? What happens if those times of day are inflexible and during prime audition hours or if you are working halfway around the world and Pacific time is the middle of the night for wherever you're filming? Is state testing required and what happens if the student books a job during state testing and can't take the tests? Is the school flexible about the days of the week and hours of the day that schooling happens? Does the school or program issue transcripts and diplomas? Have their students gone on to college? All of these questions need to be addressed in the context of the professional life of the student before you select a program that may work academically but is a nightmare when a job is booked.

—Marie Watkins

Passports

Be sure you and at least one parent or guardian have a passport. You don't want to book a job and then suddenly lose it to another actor because the job is filming outside of the United States and you don't have your passport ready to go. Things happen quickly in this industry and you need to be ready to go at a moment's notice. Be sure to read the passport application instructions carefully. If you are under 15, both parents must be present when you apply or you must have a notarized letter from the parent who cannot be there in person. Passports are required for air travel anywhere outside of the United States. Once you receive your passport, list "Passport" at the top or bottom of your resumé.

—Denise Winsor

Scams

You've read the chapter on **The Costs of Acting** and you know how to avoid scams. Please understand that—especially where young actors are concerned—those scams are turned up to hyperdrive. Scammers—or well-meaning producers who just don't know better—will tell you that child labor laws aren't a factor because their project is nonunion, and that's a lie, since *laws* are laws irrespective of union jurisdiction. Work hours, studio teacher, parent on set—these are legal requirements, not union rules. This is true whether the project is a student film or your buddy's indie project.

Again, never pay for representation; never say yes to an all-in-one photo, craft, reel, poise training package that allegedly leads to representation or a booking; never attend an audition at a private residence; never submit on a project whose principals are not verifiable as legit on IMDb-Pro; never believe a "mall scout" is your key to success in Hollywood; never be swayed by radio, newspaper, or online ads for reps coming to your town to search for the next big kid-actor-network star; and never tie your hopes and dreams up in someone who has money to earn by telling you you're a superstar. This industry is far more complex than that. You, of course, know that by now.

Safety First

According to Henry, "The California Child Performer Protection Act (AB1660) requires those service providers who work with children in the entertainment industry to get a Child Performer Permit and obtain fingerprints. This law was passed in response to a growing number of pedophilia/child abuse issues within the professional acting community. This law applies to photographers, acting coaches, dancing and singing instructors, managers, career consultants, publicists, and camp directors. It does not apply to licensed agents or studio teachers, since they already have a fingerprint requirement elsewhere in the law. Parents should make sure to ask if your service providers have obtained the proper permits and fingerprints. While having a permit is not a 100% guarantee of safety (and you should still never leave your child alone), it does tell you that the provider realizes their legal responsibility for keeping kids safe."

As you've seen earlier in this book, your Social Security Number, address, and home phone number should be kept confidential, as—until we're casting you—that data isn't relevant to your auditions or submissions. When you create your website, domain privatization is your friend (or, just use a PO Box whenever you're required to give out your address—especially online). Leave your personal details out of any posts you make as you do the social networking thing—especially if there's an NDA in place—and live as if the Internet is forever (it is).

Know the people with whom you're doing business, because it's your right to be sure you're safe on every set and at every audition. Henry added: "*Sight and sound* is a standard industry term for 'never leave your child alone—you must be within sight and sound of them.' This is the only way to make sure your child is truly safe. In some states (like CA) this is a legal requirement, and in other areas, union rules dictate parents must be within sight or sound. Sometimes shoot locations make it impossible for you to be in the room with your young actor, but production should be providing a monitor and listening device so that you can observe what is going on. In NY, the law requires a 'responsible person' that is appointed to this duty, due to tight spaces in Broadway stages. Make sure that 'sight and sound' is a priority!"

Whether it's protection under the law or common sense, please be sure you're always keeping your young actor's safety in mind. There are certain poses in young actors' headshot photos that are bait for predators. Your discarded headshots—with your contact information—could end up sold in eBay "private auctions" (*ewww*). And no child needs to be pumped up with hairspray, bronzer, or makeup, ever. We're casting *kids* and that should feel real. And safe.

Beginning Photos for Children

Parents, when you are submitting your child to different agencies for representation, a couple of good snapshots from home are all that is necessary. One close-up and one 3/4 or full-length shot are all that you need. Reputable agents actually prefer snapshots, knowing that if they should take on your child as a client, they will usually ask you to have new headshots done anyway, even if you have already had professional headshots taken. Thoughtful agents don't want anyone spending money unnecessarily and will not think any less of a prospective client for sending in snapshots. It may take a few months of submissions before your child is called in and during those months, your child will change and you'll need to update the photos. This is another good reason to wait and not have professional headshots taken too soon. Be sure to include your child's name, age, height, weight, clothing size, email address, and contact number neatly printed on the back of each photo. Use a cell phone number and not a home phone number in the event that your child's photos are discarded or lost in the mail.

Professional headshots are a good idea though, if you choose to submit your child on your own to casting directors for auditions by mail, by email, through online casting sites, or if you are taking your child to open calls. Your child is not required to have an agent to submit to any audition notices or breakdowns that are listed through public resources. Your child also does not have to be a union member to submit to a union project. If you choose to have headshots taken before getting an agent, try to find a reasonable photographer, or have a friend or relative who is handy with a camera take some photos of your child and then have those reproduced into 8x10s. The photos should be as natural-looking as possible, with no makeup for children under 12. You want the photos to represent your children for who they are. They should look like their photo when they walk through the door of any agent's or casting director's office. No glamour shots! Solid color, casual clothes are best. Think of jewel tones. Try to stay away from black, white, and busy prints or anything fancy.

—Denise Winsor

Be Prepared

Be prepared to have to leave home at the drop of a hat. Do you have family or friends who will watch your other children while you are gone? Have a plan in place for an unexpected or last-minute booking. Having a bag pre-packed with essentials is not a bad idea.

Be prepared to miss school and have work ready for a studio teacher. When your child is tutored on set, it is almost always expected that you will provide the studio teacher with work from your child's school for your child to complete on set. If your child is going to miss a lot of school, you must make a plan with your child's teachers. Some teachers feel most comfortable with providing work on a day-to-day basis. In this case, you should check that production will provide a means to get and send back work from the teacher.

Other teachers will give you lots of work in advance. In either case, it is very important to be organized and make sure that your child and the studio teacher are on top of all missed assignments.

Be prepared to be rejected... a lot. It is important to explain to your child from the very beginning that bookings do not always equate to talent. The most talented actor does not always get the job. In fact, many times, especially in the case of child actors, matching up with already-cast parents plays a larger part in casting than does talent. Try to forget about that audition, or callback, or third callback, as soon as you leave it. Throw away the sides and move on. If you book it, great! If not (which will be the case most times), it is probably not in any way a reflection on your child's acting ability. So forget about it, and move on to the next.

Be prepared to spend a lot of time waiting. Have a backpack filled with quiet things for your kids to do while waiting to be seen by the casting director, or while waiting to work on set. Realize that your child's (and your) behavior in the waiting area may impact the casting director's final decision, and that behavior on set will be remembered by everyone. Today's PA might be next year's AD! Also, remember that no audition is ever a waste of your time. Think of the business as a long and slow marathon and never a sprint. One thing generally leads to another, as it is a very small industry. Even if your child was not right for that part, casting might remember him or her next time. Or five times later. Do not ever let yourself get discouraged. Tomorrow is another day, another audition.

Be prepared to spend a lot of money. Acting is expensive! There are the obvious costs of gas, tolls, and parking; headshots; cute audition clothing; classes. And then there are the hidden costs of meals on the run, babysitting for siblings, lost revenue (if you have to take time off from your job), etc. You will accrue lots of costs, despite the fact that your child may not earn enough to cover them. Acting could end up costing you a fortune each year! Even when your child is earning money, be prepared for the fact that take-home pay is vastly different from gross salary. Before your child gets paid, the manager and agent will take their percentages. There will always be taxes. There are union dues. Although the potential for earning is there, never count your chickens before they hatch. Residuals are icing on the cake, and never are guaranteed. I have heard more stories of national commercials that never aired, or kids being downgraded (or out-graded) than I care to share. If you think that your child is going to earn his or her college fund, think again. It could happen, but it probably will not. Especially given what college costs nowadays!

Be prepared for people to think that you are crazy. Despite the fact that other parents may travel to the end of the Earth to watch their children play in soccer games, spend tons of cash on dance lessons or pitching clinics, and brag about the game-winning run, inevitably, there are going to be many people who believe that you are insane for getting involved in acting. Other kids might give your kids a hard time about it. Sometimes even members of a cast and crew look down upon the "stage parent," for no reason other than the fact that he or she is a "stage parent." As long as you and your child have tough skin, you will be just fine. But most parents of child actors will advise that the less you talk about it, with even your friends and family, the better off you will be.

Be prepared to spend hours of quality time with your child and make life-lasting memories. Traffic is a bummer, but when else do you have uninterrupted time to sit and just talk with your child? I have had lots of one-on-one time with both of my kids while traveling to auditions. Make the most of it! And don't forget to bring a camera to set to document the friends that they make along the way (but always ask before you shoot). Your kids will never forget all of the fun had on set or on location.

Finally, be careful what you wish for. You may get it all! Although the odds are greatly against it, your child just may become tomorrow's newest star. Be prepared for all that might come with that: You might have to move to NY or LA or even South Africa (if that is the location of your child's new TV show booking). Your spouse or your other children may not be as excited as you are about it. You and your child might come under public scrutiny. You may have to fight off the paparazzi. Life as you know it could change immensely, even overnight. Okay, maybe you can't prepare for any of that, but at least keep it all in mind. Showbiz is a crazy rollercoaster ride. You'll scream. You may even cry. But in the end, it will leave you laughing and full of life. Despite all of its ups and downs, it sure is a fun ride!

—Dawn Williams, parent to young actors

A Note about Premature Moves

I've stressed that avoiding premature moves at all costs is essential to an actor's healthy career, but there is one important distinction with young actors, and that's the fact that agents *are* essential sooner than they are for adult actors. According to Anne Henry of BizParentz Foundation, here's why: "Kids are legal minors, meaning they can't negotiate employment contracts for themselves. If mom is making deals on behalf of the child, they are agenting without a license in CA or NY (anybody who is procuring work for another person, or binding them to an employment agreement is doing this)."

She continued, "In contrast, adult actors can submit themselves, can negotiate their own contacts, etc. A kid technically, legally, can't. Now everyone knows that mommy is submitting on online sites, but if it came to something decent, paying, and worthwhile, an agent is needed for kids. With adults, the agent is an option, but with kids, it really isn't."

As for union membership, Henry had this to say: "The requirements for union membership are the same for kids and for adults, but they do vary from state to state. Parents will want to investigate before they are presented with 'must join' status and surprised by a very high initiation fee for their child to continue to work. A resource that kids and parents might like is youngperformers.sagaftra.org. That site was funded by grants, and includes the union *Young Performers Handbook* along with an awesome glossary of industry terms and some other fun stuff for kids and parents. Equity's *Young Performer Overview* is at actorsequity.org/benefits/youngperformers.asp currently."

Be a Castable Parent

I'm sure you're amazing. I'm sure you rock. I'm sure you want nothing but joy and success for your young actor, but more eager parents lose jobs for their kid actors than you'd like to know. Here's why: They want it *for* their kiddos. They want it really, really badly. Let your young actor want this, but treat acting like any other after-school activity. If the grades drop, it's over. If it's too stressful, it's over. If it's more your dream than your child's dream, it's over. You're hoping to raise a healthy human who *happened to do* some entertainment industry stuff—no matter how successful—once it's all said and done.

Because parents are on set, we're watching the adults at auditions as much as we're deciding how well those young actors bullseye the roles. I've seen countless well-meaning parents lose gigs for their talented youngsters by being overly involved, helicoptering, advising the young actors to do something other than what was instructed by session runners, or ingratiating themselves to the casting crew. Please don't do that. Just be cool. Be supportive. Be involved and aware, but be detached enough to let your young actor thrive.

***

As you may have guessed due to my reliance on its co-founder's wise words, one of my favorite sources for information relevant to young actors is bizparentz.org (the BizParentz Foundation). I'm also a fan of the convos going on at the Professional Actors Resource Forum (PARF), a Delphi forum located at forums.delphiforums.com/proactors. Register, introduce yourself, post your question, and get to know the ins and outs of the young actor biz. Of course, we're there for you at smfa4.com as well. Most importantly as you navigate your young actor's career, stay informed! Your power is in your own hands.

Success is divine optimism plus belligerent persistence.
—Jim Spencer, parent to a working actor

33: WHEN TO QUIT

Every now and then, a wave of "I quit-itis" flows through the acting community. Of course, for every actor who gives up on Hollywood, there's another who embraces the journey, ready to reap career rewards like never before. For every actor who actually packs it in and goes home, there's another 10 who whine about whether it's time to pack it in and go home. There are absolutely some legitimate reasons for an actor to *stop* the pursuit and move on to something else, but this is not one-size-fits-all advice. What may be a good reason to bail on acting for one person may be a cop-out for another. What I'm hoping to provide here is a nice little kick in the butt for those of you who hem and haw about leaving the biz. To paraphrase Yoda: "Leave or leave not. There is no whine."

Bad Reasons to Quit

Most of the things that bring you to the question, "Should I pack it in and go home?" are bad reasons to quit. Generally, you'll find yourself thinking about quitting when you see other actors around you doing well, when you stop getting callbacks in certain offices, when you get dropped by your agent or manager, when the haters are in attack mode, or when everyone back home asks you when you're going to give up the fantasy of making it.

When those around you are doing well, that means that you are in a peer group for which things are happening. This is a good thing. If you no longer get callbacks in offices where you were almost always going to producers, lots of things could be happening. Just keep delivering the level of work that earned you callbacks in the past with this team and trust that there will be a need for you again in the future. We all have dry spells. When you're not in demand elsewhere, create your own content.

If you're dropped by your agent or manager, look at it as an exciting opportunity to get better matched with representatives at the tier you're looking to hit. Getting dropped is not a sign that you are uncastable. It's just a part of the biz and one you'll probably experience more than once. Just like agencies don't fold when their top client leaves them for a bigger, more powerful agency, you shouldn't pack it in and go home when your agency outgrows you.

Once you're considered a public person—you're someone who has put together marketing materials, landed on IMDb, created a presence on social media, etc.—you're (by definition) seeking discussion and attention. You've invited public commentary on your very existence. There will always be people out there who enjoy the swipes they can take at you in public. There are even more people out there who enjoy *witnessing* the swipes that these folks take at public people (i.e., those who buy tabloids and who can't get enough of the Hollywood gossip sites), so, this is something that will not go away. Does an anonymous post on a random message board about your (lack of) talent mean you should pack it in and go home? Hell no! Some high-paid publicists actually go around *planting* such posts about their clients in order to get fans fired up about defending the actors. So, when someone takes a swipe at you, psychically thank them for doing you the favor of keeping your name "out there" while you stay focused on your work. If ego blows make you want to quit, you will never last in this business. The better your career is going, the more dirt they'll be slinging. Get used to it.

As for the, "When are you going to stop this foolishness and come home?" question, some of us are just blessed with such lack of support from those who know no better. There comes a time in every artist's life when you decide whether you are living your life for yourself or for everyone else. Obviously, there are considerations such as your age and responsibilities you've taken on. (Kids, mom and dad usually *do* know best!) But for the most part, we really do get to choose the life we live. Just because everyone in your family did things a certain way doesn't mean that you have to follow suit. A lot of families prize "the first in our family to go to college" or "the first in our family to own her own business." I say, let's value "the first in our family to be truly happy." And if pursuing a career in showbiz makes you happy, their opinions about what *should* make you happy are no reason for you to pack it in and go home.

What can you do to get out of actor funk, when you find yourself mired in it? First, I wouldn't advise you to rush out of it. Actor funk is an important part of your process as a creative person. You generate emotions for a living, right? Find something in this slump from which you can learn and start applying that nugget to your craft. One of the things I do when I get down in the dumps is *wallow in it*. Nothing helps you get out of a slump more efficiently than throwing yourself into it 100%. Once you let the actor funk become all-consuming (and stop fighting it), you quickly get a sense of humor about yourself. You look at yourself bawling in the mirror and think, "Am I crazy?!? In the big scheme of things, this is really no big deal!" And just like that, you're on your way out of it, lesson intact (don't forget the lesson, while you're there).

When I was pursuing acting in the early '90s, I was also taking a course at UCLA Extension called "The Art of Creative Living and Working." The instructor began the first class with the question, "Are you happy? Great! Enjoy it. It'll pass." Everyone laughed. Then he continued, "Are you sad?

Great! Enjoy it. It'll pass." While we found the "happiness is fleeting" idea of the first statement amusing, we found the second concept a little odd. How should we *enjoy* being sad? When we're sad, we all feel it will never pass, right? A-ha! That was the point. Just as happiness is a temporary emotion to enjoy, so are emotions like sadness, anger, joy, fear, and everything else for that matter. If we focus on holding on to an emotion we like (happiness, joy, excitement), we actually train ourselves to hold on to *all* emotions (including the ones we don't like holding on to). It is far more pleasant overall to find ways to enjoy *observing* the many emotions that come and go as we live our lives, not investing any more or less energy into any of them. How liberating!

Good Reasons to Quit

Believe it or not, there are some really good reasons to end your pursuit of acting in a major market. Those reasons include your level of happiness, your personal life, and your baseline of sanity. If you find that you are consistently miserable, regularly questioning whether this is your life path, and always feeling resentful about the success of others, it may be time to move on. As writer-director Jessica Bendinger told me, "The world needs more people in the world who love what they do." As an actor, what you *do* is research, audition, improve your craft, and build relationships. Sure, you also book work and act on a set or a stage, but that is a tiny percentage of what actors actually do for a living! So, if you don't love the hustle—the pursuit of the work—you may need to choose another career.

Do you covet what others have? Does the success of actors around you depress you or leave you feeling that life is unfair? If so, you need to ask yourself whether you can get okay with the fact that this business is unfair, random, and based on many factors over which you have no control. Can you get okay with that? If yes, stick it out. If no, go home. Find something that makes you happy and do that. You will not only *be happier* but you will also contribute more to the world if you choose to live as a person who *is* happy. Being a miserable person who is pursuing a dream filled with resentment doesn't serve you, and doesn't serve the world.

Other good reasons to quit include examining the results of having taken a hiatus to take stock of your life, your priorities, and your values. This industry is filled with creative artists who started out as actors and *then* realized their dream was something related but different. The folks who embrace that sort of discovery tend to be way happier than those who choose a different industry career yet still, somewhere deep inside, wish they were pursuing acting. Whatever you pursue, and wherever you pursue it, make sure it's what truly makes your heart sing. Otherwise, you'll second-guess your choices, always wonder "what if," and find yourself inherently jealous at watching others do what you wish you were doing.

A final caution on this: Remember that what you *do* as an actor most of the time is *pursue work*. So I'm not talking about finding yourself jealous of those who are succeeding in ways you were not. That doesn't count. That's like being an astronomer and finding yourself jealous that you didn't discover a new planet. Very few people have the level of success that draws people to the pursuit of acting in a major market. If you cannot be happy studying the players, pursuing the work, improving your craft, and building relationships in this industry, you absolutely should consider packing it in and going home. Do not be overly hard on yourself, should you make the decision to bail on this career. Hey, you gave it a shot and you are a better person for having done so! You have no way of knowing, today, the impact that having pursued acting in a major market will have on who you'll become as a person. And the cool thing about Hollywood is that you can always come back to it!

Endurance

> *I was exhausted. I wanted to go home. And right then, I said to myself, "Right now, someone is giving up. I may be beat down, but I'm not gonna let that someone be me. Not today." And, today, I'm still in this.*
> —Stephon Fuller

It is at the moment when you are the most wrung-dry that you have the opportunity to dig deep within and find a way to keep going. And here's why that's important: It *is* a choice. Sometimes you *will* need a break and you'll take one. That's good! And sometimes you'll somehow stick with this journey when you're sure you cannot. Perhaps the best source of inspiration at that crucial moment is the knowledge that others—when faced with the same decision—will choose to get off the treadmill, stop the hustling, take a break. Just by staying the course, you will make it to the next tier.

Now, you know I'm not one to promote the competition that's inherent to show business. Actors spend so much time focused on competition and rejection that I often find it's my duty to help actors refocus their energy on their own uniqueness and how much *acceptance* there is in this industry. But when you are *sooo* close to pulling your car over, perhaps a look in your rear-view mirror is a good idea. See all those others stacked up behind you and looking to get ahead of where you are on this next lap? They're exhausted too. No one in the industry will go hungry for your type while you take a break. So sticking it out can sometimes be "enough" to launch you ahead of the pack.

As with all things, career endurance requires good conditioning, a strong foundation, and the sheer will to *keep going*. Sure, there will be days that aren't your favorites. You'll have a tediously long day at the end of an exhaustingly long shoot and you'll still have to perform, take after take. Where do you go, to muster the strength to do that (and to do so just as well as you did it when you were really bringing your *A*-game earlier on in the shoot)? You rely on your craft, you pull from that well of passion that inspired you to give this business a go in the first place, and you see your career in terms of *your lifetime.* And that gets you through *today.* And if the knowledge that somewhere, someone else is taking this exact opportunity to pack it in and go home helps you keep your eyes on the prize, use that as fuel for your next lap.

When you feel yourself getting bogged down in actor funk, go see a play. Go to open mic night at a local comedy club and watch people hit and miss with new material. Heck, go watch someone *not* in the entertainment industry doing his job for 10 hours straight. *Most* of the time, life is not glamorous. The pop culture machine that tells you that you should be hearing your name called off the edge of the red carpet while flash bulbs pop is *lying* to you. Sure, that stuff may happen, but remember that during most hours of most days of even the most famous people in this business, that sort of thing is not happening at all.

Pick Your Hard

> *It's supposed to be hard. If it wasn't hard, everyone would do it. The* hard *is what makes it great.*
>
> —Jimmy Dugan, *A League of Their Own*

I was advising an actor who was talking about how hard the whole "moving to LA" thing was feeling. Stress from the family. Doubts introduced by well-meaning friends. Leaving behind a decent job and a network of support. Choosing to follow a dream, thousands of miles away, alone (or at least, starting over on the building up of friendships and connecting with a community).

I said, "Living your dreams is hard. Moving across the country alone is hard. Finding (and keeping) a good survival job is hard. Starting over is hard. The thing is, that's where most people stop the list. And here's what you need to know. *Not* living your dreams is hard. Staying in a place just because it's where all of your relatives are located is hard. Rolling around on a plastic pad behind a desk at a passionless job because it pays well and provides security that others in your life seem to value is hard. Staying stuck and wondering *what would've been* if you *had* chosen to live your dreams is hard. So, *pick your hard.*"

There's no one course of life that's easier, predictably, before we start out on its path. We can't know what twists and turns any of our life's choices will present to us. Just as we can't take two routes to our vacation destination simultaneously, we can only drive the road we're on, and there are times that road is going to be hard. But just as some folks prefer the "hard" of freeway traffic to surface streets, some artists prefer the "hard" of pursuing their dreams, unapologetically, sometimes alone, but focused and committed, to the "hard" of a regular paycheck, health insurance, a 401(k), and "casual Fridays."

When it gets hard—and it will—just remind yourself that you get to pick your hard. Me? I couldn't pick anything other than a creative career. I love all of this, especially the moments when I'm working so hard I can't see straight. Because I remember that the option *isn't* that there's something out there for me that's not hard, it would just be hard in a different way.

Bad audition? Stuck on a plot point in a script you're writing? Released from avail after being sure the gig was yours? Dropped by your agent just when things were starting to pick up? Edited out of the final cut of the film you told everyone you'd shot? Told you're too old or too skinny or too ethnic or too anything else for whatever particular role you really want to play? Snubbed in the casting room? Hating your reel after having spent a ton on it? Missing your family back home?

Yep. It's all hard. The only thing harder is not pursuing your dream.

> *If you have to talk to more than three people about the same problem, you don't want help; you want attention.*
> —Naomi Campbell, supermodel

If you're filled with reasons "it's too hard" and "nothing works," consider that you're arguing for your limitations. You're begging to keep them around. You're so stuck in your *story* that you refuse to consider rewriting the next chapter.

Think about that. You've chosen a creative career—one in which you crave taking on roles that force you outside your comfort zone, one in which you thrive on creating worlds that didn't exist before—yet you refuse to take steps toward thinking more creatively about your business as an actor.

Wow. Steven Pressfield—author of the excellent book *The War of Art*—calls that resistance. I call it actor Darwinism. You're guaranteeing you won't be able to reach your next tier, just by refusing to open your mind beyond your current story.

Why are you attached to "the way it is" and talking about how "they" won't let you reach your next tier? My suspicion is it has more to do with fear of success—and the need to be right—more than anything else. So, now's your chance to get honest with yourself about your blocks. Do you want to be right or do you want to be cast?

If problem-sharing is your drug of choice, honor yourself enough to put yourself in detox from it. Refuse to engage in grousing. Even if you're sure it's not that big a deal, consider that if *that* is the *one thing* standing between you and the career you've always dreamed of having, that figuring out how to *stop* engaging in your addiction to your blocks will change your life forever.

> *If you get five musicians in a room, you'll get music. Five actors, why is it only bitching?*
>
> —David Nathan Schwartz, actor-writer-coach

Good News

One of the things we do in all of our *Self-Management for Actors* classes is celebrate good news. We go around the room, or post on the private forums, to share our latest accomplishments—I got put on avail; I worked through an amazing scene in class; I got great feedback at a CD workshop; I updated my reel; I designed a postcard for a mailing; I spent 10 hours down the rabbit hole at IMDb-Pro researching my targets and updating my show bible with info flowing in from my Google Alerts; I attended a networking event and it didn't feel skeevy; I submitted on three really great projects at Actors Access; I shot a student film; I got an agent meeting—and celebrate with one another.

If you're not already down with this, you may go through that list and give me reasons these items don't qualify as good news: "but you didn't book; so what, it's just class; but did you get called in; no one watches reels anyway; mailings don't work; how does all that research *get* you anything; what results are coming from having spent those hours trying to find anyone worth talking to; submitting isn't the same as getting called in; it's just a stupid student film; they didn't offer to sign you." And to that, I'll say, sure. If you want to find a way to "but" your way out of your next tier, you're an expert, with that kind of thinking.

Let's be clear: Getting put on avail is a huge win. Thousands of others weren't put on avail. Doing hours of research on your targets *will* pay off when you have that amazing meeting you've been strategizing for months. That stupid student film could have tomorrow's Oscar-winning DP, who would love to work with you on his next big project. Moving your career forward is always a good thing. Someone else out there isn't. Good. Let the *slactors* have their free time. You've got a business to run. And that's not glamorous, but getting on set sooner, and at a higher pay rate, *is*.

Every time you feel yourself heading back into the world of that overdeveloped, Popeye-sized muscle for how that's not fun, good news isn't really good news, it won't work, it never works, and all that mess, tack on "*until now*" as an addition to every sentence. You can choose to change, now.

If *that* little trick doesn't do it for you, remember, you've gotta decide: "Do I want to be *right* or do I want to be *cast*?" Because unless you're psychic, you can't possibly know that a paradigm shift on this stuff *isn't* the difference between you feeling powerless and you hitting that next tier.

No more layering on "stories" that are only true in your mind. There's no such thing as, "It's slow." Nope. Someone is getting cast every day. Might as well be you. There's no such thing as, "They hate me in that office." Nope. If they see dollar signs, they're bringing you in. It's time to get very specific about what's within your control, what's worth celebrating about what *is* happening in your career, and why coming at the same issues differently may be the only thing standing in your way.

I don't wanna see frustrated, burned out, bitter actors who feel this business has done 'em wrong. This business is exactly as advertised—it doesn't owe any of us anything. It's tough, it's not based in fairness, and it's ridiculously rewarding for those with the talent, stamina, patience, and attitude to outlast the rest.

No matter how good you get at working through all of this, there will be days when you're sure it's all just too hard. The sacrifices you've made will feel just too massive, and your heart will tell you it's time to call it *done*, rather than soldiering on. Hey, that's okay! Better to choose happiness than heartbreak, always! And once this business starts to break you, please leave it behind, so that you can reflect on your time engaged in the pursuit with fondness for having had a go at it.

As I always say, "get down with the pursuit." In this business, you're going to be pursuing work a hell of a lot more than being paid to be on set, engaged in blissful storytelling. Can you love this business—even with all its flaws? If the answer is no, and if you will always hate some aspects of this business, please consider whether you find it worth staying in a relationship with a partner (this business) that you detest. Worth it? Heck, is it even remotely healthy to do such a thing to yourself? Absolutely not.

So, let's get healthy. Let's stay healthy. Let's start with our language about this business and all its mysteries. And let's detach from any story that isn't serving us. Let's start right now!

34: The Hyph Life

It used to be if you did anything other than acting, you weren't taken seriously as an actor. Today, if you're *only* an actor the buyers say, "Really? That's all you've got?!" Now, I'm going to celebrate your work as a hyphenate in this chapter, but this does *not* give you permission to be unfocused or scattered or so busy doing so many things that you come across as desperate. Being a hyphenate requires compartmentalization, discipline, and laser focus.

I don't cook. That's actually an understatement. I burn water. But that doesn't stop me from using an analogy about actors being master chefs. See, we often feel as if we're spinning plates in our creative pursuit, and that sometimes feels frustrating and exhausting and tedious and counterproductive. I like to reframe the "plate-spinning" analogy into one in which we're all master chefs.

Whether we're hyphenates who are juggling acting, writing, producing, directing, survival jobs, and parenting all at once or we're "just actors" who are dealing with all the work of marketing, brand-building, craft coaching, networking, and targeting, we've definitely got a lot going on. No doubt.

When you watch a cooking show, you see these chefs running throughout the kitchen, prepping one thing while moving an in-progress dish into its final stages, chopping one ingredient while bringing something else to a boil. They're frantic but in control most of the time. They're preheating the oven but they don't take their focus away from the sautéing that will go awry if they let it sit, unattended.

They're creating a *meal*—a delicious meal filled with several dishes made of many ingredients. And to bring that together, they employ the sophistication of an orchestra conductor who knows exactly when to bring each element into the foreground for its solo.

As creatives, that's what we're doing. We're crafting a *life* that's filled with daily practices, marketing strategies, self-produced content to show the buyers what we do best, and of course the delicious craft and love for storytelling that brings the whole experience together.

The next time you feel like you're spinning plates, remember that you're actually crafting a feast for everyone to enjoy. Take a breath. Take a step back. See what needs your immediate attention next. And keep on cookin'!

Crista Flanagan shared with my *SMFA* master class that she once heard this wonderful bit of advice that has stuck with her: "You need to be an amazing actor *and*. That *and* is what makes the difference."

So, that *and* could be: "You're an amazing actor *and* you're funny," or "You're an amazing actor *and* you're smart," or "You're an amazing actor *and* you're creepy," or "You're an amazing actor *and* you are the child of a studio head," or "You're an amazing actor *and* you're an amazing writer with a zillion ideas to share with the world."

Whatever comes after that *and*, according to Flanagan, that's what's gonna make the difference. Because *just* being "an amazing actor" simply isn't enough. That's baseline. Truly. We all know it's not about being the most talented actor who walks in the room. There's something more that has to click. That's where that *and* comes in. What's your *and*?

Don't feel that the *and* leads to recipes like "you have to do Twitter" or "you have to be on Facebook" or "you have to do CD workshops" or "you have to do mailings" or "you have to hurry up and get in the unions" or "you have to have an agent" or "you have to..." *anything*. It's because the *and* is unique to who you are and what you bring to the world that you needn't stress about what anyone else is doing. Seriously, don't worry about that mess. Focus on what *you* do.

The way you step up your game is not to worry about the other
guy—in any situation—'cause you can't control the other guy.
—Oprah Winfrey, hyphenate

Get Down with the Pursuit

Love what you do. Love what you do *so much* that you cannot *wait* to talk about it. If your work is something you spend most of your hours doing (which, for most folks, it is), shouldn't you be blissed out at the idea of talking about it? You should love what you do *so much* that you cannot contain yourself, when given the opportunity to gush about it. The way you light up—when you talk about your daily life—should be undeniably charismatic and attractive. Because otherwise, why *do* the thing you're spending so much of your life doing? Why devote so much of your life to something that doesn't turn you on?

Of course, for many actors, it's not their beloved *craft* that they *get* to spend most of their days doing. So, they've signed up for a career in which the majority of their time is spent *pursuing* work rather than engaging in an art they love so much. This is why living as a hyphenate can be so powerful. When you can excitedly talk about a character you're creating in a script, a new lens you're trying out on set, or the distribution process for your latest film, you aren't limited to sharing a tale from a long-ago acting gig or to discussing your most popular Facebook post.

When you're asked about what you do, you'll never have to say you're an aspiring actor or—God forbid—a struggling actor. Instead, you can tell the world you're a storyteller who proactively collaborates with fellow creatives at every turn, at higher and higher tiers each time, and that not only acting, but producing, writing, and running your *acting business* feels great, and is something to be celebrated!

One of my favorite hyphenates is Pacific Northwest actor Dan Knight. To label him geographically and as *only* an actor is to limit what is actually true. Knight works in multiple markets and not just as an actor. I asked him to share what becoming a hyphenate has taught him about his acting pursuits.

> To have a say in my acting future, I need to be willing to balance the creative and business sides of the industry and become an actor-preneur. I didn't intentionally set out to become a show business hyphenate. I just wanted to be a working actor, to make art, and to tell stories through my performances. But you don't make art in a vacuum; you make it in an environment of organized chaos. So, in addition to working on the craft of acting, I started learning more about what everyone on a film and TV project does. I pitch in and volunteer to help with non-acting stuff. I am a reader for casting directors. I schlep equipment. I help out with craft services. I do paperwork for the line producer. I hang around with the editors and cinematographers any chance I can. I ask people in the business about the challenges they face. I shut up between takes and observe what is going on. Read as many books as I can find on the business of show business. Watch biographies of successful actors, writers, producers, directors, and others in the business. Over time, my confidence in auditions and on set has increased.
>
> That adage "the more you give, the more you get" is right on the button. I am constantly amazed at how much unsolicited abundance and positivity flows back toward me after I've had a chance to provide someone with a little help. It comes in many forms: Having specific roles written for me on someone else's project; actually receiving payment from previously deferred projects; getting an instant "YES!" when a favor is needed; being honored by someone asking me to be a part of his or her project; overwhelming support and turnout when one of my own projects is shown at a festival; people willing to recommend me to their talent rep and/or to a casting director they know; someone in the industry actually accepting a phone call, replying to an email, providing a glowing reference; and on it goes.
>
> —Dan Knight

Always Be Creating

Unfortunately, one of the things that happens when you're a successful hyphenate is you attract the attention of those who are not living their dreams as fully. That time you spend hustling, creating content, building relationships, and living your dreams? They spend that same time trash-talking those of us who are changing the world with our storytelling. You can't rent mental space to those folks. It'll be tempting to engage, to defend, to attempt to explain why they're wrong. Don't bother. Logic and haters rarely intersect. Just keep creating the life of your dreams, no matter what. Because if you're in this business for more than a minute (heck, if you're in this *life* for more than a minute), you're gonna see friends come and go, you're gonna have fans love you then hate you, you're gonna experience the chill of that agent who was crazy about you suddenly forgetting you're alive, you're gonna feel a casting office go cold on you after it was hot for a nice long run.

The number one cure for even noticing the valleys that are inevitable in a creative career is having another project in waiting. Sure, you'll turn your focus to preparing for an audition, then you'll go on the audition and eagerly head straight to a pre-production meeting with your team for the next webseries you're producing. When a film you've written finishes its run on the festival circuit, you'll shift your attention to updating your website and creating marketing materials for your next bit of outreach. The day your agent drops you doesn't feel like the worst day you've ever had, because you're supervising ADR for a fellow collaborator's pet project. And as you're discovering all sorts of elements of the entertainment industry—not just what you experience as an actor—you may find you're feeling more enriched by another role in your creative career. I'm not trying to talk you out of loving your life as an actor! I'm suggesting that you feel creative fulfillment by always having something else *creative* to do, in your pursuit. It tunes out all the noise that tends to distract others.

I said it earlier and here it is again: The hyph life requires compartmentalization, discipline, and laser focus. As you explore the various beautiful elements of your creative pursuit, really examine what it is that you love about the storytelling process and spend as much time as possible doing that—whatever it is. Being blissed out by your journey is an attractive state. And *that* is castable!

In Closing

Everyone knows that this business is not about rules or absolutes. There are always magic stories, and that's what keeps the dream alive in so many aspiring performers.

When I first entered high school, there was no drama club. So, I started one! There are ways to create opportunities to do what we love no matter where we live. Location may be a barrier, but if there is a casting director who really believes in you, you'll be considered despite the distance. It's not *likely*, but that doesn't mean it's impossible. And as hyphenate Colleen Wainwright asks, as we charge into any challenge: "Are you *sure* it's impossible?" because only if you're sure there's no shot should you ever give up.

If you're not currently living in a major market, sure, consider looking into contests, competitions, and scholarships that could have high-level scouts open to looking at performers from all areas, but always remember: Research *everyone* to be sure they're legit, *never* pay to be represented, and *always* shop around for the best classes. An agent or manager gets paid only when you do—by commission. Never let your dream get soiled by the greed of others. If you have legitimate talent, there are legitimate representatives eager to sign you, legitimate coaches whose training will make you stronger, and legitimate productions being mounted in your area.

Recipe for Success

I've been pretty fortunate in our business and I have no idea of what to tell you about how or why it's happened. Preparedness linked to the right look and the right age at the right time in the right place? Who knows? I don't think there's a "formula" that works for everyone. But I think that we can increase our chances of success in the entertainment business by following some simple guidelines that, coincidentally, seem to also work pretty well in helping us lead a good life.

But first, you have to figure out if you're a chicken or a pig. Show business requires sheer, unadulterated commitment. I hear quite a few young actors talk about how involved they are in their careers. They do this and that, go here and there, and involve themselves. Really *involve* themselves. Consider what it takes, though, to put together a bacon and egg breakfast. The chicken is involved—but the pig is *committed*.

The difference is easy to see in that context, but what does it mean in our industry? Maybe, ultimately, just two things: Don't give up, and don't die. Those are our main objectives. But there are a few other seemingly inconsequential things that are always helpful in completing the recipe so that the soufflé doesn't fall.

> ➤Suit up and show up. Every day. Especially when you don't feel like it.
> ➤Apologize. Sleeping well is more important than being right.
> ➤Be where you say you'll be when you say you'll be there.
> ➤Don't ever flake. On anything or anyone.
> ➤Mind your own business.
> ➤Don't try to manipulate the outcome of any situation. The marionette's strings run both ways—the manipulator is also being manipulated.
> ➤What anyone else thinks of you is none of your business.
> ➤Forgive. Clinging to resentment is like drinking poison and hoping the other guy dies.
> ➤Be prepared for your opportunity.
> ➤After your audition, walk away and *forget about it*.
> ➤Give your best performance in the audition room, not in the car on the way home.
> ➤Live life. Have interests and activities other than performing.
> ➤Be interested in the lives of others.
> ➤Listen. Really listen. Much more than you speak.
> ➤Volunteer.

Some of these are really, really hard to do all the time. But as the New York City police officer told the tourist asking how to get to Carnegie Hall: "Practice!" Every habit we have, good and bad, is the result of consistent, repetitive behavior—when we want to and even when we don't.

A well-rounded actor is, first and foremost, a well-rounded person. I promise you that if you approach your real life with honesty, compassion, service, sacrifice, and hard work, the reward will come. It may not be stardom. Maybe it will only be having lived a good life. And would that be so bad?

—Steve Tom, actor

How to "Make It"

I was having a conversation with a series regular friend of mine about a less-frequently working actor mutual friend. He's amazingly talented and anyone would want to work with him, see him working, pay to see him working in anything. He's that great. But he's only occasionally working. He hasn't "made it." Yet.

So, why *hasn't* he made it yet? Hmm. Why hasn't *anyone* made it yet? What is it that stands between the most talented people we know and "making it" in this industry? I came up with three key elements that seem to dictate a brilliant actor's absence from any "it" list.

Directors you're getting in front of aren't ready to take a risk on you. This one is especially true for the friend we were discussing, above. I've brought him to callbacks in a few of the films I've cast and he's always a top choice. But he's not cast. The directors tend to go for more "bankable" talent (*name* actors or those who are on the rise due to their recognizable credits). They know they need to impress the money guys and the best way to do that is with a known commodity. Once these directors find themselves confidently at the career level where decisions are truly their own, perhaps they *will* take a chance on brilliant actors without *name* value.

It's not your time. No one likes this one, as it's one of those things you can't control, but you simply may not be ready for the big break that would see you "make it" right now. You could be given that opportunity (get the *dream role* you've been waiting for) and then not have the career stamina to back it up with a strong second act. How many times have we seen actors get a huge shot and then blow it all with irresponsible post-fame behavior or really sketchy choices for follow-up projects? On a less-extreme scale, how many times have you looked back at your own career path and been pleased that *not* getting a certain role allowed things to work out for the best, even though at the time you felt heartbroken?

You're still building your relationships. This one is my favorite, and it really encompasses both of the above notions. I see so many people with aspirations of connecting with "the right people" so that they can "make it" (and fast). I wish I could explain how vitally important it is for you to have a paradigm shift, if that is your perception of how it's done in this business. Making it has very little to do with meeting *today's* hot players.

I've seen actors who've spent a decade trying to get in with all of the cool kids and who still have little more to show for it than a few co-star credits on forgettable one-season series. Meanwhile, I've seen actors who started with a strong foundation of relationships based on common interests, mutual respect, working to help one another, and a collaborative spirit within their own tier who now reap great rewards by virtue of the fact that some of their best friends are *now* showrunners, filmmakers, producers, or casting directors. Did they initiate these friendships simply because they believed years down the line there would be a payoff? No. The friendships began organically (as most true friendships do) and developed over time into business partnerships in a biz where there are very few rules to making it.

Look at my casting career: I'm still new at this! Should I be sending my casting resumé out to big-name directors who've been working at the studio level for decades (and who tend to be very loyal to their casting directors from project to project)? Why would I try to break in on an existing relationship to hope I'd become someone's new casting director when they're perfectly happy with their long-term business partner? Instead, I work with filmmakers who are also at the beginning of their professional journeys and we collaborate to build the best casts possible. Sometimes I work with filmmakers who may have less experience in the industry than I do. Other times, I work with filmmakers transitioning from one type of project to another—a commercial director working on his first indie feature film, for example. We all come together to help one another reach the next tier while involved in a creative endeavor. That is how relationships begin: We believe in one another before it's popular (or hugely profitable) to do so.

A similar approach can work for actors. Continue to pursue dream jobs, for sure, but keep your current professional relationships healthy. Network— and not just with fellow actors. Connect with other industry professionals at your level and slightly above, so that you can share ideas and get (and give) a little mentoring along the way. So many actors get caught up in goal-setting for getting to the top tier that they neglect the beneficial networking that goes on at each and every tier along the way. It's not just "the top" that has payoffs. People who get to the top know this very well and will speak quite fondly of some of the projects those "lower tier" experiences and early relationships brought into their lives.

You never know when the aspiring writer in your improv workshop will sell that quirky little script written with you in mind for the lead. And who's to say what may come of that script? Festivals? Funding and major distribution? Could it all be a part of your road to making it? Who knows? But it's certainly as much a part of your job as an actor to develop industry relationships as it is to submit on major studio projects—probably more so.

If you find yourself frustrated with this industry and what surviving it entails, remember that there is no amount of hate you can throw at something that will change it. There is, however, enough love to throw at it that will change *you*. And maybe that changed version of you will find ascension to the next tier effortless.

Showfax Bob's Three-Step Program for Getting What You Want

Step One: Set clear and precise goals (one at a time is fine, too many cloud the action plan). Goals are fine but they need an action plan for you to reel them in. Without action, they're dreams. Dreams are also fine but they are just that, dreams, not the real world. So one goal at a time that you can act on can keep you rather busy.

Step Two: Paint your day. Hang a blank artist's canvas on the bedroom wall in direct path of your eyesight when you wake up in the morning. You can use a blank space of wall instead of a blank artist's canvas but the canvas is an object and that helps to maintain association. When you wake up, look at the canvas and paint your day. What do you see yourself doing today? What do you want to be doing? Remember, you set a goal in Step One. Stick with it. Stay focused. Yeah, you may be serving ham and eggs to customers in Denny's today, but that's what the *world* sees you doing. What do *you* see yourself doing today? Paint your day.

Step Three: Live into what you want (what you painted for your day). If you're driving to work at Denny's, consider instead that you're driving to the casting office for a callback. If you're walking to the corner newsstand for a newspaper, see yourself instead on the studio lot walking to the producer's office. Live into what you want.

Fill in the above apropos your aspirations: acting, directing, writing, whatever. Stick with it, stay focused, be persistent. Keep your eye on the ball and things will happen. But be forewarned, be careful what you wish for, 'cuz my Three-Step Program works.

—Robert Brody, Showfax

Traffic Jams

Consider the pursuit of your acting career as doing time in traffic. Here in LA, for instance, you may check SigAlert before you head out, and all may look clear, but when you hit The 10, suddenly it's a parking lot, and you're stuck for hours just trying to make it a few miles. Terribly frustrating, right? You thought you had your route planned and now you're either stuck with the non-moving freeway or you're gonna have to exit and find your way around using surface streets, and there's construction that your GPS hasn't databased yet. Do you stick with the devil you know or attempt to try out the one you don't know? No way to know which one will get you to your destination faster (if at all), but you've got to get there, so you're stuck in traffic.

How many times, as an actor, have you felt like you're cruising at a delightfully efficient pace, actually making really good time toward your ultimate destination (anything from fame to that first network co-star booking) and then—*bam*—there's a snag? You're suddenly in a traffic jam and now your arrival doesn't seem like it will be on schedule.

Or, more likely, the way actors spend the most frustrated time as they head down that highway, you were going above the speed limit and then things just slowed down. You're not in stop-and-go traffic, but you're certainly going more slowly than the rules of the road would allow. You're frustrated because other lanes seem to be moving faster than yours. So you change lanes. And now the lane you just left is moving faster. *Dangit!* Where is the logic in this?

Ah, that's just it. There is no logic. Identical twins could set out on their pursuit of an acting career in Hollywood and have completely different results and experiences. Still, there are actors who, in their pursuit of acting, will decide the journey—with all of the traffic, the lack of recommended tourist attractions, the inability to know for certain when to expect gridlock—is unpredictable enough to abandon altogether. That's right. There are travelers among you who will—rather than sitting patiently in traffic or attempting an alternate route to their destination—simply get out of their cars and leave 'em sitting there.

Assuming you've chosen to stay in traffic, it's at this point you have two choices: Be frustrated with the lack of control or be mystified by the wonderful journey you're experiencing. Yeah, we always have that choice. Enjoy the ride or try and force it to be like we expect it will be. Amazingly, it's when we enjoy it for what it is that the journey actually becomes much more like we would've liked to force it to be. Interesting, isn't it?

So, when you're traveling along at the "straight to producers, guest-star level, on the road to offer only status" clip and suddenly get asked to preread, don't automatically assume you're experiencing something negative. It's quite possible that, by going in on that preread, you're going to meet a casting director who wouldn't have known your work otherwise and who will sign on to cast something *huge* a week later and who will remember you from that silly preread and call to offer you a plum role in something you wouldn't even have been considered for, had you not been on that casting director's radar via that preread.

You just can't know the impact the intricacies of traffic will have on your ability to reach your ultimate destination on any particular schedule. Because the destination isn't one you can plot out on a physical map and determine the amount of time it should take to get there, it becomes all the more important that you enjoy the journey. Yes, even when you're sitting still, wondering when you'll *ever* get there.

Because the other options are *not* enjoying the journey and getting out of the pursuit of acting altogether, why not just go ahead and enjoy the ride?

How to Stay Plugged in with *SMFA*

I always love hearing from actors who've found my work helpful. It thrills me to know that—even if we've never met—I've walked along your path with you for a bit, somehow. But one of the most valuable elements in my creative journey has always been the community I've created, cultivated, curated, and committed to support. This community has taken many forms and has involved fellow creatives worldwide over the years.

As a means of keeping the fourth edition of *Self-Management for Actors* as fresh and updated as possible, we've set up a support site at smfa4.com where we regularly update and post downloadable supplements to this printed book in the form of *SMFA* Hot Sheets. We also offer regular free calls and streaming video broadcasts for tune-ups and trouble-shooting the *SMFA* principles. Most awesomely, there's a fabulous discussion forum where ninjas worldwide can talk about the journey, swap stories, offer support and encouragement, and build a community that can help change this industry into a more inclusive, positive place. All of this is free and we encourage you to take advantage of the full *Self-Management for Actors* experience!

We're thrilled to be a part of your ever-expanding circle of co-conspirators for making this creative journey the most delicious it can possibly be. Please, don't wait. Come on over to smfa4.com and become an active part of *your* beloved industry, wherever you live and at whatever tier you may currently be. Ninja badassery awaits. We can't wait to jam with you as we work to create the Hollywood we proudly call our own. Have fun; don't suck! And as always, stay ninja.

The two most important days in your life are the day you were born and the day you find out why.

—Mark Twain, author

ABOUT THE AUTHOR

Bonnie Gillespie is living her dreams by helping others figure out how to live theirs.

She casts SAG-AFTRA indie feature films and series such as the Machinima zombie smash hit *Bite Me* which made the leap from web to TV with Lionsgate in its second season. Her work on this groundbreaking series led to her membership in the Television Academy.

As a weekly columnist for actors in publications such as *Backstage* and Actors Access for more than 15 years, Bonnie has also authored several books demystifying the casting process and illuminating the business side of pursuing a creative career. The most popular of these books is *Self-Management for Actors: Getting Down to (Show) Business*, which has been named one of The Top 10 Best Books on Acting Ever Written and is featured on the Tom Cruise actor resource blog.

She tours the world teaching curriculum based on this top-selling book as a guest instructor at colleges, universities, actors' unions, and acting studios. She also works as a private coach to creatives ready to bring a sense of empowerment and joy to their storytelling journeys.

Bonnie's work has been featured on *Good Morning America*, *BBC Breakfast*, *Sunrise Australia*, UTV-Ireland, ARD-1 Germany, CBC Radio One, BBC Radio 5, E! Online, Yahoo! Movies, and in the *Wall Street Journal*, the *Washington Post*, and the *LA Times*. Her podcast "The Work" is available on iTunes with behind-the-scenes vids at YouTube.

She blissfully lives at the beach with her partner since 2001, Keith Johnson. To hop on Bonnie's mailing list, get loads of free resources, and grab your tip-filled MP3, please visit bonniegillespie.com. From here, you can also explore digging deeper with all things *SMFA*.

You can't build a reputation on what you're going to do.
—Henry Ford, industrialist

INDEX

OTHER OFFERINGS FROM TEAM CRICKET FEET

In addition to *Self-Management for Actors*, we have a companion guide (a "Bonnie in your pocket") in the form of *SMFA: The Ninja Within*. Bonnie Gillespie has also co-authored *Acting Qs: Conversations with Working Actors* with Blake Robbins. Bonnie's first book, *Casting Qs: A Collection of Casting Director Interviews*, is out of print but individual chapters and updated vid interviews with casting directors are available exclusively in **The *SMFA* Vault**.

The *SMFA* Vault is a treasure-filled collection of goodies Bonnie has created for her private coaching clients, masterminders, and creative entrepreneurs around the world and access to **The *SMFA* Vault** is for graduates of the 100-day challenge program **Get in Gear for the Next Tier**. You may begin your inspiring, empowering journey to the next tier today at bonniegillespie.com!

Also for students of **Get in Gear for the Next Tier**, Bonnie offers private coaching and ongoing mastermind group meetings virtually and in person. Application required—just visit smfa4.com to start the intake process or to explore our other ongoing mentorship packages. To order any of our books, enroll in courses, or download goodies from the *Self-Management for Actors* catalog, visit shop.selfmanagementforactors.com (you may pay via credit card or PayPal through our site).

Please call 323.397.7576 or email publisher@cricketfeet.com to arrange for bulk discounts of textbooks to bookstores and educational facilities or to order any of our offerings with check or money order by mail.

If you would like to be added to our mailing list for notification of future publications, tour cities, speaking engagements, free quarterly phone calls, and other promotional activities, please visit bonniegillespie.com and opt on in for fun BonBlasts and your free bonus MP3 filled with action items you can take to feel more in control of the business side of your creative career.

Of course, you know by now that we have a library of *Self-Management for Actors* Hot Sheet downloads to enhance your fourth edition experience. These goodies are available to you at smfa4.com (where you'll also find a thriving community of ninja actors worldwide—just check out #SMFAninjas throughout social media). Jump on in, introduce yourself to your fellow ninjas, and stay awesome! We'll see you online!